Joanna Baillie, Romantic Dramatist

Critical essays

Edited by
Thomas C. Crochunis

KV-373-041

Routledge
Taylor & Francis Group

LONDON AND NEW YORK

First published 2004
by Routledge
2 Park Square, Milton Park, Abingdon, Oxon OX14 4RN

Simultaneously published in the USA and Canada
by Routledge
711 Third Avenue, New York, NY 10017

Routledge is an imprint of the Taylor & Francis Group

© 2004 Selection and editorial matter Thomas C. Crochunis;
individual chapters the contributors
First issued in paperback 2013

Typeset in Garamond by
Rosemount Typing Services, Barjarg Tower, Auldgirth, Dumfriesshire

All rights reserved. No part of this book may be reprinted or
reproduced or utilised in any form or by any electronic, mechanical,
or other means, now known or hereafter invented, including
photocopying and recording, or in any information storage or
retrieval system, without permission in writing from the publishers.

British Library Cataloguing in Publication Data
A catalogue record for this book is available from the British Library

Library of Congress Cataloging in Publication Data
Joanna Baillie, romantic dramatist : critical essays / [compiled by]
Thomas C. Crochunis.
        p. cm.
Includes bibliographical references and index.
   1. Baillie, Joanna, 1762–1851–Criticism and interpretation.
2. Women and literature–Scotland–History–19th century.
3. Romanticism–Scotland. I. Crochunis, Thomas C., 1959–
   PR4056.Z74 2004
   822'.7–dc21

                                                2003012391

ISBN 978-0-415-29990-9 (hbk)
ISBN 978-0-415-85984-4 (pbk)

Joanna Baillie,
Romantic Dramatist

Joanna Baillie, Romantic Dramatist is the first-ever collection of critical essays on one of Britain's most prolific literary dramatists. Joanna Baillie is a playwright whose work is rapidly gaining the attention of theatre artists and scholars of eighteenth- and nineteenth-century literary history, dramatic history and women's studies, and in recent years her plays have been viewed as important evidence in our rethinking of each of these fields of study and, as more have been included in classroom anthologies and taught widely in undergraduate and graduate courses, teachers and students have drawn upon the kinds of contexts that are thoroughly considered in the essays of this volume.

This unique collection includes contributions from leading scholars of women's dramatic writing of the Romantic era and specialists across the various fields of study with greatest relevance to Baillie's playwriting. The essays range from introductory contexts for those encountering Baillie's work for the first time to thought-provoking examinations of the complex relationships between Baillie's plays and other forms of philosophical and scientific writing of her era and of Baillie's theatrical and dramatic methods, in some cases providing extended interpretations of individual plays.

Teachers and students will welcome this collection, which offers a variety of approaches to exploring the work of this important dramatist.

Thomas C. Crochunis has published essays on drama and theatre history in *Gothic Studies, European Romantic Review* and *Romanticism on the Net,* and also in several collections including *Women in British Romantic Theatre* and *Visual Media in the Humanities.* He is co-editor of the British Women Playwrights around 1800 Web project.

Originally commissioned for the Interdisciplinary Nineteenth-Century Studies series, edited by Keith Hanley and Greg Kucich

To Madeline

Contents

Contributors

Ken A. Bugajski is Assistant Professor of English at Rogers State University. He completed his dissertation, a study of Mary Robinson, Samuel Taylor Coleridge, John Henry Newman and Leigh Hunt entitled "'The Men and Women Merely Players': Performing the Self in Nineteenth-Century British Literary Autobiography," at Texas A&M University. He has presented papers at the American Conference on Romanticism and the Eighteenth- and Nineteenth-Century British Women Writers' Conference.

Catherine B. Burroughs is Associate Professor of English at Wells College and visiting lecturer in English at Cornell University. Her publications include: *Reading the Social Body* (co-ed., 1993); *Closet Stages: Joanna Baillie and the Theater Theory of British Romantic Women Writers* (1997), and *Women in British Romantic Theatre: Drama, Performance, and Society, 1790–1840* (ed., 2000).

Frederick Burwick is Professor of English at UCLA. With an interdisciplinary approach to literature, he explores the interactions of literature with art, science, music, and theatre. Author and editor of twenty books, eighty articles and twenty reviews, his research is dedicated to problems of perception, illusion, and delusion in literary representation and theatrical performance. His recent book *Poetic Madness and the Romantic Imagination* (1996) won the American Conference on Romanticism book prize. He has been named Distinguished Scholar by both the British Academy (1992) and the Keats-Shelley Association (1998).

Julie A. Carlson is Associate Professor of English at UCSB. She is author of *In the Theatre of Romanticism: Coleridge, Nationalism, Women* (1994) and guest editor of "Domestic/Tragedy" (*South Atlantic Quarterly* 98.3, 1999). She has written many essays on Romantic drama, including "Hazlitt and the Sociability of Theater" (in *Romantic Sociability*, 2002), "Remaking Love: Remorse in the Theatre of Baillie and Inchbald" (in *Women in British Romantic*

Theatre, 2000), and "Coming After: Shelley's Proserpine" (*Texas Studies in Literature and Language*, 1999). She is currently writing a book on the Wollstonecraft–Godwin–Shelley family, entitled *Public Lives: England's First Family of Writers*.

Jeffrey N. Cox is Professor of English and of Comparative Literature at the University of Colorado at Boulder, where he also directs the Center for Humanities and the Arts. His work on the drama includes *In the Shadows of Romance: Romantic Tragic Drama in Germany, England, and France* (1987), an edition of *Seven Gothic Dramas: 1789–1825* (1992), and the Broadview Anthology of Romantic Drama (2003, co-ed. with Michael Gamer). He is also the author of *Poetry and Politics in the Cockney School: Keats, Shelley, Hunt, and Their Circle* (1998).

Thomas C. Crochunis is an independent scholar whose essays and reviews on drama, theatre, and performance in Britain in the late-eighteenth and early-nineteenth centuries and on cultural performance, historiography, and media studies have been published in *Gothic Studies, European Romantic Review, Theatre Journal, Nineteenth Century Theatre*, and *Romanticism on the Net* and also in the collections *Women in British Romantic Theatre* (2000), *Beyond Nature Writing* (2001), and *Visual Media in the Humanities* (2003). He is co-editor (with Michael Eberle-Sinatra) of the British Women Playwrights around 1800 Web project.

Bruce Graver is Professor of English at Providence College. He edited Wordsworth's *Translations of Chaucer and Virgil* for the Cornell Wordsworth, and, with Ronald Tetreault, has prepared an electronic edition of Wordsworth and Coleridge's *Lyrical Ballads*, forthcoming from Cambridge University Press.

Greg Kucich is Associate Professor of English at the University of Notre Dame, where he is also a Fellow of the Nanovic Institute for European Studies. He has published articles on drama and women writers of the Romantic era. His books include *Keats, Shelley, and Romantic Spenserianism* (1991) and, with Jeffrey N. Cox, a forthcoming collection of periodical essays by Leigh Hunt. He is currently writing a book-length study on the rewriting of history by women writers of the Romantic era. He is also co-editor of *Nineteenth-Century Contexts: An Interdisciplinary Journal*.

Dorothy McMillan is currently Head of the School of English and Scottish Language and Literature in the University of Glasgow. With Douglas Gifford she edited *A History of Scottish Women's Writing* (1997). Her anthology *The Scotswoman at Home and Abroad: Non-fiction Writing 1700-1900* (1999) includes two previously unpublished memoirs by Joanna Baillie, and a chapter on Baillie also appears in the collection *1798: The Year of the Lyrical Ballads* (1998). Other editions include *Queen of Science: The Personal Recollections of Mary Somerville*, the nineteenth-century Scottish astronomer (2001).

Victoria Myers is Professor of English at Pepperdine University and General Editor of *Pacific Coast Philology*. She has authored articles on Blake, Wordsworth, Coleridge, Godwin, and on speech act theory, and has just completed the manuscript for a book entitled "Coleridge and the Ethical Argument: Character, History, and Interpretation in the Polemics of the 1790s." She is currently editing the diaries of William Godwin.

Marjean D. Purinton, Associate Professor of English and Associate Chair of the English Department at Texas Tech University, also teaches in the Women's Studies and Comparative Literature programs and serves as Chair of the Executive Council of the Teaching Academy at Texas Tech University. Purinton is the author of *Romantic Ideology Unmasked: The Mentally Constructed Tyrannies in Dramas of William Wordsworth, Lord Byron, Percy Shelley, and Joanna Baillie* (1994), as well as numerous articles on Romantic drama, early nineteenth-century women writers, and pedagogical issues. She is currently finishing a book project about British Romantic Techno-Gothic drama.

Alan Richardson is Professor of English at Boston College. His books include *British Romanticism and the Science of the Mind* (2001), *Literature, Education, and Romanticism: Reading as Social Practice, 1780–1832* (1994, American Conference on Romanticism book prize winner), and *Romanticism, Race, and Imperial Culture 1780–1834* (co-ed., 1996). He has also published numerous essays on Romantic-era literature and culture, particularly in relation to gender, childhood and education, colonialism, and early neuroscience. Major honors and awards include fellowships from the Andrew W. Mellon Foundation, the National Endowment for the Humanities, and the John Simon Guggenheim Foundation.

Judith Bailey Slagle, Associate Professor of Restoration and Eighteenth-century Literature and Chair of the Department of English at East Tennessee State University, has published editions of plays by Thomas Shadwell and edited a collection entitled *Thomas Shadwell Reconsider'd: Essays in Criticism* (1996) for *Restoration: Studies in English Literary Culture, 1660–1700*. Her research on Joanna Baillie began in a National Endowment for the Humanities seminar in 1994, continued during a research fellowship at the University of Edinburgh in 1996, and resulted in a two-volume work entitled *The Collected Letters of Joanna Baillie* (1999). Her biography *Joanna Baillie: A Literary Life*, based on archival research in the UK and US, appeared in 2002.

Acknowledgments

The longer a project takes to bring to completion, the more people contribute in small and large ways to its history.

My own work on Joanna Baillie has been inspired over many years by the knowledge and creativity of the scholars with whom I have studied. Roy Park first made British Romantic drama and theatre compelling to me. Susan Wolfson first introduced me to Baillie and her plays. William Galperin and Daniel Harris, through challenging my thinking about Robert Browning (of all people), prepared me to look beyond the obvious when reading women playwrights like Baillie. Elin Diamond pushed me to think about gender and cultural history, and I continue to value the intellectual struggles that nudge set in motion. Alan MacVey's directing and teaching showed me how intellectual work nourishes the passion of theatrical art, and Alan, along with George Levine, who continues to offer friendship and wise counsel, helped me keep my eyes on both the trees and the forest in British cultural history and in the humanities generally.

Many scholars have contributed to this volume's development, but none have been more instrumental in helping me navigate the rough waters of contemporary publishing than Greg Kucich or in expanding my knowledge of the many scholars working on Joanna Baillie than Janice Patten. It is no exaggeration to say that without Greg and Janice this volume would never have made it to print.

I am honored to know and work alongside many teachers, scholars, and theatre artists whose combination of knowledge and generosity have taught me much about research, theatre practice, and professional collegiality, in particular Alex Dick, Jane Moody, Jacky Bratton, Kate Newey, Danny O'Quinn, Judith Slagle, Marjean Purinton, Michael Gamer, Julie Carlson, Tracy Davis, Ellen Donkin, Julia Flanders, Gioia Angeletti, Mallory Catlett, and Gwynn MacDonald. Among even so valued a group of colleagues, Catherine Burroughs, Jonathan Mulrooney, Michael Eberle-Sinatra and Jeff Cox stand out as friends whose enthusiasm for shared interests and personal encouragement have helped me more than they may know.

My parents, who will be thrilled to see this book though they probably aren't expecting it, made my scholarship possible in ways neither they nor I understand. Finally, to Madeline, Catherine, and Christine, who every day make the challenges of thinking, writing, and living rewarding and beautiful, I hope that my love and support will continually repay you for yours.

* * *

The essay "A Reasonable Woman's Desire: The Private Theatrical and Joanna Baillie's *The Tryal*" by Catherine B. Burroughs is reprinted from *Texas Studies in Literature and Language* (38: 3/4, pp. 265–84. Copyright © 1996 by the University of Texas Press. All rights reserved.) Thanks to Catherine Burroughs and the University of Texas Press for granting permission to reprint.

1 Introduction

The case of Joanna Baillie

Thomas C. Crochunis

What is the best way to make a case for the importance of Joanna Baillie's dramatic writing? Does such a case need to be made?

Among certain circles – certainly British Romanticists, perhaps feminist theatre historians, and most recently among theatre practitioners – Baillie has already been given serious consideration. The major publications in these fields – *Studies in Romanticism, The Wordsworth Circle, European Romantic Review, The Keats-Shelley Journal; Nineteenth Century Theatre, Theatre Survey, Theatre Journal;* and also *Publications of the Modern Language Association* – have published essays on Baillie. She has been featured in conference sessions and papers, and several recent collections of essays on women and theatre in her era have included essays entirely or in part about Baillie. In fact, Baillie has been a fit subject for professional publication and presentation for some time now. Beginning in the summer of 2003, performance practitioners significantly increased their engagement with Baillie's plays through public readings given as part of a series in New York City, "The First 100 Years: The Professional Female Playwright," and through a performance of *Basil* staged at the 2003 North American Society for the Study of Romanticism conference at Fordham University.

More subtle has been a qualitative change in how people study and teach Baillie's plays. This change takes several forms that I have noticed. Baillie's plays, which began as an interesting sidelight for Romanticists, have increasingly become interesting to theatre historians, in part because her plays and their sparse production history raise important questions for feminist critics about the over reliance on unproblematic acceptance of theatrical production as the organizing principle of dramaturgical history. And, as a result of Baillie's role in raising questions about historiography, her work has become interesting in new ways in the context of women's studies more broadly. One further shift in how Baillie figures in the work of scholars and teachers is that, based on the anecdotal evidence I have collected over a few years, more people include Baillie's plays on their syllabi (perhaps spurred by Duthie's 2001 paperback edition of the *Plays on the Passions*), and more of those who do report pedagogical success as measured by student engagement and teacher perception that the plays helped them raise issues that fed other parts of the course. It seems that the time has come to explore the unusual case of Joanna Baillie's playwriting rather than to make a case for her importance.

And so, I will not base this introduction on a review of how the criticism that has already been published, cited frequently in the contributions to this volume, has made the case for Baillie's significance or interest. Each piece of that important past work on Baillie set its own terms, made its own kind of case, for Baillie's drama. The aim of this volume is to provide a number of different points of entry to the study of Baillie by building on a number of the directions taken in past scholarship and revisiting or pursuing them further. Collected together, these essays map a shared starting point for further exploration of Baillie through scholarship and teaching.

To examine the case of Baillie's importance now is different, of course, from studying her importance in her own time. While several essays in this volume provide valuable information on just how Baillie was regarded in the British eighteenth and nineteenth centuries, we know – as she did – that her reputation then depended in part on how she performed her artistic identity in relationship to the beliefs and perceptions of her era. It is often noted that key figures in British Romanticism knew Baillie and regarded her highly, but this observation always seems to me a peculiar sort of affirmative action by Romantic ideology. While how Baillie was viewed in her own era by Scott, Byron, or Hemans can inform our contemporary historiographic inquiry, these judgments by her contemporaries, rather than representing definitive testimony to her importance, are yet another kind of information for us to consider in filling in the details of her case.

It is also wise for those of us still interested in making a case for Baillie now to be cautious about building our arguments on the aesthetic quality or cultural richness of her texts. While there are several essays in this volume that unfold the complexities of Baillie's plays, we need to pause to consider how much of our ideas of "aesthetic quality" or "cultural richness" are constituted by previous scholarly approaches that trace at least part of their epistemologies and methodologies back to elements of Romanticism or to reactions against its (multiple) ideologies. In fact, studying Baillie's plays gives us new opportunities to question our received dramaturgical standards and expectations. For example, we might find it hard to encounter Baillie's plays without first reconsidering our post-Ibsen, post high-realist assumptions. And yet Ibsen's dramaturgy was post-Romantic (in fact, some of his plays explored Romantic dramaturgical structures), while Baillie's were (perhaps) para-Romantic. How do we make sense of a writer like Baillie who was both engaged with the literature and theatre of her era and yet exploring alternatives to styles of her era that have, from an historiographic perspective, turned out to be the ones that underlie our own inherited dramatic aesthetics?

Similarly, to engage with Baillie's sources and influences is to rethink the fields of influence that matter to literary and cultural history. Although other writers who are already considered central to her era were influenced by medicine, science, and philosophy, Baillie's drama invites us to think about cross-fertilizing influences from these disciplines in somewhat different ways since her dramas make use of these disciplines differently from works in other genres – such as lyric poetry or the novel – that have constituted the British Romantic era's literary canon. Undoubtedly, the very paradigms we have at our immediate disposal for contextualizing a writer of Baillie's time are themselves influenced by legacies of the British Romantic era that live on in our scholarship and teaching in spite of continued attempts to question them. We need to bring varied methods and contexts to bear when investigating the case of Joanna Baillie at least in part because no writer of her era pursued a career-long project quite like hers.

For sheer quantity of highly crafted dramatic work produced she is unmatched in her era. Her collected plays represent a lifetime commitment to dramatic writing in pursuit of a cogently articulated aesthetic purpose. Baillie's dramas were, if not perfectly suited to the theatre institutions or audiences of their day, carefully structured and skillfully executed. In fact, she exhibited remarkable tenacity and a high degree of craft in writing for *both* stage and page, something often lost amidst quibbles over the stageability or unstageability of her plays. Baillie was nothing if not "a professional" in her approach to dramatic writing, even if her plays weren't professionally produced with any regularity. What might her presence as a cultural figure – a prolific woman dramatist, committed to writing for the stage and yet resiliently publishing a lifetime's worth of drama while enduring fifty years of sparse production – have meant to other women writers and theatre artists of her era?

We should test the contours of Baillie's dramatic career against our own scholarly and pedagogical paradigms by asking what challenges face us as we try to make a space for her within our existing curricula and histories of the Romantic era. Baillie is ill suited to become one of many other small figures in the newly open canon – the scale of her written production and sustained broad significance as a public figure hardly suit "minor writer status." However, she would also be an odd candidate for a newly expanded major figures canon – she was a dramatist, an unmarried woman, a writer who made little compromise of her authorial purposes for the public and yet showed little disdain for those who received her work with hostility or indifference. So, although Baillie would be miscast as one of a chorus of minor writers of the period, she arrives too late – historiographically speaking – and is too odd in her professional orientations and style to become a major figure without scholars of the era undertaking some substantial rethinking of the cultural field. Furthermore, while Baillie has primarily received attention from scholars of British Romanticism, it would seem paltry to offer her no more than a place in some new version of this sub-discipline's canon, particularly when her potential significance within women's literary history or within dramaturgical history has yet to be sufficiently explored for reasons having to do with the paradigms and predilections that currently shape feminist literary history and dramaturgical history. Work on Baillie needs a bigger space than British Romanticism studies can provide, in part because of the expansiveness of Baillie's work and the wide influences she drew upon. Her peculiar situation in relation to our own era perhaps sheds light on her predicament in her own.

As this volume shows, Baillie's writing has strong connections to many significant discourses of her era. With her family background in medicine and physiological psychology, she writes dramas that merge the rhetorics of case study, clinical observation, and instruction. Widely read in eighteenth-century political and aesthetic philosophy, Baillie employs the figure of the stage – and hopes to employ the actual institution of the theatre – to enact characters, actions, and scenes that might engage the public and affect civic emotions and thought. Baillie's connection to these varied discourses offers us opportunities as scholars and teachers of British literature, theatre, and culture to embed our work with British Romantic texts, performance history, and public culture within a broader web-work of connections. In the essays in this volume, a series of Baillie scholars choose avenues of inquiry with dual purposes – they explore particular aspects of Joanna Baillie's career and fill in pieces of a complex jigsaw of contexts to inform further study of her works. These experiments in ways of knowing Joanna Baillie's drama provide both the evidence and the argument for Baillie's importance to our work.

In the first three chapters in the volume, contributors explore Baillie's life, influences, and contemporary reception. Judith Bailey Slagle, editor of Baillie's letters, gives a short biography of Baillie and an overview of the parts of the Baillie life story that can be found in existing correspondence and unpublished manuscripts. In addition, in her chapter "Evolution of a writer: Joanna Baillie's life in letters" Slagle traces some of the background to Baillie's literary career and touches upon the highlights of her literary relations. Bruce Graver takes Baillie's acquaintance and correspondence with an American diarist and professor as his subject in "Joanna Baillie and George Ticknor." By tracing their knowledge of each other from a first meeting in July of 1835 to Baillie's sending a copy of her 1851 plays that arrived after her death, Graver reveals aspects of Baillie's reputation in America, showing how her plays were understood by many to be a touchstone of the era's literary dramaturgy. In his chapter, "Joanna Baillie, Matthew Baillie, and the pathology of the passions," Frederick Burwick parallels Joanna Baillie's plays with two of her brother Matthew's

works, the supplements to his book *Morbid Anatomy* and his Gulstonian
Lectures. Burwick demonstrates that both Baillies give attention to the
internal sources of the disorders of the mind, and through his comparison
Burwick reveals that Baillie's plays were indeed based on a different set of
assumptions than those of classical tragedy, a point that Baillie herself
made in critical defenses of her plays during her career. By elaborating on
different aspects of Baillie's life context, these chapters reposition Baillie's
plays within her wide range of intellectual and social relationships.

The four chapters that follow apply a series of key contexts to Baillie's
plays, showing how her dramaturgy and themes draw upon a number of
influences and discourses of significance to her era. In "Unromantic
Caledon: representing Scotland in *The Family Legend*, *Metrical Legends*,
and *Witchcraft*," Dorothy McMillan considers diverse facets of Baillie's
"Scottishness" – from her accent to the possible significance of Baillie's
Scottish plays – for our understanding of her personal and political
values. Through close attention to Baillie's Scottish themes and their
context, McMillan gives a sense of Baillie's responses to her British socio-
political context, an important opening to further consideration of Baillie
as a woman of her time. Victoria Myers extends the volume's discussion
of Baillie's relationship to eighteenth-century writers on sympathy and
politics such as Adam Smith and David Hume, showing that Baillie's use
of the term "sympathetic curiosity" allows her to use representations of
the passions for potent dramaturgical effects. In "Joanna Baillie's theatre
of cruelty," Myers provides us with a way to see Baillie's dramaturgy of the
passions within the context of British discussions of political philosophy,
discussions that Baillie's plays rewrite at a particularly complicated
political moment in British culture. In his chapter " Joanna Baillie and the
restaging of history and gender," Greg Kucich connects Baillie's uses of
history to the historiography of key women writers of the era – such as
Wollstonecraft, Austen, and Catherine Macaulay – and to stagecraft, acting
manuals, and the performances of Emma Hamilton. Kucich explains the
sources and significance of the stagecraft of Baillie's complex tableaux
that arrest the progress of historical narrative and expose the social
dynamics of certain key moments in her plays. Drawing from a very
different – but equally important – set of intellectual contexts, in "A neural
theatre: Joanna Baillie's 'Plays on the Passions'," Alan Richardson both
differentiates Baillie's dramatic writing from other examples of Romantic
"mental theatre" and shows how her plays can enrich our understanding
of Romanticism's relationship with its era's theories of the mind.
Richardson focuses on the embodied nature of passion in Baillie's *Count
Basil*, revealing how her dramaturgy makes bodily enactment of feeling
both its means and its subject. These chapters provide examples of how
Baillie's plays engage political, intellectual, and social concerns, showing
how her works can provide a viable countertext to readings in the major
historical issues of her time.

The next four chapters offer ways of interpreting the structures, strategies, and purposes of Baillie's plays. Jeffrey N. Cox explores the important role theatrical spectacle plays in Baillie's drama in his chapter "Staging Baillie." Challenging the view that Baillie wrote for either the closet or an alternative more intimate theatre than the public theatres of her era, Cox explains that Baillie's use of spectacular scenes supports other elements of her dramaturgy – her emphasis on character rather than plot, for example – while also making it difficult for Baillie's plays to achieve their stated moral purposes. Carefully examining the production strategies used to mount *De Monfort* and *The Family Legend*, Cox explores the complex relationship between stage spectacle and authorial intent in the Romantic era. In my chapter, "Joanna Baillie's ambivalent dramaturgy," I consider the mixture of desires at the heart of Baillie's drama for both page and stage. Questioning the historiographic need to resolve Baillie's ambivalence, I consider parallels between Baillie's mixed dramaturgy and the psychological structures of sexual ambivalence, and demonstrate how her dramaturgical strategies influenced the public's experience of her plays and the passions they dramatize. By placing Baillie's *The Tryal* within the context of women's private theatricals, Catherine B. Burroughs' " 'A reasonable woman's desire': the private theatrical and Joanna Baillie's *The Tryal*" (reprinted with kind permission from *Texas Studies in Literature and Language*) invites us to read Baillie's play as an exploration of theatricality's potential for rewriting gender relations. Burroughs' interpretation of Baillie's first published comedy sheds light on women's reasons for participating in private theatricals and on domestic politics. In her chapter "Baillie's *Orra*: shrinking in fear," Julie A. Carlson establishes Baillie's credentials as a "hauntologist," showing that Baillie directly addresses societal ghosts that others would rather encounter second hand – in *Orra* patriarchy's pressure on women. Placing Baillie in the context of recent critical theory on the figure of the ghost in histories of oppression, Carlson offers a new way of parsing Baillie's trafficking with ghosts.

This collection concludes with two contributions that help scholars and teachers pursue further work on Baillie. Marjean D. Purinton, in "Pedagogy and passions: teaching Joanna Baillie's dramas," looks at how we might teach Baillie, examining both what resources exist and how we might link Baillie to current themes in our curricula. Ken A. Bugajski's contribution to the volume, "Joanna Baillie: an annotated bibliography," gathers together in one resource a wide range of citations that facilitate further study of Baillie. Bugajski's bibliography includes recent criticism, information about editions and reviews of Baillie's published works, and reviews of theatrical productions of her plays in her lifetime. Together, the collection's contributions take a wide range of theoretical and pedagogical approaches to Baillie, showing the multiple contexts and strategies that can be applied to her plays.

Exploring the case of Joanna Baillie can be both beneficial and challenging for contemporary scholar-teachers in British Romantic, theatre history, and women's history studies. Her plays provide us with both teachable content and examples of the complexity of one writer's engagement with the cultural venues of her era. Studying Baillie gives us every opportunity to rethink the paradigms that shape how we construct historiographically the meaning of literary publishing and theatre. To make space for Baillie in our thinking, we must shuttle between examining her life, works, and influences, and rethinking our own historiographic practices and beliefs. In effect, we learn about Baillie's potential importance to our fields of study by allowing ourselves to question our own assumptions, pedagogies, and historiographic methods – as we frequently must when considering her work.

For example, the odd relationship between Baillie's dramatic strategies and her "politics" (a subject both Jeffrey Cox and Victoria Myers illuminate in this volume) reminds us how "feminism," as an orientation toward subjects of inquiry explored and kinds of influence sought, cuts across a wide spectrum of political positions on the public issues of Baillie's day. Greg Kucich (in this volume) invites us to ask whether, when it comes to gendered spheres of knowledge and action, Baillie's dramatic method is representational or guided by a theory of influence that hopes to change audience knowledge and action. For Baillie's era, however, her difference in method from comparable dramatists can rightly be termed "feminist" without having to claim that her writing aimed to serve a historically recognizable feminist politics in the public sphere. Through provocatively juxtaposing its particular chapters on Baillie, this volume seeks to raise these kinds of broader complications for our scholarship and teaching.

One cannot remain content with existing British dramaturgical histories or women's literary histories once one considers how Baillie's writing turns inside out our assumptions about what constitutes a good or stageable play or what motivated professional women writers. As scholars and thinkers, we need Joanna Baillie's drama before us as a challenge to our practices and beliefs. The case of Joanna Baillie lures us into putting at risk all that our disciplines and canons rely on in order to understand her work. This volume invites its readers to begin to take that irresistible risk.

2 Evolution of a writer

Joanna Baillie's life in letters

Judith Bailey Slagle

The following biographical work on Joanna Baillie began in a 1994 National Endowment for the Humanities summer seminar held at the London Public Record Office and directed by Professor Paula Backscheider. The cache of more than 800 letters in *The Collected Letters of Joanna Baillie* (1999), which resulted from the initial research, represents the vast majority of Baillie's correspondence in American, British and Scottish repositories and provides the background for this essay and for *Joanna Baillie: A Literary Life* (2002).[1]

In 1757 Joanna Baillie's father, the Reverend James Baillie (1722–1778), married Dorothea Hunter (1721–1806), sister of the famous Hunter physicians of Edinburgh.[2] Their first child, James [William] Baillie, died in infancy. Their second child was Agnes Baillie (1760–1861), the next Matthew Baillie (1761–1823), and the last Joanna Baillie (1762–1851), the sister of a twin who died a few hours after their premature delivery on 11 September 1762 (Crainz 1995: 9).[3] The parents had recently moved to the manse of Bothwell in Lanarkshire, Scotland, because the Rev. Baillie had left a less desirable position in the parish of Shotts. In a Wellcome Institute letter dated 22 February 1838 to her nephew William Hunter Baillie (1797–1894), Joanna answered some of his questions about the Baillie descent as it was partially traced by her friend John Richardson;[4] for during the 1830s both her family and her friend Mary Berry (1763–1852) were encouraging Baillie, already seventy, to leave them with some form of memoir, along with information about her ancestors. In such an autobiographical manuscript (1831), written at the request of her friend and writer Mary Berry, Baillie related her earliest memories of childhood:

> The farthest back thing that I can remember is sitting with my Sister on the steps of the s[t]air in Bothwell Manse, repeating after her as loud as I could roar the letters of the Alphabet while she held in her hand a paper on which was marked in large letters the A B C &c. I was then about 3 years old, and this was, I suppose the very beginning of

my education . . . not being able to read but in a very imperfect manner at the age of eight or nine . . . I was sent to day-school at Hamilton where my Father was then settled as Clergyman, but even the sight of a book was hateful to me . . . I was an active stirring child, quick in apprehending & learning any thing else.

(Royal College of Surgeons of England manuscript HB.ii.56c;
Slagle 1999: 3)

In a similar manuscript ("Memoirs Written to please my Nephew William Baillie") Baillie further elaborated:

My first faint recollections are of Bothwell where I was born and passed the first four years of my life. They are chiefly out of door recollections – running in the garden and looking at the flowers and seeing pigeons flying in the air or gathered on the round roof of a pigeon house that belonged to the manse and above all an occasional walk to the Clyde with my Sister, when our Nurse-maid put us both into the water to be <u>douket</u>[5] and dance & splash about as we pleased. It is curious enough that remembering these little circumstances pretty vividly, almost every thing that passed within doors are almost entirely lost; and that the important change of going to a new residence – Hamilton is in my mind a blanc [*sic*] altogether. My being sent to the reading-school I dont remember, but well do I remember sitting there on a weary bench day after day working on letters & stories which I did not understand and had no desire to know – the worst or one of the worst scholars in the School. My only bright time was when playing out of doors with other Children – playing at make-believe grown people or Gentlemen & Ladies, generally in some open cart or wagon that served us for a house. It is such a common pastime with Children that it would scarcely be worth while to mention it only that I was so particularly fond of it and my Sister who could read and amused herself with books never entered into it at all. But there was one occupation which we both joined in with equal avidity – listening to Ghost stories told us by the sexton of parish who, frequently came to the house of a winter evening and sat by the Kitchen fire. We always, I dont know how, contrived to escape from the parlor when we heard that John Leipen, so he was called, was in the house. His stories excited us much, and as the house we lived in was said to be haunted by the ghost of a man who had in former years hanged himself in the Garret, we became so frighten'd that we durst not go up stairs alone even in broad day light.[6]

Baillie confirmed to Berry that ghost stories had a great deal to do with arousing her and Agnes's imaginations, making them fear the dark as children: "My Father & Mother were never aware of the state of our minds in this respect," she explains, "for we durst not acknowledge it lest we should be obliged to be alone & in the dark to get the better of our timidity" (Royal College of Surgeons HB.ii.56c; Slagle 1999: 4). Certainly, this early penchant for ghost stories may well have been the basis for Baillie's attraction to the Gothic.

Baillie also recalled one of her first "play-fellows," the only daughter (unidentified) of a nearby farmer, whose house she often visited on winter days; it was in this house that the two girls engaged in make believe and spent many pleasant hours together. Both Joanna and Agnes Baillie were obviously well liked by their neighbors and by others who knew of the family, for Joanna reported that "when visitors from a distance" came to her father's house and asked that the sisters be allowed to accompany them to local sites and gardens, "it was also a delightful thing," the pictures in nearby palaces opening their imaginations. These visits, along with excursions into the old forest, explained Baillie,

> did my fanciful untaught mind much good . . . but into the Town itself I never looked to go except in a Fair-day when the streets were crowded with country people & Lads & Lasses, dressed in their holiday gear . . . where the sound of fiddles & dancing gave notice of the merry-making within, to say nothing of the booths with all their tempting treasure.
> (Wellcome Institute Ms 5613/68/1–6; Slagle 1999: 4–5)

Joanna and Agnes went away to boarding school in Glasgow in 1772, where, Joanna conceded, she finally developed an interest in learning to read before she began school. This she did in order to avoid embarrassment but found that she still had no real pleasure in books, proving to be very much like her uncle John Hunter in her proclivity for experimentation rather than sophistic exercise. It happened, however, that shortly before her venture to boarding school she stumbled on some broken bottles one day, cut her ankle, and was required by the doctor to lie upon the sofa for several weeks:

> Agnes, like a kind Sister came to me with books in her hand and coaxed me to try reading some story . . . in this way Oceans [Ossian's] Poems became the first book I ever read of my own good will without being obliged to do it. . . . I then read of my own accord various poetical works & afterwards prose, though I had not pleasure enough in the occupation to sit at it long at a time. What first induced me to read history was the pleasure of reading by my Brother, sitting by his side & doing as he did, my love for him was beyond all the affection I felt for any body else. . . . When the summer was ended, he went to College and I was put to a boarding school at Glasgow. This great

change of scene and mingling with so many new companions, quickened my mind & opened my ideas & notions in many respects. (Wellcome Institute Ms 5613/68/1–6; Slagle 1999: 5)[7]

To her surprise, at boarding school Joanna found herself as good a reader as the other young girls; this resolved her insecurity somewhat, but her spelling was still imperfect: "This defect has made me all my life an uneasy bad writer of letters," she later wrote in her memoir for Berry, and she also cited difficulties in setting verses to memory. Even as a child Baillie's strength lay in action, and she showed little tolerance for dull assignments.

The Baillie family had moved to Glasgow after the Reverend James Baillie's appointment as professor of divinity at the University of Glasgow in December 1775, and he died suddenly in Glasgow on 28 April 1778.[8] Being left with only a small inheritance, Dorothea Hunter Baillie and her three children were now supported by the generosity of Dorothea's famous brother Dr. William Hunter, who provided them a home at Long Calderwood in Scotland; but Matthew Baillie had received a fellowship in Balliol College, Oxford, so he left the family home for England and soon became a lecturer in anatomy at William Hunter's medical school in Great Windmill Street, London.[9] John Hunter had also become a prominent London surgeon, but the brothers had reportedly had professional differences earlier. A famous argument between the two Hunters over William's supposedly using a discovery of John's without giving proper credit has been made much of, but representatives at the Hunterian Museum, Royal College of Surgeons of England, believe it has been exaggerated.[10] In a letter to Dr. Andrews Norton, however, Joanna revealed that she knew only her uncle John Hunter, never having met her uncle William, who was reportedly as jovial as he was brilliant (Houghton Library MS Eng 944 [8] to Norton; Slagle 1999: 923). William was already dead when Joanna moved to London around 1784, where both he and John had been since before her birth, and there she maintained a close relationship with John Hunter and his wife, the poet Anne Home Hunter, as well as with their daughter Agnes, later Lady Campbell. It was Anne Hunter who first inspired Baillie to write poetry, for Joanna read everything that came from her aunt's imagination.

Shortly after Dr. William Hunter died in 1783, Joanna, Agnes and their mother Dorothea moved to London to be with and keep house for Dr. Matthew Baillie. After Dr. Baillie's marriage in 1791 to Sophia Denman (1771–1845), the daughter of Thomas Denman and Elizabeth Brodie Denman, the two sisters and their mother changed residence several times, moving first to Sunbury, then to Hythe, next to Maldon, and finally settling in Colchester (Slagle 2002: 60). Around the late 1790s the three moved to Hampstead, where they remained the rest of their lives.[11] It was at her initial move to London around 1784 that Joanna Baillie, then 22, seems to have begun to write seriously; but in an account of her earliest writing inspiration, she told Mary Berry:

> My Father had a man-servant who was very vain & particular about his dress though at the same time very uncouth. . . . My first verses were composed in ridicule of him and sung by myself & others to a ballad tune to his great mortification & annoyance. . . . he came privately to me, beseeching me not to sing it, and promising in return to give me a ride behind him every time he took my Father's horse to be watered. I consented: he kept his promise; and this was the first reward I received for what might be termed literary labours. . . . my Brother came one day from the Grammar school, some what disturbed by the Master's having enjoined him & some of his boys of his class to compose a few couplets on the seasons, – My Father saying to him, "tut man! Jack (the name I then went by) could do that.["] I was set to it forthwith and composed a few common-place lines upon the subject, the copy of which has happily been long since lost. . . . However my Mother very sensibly knocked that on the head, by saying to me when I had completed my tenth year, "Remember you are no longer a child and must give up making verses."
> (Royal College of Surgeons HB.ii.56c; Slagle 1999: 7)

After this suggestion, "I followed her advice," wrote Baillie, "and thought no more at that time & long after, of writing verse." During the years of her teens, however, Baillie began to read plays; "a love for the Drama took hold of me," she explained, "and I began to borrow Play books and to read them with great avidity. . . . The only Dramatic books which my Father's library afforded – a copy of Shakespear[e] with no pictures in it was sadly overlooked & neglected" (Royal College of Surgeons HB.ii.56c; Slagle 1999: 7).[12] But then, after her father's election to the Divinity Chair in Glasgow, Baillie related, a gentleman of the town often stayed at the house of her friend Miss Graham and had in his possession a copy of *Bell's Theatre*, with engravings of actors and actresses in stage costumes. This work, certainly more intriguing for a young girl than the unilluminated Shakespeare edition, enhanced her interest in tragedy and comedy. About one of her first girlhood theatrical experiences in Glasgow, she wrote in 1831:[13]

> I now beheld a lighted up Theatre with fine painted scenes and gay dressed Gentlemen & Ladies acting a story on the stage, like busy agitated people in their own dwellings and my attention was riveted with delight. It very naturally touched upon my old passion for make-believe, and took possession of me entirely. The play was a singing sentimental comedy not very interesting in itself but the after-piece was one of Foott's Farces. . . . I with my young companions went

home with our heads full of it; each repeating all the scraps from it she could possibly remember.

(Wellcome Institute Ms 5613/68/1–6; Slagle 1999: 8)

The later move to London and Baillie's ability to see "M<u>rs</u> Siddons and other accomplished Actors in Theatres" increased her love for drama, and one day she explained:

> seeing a quantity of white paper lying on the floor which from a circumstance needless to mention had been left there . . . it came into my head that one might write something upon it . . . that the <u>something</u> might be a play. The play was written or rather composed while my fingers were employed in sprigging muslin for an apron and afterwards transferred to the paper, and though my Brother did not much like such a bent given to my mind, he bestowed upon it so much hearty & manly praise, that my favorite propensity was fixed for ever. I was just two & twenty when we first came to London and this took place I believe the following summer about 9 months afterwards.
>
> (Royal College of Surgeons HB.ii.56c; Slagle 1999: 8)

Baillie demonstrated in her memoir to William that it was a great transition from her somewhat retired country home in Scotland to the dark, narrow streets of London, and the move did little to awaken her imagination. She remained curious about places she had read of and had seen in pictures, but creative inspiration came largely from her aunt Anne Home Hunter (the daughter of surgeon Sir Everard Home), who had written many beautiful and popular songs and read to Joanna "every new composition as it came from her pen":

> To write as she did was far beyond any attempt of mine, but it turned my thoughts to poetical composition. . . . One dark morning of a dull winter day, standing on the hearth in Windmill Street and looking at the mean dirty houses on the opposite side of the street, the contrast of my situation from the winter scenes of my own country came powerfully to my mind. . . . and with little further deliberation I forthwith set myself to write the "Winter day" in blank verse.
>
> (Wellcome Institute Ms 5613/68/1–6; Slagle 1999: 9)[14]

Years after Anne Hunter's death, Baillie still praised her work and her support of women writers.

From the British Library, Joanna began to borrow the dramatic works of French poets Corneille, Racine, Voltaire and Molière, and she later added the plays of Beaumont and Fletcher and older English dramatists: "However," she elucidated, "I did not find much in our old plays to interest me . . . I proceeded in my work, following simply my own notions of real nature, I began to feel imaginary scenes & Theatrical representation."[15] About this time Baillie published her first work, a small volume entitled POEMS; *wherein it is attempted to describe* CERTAIN VIEWS OF NATURE *and of* RUSTIC MANNERS; *and also, to point out, in some instances, the different influence which the same circumstances produce on different characters* (London: Printed for J. Johnson, St Paul's Church-Yard, 1790), which would later become part of her *Fugitive Verses* (1840). But the volume, born of the disparity between Baillie's native Scotland and urban London, evidently garnered little attention, even though it would later influence Wordsworth and Coleridge's more famous *Lyrical Ballads*.[16] Having spent a year back in Scotland, Baillie continued to expand her talent, at the same time increasing her circle of literary acquaintances to include the Barbaulds, Samuel Rogers and Lucy Aikin, who said that "the first thing which drew upon Joanna the admiring notice of Hampstead society was the devoted assiduity of her attention to her mother, then blind as well as aged, whom she attended day and night" (Le Breton 1864: 8).[17]

After 1798, however, Baillie's fame sprang from another source, as Volume 1 of *A Series of Plays: in which it is attempted to delineate the stronger passions of the mind, each passion being the subject of a tragedy and a comedy* was published anonymously in London, including her famous introductory discourse on drama and *Count Basil*, *The Tryal*, and *De Monfort*. Subsequent word of her authorship made her company arguably the most sought after in London literary circles. Thereafter Baillie's was not the sheltered life that some critics have mistakenly indicated,[18] and Lucy Aikin remembered her, excepting Mrs. Barbauld, as making "by far the deepest impression" on her when they finally met:

> I was a young girl when I first met her at Mrs. Barbauld's, to whom she had become known through her residence at Hampstead, her attendance on Mr. B.'s ministry, and her connection with the Denman family. Her genius had shrouded itself under so thick a veil of silent reserve, that its existence seems scarcely to have been even suspected beyond the domestic circle, when the 'Plays on the Passions' burst on the world. The dedication to Dr. Baillie gave a hint in what quarter the author was to be sought; but the person chiefly suspected was the accomplished widow of his uncle John Hunter. Of Joanna no one dreamt, on the occasion.
>
> (Le Breton 1864: 7)

Acquaintances would soon include Walter Scott, Robert Southey, William Wordsworth, Lord Byron, Maria Edgeworth and others. While fame brought her new admirers, however, Baillie later revealed to nephew

William the prejudice she encountered on ultimately confessing authorship:

> The first vol of Plays lay for some months at the Booksellers, who had refused to publish them at his own risk and cared very little about its success, without being called for or noticed, notwithstanding a review of them full of the highest & most liberal praise, published in the first Review for reputation in those days, the writer of it being equally ignorant of the Author. . . . None of those literary persons, as far as I know, took any notice of it but Miss Berry, who saw much company at her house and spoke in the highest terms of it to every body. To her zeal in the cause I have always felt myself to be a debtor. Thus, after a time, it got into circulation, became a subject of conversation in the upper circles, and John Kemble through the medium of my book sellers, asked leave to bring out De Monfort at Drury lane. . . .[19] Thus envigorated, without being intoxicated, I began to write Ethwald . . . so passed away the earlier & brightest part of my career, till the feeble success of de Monfort on the stage, and the discovery of the hitherto conceald [*sic*] Dramatist being not a man of letters but a private Gentlewoman of no mark or likelihood, turned the tide of publing [public] favour, and then influential critics and Reviewers from all quarters North & South, attacked the intention of the work as delineating in each of the Dramas only one passion, and therefore quite unnatural & absurd. . . . the inferences drawn from their <u>own</u> remarks was all that they deigned to lay before their Readers.
>
> (Wellcome Institute Ms 5613/68/1–6; Slagle 1999: 11–12)[20]

Two more volumes, this time bearing the author's name, followed between 1802 and 1812. Volume 2 contained *The Election, Ethwald* (parts 1 and 2), and *The Second Marriage*; Volume 3 contained *Orra, The Dream, The Siege*, and *The Beacon*. When Volume 3 was brutally reviewed by critic Francis Jeffrey in 1812, who just a year before had written that "Southey, and Wordsworth, and Coleridge, and Miss Baillie have all of them copied the manner of our old poets; and, along with this indication of good taste, have given great proofs of original genius" (Greig 1948: 194), Baillie was not unscathed by his attack.[21] For in a letter relating to her friend Fanny Head's translation of Klopstock's *Messiah*, she disclosed to Scott in 1826 that a woman writer's gravest mistake was in revealing her identity:

> She [Miss Head] would fain have kept her name & sex unknown, if her friends would have allowed it, and they were not very wise friends who thwarted her on this point. I speak feelingly on this subject like

a burnt child. John any-body would have stood higher with the critics
than Joanna Baillie. I too was unwisely thwarted on this point.
(National Library of Scotland Ms 3903 ff.131–133 to Scott [13
October 1826]; Slagle 1999: 439)

Baillie had learned from her eighteenth-century predecessors that
anonymity was the best path for a woman writer; and, argues Catherine
Burroughs, even in the nineteenth century, "British female playwrights
were still being regarded as 'culprits'" (Burroughs 1997: 74).

Nevertheless, Baillie continued in a flourish of creative activity,
engaging in a long correspondence with music publisher/historian
George Thomson in 1804 and contributing literally dozens of lyrics for his
Scottish, Welsh, and Irish collections (eleven volumes in all, culminated
by a royal octavo edition of six volumes in 1822) which appeared over two
decades. In 1804 Baillie's volume of *Miscellaneous Plays* (London:
Longman, Hurst, Rees, and Orme) also appeared, containing *Rayner*, *The
Country Inn*, and *Constantine Paleologus*. These plays were later
followed by historical verses entitled *Metrical Legends of Exalted
Characters* (1821), a work greatly inspired by her friendship with Scott
and his historical romances:[22]

> In the great & deserved sensation of admiration excited by the Poems
> of Walter Scott, a few years later, I had my share, and the generous
> encouragement I always received from him was certainly of great use
> in keeping me to my work. The fascination of his heroic Ballads made
> the drama less interesting for a time and then an idea of Metrical
> Legends of exalted Characters, in which there should be no mixter
> [*sic*] of fiction in the events . . . first came into my head. . . . You know
> that I have been in Switzerland and have seen objects there which you
> would naturally expect me to notice but during the short time I was
> in that sublime region, my mind was occupied with anxious thoughts,
> and . . . I carried nothing home with me to add to the indwelling
> treasures of my heart. . . . I did not carry home with me what I might
> have done under different circumstances. The clouds seen in my
> youthful days floating across Benlomon[d] . . . as seen from the high
> lands of Longcalderwood, were my chief store of mountain-Ideas and
> continued so through life.
> (Wellcome Institute Ms 5613/68/1–6; Slagle 1999: 13)

Certainly, Baillie's close collaborative relationship with Scott, to whom
she was introduced in 1806 by writer and friend William Sotheby, touched
her both personally and professionally. Their exchange of criticism and
gifts, along with the unaffected tone in which the two corresponded,
imparts an intimacy neither shared with other correspondents. Baillie also
met the Benthams some time before 1810,[23] William Wordsworth in

1808,[24] and Lord Byron between 1813 and 1815, having become friends with Anne Isabella Milbanke—Annabella to her friends—in March 1812. While her relationship with Wordsworth over the years seems indifferent, her early professional relationship with Byron was quite intense, ended only by his abuse of her friend Annabella. Even afterwards, it was primarily Byron's poetry that Baillie read and criticized in her letters to Scott. And in one of her finest letters, she harshly reprimanded Scott for what she considered his undue praise of *Childe Harold* in the *Quarterly Review*:

> O! why have you endeavoured to reconcile the world in some degree with that unhappy man at the expence of having yourself, perhaps, considered as regarding want of all principle and the vilest corruption with an indulgent eye? indeed my good, my kind, my unwearied friend, this goes to my heart! I truly believe that you have done it to cheer in some degree the despair of a perishing mind and rouse it to make some effort to save itself; but this will not be: you cannot save him tho' by that effort you may depress, a most worthy character who has been already so sinned against, and who bears the deepest part of her distress in silence. And now that I am taking the privilege of a Friend I had almost said of a Mother to rate you thus, let me ask why you have reviewed Lord Bs poetry in a strain of praise which in my simple opinion is far beyond its real merit? I may not think you insincere and therefore I must even believe that your wits have been a wool gathering. I shall give but one instance of it as I would not prolong my letter: the thunder storm on the Lake which you praise as the most sublime discription [*sic*]

> > "Far along – From peak to peak the rattling crags among,
> > Leaps the live thunder! Not from one cloud alone
> > But every mountain now hath found a tongue
> > And Jura answers thro' her misty shroud
> > Back to the joyous Alps who call to her aloud."

> > "And the big rain comes dancing to the earth
> > And now again 'tis black – and now the glee
> > Of the loud hills shakes with its mountain mirth."
> >   [Canto III, XCII and XCIII]

These familiar personifications give meanness instead of sublimity to the discription (if discription it may be called) besides being far-fetched & fantastical. I have transcribed these lines from the Edin͞ review which also greatly praises this passage, but nonetheless my opinion is the same in spite of two such high authorities. What I should consider as bad in Wordsworth I can never believe is good in Lord Byron.

(National Library of Scotland Ms 3888 ff.37–9 to Scott; Slagle 1999: 362–4)[25]

While Baillie's candor with Scott is unmistakable in her letters, her fascination with his historical romances and with his natural settings is also unmistakable and clearly influenced her own *Metrical Legends*. After *Metrical Legends*, however, Baillie directed her creativity toward poetry and "charitable" editing for a while.[26]

In 1822, soliciting unpublished works from her close circle of creative companions, Baillie proposed to edit a volume of poetry for the benefit of a needy friend, Mrs. James Stirling, and to call it *A Collection of Poems, Chiefly Manuscript, and from Living Authors* (London: Longman, Hurst, Rees, Orme, and Brown, 1823). Most of her letters from 1822–23 refer to this edition, which contained poems by Walter Scott, Thomas Campbell, Anne Home Hunter, Robert Southey, William Wordsworth, George Crabbe, Anna Laetitia Barbauld, Samuel Rogers, Felicia Hemans, Anna Maria Porter, Anne Grant of Laggan, herself and many others, earning well over £2,000 with its subscription. Baillie's letters throughout this task reveal her good business sense, tenacity, critical perceptiveness, and tactful editing, for she had no compunction about sending bad poetry back for revision. This enthusiastic period was dampened, however, by the unexpected death of her brother Matthew on 23 September 1823, from which her spirits never seem to have entirely recovered. Because of her longevity, Baillie witnessed the deaths of most of her closest friends and many family members, but a major blow also came with the death of Sir Walter Scott in 1832. In one of Scott's last visits to London (1828), he recorded a meeting with his old friend:

> Breakfasted with Joanna Baillie and found that gifted person extremely well and in the display of all her native knowledge of character and benevolence. She looks much more aged however. I would give as much to have a capital picture of her as for any portrait in the world. She gave me a Manuscript play to read upon Witchcraft.[27]
>
> (Anderson 1972: 460)

Even in these later years, Baillie's interest in religious dogma (*A View of the General Tenour of the New Testament Regarding the Nature and Dignity of Jesus Christ*, 1831) and in literary enterprises persisted. She published major British and American editions of *Dramas* (3 vols) in 1836, *Fugitive Verses* in 1840, *Ahalya Baee: A Poem* in 1849, and *The Dramatic and Poetical Works of Joanna Baillie* in 1851, the last volume (composed specifically for her heirs) over which she had control.

And control was, in fact, what Baillie assumed in her life and work. While she was realistic about the plight of a single woman in nineteenth-century Britain, she chose to remain unmarried. When in 1806 her friend Mary Berry was pursued by a certain "Gentleman of Yorkshire," Baillie had advised:

> You wish for employment, and you wish to be useful in the world: as the Wife of a man of fortune you will have this much more in your power than you are ever likely to have by remaining single. . . . This is enough in the mean time to set you thinking upon it seriously which is all I want. – Now in what I am saying to you I am most disinterested, for every single woman, who is to remain so, has great pride in seeing such a woman as you of her Sister hood, and cannot possibly see you quitting the ranks but with considerable regret.
>
> (Wellcome Institute Ms 5616/64 to Mary Berry dated 25 December 1805; Slagle 1999: 156–7)

For the unmarried Joanna Baillie a constant source of pleasure came not only from work, friends, writers and frequent visitors to Hampstead, but from her immediate family. Joanna's brother Dr. Matthew Baillie had become a prominent London physician and one of the court physicians to George III, attending him during many years of illness. He was well paid for his services, his accounts showing that from 1813 to 1820 he received £23,327 from His Majesty (Crainz 1995: 143). Matthew was requested to be present for the birth of Princess Charlotte's child, George IV's grandson and heir to the throne; and as he arrived reluctantly, he spent the day in the library, and was reportedly not responsible for the bungling that caused the death of both mother and son. Before his stay in Gloucestershire, convenient to Windsor, the Baillies purchased Duntisbourne House in 1806, first used as a country retreat but later becoming a permanent home which William Baillie would inherit (Carver 1966: 27). Dr. Baillie was at Duntisbourne as Queen Caroline lay dying and was implored to go at once to London to attend her. As he had always sympathized with the Queen, he set out, later writing his granddaughter that there was nothing he could do for the poor woman, "who died in poverty and unbefriended" (Carver 1966: 32). This series of events and illnesses at court is outlined mostly in Joanna's letters to Scott, in which she exhibited nothing but sympathy and affection for George III during the difficult years of his reign. A declared Whig, her attention to politics and to the Royal Family continued through the reigns of George IV and Queen Victoria, about whom she wrote in many letters.

Joanna's brother and sister-in-law, Dr. Matthew and Sophia Baillie, were the parents of three children, of whom only one, James Baillie (1792–93), did not survive them. Their daughter Elizabeth Margaret Baillie Milligan (1794–1876) and son William Hunter Baillie (1797–1894) were continuous topics of Baillie's letters, and they appear an affectionate family. Baillie's niece Elizabeth Margaret was from the beginning a favorite of aunts Joanna and Agnes and was reportedly fond of both music and poetry. She became a companion of Sir Walter Scott's oldest daughter Sophia (later Mrs. John Lockhart) whenever Sophia accompanied her father to London. In 1816 the Baillie family was initially devastated at her desire to marry Capt. Robert Milligan, a mere soldier, evident in Joanna's letter to Scott in July of that year. But the couple appear to have been very compatible and lived most of their lives with their only daughter, Sophia Milligan (1817–82) near the coast at Ryde, where all the Baillies often visited.

Joanna's nephew William became the Squire of Duntisbourne Abbots in 1823. He had been provided an expensive education at Westminster School and at Oxford and was later called to the Bar. William was clearly attached to his aunts Joanna and Agnes and visited them almost every day in their last years, while keeping his own family close to them. He knew a variety of engaging people, many of them friends of Joanna, such as Maria Edgeworth and Sarah Siddons. That he was interested in genealogy is indicated in Joanna's letters to him, and he was responsible for having his great-uncle John Hunter's body moved from the vaults of St. Martin's in the Fields to Westminster Abbey. He was present at the trial of Queen Caroline, whom his uncle Thomas Denman defended, and later acted as Judge's Marshal to him when he advanced to the bench;[28] but apparently William never practiced law, mostly traveling and managing his estates. He married Henrietta Duff, the daughter of a Scottish Minister, in 1835, shortly after being introduced to her at the house of Dr. Baron in Margaretta Terrace, Cheltenham;[29] and Dr. Baron later willed his house to the young couple.[30] William and Henrietta were the parents of eight children, but only three outlived their father (William Hunter, Helen Mary Henrietta, and Agnes Elizabeth); and when Henrietta Baillie died in 1857 at the age of 49, William never remarried.

It is disappointing that no early letters survive in Baillie's hand (at least I found none among the hundreds I transcribed) to afford a clearer picture of her young adult life, but from 1804 to her death, her correspondence provides a distinct picture of her life, friends and passions. The letters are a record of her life and should be studied as such. Around 1840, in her later years, Baillie's old nemesis Francis Jeffrey visited her in Hampstead and remembered her as follows: "I found her as fresh, natural, and amiable as ever, and as little like a tragic muse." Two years later he described her as "marvellous in health and spirits, and youthful freshness and simplicity of feeling, and not a bit deaf, blind, or torpid . . . the prettiest, best-dressed, kindest, happiest beauty of fourscore that has been seen since the flood" (qtd. in Lockhart 1837–38: 5, 336).

Joanna Baillie died in Hampstead on 23 February 1851 at the age of 88. As an end to this biographical sketch, I offer the following letter from her nephew William Baillie to her old friend Samuel Rogers:

Tuesday Feby 23 [1851]

4 Upper Harley Street

My dear Sir

I cannot bear that you so old a friend of our family & so much attached to my dear Aunts, should hear an event from the newspapers which I am sure will afflict you very much – My dear Aunt Joanna drew her last breath this day. She was much the same yesterday as she has been for sometime, but after being in bed complained of a pain in her back & chest, & sank till this afternoon about four o'clock when all was over. The pain & weariness she suffered were slight & a more placid termination of life could not be. She only ceased to breathe.

My Aunt Agnes behaved with the utmost firmness & seemed afterwards pretty well. She was in some degree confused, but I trust this was only the consequence of agitation, & a perfectly sleepless night. She took some dinner, & afterwards slept, & I left her sleeping. She was to be conveyed to bed as soon as possible, & Dr Evans was to see her the first thing in the morning.

I am sure you will be interested in all these particulars & remain

Dear Sir

yrs very truly

WHBaillie

(Ms. 14/55, University College London's Sharpe Collection, "Letters from Well-Known People"; Slagle 1999: 18–19)

Various obituaries followed. Below is an excerpt from the newspaper reprint of *The Living and the Dead*, this copy owned by Dr. Williams's Library in London (Ms 8.27), which was reprinted on Joanna's death:

There is something exceedingly striking in the appearance of Joanna Baillie. Though she is no longer young, and her features have lost the glow and freshness of youth, the rays of beauty still linger about her countenance, and over its expression the tyrant has had no power. Her face is decidedly tragic, not altogether unlike that of Mrs. Siddons – and capable of pourtraying the strongest and deepest emotion. Her air is lofty and reserved; and if there be a dash of hauteur in her manner, amounting, at times, almost to sternness, there is, on the other hand, something delightfully winning in the tone of her deep fine voice. Her eye – I hesitated long before I could decide its hue, and, after all, I am not quite certain whether it be dark blue or hazel – has a most melancholy expression; though time has not quenched its fire, or bent, in the slightest, her erect but attenuated form. She appeared about 50; thin, pale, and dressed with a Quakerlike simplicity; and though some might be inclined to say she is too conscious of her powers, and to quarrel with the precision of her manner, there is much of the majesty of a genius about her, and, in person altogether, she is one, who once seen, is not easily to be forgotten.

This would not, however, be Baillie's last memorial, for in the 1890s James Donald would erect the beautiful monument that still stands at St. Bride's Church, Bothwell, Scotland, in her honor.

Playwright and theatre theorist Joanna Baillie was a vibrant woman born into a patriarchal world. Her life spanned the second half of the eighteenth century and the first half of the nineteenth. Aside from her twenty-seven published plays, eight metrical legends and dozens of songs and poems, her great legacy lies in hundreds of eloquent letters from which historians and literary scholars can formulate a sense of the intellectual society emerging with early Romanticism. Baillie witnessed times of social, political, and intellectual change, prompted not only by two major revolutions, but also by important shifts in literary style and focus. She was not only an original drama theorist, but, as Jeffrey Cox asserts, she was central to the Gothic tradition (Cox 1992: 51). Joanna Baillie participated in her era, commenting on relevant issues of her time, issues such as chimney sweeping, animal abuse, and temperance. She was an actor in many ways, not simply a spectator. To conclude, as some writers have, that her life was uneventful and her later years pitiable is both uninformed and critically naive; for even Baillie's later letters reveal a tenacious and ambitious woman, receiving visits from friends and family, publishing *Ahalya Baee: a poem* in 1849, and editing her complete works nearly to the time of her death in 1851 at the age of 88.[31] What is sad, however, is Baillie's lack of genuine acceptance in a male-dominated literary society which, while it may have accepted her as an accomplished "gentlewoman," marginalized her critical intelligence and afforded her visibility mostly through her relationships with famous men, from her uncles and brother to Sir Walter Scott and onward. Yet Joanna Baillie somehow prevailed, successfully balancing her feminism with her nationalism and conservatism.

Notes

1 All manuscript letters cited herein are included in *The Collected Letters of Joanna Baillie* (Slagle 1999). More detailed biographical information may be found in *Joanna Baillie: A Literary Life* (Slagle 2002). I have retained the spelling and punctuation Baillie uses in her letters.

2 Important Hunter/Baillie biographies include the following: Crainz 1995; Dobson 1969; Kobler 1960; Mather 1894; and Peachey 1924 (see Works Cited at the back of this volume for complete bibliographical information).

3 Although this is commonly recorded genealogical information, I have verified dates, etc., through the genealogical data bank maintained by the Church of Jesus Christ of Latter-Day Saints in their London Public Record Office location during summer 1994. There is some discrepancy about the name of the first-born son; biographer Crainz lists him as James, while Hunter House Museum lists him as William.

4 John Richardson (1780–1864) was a parliamentary solicitor and for 30 years discharged the duties of crown agent for Scotland, reputed to be the most learned peerage lawyer of his time. He had literary tastes and in 1821 was introduced to George Crabbe in Joanna Baillie's house; he regularly corresponded with Walter Scott, whose deathbed he attended shortly before Scott's demise. He married Elizabeth Hill, a close friend of Thomas Campbell, in 1811 and had several children (*Dictionary of National Biography* 1938–: XVI, 1118–19). Richardson submitted "Song – Her features speak the warmest heart" for Baillie's 1823 *Collection of Poems, Chiefly Manuscript, and from Living Authors* and, in a letter dated 18 January 1842, tells Baillie that "It is, as it has long been, a great pride and gratification to me to have enjoyed your friendship; a few circumstances of my life have afforded me more real pleasure" (National Library of Scotland Ms 3990; Slagle 2002: 36).

5 Douk or douke: to dive or dip forcibly under water (*Scottish National Dictionary*).

6 This comes from the Wellcome Institute for the History of Medicine Ms 5613/68/1–6 which has no address but a note from William Baillie as follows: "This version must not be published or allowed to be read out of the family, May 25, 1860." There does not appear to me to be any reason for William Baillie's secrecy, for the brief and incomplete memoirs, clearly written in Joanna's hand, only reinforce her powers of imagination even in childhood; I will, however, honor his request and only summarize and provide some excerpts from the manuscript (Slagle 1999: 3–4).

7 Matthew Baillie matriculated at Glasgow University in 1774 (Crainz 1995: 173).

8 Lucy Aikin writes that Agnes remembered the Rev. James Baillie as an excellent parent; once when Joanna was bitten by a dog thought to be rabid, he sucked the wound at the hazard of his own life. But Aikin also reports that he never gave Joanna a kiss, though she yearned to be caressed as a child (Le Breton 1864: 8). Baillie, however, does not mention anything like this in any of her letters.

9 Matthew Baillie's degrees are as follows: BA January 1783, MA June 1786, BM July 1786, MF 1789 (Crainz 1995: 25).

10 The brothers' correspondence is housed in the Royal College of Surgeons Library and in the Wellcome Institute for the History of Medicine.

11 There is a great deal of discrepancy in addresses recorded for Agnes and Joanna Baillie after their move from Dr. Baillie's home. Guildhall Library Pamphlet FO 3155 reports that they moved to Red Lion Hill with their mother in 1802 and after her death in 1806 settled at Bolton House, Windmill Hill,

Hampstead, where they remained the rest of their lives. But letters 11 and 12 to Margaret Holford Hodson dispute this record: "But it seems to be a season of change – with us, for Agnes & I also are about to quit the house in which we spent 21 years, and my Brother has at last been released from his long attendance at Windsor" (no. 11 dated 12 February 1820). The letter following provides a more specific address: "If I were as strong as I have been I would walk to Hendon to see you, for our new house is nearer you than the old one, being on what is called Holly Bush hill & very near the heath, but besides old age & fatigue from moving &c has made me a very poor creature at present" (no. 12 dated 29 March 1820). Baillie, by her own account, moved to the country and then to Colchester with her mother and sister after Dr. Baillie married Sophia Denman in 1791 (Wellcome Institute Ms 5613/68/1–6). The Baillies do not appear in the Rate Books (tax records) for Hampstead until early 1799, then listed in the general area of Nag's Head Side (probably taking in Red Lion Hill). She moves from that address to Holly Bush Hill (probably Bolton House) in 1820 but does *not* live in Bolton House, as reported by historians, for over 50 years (Slagle 1999: 556–7; and Slagle 2002: 207–8).

12 As was the general practice in the eighteenth and nineteenth centuries, Baillie often uses variant spellings of Shakespeare (Shakespear and Shakespere).

13 Bell's edition of Shakespeare's Plays, As they are now performed at the Theatres Royal in London was published by John Bell in 1774. Each play was prefaced by a picture of actors in full costume from a specific scene of the play that followed. Baillie explains further, "I have mentioned Bell's Theatre & Shakespere, but nothing in a dramatic form ever charmed me so much as Milton's Comus which I read (I forget exactly when) a year or two before we left Scotland" (Wellcome Institute Ms 5613/68/1–6; and Slagle 1999: 8). She confirms to Berry that when she was about 15,

> having heard a great deal about Milton I thought I must read Paradise Lost, but after going through the two first books, I could not proceed; it was beyond the level of my mind at that time. But when I was about 3 years older I fortunately met with Comus, and read it with so much delight that I took courage and began again to try Paradise; then indeed I did perceive the grandeur, sublimity & beauty of the Poem, and read through it with great admiration & interest, though the many learned allusions & the Theology did often make it heavy, and I could not help wishing that the great Poet had been a less learned man.
>
> (Royal College of Surgeons HB.ii.56c; and Slagle 1999: 8)

14 "A Winter's Day," later published in Baillie's *Fugitive Verses* (1840, dedicated to Samuel Rogers), begins:

> The cock, warm roosting 'mid his feather'd mates,
> Now lifts his beak and snuffs the morning air,
> Stretches his neck and claps his heavy wings,
> Gives three hoarse crows, and glad his task is done,
> Low chuckling turns himself upon the roost,
> Then nestles down again into his place.
>
> (J. Baillie 1851: 772)

15 In this long memoir, Baillie goes on to explain briefly how she was inspired for plays she later wrote (Wellcome Institute Ms 5613/68/1–6; and Slagle 2002: 67).

16 In her last year, editing *The Dramatic and Poetical Works of Joanna Baillie*, Baillie acknowledged the little volume in the preface to the section titled *Fugitive Verses* after the 1840 publication of the same title:

> The early poems that stand first in the arrangement of this book, I now mention last. They are taken from a small volume, published by me

anonymously many years ago, but not noticed by the public, or circulated in any considerable degree. Indeed, in the course of after years it became almost forgotten by myself, and the feelings of my mind in a good measure coincided with the neglect it had met with. A review, of those days, had spoken of it encouragingly, and the chief commendation bestowed was, that it contained true unsophisticated representations of nature. This cheered me at the time, and then gradually faded from my thoughts.

See Preface to *Fugitive Verses* (J. Baillie 1840) and *The Dramatic and Poetical Works of Joanna Baillie* (J. Baillie 1851: 771). In his 1994 edition of *Poems, 1790*, Jonathan Wordsworth argues that: "It is clear that Baillie's thinking in the Introductory Address was known to Coleridge and Wordsworth as they worked on *Lyrical Ballads*, and influenced the wording of the Advertisement" (Wordsworth 1994: Introduction).

17 Dorothea Hunter Baillie died on 30 September 1806, not 1808 as Carhart states, and was blind for three years before her death (Mitchell Library MS 212c to Lady Davy; and Slagle 1999: 507).

18 For unaccountable reasons, such is suggested both in Carhart's brief 1923 biography of Baillie and in "The Cool World of Samuel Taylor Coleridge: The Question of Joanna Baillie" (Zall 1982: 17–20).

19 *De Monfort* appeared for eight nights, beginning 29 April 1800, at Drury Lane (Cox 1992: 231); Baillie's *The Family Legend*, however, was more successful in Edinburgh. Though Scott's insistence put *The Family Legend* on stage, on 29 January 1810 the curtain rose to a packed house there, and the highland play scored a tremendous success for three weeks, followed by a revival of *De Monfort* (Johnson 1970: 223–4; and National Library of Scotland letters to Scott during 1810–11).

20 One such attack came from the *Edinburgh Review*'s Francis Jeffrey. See Brewer (1995: 165–81) and Donkin (1995: 159–83) for details on Byron's help with reviving *De Monfort* and suppositions about Baillie's failure on the stage.

21 On the publication of Baillie's third volume of plays in 1812, Francis Jeffrey wrote in the *Edinburgh Review*: "Miss Baillie, we think, has set the example of plays as poor in incident and character, and as sluggish in their pace, as any that languish on the Continental stage, without their grandeur, their elegance, or their interest" (Jeffrey 1812: 265–6).

22 The admiration was mutual, and they remained friends until his death. Much of Scott's voluminous correspondence is to Baillie, and he also sent her several gifts, including a brooch set with a sacred green pebble from Iona. The brooch appears in the earliest portrait of Baillie, catching the scarf at her neck. She knitted Scott a purse in return and enclosed a lock of hair from the head of Charles I, with the words "Remember" surrounding it (Guildhall Library Pamphlet FO 2218; and Slagle 1999: Letters to Scott).

23 Baillie mentions Samuel Bentham, younger brother of Jeremy Bentham, often in her letters. Jeremy Bentham writes on 20 November 1810 that he "dined at the Miss. B.'s who had been to see their brother the Dr at Windsor"; Samuel encourages his uncle on 2 January 1813 that: "If you will be so good to come you shall lead down the first dance with Miss Joanna Baillie" (Conway 1994: 83, 300).

24 Baillie describes meeting Wordsworth and Southey in the Lake District in 1808. She writes to Scott in October 1808 about meeting Wordsworth (and Southey) on her visit to the Lakes:

He is a man with good strong abilities and a great power of words, but I fear there is that soreness in regard to the world & severity in his notions of mankind growing upon him that will prevent him from being so happy as he deserves to be, for he is I understand a very worthy man.

(National Library of Scotland Ms 3877, f. 158–61; and Slagle 1999: 240)

Wordsworth provided two sonnets, "Not love nor war" and "A volant tribe of bards," for Baillie's 1823 *Collection of Poems*.

25 In his *Quarterly Review* article from October 1816, Scott had given Canto III of Byron's *Childe Harold's Pilgrimage* a just and generous review, though many of Lady Byron's friends resented it. Byron was deeply moved, and told Murray that Scott "must be a gallant as well as a good man" (qtd. in Johnson 1970: 562).

26 Meanwhile, *Constantine Paleologus* had been performed in Edinburgh in 1820, and *De Monfort* had been brought out by Kean at Drury Lane in November 1821 (Slagle 1999: 559, 569).

27 See Scott's 18 April 1828 entry in Anderson's *The Journal of Sir Walter Scott*. Baillie's play was entitled *Witchcraft: a Tragedy in Prose*. Scott and Baillie met for the last time in the autumn of 1831.

28 George IV's wife Caroline was the daughter of George III's sister, thus George IV's cousin and wife. It was a loveless marriage of convenience, and the couple separated after the birth of their first child, Princess Charlotte. After George IV's accession Caroline came back from Italy to claim her rights as Queen. A bill to dissolve the marriage based on her alleged adultery was proposed to the House of Lords but never put to vote; she died on 7 August 1821.

29 John Baron, MD (1789–1851), was a physician who spent much of his life in Cheltenham and a friend of Dr. Matthew Baillie (*Dictionary of National Biography* 1938–: I, 1189).

30 See both Crainz and Carver, though Carver states incorrectly that only two children survived their father William.

31 For whatever reason, Carhart states that Baillie's closing years were "pathetic" (Carhart 1923: 66).

3 Joanna Baillie and George Ticknor[1]

Bruce Graver

Throughout the last three decades of her life, Joanna Baillie maintained close relations with a group of New England Unitarians, most of them associated with the Federal Street meeting-house in Boston. She was especially close to William Ellery Channing, senior pastor of the meeting-house, whom she regarded as the finest living writer of English prose, and Andrews Norton, the Unitarian theologian and biblical scholar.[2] Through them, she became acquainted with several other members of the Federal Street congregation: Channing's assistants, Orville Dewey and Ezra Stiles Gannett,[3] and Norton's friend and brother-in-law, George Ticknor, the accomplished diarist and Harvard professor of modern languages. The Ticknor Collection at Dartmouth College contains several books and manuscripts that document Baillie and Ticknor's friendship: three letters from Baillie to Ticknor, journal accounts by both George and Anna Ticknor of visits to Baillie in 1835 and 1838, Ticknor's collection of Baillie's published works, including one presentation copy, and letters by Ticknor's friends or acquaintances that contain references to the playwright. From them emerges a clear narrative of the friendship of Baillie and Ticknor, a friendship that provides an interesting glimpse of Baillie herself and calls attention to the significance of her literary reputation in America.

First meeting

When he came to London with his family in 1835, at the beginning of a three-year European tour, George Ticknor set out to re-establish ties formed two decades earlier when he had lived and studied in Europe for four years.[4] Then he had sought out prominent politicians and writers and recorded his impressions, with revisions, in a diary that he was accustomed to share with family and friends. Upon his return to Europe in the 1830s, he renewed his former acquaintances, if they were still alive, but also sought out new ones, particularly among important women writers whom he seems to have ignored first time round. He visited Maria Edgeworth at her home in Ireland, Mary Russell Mitford, and attempted a visit to Channing's close friend and correspondent, Lucy Aikin (Ticknor and Hillard 1876: I, 418–19, 426–32). But, if his journal account is accurate, by far the most engaging of his new acquaintances was Joanna Baillie. In May, 1835, a month before the Ticknors' arrival, Baillie wrote Andrews Norton that "a Sister of your or M<u>rs</u> Norton is on her way to England" and that "we take for granted that when she comes to London she will either honour us with a visit or let us know where we can wait upon her" (Houghton Library MS Eng 944 [11]; Slagle 1999: 931).[5] A few weeks later, she got her wish: on 18 July, bearing a letter from the Nortons, the Ticknors drove out to her home in Hampstead to pay a call. Both George and Anna Ticknor wrote diary accounts of the visit.

George Ticknor's journal[6]

43ᵛ	44ʳ
July 18. Joanna Baillie	July 18. – We had a morning of much less excitement than the evening that had preceded it; but I cannot say it was less agreeable. At XII. o'clock, by appointment, we drove out to Mrs. Joanna Baillie's, at Hampstead – took our lunch with her; – and passed the time at her house till IV. o'clock. The weather was beautiful & the drive out of town & up Hampstead hill afforded us constantly those fine views of London & its environs, which are the subjects of the prints we see at home. We found her living in a small
44ᵛ	**45ʳ**
1835. July 18. Joanna Baillie. *She has a sister, about her own age, living with her – but she was now on a visit at London. We intended to have visited the same morning Miss Lucy Aikin; but she, too, was gone to town. Her usual residence is Hampstead.	and most comfortable, nice, unpretending house, where she has dwelt for above thirty years.* She herself is now above seventy, and, dressed with an exact & beautiful propriety, received us most gently & kindly. Her accent is still Scotch; her manner

strongly marked with that peculiar modesty, which we sometimes see united to the venerableness of age & which is then so very winning; and her conversation, always quiet & never reminding you of her own claims as an author, is so full of good sense, with occasionally striking & decisive remark & occasionally a little touch of humour, that I do not know, when I have been more pleased & gratified than I was by this visit. She lives exactly as an English Gentlewoman of her age & character should live, & everything about her was in good taste & appropriate to her own position – even down to the delicious little table she had spread for us in her quiet parlour. – When I asked her about her own works, she answered my questions very simply & directly; but without any air of authorship; and I was very glad to hear her say, that, in the autumn, she intends to publish the three remaining volumes of her plays, which have been so many years in MSS. thinking, as she said "that it is better to do up all her own work, as she has lived to be so old, rather than to leave it, as she originally intended, to her Executor."[7] She led us a short distance from her house & showed us a magnificent view of London,[8] in the midst of which, wreathed in mist, the dome of

45ᵛ	46ʳ
1835. July 18. 19. London – Leslie[9]	St Paul's towered up like a vast spectre to the clouds & seemed to be the controlling power of the dense mass of human habitation around & beneath it. It is the most imposing view of London I have ever seen; and when we had enjoyed it for some time, we walked slowly back with our kind & venerable hostess & then returned to town. – On our way, we stopped to see Leslie, who is little changed & always simple & pleasant. He had nothing to show us except a sketch on his easel of Autolycus roaring out the ballad in Winter's Tale, while he opens his pack to the astonished peasants. We could hardly foresee what effect it will produce[d *del*] – so little is it now advanced – after our return he made us a visit – very agreeable indeed, – and we dined at home afterwards, with Mr. & Mrs. Richards & Mr. Treadwell which we found truly refreshing, for it is the first time I have done so, since the day of our arrival in London, except to go to the Opera.

Anna Ticknor's journal

83ʳ

1835. July 18.ᵗʰ London.

– This morn. Sydney Smith had promised to breakfast with us, & I was much disappointed when we received an excuse.[10] But we had the more time for a drive to Hampstead, to visit the Miss Baillies, where we were most kindly received, & passed three most agreeable hours. Both

Miss Baillies are the most charming old ladies possible; – calm, intellectual, refined – affectionate to each other, cordial to strangers; with a gentle shyness, entirely controlled by good manners, which is most graceful. They knew so many of our acquaintance & friends at home, that they seemed like old friends themselves. We walked with one of the ladies to the top of the hill, to see the view, & when we came back, found a delicate lunch ready. Their appearance, & manner of living just realises my ideal for two such ladies.

Anne & Mr Richards, who went with us to Hampstead, dined with us, & we tried to keep Mr Leslie, who made us a long pleasant visit just before dinner. We had made him a short call on our way home from Hampstead, & found him in rather a cheerless house, on a new road, outside of London, & with few things to show us. Mrs Leslie was not at home.

There are discrepancies between these two accounts: according to George Ticknor, Agnes Baillie was not at home, whereas Anna Ticknor seems to remember "the Miss Baillies," and refers to Joanna as "one of them." This discrepancy is almost certainly due to Anna Ticknor's method of composition. She normally would make short memoranda of her experiences, almost on a daily basis; some time later, perhaps as late as her return to Boston, these memoranda were worked into a coherent narrative, and that narrative was copied, in her best fair hand, into the leather-bound journal.[11] In this case, she seems to have conflated the 1835 visit with her subsequent one in 1838, when both Agnes and Sophia Baillie, widow of Mathew Baillie, the famous physician, were present (Anna Ticknor's journal breaks off before the 1838 visit took place). In any case, the Ticknors regard Baillie rather differently. For Anna Ticknor, the trip to Hampstead is a pleasant visit to the home of interesting elderly women; she seems almost wholly unaware that one of them is an important writer, nor does she differentiate between Joanna Baillie, her sister, and her sister-in-law. Mainly, she is struck by how well-mannered they are and how many of her American friends they know. From her account, we can surmise either that she had not read Baillie's works, or that the fact of authorship did not concern her much. George Ticknor, on the other hand, is more precise and more purposeful. For him, it is a visit to see the famous writer whom he has read and admired; he sets out to record her manners, appearance, and opinions, and to establish the kind of warm, friendly relations with her that he might use to advantage at a later date. At the same time, he is genuinely delighted by the visit, as is his wife, and seems almost reluctant to leave. Particularly striking is the account he gives of their walk on Hampstead Heath: the genteel, unassuming Joanna Baillie is the agent through which sublime power is revealed.

Baillie's own account of the visit survives in a letter to Andrews Norton of 20 August 1835 (Houghton Manuscript Eng 944: 12; Slagle 1999: 932–3), and has little to do with either the sublime or the literary. Norton had given the Ticknors a letter to deliver, which was apparently both a response to an earlier letter of hers and a letter of introduction. She teases him about his slowness to reply, and then writes:

> M[r] and M[rs] Tickner seem to merit all that you have said of them and we have only to regret that their visit passed so soon away and that it has not been repeated. They talked of going to Scotland & I think Ireland also, and I suppose did leave London soon after we saw them.[12] They are clever, well informed, conversable people, and will make themselves friends wherever they go. I was glad to hear they had been at Lansdown House[13] and some other fine places of fashionable resort which is always a desirable thing for strangers. They brought a very pretty little Girl with them, their Daughter, who seemed quite delighted with the amusement she found here under the direction of their friend Mr Richardson[14] who with his Lady came along with them, viz. a ride upon a Donkey over Hampstead heath. I trust we shall see them again on their return from the North and find that they have gained both health & pleasure from their Travels. I tried to find a resemblance in Mrs Tickner's face to her Sister Mrs Norton, but I could scarcely make it out; the voice is somewhat similar.

Baillie's focus is much more like Anna Ticknor's: manners and family concern her, and the walk on Hampstead Heath has more to do with a little girl's donkey ride than picturesque views. At the same time, she sees pretty clearly what the Ticknors are up to: they are here to "make themselves friends" in "places of fashionable resort," and they seem to be good at it. What is more, she knows that such connections can be mutually beneficial, as she reveals in another letter to the Nortons written a year later, just after the publication of her three-volume *Dramas*:

> My tide of public favour is now, I fear, somewhat on the ebb, but it will not, I hope, leave me entirely aground. You & my other American friends must speak as well of me as you can, that I may retain some degree of reputation where I am particularly ambitious of doing so. – I thank you for mentioning your connections Mr and Mrs Tickner. I am pleased to know that *they* were *pleased* with their short visit to Hampstead, and am glad to think there is a hope of seeing them here again.
>
> (MS Eng 944: 13; Slagle 1999: 935–6)

Baillie understood, then, that friendships with Americans like the Nortons, the Ticknors, and (as she implies elsewhere in the same letter) the Channings were crucial to her literary reputation. America is a vast country with vastly more readers than Britain: she is "particularly ambitious" that its inhabitants appreciate her works.

Second meeting

The Ticknors left London for the continent in late October 1835, and did not return to England until late in March 1838. At that time, they revisited old acquaintances, and among the first they called upon was Joanna Baillie. Records of the visit in the Ticknor Collection include Baillie's letter of invitation, postmarked 3 April 1838, and George Ticknor's journal entry for 7 April.[15]

Joanna Baillie to George Ticknor

Address: George Ticknor Esq.
                Brunswick Hotel
                Hanover Square
Postmark: 3 April 1838

Hampstead tuesday morning

Dear Sir,
I am very much obliged to you for your friendly note of yesterday which I have received this morning and now answer by return of Post. You are very kind to us indeed, and we shall be most happy to see you & M͟r͟s Tickner on Saturday morning, before two o'clock, when I hope we shall have the pleasure of finding you well after your long absence. I regret that we cannot name an earlier day in the week, but at this season of the year many engagements come in the way.

    With best remembrances to Mrs Tickner in which my Sister begs to join, I rest, dear Sir,

Your truly obliged &c

J Baillie

(Manuscript Ticknor 001473; Slagle 1999: 1077–8)

George Ticknor's journal records the visit, one among several on a very busy day. They stopped to see Leslie on the way to Hampstead, visited Baillie's neighbor, Lucy Aikin, in the late morning, the Baillies in the afternoon, and stopped at the H. N. Coleridges', in Regent's Park, for dinner. I present here the entire journal entry, omitting only the dinner at

Coleridge's, which was published with only a slight abridgement in Ticknor's *Life* (Ticknor and Hillard 1876: II, 153). Ticknor intends his readers to contrast the various people with each other, and it seems best to preserve that effect here.

George Ticknor's journal

30ᵛ	31ʳ
1838. April . . . 7. . . Leslie	April 7. This is the season for visiting the Artists in their ateliers, as they have all finished their pictures for the Exhibition, which is soon to open & are glad to show them, in their own way, to their friends privately. So, at his invitation, we went this morning to see Leslie. Falstaff's dinner at Page's – the scene intimated but not given in the Merry Wives of Windsor, – was the principal thing he had to exhibit. It seemed to us to have considerable defects – and what
31ᵛ	**32ʳ**
1838. April 7. London. Leslie. Miss Lucy Aikin.	much surprized us, a defect in the perspective, of the table – as well as the chalky, sketchy manner, to which he has given himself of late. But Sir John himself is a happy hit & so are some other things in the picture. – He had besides two pic-tures in the Flemish manner – a Lady receiving privately a letter from her lover; – and the same lady walking with her father, & meeting the lover, whose some-what fashionable but very respect-ful bow, the father returns with a very formal & wondering saluta-tion, touching his three cornered hat, with admirable surprize & alarm. – But after all, I enjoyed

Leslie more than I did his pictures. His simplicity, his bon-hommie; & a slightly picturesque way he has of telling stories not unlike Allston,[16] are quite delightful.

When we left him, we drove on to Hampstead, and made a visit to Miss Lucy Aikin. But we lost our simplicity which in Leslie had been so winning. She talked with great formality, looking strangely up at the ceiling all the time, and seemed to like to listen to herself. On Canada & Canadian affairs she was quite diffuse – not, I thought, very acute or very accurate.[17] It is hard to judge a person, by a first visit, made with some awkwardness; but whatever may be her other merits, I should be surprized, if, on

32ᵛ	33ʳ

1838. April 7. London. Joanna Baillie

a more considerable acquaintance, she were to prove agreeable.

At the other end of the village, however, we made a most delightful visit to Miss Joanna Baillie. The neatness and propriety of her establishment – her own most nice & most suitable dress – even the delicate little lunch she gave us – everything was in keeping with her own character, position in life, and genius. She might be taken as the model of an English Gentlewoman.[18] Her conversation, too, was like herself – modest & gentle, yet with a decided expression of her own opinions and sometimes a little Scotch humour which mingles

	admirably with her slightly Scotch accent. She talked of Scott with a tender enthusiasm that was [very *deleted in pencil*] contagious & of Lockhart with a kindness that is [rare *del in pencil*] [uncommon *inserted in pencil*], when coupled with his name, & which seemed only characteristick of her benevolence.[19]
	It is very rare that old age or indeed any age is found so winning & agreeable. I do not wonder after thus seeing her two or three times, that Scott in his letters treats her with more deference and writes to her with more care & beauty than he does [to *inserted in pencil*] any other of his correspondents however high or titled.[20] Nor could it well be otherwise. Her presence or even the thought of her would rebuke any feeling not entirely respectful.
33ᵛ	**34ʳ**
1828. April 7. London. Joanna Baillie. Dinner with H. Nelson Coleridge.	Her sister was there, whom I had never seen before – a venerable & kindly person, for whom Joanna showed both affection & respect, consulting her opinion on matters where her own was necessarily decisive. – And finally, Mrs. Baillie, – the widow of the great Doctor was there – but really I was so much occupied & fascinated by the [great *deleted in pencil*] poetess, & her most winning & pleasant talk, that I can give little account of Mrs. Baillie, except, that she returned to London, while we were at lunch; – [& that *del*] An hour later &, in a drenching rain, we followed her; – sorry, very sorry, that we shall hardly again see the delightful, venerable Joanna.

Louisa Park and *Miriam*

Ticknor did not see the "venerable Joanna" again but did correspond with her over the next few years. Two further letters from Baillie survive. In the first, she sends her criticisms of the verse drama *Miriam*, by Louisa Jane Park of Worcester, Massachusetts. Park had written the play in 1825 while living in Boston, circulated it among friends there, and only with considerable reluctance was persuaded to publish it (Duyckinck and Duyckinck 1856: II, 382). The first edition appeared anonymously in 1837, and the corrected second edition, a copy of which Ticknor owned, appeared the following year.[21] Shortly after his return to America,[22] Ticknor sent Baillie a copy of the play; her letter thanks him for the gift and offers warm encouragement for Park's efforts.

Joanna Baillie to George Ticknor

address: George Ticknor Esq[r].
         Boston
postmark: none

Hampstead March 29.th 1839

My dear Sir,

I am very much pleased with your kind & friendly recollection of me and the acceptable present you have made me of Miss Park's "Miriam." I am very glad to have an opportunity of reading new works of real merit, particularly when they come from a foreign country and from the pen of a woman. The Drama is well & elegantly written, and there is much heroic feeling & tenderness & refinement in the principle Characters. The circumstances of the plot too are very well imagined & interesting, and would, I should think, have produced a good effect in acting had that been the object of the writer. The speeches are often too long and the sentiments & thoughts sometimes those of a third person or the Poet [rather *inserted*] than those of characters in real action, but this in a Dramatic *Poem*[23] is very allowable. I hope she will be encouraged to employ her fine Talents in other poetical works and take an honourable place among the distinguished Literary Ladies of your Country. My Sister is also very much pleased with Miriam, and I shall presently lend the work to our accomplished Neighbour D[r] Park,[24] who will I am sure be very proud of his name-sake.*

We thank M[rs] Ticknor & your Daughter very much for their kind remembrances. I hope they have not lost any of the improved health with which they returned to America after their travels in Europe. It really did us good to see them both look so well when we had the pleasure of seeing them last. I am sure they will be pleased as well as yourself to know that my Sister & I have got over the winter upon the whole pretty favorably. Formerly I did not use to say a word about our own health, even to distant correspondents, but now at our advanced age, I take it for granted that a word or two on that point may be acceptable. – I hope D^r & Mrs Norton & their family are well. I hope to have the pleasure of hearing particularly of them in the course of the Summer by Miss Sedgewick,[25] who is (Mrs Jameson[26] informs us) to be in England soon. Mrs Jameson will be kind enough to bring her to Hampstead and I allow myself to think that she will not be unwilling to be brought. Her name is so well known in this country that her general reception cannot fail to be very gratifying. What a clever pleasant book Mrs Jameson has made of her Winter Studies & Summer Rambles in Canada; particularly the last part of it. As I am not a german Scholar nor very conversant in works of art, I cannot well appreciate the Winter Studies as they deserve. She is a very agreeable, amusing woman in herself, and has deservedly become a popular writer in this country, where popular books & popular writers abound. – Again let me thank you for your kind letter & present, and believe me very Sincerely, my dear Sir,

Your obliged friend & Servant

J Baillie

* Miriam appears to me to possess a similar character of poetical beauty with that which has been so much & justly admired in Sergeant Talfourd's Ion.[27] –

(Manuscript Ticknor 839229/1; Slagle 1999: 1078–80)

Baillie's praise and encouragement were communicated by Ticknor through his relation Thomas B. Curtis, who was a friend of Louisa Park.[28] Her reaction is preserved in a letter to Curtis, also found in the Ticknor Collection, dated 28 May 1839 (Manuscript Ticknor 839328/2). The letter is worth quoting at length, as a record of Baillie's literary reputation among younger American writers.

I am much gratified by the thoughtful kindness which prompted you to send me Mr Ticknor's note; and assure you that few occurrences in a singularly happy life have given me more pleasure. To be spoken of at all in a correspondence between two such individuals is flattering; my reverence for Miss Baillie's character as a woman, independently of her high literary reputation, gives a peculiar value to her praise. Its effect, I trust, will be not to stir up any vain emotion, but to stimulate one conscious of her deficiencies to efforts at improvement. – I need not explain to you how much I enjoyed as a daughter in handing your communication to a certain *"Dr. Park"* in these regions.[29] Allow me to thank you for an enjoyment whose source lies so deep; but be assured that I cannot neglect the judicious caution of Mr Ticknor. – I feel indebted to you also for the goodwill which prompted you make me known even in the very land of song; and am glad that the reception of the little nondescript "Miriam" did not make you ashamed of the introduction.

Louisa Park did continue to write, although her production slowed somewhat after her marriage, in 1840, to the Unitarian minister Edward B. Hall.[30] Perhaps because of Baillie's encouragement, her reluctance to publish diminished, and her works appeared regularly under her own name. They include plays, novels, a biography, an elegy in memory of Channing, hymns, and stories and poems for children.

James Hillhouse's *Dramas, Discourses, and Other Pieces*

Baillie's last surviving letter to Ticknor was also written in thanks for a book he had sent her, this time *Dramas, Discourses, and Other Pieces* (Boston, 1839) by James Abraham Hillhouse. Hillhouse, whose father was treasurer of Yale College and a prominent Connecticut politician, had early made a name for himself as a poet, primarily for his poem "The Judgment," which he read at the annual meeting of the Phi Beta Kappa Society in 1813. He subsequently prepared for a business career in Boston, spent a year in Europe, then returned to New York City to work as a hardware merchant. But his first love had always been poetry, especially dramatic poetry, and in 1823 he returned to New Haven, taking up residence at Sachem's Wood, where he lived a life of cultured leisure (Duyckinck and Duyckinck 1856: II, 118). Ticknor had known Hillhouse since at least 1820 (they may have met during Hillhouse's residence in Boston), corresponded with him regularly, and owned several presentation copies of Hillhouse's works. In 1839, as Hillhouse was preparing to publish his collected works, he enlisted Ticknor to negotiate with publishers, oversee the printing, file copyright papers, and even to read proof.[31] Ticknor obliged and, just as the volumes were about to appear, volunteered to send copies of the plays to his literary acquaintances in England. "I shall be glad," he wrote in a letter of 11 September 1839, "to send to Wordsworth,[32] Southey, Rogers, Miss. Baillie, L^d. Holland, Prof. Smyth of Cambridge,[33] [Milman, *inserted*] & as many more as you like to spare for such purposes" (Manuscript Ticknor 839511). Hillhouse replied on 24 October, after receiving the first printed copies: "I feel special good will to all who have worthily attempted dramatic writing – Taylor,[34] Talfourd – Miss Baillie preeminently – Walter Savage Landor – for his Count Julian – &c &c" (Manuscript Ticknor

839574). In fact, the Ticknor Collection includes letters of thanks for Hillhouse's plays from Talfourd, Samuel Rogers, Lord Holland, Henry Hart Milman, Henry Taylor,[35] William Smyth,[36] and, "preeminently," Joanna Baillie.[37]

Joanna Baillie to George Ticknor

address: none
postmark: none

My dear Sir

Hampstead Jan[y]. 16th. 1840

You have been exceedingly kind to me in sending me a Copy of the Dramas &c of your gifted friend M[r] Hillhouse, and I am doubly gratified that it was his own wish also that I should have a copy. I have indeed great cause to be pleased with the present, for it has already afforded me several evenings very interesting reading, and will be kept in store for after perusal when it will not be found, I daresay, to have lost any of its attractions. As a dramatic writer, besides the beauties of his imagery & verse, he has the good quality (too rare a one) of seldom departing from real nature to produce fanciful effect. The character of Demetria[38] is delicately & beautifully drawn, and with her distress one can perfectly sympathize, and with the situation of the sister also in some degree ; though it may, perhaps, be objected as to general effect that the servile Confidant – the female villian should [be *deleted*] have occupied so much of [the *inserted*] dramatic Canvas, I should[39] the picture as a whole is considerably injured by it, but of this I shant be quite sure till I have read it again.[40] Hadad is certainly a work of great power. My Sister in reading it was struck with its merit and so was I, though I have a particular dislike to supernatural beings of any kind turned into passionate Lovers of the fair Daughters of men. I like no such stories either from the pen of Moore, Byron, Edmond Reide[41] or M[r] Hillhouse. I say nothing of Southey in his Curse of Kehema, for that is a professed embodying of eastern mythology altogether. Percy's Masque[42] is written with great spirit and I read it throughout with much pleasure. The interest is kept up & encreases to the very end. If I had a memory to retain what strikes & pleases me in detail, I should quote many beautiful passages from your friends work, for your satisfaction as well as my own, but alas alas! old age has made my bad memory still worse, and a general impression of beauties is all that remains with me after the lapse of a few days, nay sometimes a few hours. – Your book of Charade has amused me, for they are good of their kind and well versified, and probably I should have tried to find out some of them, though I am rather dull at the exercise, but having the key so conveniently at the end, I gratified my curiosity more speedily. – Well; many thanks to yourself & to Mr Hillhouse! I am much endebted to you both.

You are very kind in enquiring after our health and I am very thankful that I can answer it satisfactorily. [E]xcept slight, passing ailments, we have had little the matter with us all the winter, as far as it is passed, and it has generally speaking been very rainy & foggy & damp and by no means favorable for old people taking either air or exercise. My Sister in law whom you so obligingly mention has by no means forgot the agreeable American who conversed with so much animation, and had afterwards the gallantry to take care of her *reticule.* She will be pleased with your recollecting her when I have an opportunity of telling her. She is just recovered from a short but severe bilious attack, and we are to spend some days with her next week, when I hope we shall find her perfectly restored; she is an excellent, intelligent & amiable woman, I wish you were better acquainted with her. She has been one of the greatest blessings of our life ever since she became our Sister in law, – an old story now! – I hope this will find yourself, Mrs Ticknor & your Daughter, well and my Sister begs to unite with me in best regards & wishes to you all. – I say nothing of other American friends, for I am going as soon as a weak eye will permit me again to look on white paper, to write to Mr Norton, and perhaps through this convenient BookSeller of yours, you may not think me too bold in putting the letter under cover with this.

I believe you are personally acquainted with Miss Edgeworth, who is estimated as she ought to be in your Country: I had a letter from her last night with a good account of herself every way. Still writing but very doubtful as to publishing any thing more in her life time. However this may be, her bright mind is still in healthy conditions.

Believe me, my dear Sir, your truly obliged & grateful

J Baillie
(Manuscript Ticknor 840116; Slagle 1999: 1080–82)

As was his custom, Ticknor communicated Baillie's remarks to Hillhouse in a letter of his own, or so we can assume from Hillhouse's response, dated 30 July 1840. Interestingly enough, Ticknor does not seem to have repressed the negative comments, at least those about *Demetria*. And Hillhouse, like Louisa Park, gives another, more effusive indication of how highly Baillie was regarded by American authors.

Miss Baillie's complaint of the female villain's occupying to[43] much of the 2^d & 3^d acts of D. and in that way injuring the work is so true that in years past when I glanced at it, I have been so forcibly struck with the fault as rather to have thought the piece not worth furbishing up. Two reasons only decided me differently – the first, having fixed on no other subject – the second, having always [had *inserted*] a kind of passion for the heroine herself. Miss B.s acknowledgment on the other hand of an adherence to Nature in my attempts is the commendation of all others which I am best pleased to receive at her hands. She has herself striven with a resolute and honest purpose to keep close to the Great Pattern, and she is a competent judge of the success of others in that respect. If I could see her letter I would kiss it, and lay it on my head or my heart whichever is the profoundest token of respect; for I have read her and thought of her from my youth, till I fancied I knew how she looked, & could identify her eyes & voice. Does she not write with *very* black ink, and in a sort of dagger-pointed hand? Perhaps some day you will lend me a letter of hers for a little while. It shall be carefully treated & honorably returned. You may safely send me as you say praise or censure – I will endeavor to profit by it.[44]

(Manuscript Ticknor 840430.)

Whether Ticknor ever allowed Hillhouse his bit of extravagance we may never know, but it seems highly unlikely. Nor will we know what effect Baillie's criticisms might have had on Hillhouse's future dramatic output. The now-forgotten author of *Hadad* and *Demetria* died of consumption in January of the next year.

Last contacts

The correspondence between Baillie and the Ticknors slowed after 1840; no letters from her survive from this period, although she regularly mentions them in her correspondence with the Nortons. On one occasion, in late July 1848, she sent the Nortons a number of presentation copies of the second edition of her theological work, *A View of the General Tenour of the New Testament regarding the Nature and Dignity of Jesus Christ* (London, 1838), and specifically directed that copies be given to "Mr Dewey, Mrs Lee, Mr Ticknor & Dr Ware."[45] Ticknor's copy, inscribed "From the author," is preserved in the Ticknor Collection. Her last letter to Norton, dated 11 January 1850, indicates that Ticknor had recently written to her again and sent as a present his massive *History of Spanish Literature* (3 vols, New York, 1849). "I may now say," she wrote, "how much we are pleased with your friend Mr Ticknor's work on Spanish Literature; it is a treasure for any Library and he has been very bountiful in bestowing it upon me. My love for Chivalry & ballads will follow me to the grave" (Houghton Library MS Eng 944 [39]; Slagle 1999: 988). A note of thanks seems also to have been sent to Ticknor, for a letter cover in her autograph, watermarked J WHATMAN / 1849, addressed to Ticknor and bearing a postmark of 7 January 1850, is preserved in the Ticknor Collection.[46] Unfortunately, the letter itself does not seem to have survived. But it is important to note that, just before her death, as the one-volume Longman edition of her works (1851) was being published, her thoughts were again with her American friends. A letter from Norton to Ticknor preserves the record.

Andrews Norton to George Ticknor

address: none
postmark: none

Cambridge 9 Sep[r]. 1851

My dear sir
A short time before Miss Baillie's death she sent me a number of copies of the new edition of her works. I presumed them to be intended for distribution among her friends in this country. But they are unaccompanied by any letter. After her death, I wrote to her sister for directions; and from a letter in reply (received at Newport) I have no doubt that I shall be complying with Miss Baillie's wishes in sending a copy to you and Mrs Ticknor.[47]

Very truly yours
Andrews Norton

G. Ticknor Esq.
(Manuscript Ticknor 840464)

Joanna Baillie's friendship with the Ticknors is neither the most extensive nor the most interesting of her American connections. Many more letters, over a much greater length of time, were exchanged between her and the Nortons and the Channings, and Channing was a much greater writer than Ticknor, and Norton nearly as important a scholar. But because the Ticknor family and their descendants, the Dexters,[48] preserved so much of the evidence and had the wisdom to keep almost all of it together, we can trace in Dartmouth's Ticknor Collection details about Baillie's influence and reception in America that are difficult to find elsewhere. A steady stream of books, letters, and visitors crossed the Atlantic between Boston and Hampstead; through the efforts of her American friends, Baillie's works and critical remarks were circulated widely and integrated into the emerging body of American literature. If the Unitarian movement in New England and its Transcendentalist heirs looked to Wordsworth as its poet and Coleridge as its sage, it also looked to Baillie as its dramatist.

Ticknor's "venerable Joanna" thus helped to shape American literary culture in ways that we have yet to comprehend.

Notes

1   I am grateful to Philip Cronenwett, Curator of Manuscripts, for permission to quote from or publish manuscripts in the Dartmouth College Library. I am especially grateful to Judith Bailey Slagle, who generously supplied me with a typescript of Baillie's letters to the Nortons, from a draft of her *Collected Letters of Joanna Baillie*. That edition has subsequently been published, and page references to it are cited in the text.

2   Baillie and Channing never met; their correspondence began in the mid-1820s and continued until shortly before Channing's death in 1842. His letters to her were published, in part, in Channing's *Memoir*, and transcriptions of them used in preparing the *Memoir* are now at the Massachusetts Historical Society; her letters to him have never been published, and their whereabouts are unknown. Thirty-nine letters from Baillie to Andrews and Catharine Norton are preserved in the Houghton Library (MS Eng 944 [1–39]); a transcription of another, in the hand of Charles Eliot Norton, is also in the Houghton Library, catalogued with the Widener Manuscripts. Baillie's estimate of Channing can be found in several places, including Ticknor's letter to William Prescott, dated 8 February 1836, and published in Anna Ticknor and George S. Hillard's *Life, Letters and Journals of George Ticknor* (1876: I, 37).

3   Dewey was Channing's associate from 1821–23, after which he was pastor at several Unitarian churches in Massachusetts and New York. He probably met Baillie during a visit to Europe in 1833, and renewed his acquaintance a decade later on a second visit, 1841–43. Gannett was Channing's assistant from 1824 to 1842, the year of Channing's death; he then succeeded Channing at Federal Street (*Dictionary of American Biography*).

4   The occasion of Ticknor's return to Europe was in fact an unhappy one: his son, George, had died the previous summer, and his wife's health had been seriously deteriorating (Ticknor and Hillard 1876: I, 394–401).

5   Baillie's informant was probably William Ellery Channing, several of whose relations were visiting England at this time. In an unpublished letter to Lucy Aikin (Houghton Library bMS AM 1428 [9]), dated 15 April 1835, Channing wrote: "I have said to Mrs Baillie, that I should be glad to have my friends introduced to Mrs Jamieson, Somerville, Austen, & any other ladies whose names & writings are familiar to them."

6   Ticknor regularly entered his journal narratives on the recto pages of his writing notebook; he reserved the verso pages for reference information: dates, notations about people met or places visited, and brief corrections or additions to the original journal entry. I have attempted to reproduce here the appearance of the journal pages by setting recto and verso side by side in parallel columns.

7   Baillie is referring to her *Dramas*, 3 vols (London, 1836). Ticknor acquired this edition of her plays, which is now in the Ticknor Collection.

8   Baillie lived at the top of Holly Bush Hill in Hampstead, just a short walk from Hampstead Heath, whence this view could be seen.

9   Charles Robert Leslie, the American painter and friend of John Constable. Leslie corresponded with the Ticknors regularly and later sent a prospectus for his memoir of Constable, asking them to subscribe (Manuscript Ticknor 832679).

10 The Rev. Sydney Smith, co-founder of *The Edinburgh Review*, one of Ticknor's favorite London friends, whom he had first met in 1819. Twelve letters from Smith are preserved in the Ticknor Collection (Manuscript Ticknor 835422), including the letter of excuse mentioned here. The Ticknors had visited Smith the previous day and on 19 July 1835 heard him preach at St. Paul's Cathedral.

11 At the end of her journal, a number of such jottings are present that are not worked up into coherent entries. Her writing process is described in Allaback and Medlicott (1978: 84).

12 They in fact left London on July 25 and traveled to Ireland and the north of England, returning to London in mid-October (Ticknor and Hillard 1876: I, 418–45).

13 The previous evening, July 17, the Ticknors had attended a concert at the Marquis of Lansdowne's house in Berkeley Square. It was an occasion, wrote Ticknor, "on the highest scale of London magnificence and exclusiveness" (Ticknor and Hillard 1876: I, 413).

14 Baillie's error for "Richards."

15 Anna Ticknor's journal breaks off in January 1838.

16 Washington Allston, the American painter who, like Leslie, spent much of his professional life in London.

17 Ticknor and Aikin were discussing the border dispute between Maine and New Brunswick known as the Aroostook War. The dispute was halted without bloodshed by Winfield Scott in 1839 and ultimately resolved by the Webster-Ashburton Treaty of 1842.

18 Ticknor here may be echoing Wordsworth, who said the same thing about Baillie to Henry Crabb Robinson in 1812 (Robinson 1869: I, 386), The Ticknors had seen a good deal of Wordsworth and Robinson the previous year during their continental tour; they ran into each other by chance in Rome, shared a gondola ride in Venice, and traveled north to Germany at about the same time. They probably discussed Baillie, since, according to Baillie's letter to Catharine Norton of 6 September 1837, when Wordsworth returned to London he sent her greetings from the Ticknors (Slagle 1999: 942; Houghton Library MS Eng 944 [16]).

19 Ticknor had seen Lockhart the previous week at John Murray's; he had, wrote Ticknor, "the coldest and most disagreeable manners I have ever seen" (Ticknor and Hillard 1876: II, 147).

20 Ticknor had been reading Lockhart's *Life of Scott*, as had Baillie herself, for she and Channing discuss the work in their 1838 correspondence (Channing 1848: II, 358–60).

21 A few months later, Andrews Norton also sent Baillie a copy of *Miriam* as well as Park's historical novel, *Joanna of Naples*. Baillie acknowledged the gift in a letter dated 9 August 1839 (Slagle 1999: 947; Houghton Library MS 944 [19]).

22 The Ticknors sailed for home on 6 June 1838.

23 *Miriam* is subtitled *A Dramatic Poem*.

24 Dr. Park is Dr. John Ranicar Park, the surgeon, who was a neighbor and close friend of the Baillies (*Dictionary of National Biography*).

25 Catharine Maria Sedgwick, the prominent novelist from Stockbridge, Massachusetts (Duyckinck and Duyckinck 1856: II, 292).

26 Anna Jameson, the miscellaneous writer who had just returned to England from Canada, where her estranged husband was a prominent government official. Her *Winter Studies and Summer Rambles in Canada* was published in 1838 (*Dictionary of National Biography*). According to the author's

"Preface," Louisa Park had based her historical novel, *Joanna of Naples* (Boston, 1837), on Jameson's *Lives of Female Sovereigns*.

27   Baillie had seen the premiere performance of Talfourd's *Ion* in May 1836; Wordsworth was seated in the next box (Carhart 1923: 37–8).

28   Ticknor's letter to Curtis, dated 20 May 1839, is preserved among the Hall autographs at the Massachusetts Historical Society, as is a letter from Andrews Norton to Louisa Park, dated 7 December 1839, which also conveys Baillie's praise of *Miriam*.

29   Her father, Dr. John Park (Duyckinck and Duyckinck 1856: II, 382).

30   Hall became pastor of First Congregationalist Church (later to change its name to First Unitarian) on Benefit Street in Providence, Rhode Island. He published regularly on theological matters, became active in the anti-slavery movement, and at his death in 1866 was a leader in the Rhode Island Freedman's Association, which was organized to help relocate freed slaves. His published works can be found in the library of the Rhode Island Historical Society.

31   Hillhouse's letters survive in the Ticknor Collection. He was sensitive about the page layout of his plays, and in a letter of 15 March 1839, wrote: "I think I would rather not have my Book printed at all than to have the heading of each Scene in capital letters as in Carey's Ed. of Miss Baillie." He refers to the American edition of Baillie's complete works, *The Complete Works of Joanna Baillie* (Philadelphia, 1832) (Manuscript Ticknor 839215).

32   The sale catalogue of Wordsworth's personal library listed "Hillhouse's (J. A.) Haydad, a Dramatic Poem, 8vo, 1825" (*Transactions* 1966: 247). The Shavers (1978) list no other work by Hillhouse, so it seems likely that Ticknor did not send Wordsworth a copy of the 1839 collection.

33   William Smyth, the Professor of Modern History at Cambridge, who was also a friend of Lucy Aikin and Baillie (*Dictionary of National Biography*).

34   Henry Taylor, author of *Philip van Artevelde* and other plays.

35   Manuscript Ticknor 840151/1, 838253.2, 840466, 838354.4, and 8839678, respectively.

36   Manuscript Ticknor 839413. Smyth mentions the Hillhouse volumes in letters of 8 July and 1 November 1840; like Baillie, he sent an extended critique of the plays, which he did not much like.

37   Andrews Norton also sent Baillie a copy of Hillhouse's works, which she thanked him for in a letter postmarked 2 September 1840, and another dated 8 December 1840. Orville Dewey may have sent her another copy, giving her three (Slagle 1999: 951–4; Houghton Library MS Eng 944 [21–22]).

38   The title character of a play first written about 1815, but not published until 1839.

39   Baillie has omitted a word here, probably "think."

40   To Norton, Baillie is more blunt about the defects of Demetria. "I like [it] least of all, because the Heroine, or rather her envious sister is such a fool as to allow herself to be duped by that gratuitously wicked chamber-woman" (Slagle 1999: 954; Houghton Library MS Eng 944 [22]).

41   John Edmund Reade, poet, dramatist, travel writer, and plagiarist. His *The Deluge, A Drama, in Twelve Scenes* was published in 1839; his travel poem *Italy* appeared in 1838 and plagiarized *Childe Harold's Pilgrimage*. Henry Crabb Robinson (Morley 1938: 615) described Reade as "a vain poet whose works nobody will read."

42   A play based on the ballad "The Hermit of Warkworth" from Percy's *Reliques*.

43   For "too."

44   For the record, Baillie's hand is nothing like what Hillhouse imagined.

45   This letter (Slagle 1999: 981–2; Houghton Library MS Eng 944 [3]) was
     included in the parcel of books and repeated directions sent in a letter of 28
     July 1848 (Slagle 1999: 982–3; Houghton Library MS Eng 944 [35]). The 31
     July letter has been misdated as [1828?] in the Houghton Library catalogue.
     Dr. Dewey is Orville Dewey, Mrs. Lee is Hannah Lee, a prolific writer of
     miscellaneous prose (Duyckinck and Duyckinck 1856: II, 295), and Dr. Ware
     is Dr. John Ware, a prominent physician and brother of Dr. Henry Ware, the
     Unitarian theologian (*Dictionary of American Biography*). Lee, Dewey, and
     Ware had all visited Baillie during the 1840s.
46   The letter wrapper is filed with the letter of 3 April 1838 (Manuscript Ticknor
     001473). The wrapper is sealed with a stamp bearing Agnes Baillie's
     monogram.
47   Oddly enough, the copy Norton sent is not in the Ticknor Collection.
48   The Ticknors' youngest daughter, Eliza, married William Dexter in 1856
     (Ticknor and Hillard 1876: II, 321); the Dexter family presented the Ticknor
     collection to Dartmouth College in 1942.

4 Joanna Baillie, Matthew Baillie, and the pathology of the passions

Frederick Burwick

In the "Introductory Discourse" to her "Plays on the Passions" (1798), Joanna Baillie described her intention to reveal how a character succumbs to a compulsive emotion, which then wreaks its dramatic consequences. She also emphasized the "sympathetic propensities" which prompt a "strong curiosity" to observe the changing moods of others. In her plays, dramatic action involves not just the audience but the characters themselves in watching those changes unfold. She chose to represent dramatic character not in terms of traditional literary models, but rather in relation to the accounts of mental pathology in contemporary medical science.[1] Although she was by no means limited to the works on pathology by her brother, Matthew Baillie, she shared in her early endeavors the typology of mania that her brother had forwarded in his lectures on the "Anatomy and Physiology of the Nervous System" (1794).

After the death in 1778 of his father, Rev. James Baillie, Professor of Divinity at the University of Glasgow, Matthew Baillie, who had commenced his studies at Glasgow, was sent to Oxford, where his uncle, the celebrated anatomist Dr. William Hunter, took charge of his medical studies (Wardrop 1825: I, viii–ix, x–xv; M. Baillie 1896: 51–65).[2] Upon William Hunter's death in 1783, Dorothea Hunter Baillie and her daughters Joanna and Agnes, who had been living during these five years in the Hunter family home at Long Calderwood, moved to Great Windmill Street, where William Hunter had his home and school. Matthew Baillie commenced teaching at the school, served as physician at St. George's Hospital in 1787, completed his doctorate in medicine in 1789, became a fellow of the Royal College of Physicians and was elected to the Royal Society in 1790. With his career now secured, Matthew Baillie married Sophia, daughter of Dr. Thomas Denman (J. Baillie 1853: ix).[3]

Joanna Baillie began her literary career while living with her brother in Great Windmill Street. Here she wrote and published her *Poems* [. . .] *of Nature and Rustic Manners* (1790); here, too, "whilst imprisoned by the heat of a summer afternoon and seated at her mother's side engaged in needlework, [. . .] the thought of essaying dramatic composition burst upon her" (J. Baillie 1853: x). She spent three months composing her first tragedy, "Arnold," which, according to her sister, "contained much fine poetry." That play has been lost, or perhaps rewritten. *Basil, The Tryal*, and *De Monfort*, were written in the following years. In 1798 they were published as *A Series of Plays: in which it is attempted to Delineate the stronger Passions of the Mind; each Passion being the subject of a Tragedy and a Comedy.*

The second series of the "Plays on the Passions" (1802) she dedicated to Matthew Baillie, "for the unwearied zeal and brotherly partiality which have supported me in the course of this work." This second volume included *The Election, Ethwald*, and *The Second Marriage*. Shortly before its publication, Joanna, her sister, and her mother moved to Red Lion Hill, Hampstead,[4] where she prepared a volume of *Miscellaneous Plays* (1804) with two tragedies and a comedy (*Rayner, Constantine Paleologus*, and *The Country Inn*). Upon the death of her mother in 1806, she and her sister moved to Bolton House, Windmill Hill, Hampstead. The third volume of "Plays on the Passions" (*Orra, The Dream, The Siege, The Beacon*) appeared in 1812, and a final installment (*Romiero, The Alienated Manor*, and *Henriquez*) in 1836.

For each of the subsequent volumes, she wrote a preface reaffirming her endeavor to represent the effects of a dominant passion, and briefly delineating the passions she had selected for each play in the collection. The "Introductory Discourse" to the first volume, however, stands as the most thorough exposition of her theory of drama. Drama arouses interest, she wrote, through its appeal to "that strong sympathy which most creatures, but the human above all, feel for others of their kind." "Nothing," Baillie declares, "has become so much an object of man's curiosity as man himself." In the effort to comprehend its own nature, the human mind, even its daily social occupations, seeks to trace "the varieties of understanding and temper which constitute the characters of men." Fundamental skills at deciphering character are acquired in childhood. Even persons of little educational or social advantage may become astute at penetrating the attempts of others to conceal or disguise their thoughts and motives. Amongst the "common occurrences of life," evidence of "vanity and weakness put themselves forward to view, more conspicuously than virtues," and behavior that is "marked with the whimsical and ludicrous will strike us most forcibly." Thus it is that mind is attracted to scenes of affliction:

> If man is an object of so much attention to man, engaged in the ordinary occurrences of life, how much more does he excite his curiosity and interest when placed in extraordinary situations of difficulty and distress? It cannot be any pleasure we receive from the sufferings of a fellow-creature which attracts such multitudes of people to a public execution, though it is the horror we conceive for such a spectacle that keeps so many more away. To see a human being

bearing himself up under such circumstances, or struggling with the terrible apprehensions which such a situation impresses, must be the powerful incentive that makes us press forward to behold what we shrink from, and wait with trembling expectation for what we dread. [. . .] there are very few who will not be eager to converse with a person who has beheld it; and to learn, very minutely, every circumstance connected with it, except the very act itself of inflicting death. To lift up the roof of his dungeon, like the *Diable boiteux*, and look upon a criminal the night before he suffers, in his still hours of privacy, when all that disguise is removed which is imposed by respect for the opinion of others, the strong motive by which even the lowest and wickedest of men still continue to be actuated, would present an object to the mind of every person, not withheld from it by great timidity of character, more powerfully attractive than any other.

(J. Baillie 1853: 2b)[55]

Curiosity and sympathy are the driving impulses in Baillie's theory of the drama, and her subject is the exposure of a person in the thrall of strong emotion. The theatre provides an acceptable arena for the voyeurism that can otherwise be satisfied only by chance and stealth:

How sensible are we of this strong propensity within us, when we behold any person under the pressure of great and uncommon calamity. Delicacy and respect for the afflicted will, indeed, make us turn aside from observing him, and cast down our eyes in his presence; but the first glance we direct to him will involuntarily be one of the keenest observation, how hastily soever it may be checked; and often will a returning look of inquiry mix itself by stealth with our sympathy and reserve. (3a)

To witness a fellow being in the throes of extreme mental agitation and emotional turmoil holds a powerful attraction over our "sympathetic curiosity." Whenever passions are displayed, the gaze must follow. Unlike the momentary sensations of joy or pain, the emotions of fear, despair, hatred, love, jealousy embed themselves deeply into mind and character, influencing all a person's thoughts and actions.

Anger is a passion that attracts less sympathy than any other, yet the unpleasing and distorted features of an angry man will be more eagerly gazed upon by those who are in no wise concerned with his fury, or the objects of it, than the most amiable countenance in the world. Every eye is directed to him; every voice hushed to silence in his presence: even children will leave off their gambols as he passes, and gaze after him more eagerly than the gaudiest equipage. The wild tossings of despair; the gnashings of hatred and revenge; the yearnings of affection, and the softened mien of love; all the language of the agitated soul, which every age and nation understand, is never addressed to the dull or inattentive. (3b)

In our experience of watching the turbulent passions, we soon learn to detect the advance signs of inner turmoil, the tell-tale facial expressions and physical gestures that indicate the struggle to conceal anxieties or desires. Social intercourse requires every individual to be alert to the nuances of disturbance and deviation in others.

> It is not merely under the violent agitations of passion, that man so arouses and interests us; even the smallest indications of an unquiet mind, will set our attention as anxiously on watch, as the first distant flashes of a gathering storm. When some great explosion of passion bursts forth, and some consequent catastrophe happens, if we are at all acquainted with the unhappy perpetrator, how minutely shall we endeavour to remember every circumstance of his past behaviour! and with what avidity shall we seize upon every recollected word or gesture, that is in the smallest degree indicative of the supposed state of his mind, at the time when they took place. (3b)

With her insistence that drama should address the power of emotions to dictate behavior and to compel the overwrought individual to acts of irrational excess, Joanna Baillie enters into the very same province of aberrational psychology that Matthew Baillie had begun to explore in his 1794 lectures on the nervous system. She, too, seeks to ground her analysis of behavior on empirical observation, and to identify the symptoms which foreshadow an impending emotional crisis: "the restless eye, the muttering lip, the half-checked exclamation and the hasty start." Neither of them has confidence in the adequacy of introspection. Because actions in a state of excitement may override volition and even conscious awareness, they can be studied only in the observation of others.

In the first of his Gulstonian Lectures, read before the Royal College of Physicians in May 1794, Matthew Baillie discussed the "Anatomy of the Nervous System," delineating the mechanism of sensory response and what had been discovered of the coordination of motor functions within the cerebellum and of sensory responses within the cerebrum.[6] The second and third lectures, on the "Physiology of the Nervous System," define the conditions of normality and abnormality, repeatedly acknowledging the difficulty of making such discriminations on a physiological basis.[7] Only an autopsy might determine whether the causes of madness were "original" (a disorder of the mind) or "consequential" (a result of some physical cause, such as a tumor, aneurysm, etc.).[8] Such symptoms as confusion or delirium might arise from either cause. In his *Morbid Anatomy,* and in his shorter papers on brain and spinal injuries, Baillie devoted his investigations to the physiological causes (M. Baillie 1797: 454–60; 1792–1802: "The Tenth Fasculus"; 1825a: 165–71; 1825b: I, 1–21). Yet he also conceded that no simple discrimination of mind and brain, of psychological and physiological causes, was possible. Extreme emotional duress could cause spasms that might result in inflammation of the *dura mater*, or bleeding aneurysm in the *pia mater*; furthermore, a persistent emotional condition could also produce a detrimental alteration of the brain.[9] Under circumstances of disease or nervous agitation, the brain may no longer be able to respond to external impressions, and may even generate hallucinatory impressions from within its own disordered condition. Because such "false impressions" occur "in many instances of mania," he asserts, "we may suppose that there are certain changes by which it may be incapacitated from receiving impressions distinctly, or perhaps from receiving them at all" (M. Baillie 1825a: 130). In addition to the effects of physical disease or injury upon the brain, its operations can be altered by habit[10] and its normally healthy response can also be undermined by exacerbation of the nerves.

Concluding his second lecture with attention to the "variety of sensations produced, not by external objects, but by the general affections of our nature," Baillie acknowledges a source of pleasure and pain elicited through moral sympathy. He declares that introspection allows us to become "conscious of the various operations of our own mind, which may be said to produce another class of sensations" (M. Baillie 1825a: 139). The third lecture, devoted to interactions of muscles, nerves, and mind, attempts to explain the effects of strong emotions. The nerves not only convey sensations to the brain, they also convey "the influence of the brain to the different parts of the body which are capable of being excited into motion" (M. Baillie 1825a: 140). Much of this action is independent of any conscious awareness or volitional control.

> The different emotions of the mind are also conveyed along the nerves to different muscles of the body, exciting them into contraction. Each emotion, when raised in a considerable degree, sets in action its appropriate muscles, producing a change in the countenance and attitude, which is expressive of the emotion. This becomes a natural language, and is perfectly understood in all countries; for it depends upon a universal principle in human nature, and is not connected with any arbitrary customs of society. The expressions of the countenance and attitude in anger, revenge, fear &c., when strongly excited, are the same in every country, and are universally understood. Volition has no share in these actions: they may indeed be sometimes repressed by volition, when in moderate degree; but when raised to high pitch, they readily overcome its opposition, which is then very feeble, and produce their full effects.

Muscles are capable of being thrown into a much greater degree of contraction by emotions of the mind than perhaps by any other cause; and it is this circumstance which gives the astonishing strength sometimes exerted by maniacs.

(M. Baillie 1825a: 146–7)

Within a certain range, emotional behavior may be acceptable, but under the sway of stronger passions these involuntary and spontaneous responses can become erratic and dangerous. As in Joanna Baillie's "Introductory Discourse," the "natural language" of the countenance is considered a reliable index of the emotional impulses. While it is possible to engage "natural language" in a dialogue of mimicry (returning a smile, for example), it is not a language over which one can always exercise volitional control.[11] Like other physical responses initiated by the passions, it may occasionally exercise a will of its own (De Monfort, for example, in his responses to Rezenvelt). Disorientation and confusion, the first stages in the onset of delirium and delusion, are often revealed through mimic distortions of "natural language."

Matthew Baillie's most significant contribution to the medical studies of his age was his *Morbid Anatomy* (1793), which provided a detailed summary of the diseased condition of organs of the abdomen, chest, and head. To the second edition (1797) he added an account of the attendant symptoms.[12] Because the condition of the vital organs could be observed only by autopsy, it was crucial for the doctor to diagnose the symptoms early if there was to be any hope for treating a patient. Symptoms not overtly manifest could be determined only through the patient's own account. But patients, swayed by their own fears and prejudices, were not always reliable narrators.[13] Baillie developed "so distinct and systematic mode of putting questions, that their answers often presented a connected view of the whole ailment." In spite of "his sagacity in detecting diseases," he confessed his frequent predicament in being able to do no more than watch in frustration as a disease took its dreadful course: "I know better perhaps than any other man, from my knowledge of anatomy, how to discover a disease, but when I have done so, I don't know better how to cure it" (Wardrop 1825: I, xl–xli).

The plight of the helpless onlooker, who must witness a pathological obsession work its relentless destruction in the mind of a loved one, is a crucial characteristic of Joanna Baillie's tragic heroines. Many of her critics, failing to recognize her radical shift in dramatic focus, presumed that she had simply lacked adequate skill as a playwright to create an heroic character whose fall derives from some "tragic flaw." In mistaking De Monfort, because of his obsessive hatred for Rezenvelt, as a character conceived in terms of the classical model, critics were baffled by Baillie's failure to develop a dramatic struggle with that "flaw." Thomas Campbell, in his *Life of Mrs. Siddons* (1834), summarized the critical complaint:

If Joanna Baillie had known the stage practically, she would never have attached the importance which she does to the development of single passions in single tragedies; and she would have invented more stirring incidents to justify the passion of her characters, and to give them that air of fatality which, though peculiarly predominant in the Greek drama, will also be found to a certain extent in all successful tragedies. Instead of this, she contrives to make all the passions of her main characters proceed from the wilful natures of the beings themselves. Their feelings are not precipitated by circumstances, like a stream down a declivity that leaps from rock to rock, but, for want of incident, they seem like water on a level, without a propelling incident.

(Campbell 1834: II, 254)

In her "Remarks" to *De Monfort*, Elizabeth Inchbald also responded to this prevailing criticism. The spectator, she wrote, "plainly beholds defects" in De Monfort's character and "asks after causes." Since the causes are concealed within the pathological condition of De Monfort's mind, "the hero of the tragedy" seems "more a pitiable maniac, than a man acting under the dominion of a natural propensity." Inchbald has grasped the truth of the matter: the mistake lay in the effort to see De Monfort as "the hero of the tragedy," when he is in fact "a pitiable maniac" (Inchbald 1806–09: XXIV, 2–6). This is not a play with a hero. It is a play with a heroine: Jane de Monfort. She is the one who struggles vainly to rescue her brother from the inexorable progression of his destructive mania. Sarah Siddons recognized this truth when, after her performance in the role at Drury Lane in April 1800, she declared to Joanna Baillie: "Make me some more Jane de Monforts." The suffering heroine, a role she had played with compelling power as Jane Shore and as Mrs. Beverly in *The Gamester,* was one that Siddons found admirably developed in the character of Jane de Monfort.

Among all the attributes of her boldly innovative "Plays on the Passions," none is perhaps more distinctive, or more crucial to understanding her exposition of dramatic character, than the fact that the central character whom she depicts as victim of a manic obsession is not conceived as a tragic hero. The dramatic interest, as she has clearly and emphatically explained in her "Introductory Discourse," resides in the need to observe the influence of the strong passions. Her "Plays on the Passions" provide case studies in obsessive-compulsive, delusional, and phobic disorders. To document her methods of dramatic exposition, I have selected two very different examples: in *De Monfort*, the mind of the male protagonist is overwhelmed by his own obsession; in *Orra*, however, the mental stability of the female protagonist is destroyed by deliberate abuse perpetrated by her male "protectors." Scene by scene, other characters in each play are made to witness the manifestations of confusion, erratic and non-volitional responses, and the "natural language" of gesture and facial expression. Baillie gives to other characters the task of mediating audience response by observing the advent and progression of manic behavior. Not just the symptoms, as described by Matthew Baillie, but also the attentive observation, the deliberate questioning as in doctor–patient dialogue, are part of her dramatic exposition.

From the very opening scene of *De Monfort*, Baillie reveals that the mind of her central character is unsettled. "He is not the man he was," his servant, Manuel, tells the landlord, Jerome. He has become "difficult, capricious, and distrustful." Jerome, too, recalls De Monfort's "unjust suspicion," his acting "haughty, and ungraciously." Both agree that these dark moods are intermixed with "bursts of natural goodness." Jerome suggests that "Something disturbs his mind," but neither can identify a cause. The first signs of De Monfort's moodish or peevish eccentricity might well have been subtle enough to have been ignored, had not Baillie in this opening dialogue prepared her audience to anticipate them. Jerome brings De Monfort "a little of the fav'rite wine" made by his wife. When De Monfort inquires after her, Jerome tells him that she is dead. De Monfort's reply, "Well, then she is at rest," seems aloof and unfeeling. Jerome expected some expression of grief or consolation. De Monfort perceives his unwitting error and apologizes. Starting with this merely inattentive *faux pas,* Baillie gradually adds to the signs of De Monfort's disturbance. The incremental effect, even within the opening scene, is alarming.

Although he has just arrived at the inn himself, De Monfort angrily protests the arrival of other late visitors:

> [Loud knocking without.
> De Monfort.
> What fool comes here, at such untimely hours,
> To make this cursed noise? (To Manuel.) Go to the gate.
> [Exit Manuel.
> All sober citizens are gone to bed;
> It is some drunkards on their nightly rounds,
> Who mean it but in sport.
>
> (I.i.130–134)

The newly arrived visitors are Count Freberg and his lady, who warmly greet De Monfort, who grows progressively more bewildered during the ensuing conversation. To Freberg's query why he has not let them know of his coming, De Monfort has only a vague reply:

> O! many varied thoughts do cross our brain,
> Which touch the will, but leave the memory trackless;

And yet a strange compounded motive make,
Wherefore a man should bend his evening walk
To th' east or west, the forest or the field.
Is it not often so?

(I.i.149–154)

More astonishing, when Freberg expresses his regret that Jane De Monfort has not accompanied her brother and asks how she fares, De Monfort, confused, can scarcely stammer a reply: "She is – I have – I left my sister well" (159). Lady Freberg at first thinks her husband's neglect of the title, "Lady Jane," has prompted De Monfort's confusion. She then notes that he appears fatigued. "Your face is pale," Freberg also observes, "have you been ill?" "No," De Monfort half-heartedly protests, "I think I have been well." Shaking his head, Freberg responds, "I fear thou hast not, Monfort – Let it pass./ We'll re-establish thee: we'll banish pain." (170–171). The first scene closes with Freberg's promise to cheer his friend's spirits by introducing him to "A most accomplish'd stranger: new to Amberg;/ [. . .] so full of pleasant anecdote,/ So rich, so gay, so poignant is his wit,/ Time vanishes before him as he speaks" (190–195). In the monologue at the close of this scene, De Monfort exposes to the audience his incapacity to reciprocate proffered friendship: "my heart stands back,/ And meets not this man's love." Perversely, he wants not friendship but "proscription, yea abuse."

The second scene opens at breakfast the next morning. De Monfort is half-convinced that his landlord's affections are not feigned: "He serves as though he lov'd me." For the moment, he feels release from his paranoic sense that he is surrounded by fawning hypocrites:

This pure air

Braces the listless nerves, and warms the blood:
I feel in freedom here.
[. . .]
Here can I wander with assured steps,
Nor dread, at every winding of the path,
Lest an abhorred serpent cross my way,
To move – (stopping short.)

(I.ii.4–9)

Here his servant, Manuel, alarmed at the malignant turn in his master's thoughts, interrupts: "What says your honour?/ There are no serpents in our pleasant fields." The brief interlude of content has passed. De Monfort resorts to his conviction that he is surrounded by enemies who plot to undermine his health and peace of mind:

But those who slide along the grassy sod,
And sting the luckless foot that presses them?
There are who in the path of social life
Do bask their spotted skins in Fortune's sun,
And sting the soul – Ay, till its healthful frame
Is chang'd to secret, fest'ring, sore disease,
So deadly is the wound.

(I.ii.14–18)

In response to Manuel's prayer that his master may be protected from "such horrid scath," De Monfort describes the persecuted victim: "We mark the hollow eye, the wasted frame,/ The gait disturb'd of wealthy honour'd men." Although De Monfort himself is apparently unaware of this self-description, Manuel immediately recognizes it: "'Tis very true. God keep you well, my lord!"

The precarious equilibrium that Manuel has managed to restore is totally disrupted with the announcement that the Marquis Rezenvelt has arrived. De Monfort falls into a violent rage, pounding the table with his fist, sending the breakfast service crashing to the floor, and threatening to kill the servant who has brought the news. In the ensuing monologue, De Monfort reveals his obsessive fear of Rezenvelt's presumed malice:

He haunts me – stings me – like a devil haunts –
He'll make a raving maniac of me – Villain!
The air wherein thou drawst thy fulsome breath
Is poison to me – Oceans shall divide us! (Pauses.)
But no; thou thinkst I fear thee, cursed reptile;
Though my heart's blood should curdle at thy sight,
I'll stay and face thee still.

(I.ii.68–74)

At this moment Freberg arrives to inquire how De Monfort has passed the night. He expects to find him refreshed, but observes instead that he is even more agitated than on the previous night: "Thy looks speak not of rest. Thou art disturb'd." To De Monfort's claim that he is merely "ruffled from a foolish cause,/ Which soon will pass away," Freberg replies that "something in thy face/ Tells me another tale." He begs his friend to confess what "secret grief" distracts him. De Monfort brusquely asserts that one displays only "the splendid foppery of virtue," while hiding the

secret soul,
With all its motley treasure of dark thoughts,
Foul fantasies, vain musings, and wild dreams.

(I.ii.95–97)

For De Monfort, the pretense of trust and shared confidences is "delusion." Freberg proposes to cheer his friend by introducing "thy townsman, noble Rezenvelt." De Monfort responds to Rezenvelt's greeting with studied aloofness, and to all his overtures of wit and comradery with cold disdain. Failing in a forced attempt to address Freberg and draw the conversation away from Rezenvelt, De Monfort falls into confusion, forgets the time of day, calls for his horse, then declares he has no intent to ride. Rezenvelt affably turns aside his insults, then gently excuses himself. He departs with Freberg, leaving De Monfort alone, "tossing his arms distractedly," and raging over the abuse he has suffered:

> Hell hath no greater torment for th' accurs'd
> Than this man's presence gives –
> Abhorred fiend! he hath a pleasure too,
> A damned pleasure in the pain he gives!
> Oh! the side glance of that detested eye!
> That conscious smile! that full insulting lip!
> It touches every nerve: it makes me mad.
> What, does it please thee? Dost thou woo my hate?
> Hate shalt thou have! Determin'd, deadly hate,
> Which shall awake no smile. Malignant villain!
> The venom of thy mind is rank and devilish,
> And thin the film that hides it.
> Thy hateful visage ever spoke thy worth:
> I loath'd thee when a boy.
> That men should be besotted with him thus!
> (I.ii.193–207)

By the close of the first act, Manuel, Jerome, the Count and Countess Freberg, as well as Rezenvelt, whom De Monfort considers his hell-sent nemesis, have all witnessed De Monfort's tormented behavior.

Jane de Monfort is reunited with her brother in Act II. As in *Basil*, Baillie relies on the artifice of a mask-scene. She provides a rationale for the disguise by having Jane de Monfort, "in quest of a dear truant friend" (II.i.57), arrive from her travels in "homely dress" in the midst of a gala festivity. Freberg, who has just praised "noble simplicity," falls into such lavish praise for Jane's "nobly simple" beauty that the Countess takes his preference as a personal slight. Jane's first concern is her brother's health. Freberg's report that De Monfort is "joyless" confirms her own diagnosis:

> It is the usual temper of his mind;
> It opens not, but with the thrilling touch
> Of some strong heart-string o' the sudden press'd

Freberg's observation that De Monfort has grown "suspicious," however, is answered by an emphatic rebuke. Jane offers a kinder interpretation of her brother's "strange and scowling eye" (II.i.67–70).

In Act V, that she may attend the feast, the Countess offers her a veiled costume from her own wardrobe, which Jane accepts in order that she might "unknown [. . .] speak to him/ And gently prove the temper of his mind" (II.i.103–4). Upon her veiled reappearance, she immediately attracts the attention of both Rezenvelt and her brother. In her disguise, she relates to De Monfort her tale of a brother "who, alas! is heedless of my pain":

> he, who has, alas! forsaken me,
> Was the companion of my early days,
> My cradle's mate, mine infant play-fellow.
> Within our op'ning minds, with riper years,
> The love of praise and gen'rous virtue sprung:
> Through varied life our pride, our joys were one;
> At the same tale we wept: he is my brother.
> (II.i.213–219)

De Monfort's impassioned account of his sister so overwhelms her that she forgets to disguise her voice; she replies "in a soft natural tone of voice" which he recognizes. He no sooner attempts to withdraw her veil than Rezenvelt, mistaking the action as an impolite presumption, intervenes. The two almost come to blows before Jane can reveal her identity.

Retiring from the feast to be alone with her brother, Jane questions him about his sudden departure. She received a letter informing her of his duel with Rezenvelt, a duel in which Rezenvelt disarmed him, and then, in a gentlemanly gesture, returned his sword to him. De Monfort explains his sense of humiliation, and, after much persuasion, confesses his hatred for Rezenvelt (II.ii). Throughout Acts II and III, Baillie shows Jane's nurturing and calming influence. Her efforts at reconciliation go awry when De Monfort refuses Rezenvelt's embrace, offering him only his hand (III.ii). Rezenvelt, now resigned to the continuing enmity, admits to Freberg that he has always loathed De Monfort's officious manner and air of superiority (IV.i). In the next scene, De Monfort attacks Rezenvelt with a sword. As in their previous duel, Rezenvelt, the superior swordsman, disarms him, then offers to return the weapon when his opponent is calmer (IV.ii). But no calm comes to De Monfort; rather, he continues to rave in mounting delirium. Rezenvelt is last seen wandering alone in the woods.

In Act V, Baillie provides a Gothic setting: a convent in the woods, torches burning over a grave, lightning flashing at the windows, sounds of wind and thunder. "A young pensioner, with a wild terrified look, her hair and dress all scattered," rushes in upon the assembled nuns to report hearing horrid cries of "murder!" echoing from the woods. Her entry is followed by that of Brother Bernard, who has discovered a "a murder'd corse, stretch'd on his back,/ Smear'd with new blood." This news has scarcely been delivered when another monk returning from the wood tells of his encounter with a distraught revenant:

> Turning my feeble lantern from the wind,
> Its light upon a dreadful visage gleam'd,
> Which paus'd and look'd upon me as it pass'd;
> But such a look, such wildness of despair,
> Such horror-strained features, never yet
> Did earthly visage show. I shrank and shudder'd.
> If a damn'd spirit may to earth return,
> I've seen it.
>
> (V.i.82–89)

Found and brought to the convent, De Monfort reacts with "violent perturbation" when the corpse is shown to him. Left alone with the murdered Rezenvelt, he is overcome with frenzied anguish and attempts suicide:

> Come, madness! come unto me, senseless death!
> I cannot suffer this! Here, rocky wall,
> Scatter these brains, or dull them!
> [Runs furiously, and dashing his head against the wall, falls
> upon the floor].
>
> (V.ii.91–93)

Temporarily roused from his senseless stupor, De Monfort declares that, in comparison to the mental torment he has endured, comatose mindlessness is a blessing:

> O that my mind in mental darkness pent,
> Had no perception, no distinction known,
> Of fair or foul, perfection or defect,
> Nor thought conceiv'd of proud pre-eminence!
> O that it had! O that I had been form'd
> An idiot from the birth!
>
> (V.iv.4–9)

He wishes for "still unconsciousness," that he might become a "senseless clod." Arrested and bound in chains, he bids his sister farewell. Before he can be led off to prison, De Monfort's wish is granted: he suffers a final paroxysm and falls dead with blood gushing from his mouth.

Baillie, in a note at the close of the scene of De Monfort's arrest (V.iv), states that this would be an appropriate moment for the curtain to drop: "our interest for the fate of De Monfort is at an end." This statement, of course, fully accords with the thesis in her "Introductory Discourse" that dramatic interest is sustained by the compulsive human need to observe "the violent agitations of passion." But her own authorial instincts did not allow her to close the play without providing a finale in which Jane de Monfort may reassert her dignity and her proud devotion to her brother. After dismissing the arresting officers, she requests Freberg to attend to the funeral of Rezenvelt, and from the nuns of the convent she begs permission

> That I, within these sacred cloister walls,
> May raise a humble, nameless tomb to him,
> Who, but for one dark passion, one dire deed,
> Had claim'd a record of as noble worth
> As e'er enrich'd the sculptur'd pedestal.
>
> (V.vi.137–141)

Baillie felt constrained to add a note explaining that these final lines of the play were not intended as a defense of the "true character of De Monfort" but rather "to express the partial sentiments of an affectionate sister, naturally more inclined to praise him from the misfortune into which he had fallen." She has presented him not as a hero with a "tragic flaw," but as an individual whose mental stability has been undermined by manic obsession. Even without that obsession, his good qualities were compromised by a manner which Baillie describes as "proud, suspicious, and susceptible of envy" (J. Baillie 1853: 104).[14]

The role performed by Jane de Monfort in her steadfast loyalty to her brother throughout his progressive mental deterioration has no parallel in *Orra*. In depicting a female character victimized by madness, Baillie is more concerned with revealing her plight as caused more by the ruthless abuse of male authority, than by inherent fragility of mind. To be sure, she has the love and loyalty of Theobald, but the machinations of Rudigere, the villain, succeed in secluding Orra from his intervention. Orra, heiress to the fiefdom of her deceased father, lives as a ward to her uncle, Hughobert, who seeks to marry her to his son, and thus unite the two branches of the Aldenberg estates. Orra, however, recognizes the selfish motives and steadfastly rejects the suit of her cousin. A strongly independent woman, she struggles against male domination. With sarcasm, she scorns the attempts to usurp her "lands and rights" through marriage:

> And so, since fate has made me, woe the day!
> That poor and good-for-nothing, helpless being,

Woman yclept, I must consign myself
With all my lands and rights into the hands
Of some proud man, and say, "Take all, I pray,
And do me in return the grace and favour
To be my master."

(II.i.1–7)

In spite of her forthright assertiveness, Orra, no less than other characters
in Baillie's "Plays on the Passions," has her mental weakness. She
possesses an easily excited sensibility. Readily captivated by ghost stories,
her superstitious imagination cannot resist their horrid delights. She
confesses her fascination with tales of terror:

when the cold-blood shoots through every vein:
When every hair's-pit on my shrunken skin
A knotted knoll becomes, and mine ears
Strange inward sounds awake, and to mine eyes
Rush stranger tears, there is a joy in fear.

(II.i.170–174)

Aware of her susceptibility to superstitious lore, Rudigere conceives of a
plot to possess her. He convinces Hughobert that his hopes to marry her
to his son, Glottenbal, will soon be blighted because she has taken a fancy
for Theobald of Falkenstein, who lingers about the castle seeking
opportunities to meet with Orra. He convinces Hughobert to present
Orra with the ultimatum to accept Glottenbal as her husband. If she
refuses, she must be sent to the family's long-vacant, half-ruined castle in
the Black Forest until she reconsiders. Rudigere offers his service to act as
her protector during her banishment to the Black Forest, a banishment,
he predicts, that will be short-lived because she will promptly repent her
stubbornness and eagerly return to marry Glottenbal.

Catherina, who attends Orra on this journey, has been blackmailed into
obedience to Rudigere for some impropriety which he threatens to
expose. Thus Orra, once she has arrived in the isolated castle, has no
companion to help her avoid Rudigere's sexual advances. Unable to assail
her dignity and integrity, he seeks to undermine her courage by arousing
her superstitious fear. He tries to convince her that he, too, dreads the
spectre that haunts the place. He longs for her companionship to dispel
the gloom:

To hear thy voice, makes ev'n this place of horrors, –
Where, as 'tis said, the spectre of a chief,
Slain by our common grandsire, haunts the night,
A paradise – a place where I could live
In penury and gloom, and be most blessed.

Ah! Orra! if there's misery in thraldom,
Pity a wretch who breathes but in thy favour:
Who, till he look'd upon that beauteous face,
Was free and happy. – Pity me or kill me!

(III.i.83–89)

By exacerbating her fears, he thinks to make her so terrified that she will shrink from being left alone and choose to spend the night in his chamber.

The Gothic romance, as critics have often observed, uses the conventions of supernaturalism as a disguise for an exposition of sexual exploitation.[15] Baillie assembles the conventions: the wicked villain, the maiden in distress, the Gothic castle, the rumors of a ghost. But she resorts to no supernatural disguise. Nor is the advent of Orra's madness but a substitute for supernaturalism. Rudigere's threat of sexual assault combines with the "real agony of fear" to drive Orra to the brink of madness. Finding no escape left to her, she is plunged into insanity. Theobald arrives to rescue her – but too late. In *De Monfort* Baillie delineated the gradual course of the obsession which destroyed her character's mind; in *Orra* madness comes suddenly. In Act V Baillie reveals the devastating affliction. The cause, as surmised by those who see her, was some seizure of the brain:[16]

not her mind? – Oh direst wreck of all!
That noble mind! – But 'tis some passing seizure,
Some powerful movement of a transient nature;
It is not madness?

(V.ii.33–36)

But Orra responds not to attempts to release her from her delusions. She sees herself captive in a borderland where the spirits of the dead intermingle with the living. She rejects the friends who arrive from her uncle's court. Hartman, Theobald's friend, attempts that "*coup d'œil*" which Dr. Francis Willis was reputed to have successfully practiced upon George III in 1789 (Porter 1987: 209–11). When he fixes his gaze upon her, she first seeks to avoid his gaze, then surrenders to his commanding eye. The effect, however, is only to force her into helpless submission.

Take off from me thy strangely-fasten'd eye:
I may not look upon thee, yet I must.
　　　[Still turning from him, and still snatching a hasty look at him as before.
Unfix thy baleful glance: art thou a snake?
Something of horrid power within thee dwells.
Still, still that powerful eye doth suck me in

Like a dark eddy to its wheeling core.
Spare me! O spare me, being of strange power,
And at thy feet my subject head I'll lay!
    [Kneeling to Hartman and bending her head submissively.
                                            (V.ii.106–113)

Neither the stringencies of a moral cure nor the sympathetic
ministrations[17] of Theobald's loving kindness are capable of dispelling
her madness: "Her mind within itself holds a dark world/ Of dismal
phantasies and horrid forms!" The uncle who had abused his
responsibility as her guardian is compelled to listen to, and share, her
vision of her avenging father who comes with hordes of the dead to wreak
his retribution. With "all the wild strength of frantic horror," she takes
hold of Hughobert and Theobald and, as the curtain drops, pulls them
back with her into the dark recesses of the stage.

At the time when *Orra* was published in "Plays on the Passions,"
volume three (1812), Matthew Baillie had already commenced his service
as physician to the deranged George III (M. Baillie 1896: 59–60). During
the years immediately preceding, the physical and emotional demands of
his medical practice began to take its toll: "my health became at length
very much dilapidated, and I had nearly sunk altogether under excessive
labour and great anxiety of mind" (1896: 58). Baillie's own health did not
improve during the ten years he spent looking after the deteriorating
mental and physical health of the king. Like Orra in her madness, the king
imagined himself surrounded by spirits of the dead: "He imagines [. . .]
that he can call from the dead whomsoever he pleases, and makes them
of any age."[18] Deafness, blindness, and increasing dementia did not
retard his manic-depressive mood swings. As late as 1819 he would still
launch into talking fits that continued non-stop for sixty hours. In
November 1819, just two months before his death, the Duke of York
found his father "amusing himself with playing on the harpsichord and
singing with as strong and firm a voice as I ever heard" (Aspinall 1938: II,
298–9). Over the Christmas holidays, however, a final bout of paroxysms
left him bed-ridden. The king died on 29 January 1820. His physician
outlived his patient by only a few years. Exhaustion and emaciation had
utterly incapacitated him by the summer of 1823. On 23 September 1823
Matthew Baillie died.

Joanna Baillie, of course, was to survive her brother by twenty-eight
years. In 1836 she published her fourth volume of the "Plays on the
Passions," and she continued to respond with confident conviction to the
critics who found her focus upon the pathology of mind at odds with the
development of heroic character. Reviews in both the *Quarterly Review*
(January 1836) and *Fraser's Magazine* (February 1836) asserted that the
very subject of *Romiero*, obsessive jealousy, required a comparison with
Shakespeare's *Othello*, a comparison that underscored the inadequacy of

Baillie's exposition of dramatic character. Baillie's defense, "On the Character of Romiero," resorts to the same argument that she had expounded in her "Introductory Discourse." Her concept of dramatic interest is not based on admiration for the masculine ideal of the heroic – an ideal which she has Orra dismiss in her dialogue with Hartman and Theobald (II.i.51–58), Alice and Cathrina (II.i.113–119), Hughobert and Glottenbal (II.iii.101–111). Rather, Baillie grounds her conception of character on human sympathy and a natural curiosity about the peculiarities of the mind. Shakespeare, she replies to her critics,

> goaded his hero to the fatal catastrophe by the machinations of a villain, whose falsehoods he never, or but very slightly, at any time distrusts; and, with such strong faith in Iago, he does conceive that his wife has been grossly false, and, in his rage, calls her by the vile name he believes her to deserve. But must every man, to be entitled to our sympathy when jealous, have his jealousy fastened upon him from without, by the evil agency of another? I thought not; and was not aware that, in representing this passion as suspicious and watchful over small indications of change in the affections of a beloved object, I should make it unworthy of human sympathy.
>
> (J. Baillie 1836: 749)

Here, again, is the crux of Baillie's dramaturgy: like her brother, her attention is addressed to the pathology of the passions. She is not the playwright of the heroic struggle against external opposition; rather, she is the playwright of the more subtle, more devastating enemy within.

Notes

1 When I referred to Joanna Baillie's "Plays on the Passions" in *Madness and the Romantic Imagination* (1996: 11), I cited Janice Patten's "Dark Imagination: Poetic Painting in Romantic Drama" (1992) as pointing to the relevance of Matthew Baillie's studies in pathology. Dorothy McMillan, in " 'Dr' Baillie," has admirably documented the similarities between Joanna Baillie's work and the medical theories of her brother and her uncles, John and William Hunter. In this essay I investigate the relevance of those works which McMillan and other commentators on Joanna Baillie's dramatic theory and practice have not cited: Matthew Baillie's Gulstonian Lectures (read before the Royal College of Physicians, May 1794); the supplements to *Morbid Anatomy* (1795), including the symptomatology added to the second edition (1797) and published separately as *An Appendix to the first edition of the Morbid Anatomy* (1798); and *A Series of Engravings, accompanied with Explanations, which are intended to illustrate The Morbid Anatomy* (1799–1802).

2 At Glasgow Matthew Baillie studied Logic and Moral Philosophy under Thomas Reid. At Oxford he acquired a classical education; for his study of medicine, however, he attended William Hunter's lectures on anatomy and

surgery, George Fordyce's lectures on chemistry, and Thomas Denman's lectures on midwifery.

3   Dr. Denman, obstetrician, studied at St. George's Hospital, was physician accoucheur to the Middlesex Hospital, 1769–1783, and became licentiate in midwifery of the College of Physicians in 1783. Joanna Baillie provides an affectionate description of her sister-in-law in "Verses sent to Mrs. Baillie on her Birthday, 1813" (J. Baillie 1853: 812).

4   The move to Red Lion Hill was precipitated by Matthew Baillie's failing health. Because of quarrels with William Cumberland Cruikshank, his associate at the Great Windmill Street School, he resigned, delivering his last lecture on 18 April 1799. Cruikshank died in 1800. On 5 March 1800 he resigned as well from St. George's Hospital (Crainz cites the unpublished diary of Mrs. Thomas Denman, Matthew Baillie's mother-in-law, now the property of the Rt. Hon the Lord Croft). Judith Slagle, whom I thank for assistance with dates, has found that in a letter addressed from Hampstead to her friend Anne Millar (December 1801; National Library of Scotland 9236 ff.3–7), Joanna Baillie refers to an intended visit to friends on Windmill; in 1804 she uses the Grosvenor address. The evidence Judith Slagle has gleaned from the letters confirms that by December 1801 Joanna, her mother and sister had moved to Hampstead; she has not yet determined the date when Matthew and Sophia moved to Grosvenor Street (Wardrop 1825: I, lii; M. Baillie 1896: 55–6, 58–9; Crainz 1995: 21).

5   When citing Baillie's prose in the 1853 collected works, I provide both page and column; plays are cited by act, scene, and line rather than page number.

6   "Although we may be considered as totally unacquainted with the uses of the particular modifications of structure within the nervous system, yet the chief purposes to which this system in general is subservient are not unknown to us. It is the system through which impressions are communicated from the different parts of the body to the brain, thereby producing sensations; and it is the system through which the influence of the mind, as connected with the brain in volition and various excitements, is communicated to many different parts of the body" (M. Baillie 1825a: 123–4).

7   "When an impression is carried along nerves to the brain, we are totally unacquainted with the change produced there, in order that sensation may take place. We cannot tell whether it is a change produced only at the origin of the nerves along which the impression had been conveyed, or whether it is a change diffused over the whole mass of the brain. We may be said, if possible, to know less of the various changes produced by the various modes of impression, from when the great variety of sensations, of which the body is capable, is derived. Notwithstanding the state of our ignorance upon this subject, we know by experience that several circumstances may take place in the brain, by which it may either be unfitted to receive impressions at all, or will receive them very imperfectly" (M. Baillie 1825a: 128–9).

8   The distinction between "original" and "consequential" madness had been introduced by William Battie, *A Treatise on Madness* (1758).

9   "The brain has sometimes been found more firm and elastic than is natural in cases of mania. I have been informed, however, lately, from the best authority, that this state of the brain is not common in maniacs; and that in them it is generally not more firm, nor more elastic, than in people whose minds have always been sound." Baillie refers to evidence at odds with an older "somatic" notion which presumed that the aberration of thought or behavior corresponded to the physical condition of the brain. Loss of memory, for example, would be evident upon autopsy by loss of brain cells, visible holes in the cerebrum. "Mania," the term referring to an obsessive preoccupation,

had been presumed to be related to a loss of "elasticity" in the brain structure (M. Baillie 1797: 457).

10 Habit has considerable influence in regulating our sensations, as well as many other functions of the body. In general it diminishes the force of sensations according to the degree of the habit, or the frequency of their being excited. It connects sensations with objects with which they are not naturally associated. It can change the nature of sensations, rendering those which were originally agreeable indifferent, or perhaps even disagreeable; and, to the contrary, rendering those at length pleasant which were originally disagreeable to us" (M. Baillie 1825a: 137).

11 "The principle of imitation is also another cause of the action of muscles. This may be said on most occasions to be influenced by volition, for we generally imitate what we previously willed to imitate; but the principle of imitation of any gesture or motion which may have been singular, and may very much have called up the attention of the mind. The state of the mind acts through the intervention of the nerves upon certain muscles, exciting them into action, and producing an imitation of the particular motion or gesture. This is so far from being dependent on volition, that the mind is often not conscious of its taking place; and whenever it becomes so, the imitation is repressed by an exertion of volition" (M. Baillie 1825a: 147–8).

12 "I was led to this publication because I had observed with much attention the morbid appearances in the numerous bodies which were brought into the dissecting room, as well as in the bodies examined at St. George's Hospital, and because I thought that the books hitherto published upon this subject were too diffuse and the descriptions of the diseased appearances were often indistinct and very inaccurate" (M. Baillie 1896: 61).

13 "Patients often explain very imperfectly their feelings, partly from their feelings, partly from their natural deficiency of language, and partly from being misled by preconceived opinions about the nature of their complaints. Medical men also, in examining into the symptoms of diseases, sometimes put their questions inaccurately, and not infrequently mislead patients into a false description, from some opinion about the disease which they have too hastily adopted. All of these are formidable difficulties, which obstruct the progress of our knowledge of the symptoms of diseases" (M. Baillie 1797: xv).

14 Also see Baillie's comments on her later play, *Romiero*, in *Fraser's Magazine* (J. Baillie 1836: 748–9).

15 A major work delineating sado-masochistic motifs, Mario Praz's *The Romantic Agony* (1951), has been followed by a vast number of studies on sexual desecration in Gothic fiction. William Patrick Day, for example, states that "the specific material that made it [the Gothic] so compelling for contemporary readers" was the concern with "masculine and feminine identity" and problems challenging "conventional concepts of identity and family that dominated nineteenth-century middle-class life" (1985: 5).

16 In his account of "Complaints of the Head" (1825a: 165–71), Matthew Baillie reviews the possibility that severe emotional shock as well as physical trauma may cause apoplectic or epileptic seizures. In "The Causes of Madness," *A Treatise on Madness* (1758), William Battie had earlier declared that "the fixed muscular marks of passion discover indeed in their operation that the turbulent storms of joy or anger, which in consequence of pressure upon the nerves, are as much the remoter causes of Madness, and indeed sooner or later are as destructive to every animal power" (1758: 44–5)

17 Vieda Skultans (1975: 9–20, 98–139), Andrew Scull (1993: 56–87), and William Bynum (1981: 35–57) survey major approaches to the treatment of the mad: moral management (imposing a strict regimen of work and

obedience), physical restraint (chains, braces, strait jackets); hydrotherapy (immersion, showers, wet-wraps); and domestication (recreating household routine and social interaction).

18   Lord Auckland, quoted in Ida Macalpine and Richard Hunter (1969: 160–1).

5 Unromantic Caledon

Representing Scotland in *The Family Legend*, *Metrical Legends*, and *Witchcraft*

Dorothy McMillan

Introducing Mrs Hemans's prize-winning poem, "Wallace's Invocation to Bruce," in *Blackwood's Edinburgh Magazine* in September 1819, John Wilson writes: "Scotland has her Baillie – Ireland her Tighe – England her Hemans" (*Blackwood's*, 1819: 686). The £50 prize had been offered by a philanthropic Scotsman who gave it as part of a package which included £1000 towards the erection of a monument to Sir William Wallace. Honouring Hemans in this way, Wilson was taking part in the debates and discussions about national characteristics, in and out of writing, which had gone through various stages of intensity for more than 100 years, and which, for the Scots, had peculiarly mattered since the Union of 1707. Debates about Scottishness often proceeded, of course, in tandem with the related pressure and desire to feel British. It is a commonplace since Linda Colley's *Britons* (1992) that British national identity and the notion of Great Britain "was an invention forged above all by war" (Colley 1992: 5). There were also, as will emerge, more positive reasons for being British but it was certainly an anti-radical stance, proclaiming commitment to an idea that transcended factional and class interests.

In 1819, then, four years after the end of the Napoleonic Wars, Wilson was comfortable in claiming Hemans as an English national writer at the same moment as celebrating her "Scottish" poem. Hemans is permitted to appropriate Scottish history, just as Joanna Baillie had appropriated English history in her two-part, ten-act tragedy *Ethwald*. But *Ethwald* was largely an invention, whereas Wallace was repeatedly celebrated as *the* exemplary national hero by English and Scots alike: Jane Porter's *The Scottish Chiefs* was published in 1809, Joanna Baillie's Metrical Legend of *Wallace,* which draws on Porter's novel, appeared in 1821, although it was written before Baillie was able to read Hemans's poem. Baillie refers, however, to Hemans's poem and to David Anderson's rather weak play which nevertheless had sixteen performances at Covent Garden, probably a tribute to the popularity of the subject rather than the quality of the theatrical piece (Genest 1832: IX, 49). It does seem as though, at least in the years following the end of the French wars, it was possible for an English writer to celebrate a Scottish subject and to win a Scottish prize without being felt to have stepped out of line, a point tellingly made by the *Edinburgh Monthly Review*:

> On this animating theme (the meeting of Wallace and Bruce), several of the competitors, we understand, were of the other side of the Tweed [. . .] Mrs. Hemans's was the first prize, against fifty-seven competitors. That a Scottish prize for a poem on a subject, purely, proudly Scottish, has been adjudged to an English candidate, is a proof at once of the perfect fairness of the award, and of the merit of the poem. It further demonstrates the disappearance of those jealousies which, not a hundred years ago, would have denied to such a candidate anything like a fair chance with a native – if we can suppose any poet in the south then dreaming of making the trial, or viewing Wallace in any other light than that of an enemy, and rebel against the paramount supremacy of England. We delight in every gleam of high feeling which warms the two nations alike; and ripens yet more that confidence and sympathy which bind them together in one great family.
>
> (*Edinburgh Monthly* 1819: 575)

The *Edinburgh Monthly* might additionally have pointed out that Mrs Hemans was born in Liverpool, had a father who was a native of Ireland and a mother of mingled Italian and German descent and had spent her early life in Wales. In 1819 social, political and literary miscegenation seemed "a good thing." But, of course, literary, social and political relationships among the countries of Britain had been before, and would again become, much more edgy than this.

Certainly, national relationships were widely discussed. Reading the letters, memoirs and diaries of the period leaves one with the impression that national differences, and the relative merits of the intellectuals of Scotland and England particularly, were persistent subjects of conversation; and it is common to find reflections in essays and reviews about what constitutes national character in lives and works.

Nationality and national differences, shortcomings or superiorities seem to have been often on the agenda in the Hampstead literary circles in which Joanna Baillie moved, in the correspondence of the various groups to which Joanna Baillie was attached and in the public writings of Joanna Baillie herself and, of course, her close friend Walter Scott. The interest in the matter of nation was naturally stimulated by the interaction of visitors from Scotland and Scottish expatriates. As early as 21 April 1791 Samuel Rogers reports a conversation at the house of Miss Williams in Hampstead occasioned by a visit from Henry Mackenzie, author of *The Man of Feeling*: it may be taken as exemplary. The conversation unsurprisingly turned to Scotland and Mackenzie held forth:

"I believe," said he, "conversation is more cultivated there [Edinburgh] than here. In London the ardour of pursuit is greater. The merchant, the lawyer, and the physician are enveloped in their different professional engagements, but the Scotchman will retire early from the counter or the counting-house to lecture on metaphysics, or make the grand tour of the arts and sciences. I believe we have a more contemplative turn than you, and it arises partly from a defect – the little commerce and agriculture we have among us. We are also more national, and there is not a labourer among us that is not versed in the history of his country."

Mackenzie then tells an anecdote about "an innocent trick that was once played on an Englishman" who was induced to believe that Wilkie, "the celebrated author of the 'Epigoniad'" and an eccentric who dressed like a labourer, was indeed an ordinary peasant. Yet Mackenzie concedes that Scottish learning perhaps does not always go deep:

> "But after all," said Mr. Mackenzie, returning to his subject, "Dr Johnson was perhaps right when he said of us that every man had a taste, and no man a bellyful."
>
> "And yet you will allow that there are many exceptions to the last rule, sir?" said Miss Baillie, a very pretty woman with a very broad Scotch accent. "Mr. Adam Smith – "
>
> "Yes, ma'am," Mr. Mackenzie interrupted with a warmth he seldom discovered, "Mr. Smith was an exception. He had twice Dr Johnson's learning – who only knew one language well, the Latin – though he had none of his affectation of it."
>
> (Clayden 1887: 165–7)

Adam Smith was a friend of Joanna Baillie's uncle, the anatomist and surgeon William Hunter, and Smith's *Theory of Moral Sentiments* almost certainly informs her preface to her *Plays on the Passions*. The whole exchange exemplifies the way in which such conversations were conducted, with generalizations being made and specific counter-instances being adduced. The interest in accent is also a feature of all these discussions of national characteristics.

I shall return to the retention of a Scottish accent by Joanna Baillie and her sister, Agnes, but they were not the only Scottish expatriates to continue to sound like Scots throughout a long life spent outside the native country. The mathematician Mary Somerville, eighteen years younger than Joanna Baillie, seems also to have sustained her Scotticisms throughout her life. Mary Somerville was intimate with the Baillies after she moved to London in 1816. Her reminiscences display the kind of problematic relationship with Scottishness that was typical of expatriate

Scots. In her *Recollections* she speaks of one of the games at her boarding school, kept by Miss Primrose at Musselburgh:

> In our play-hours we amused ourselves with playing at ball, marbles, and especially at "Scotch and English", a game which represented a raid on the debatable land, or Border between Scotland and England, in which each party tried to rob the other of their playthings. The little ones were always compelled to be English, for the bigger girls thought it too degrading.
>
> (Somerville 2001: 19)

But Mary Somerville seems to have made more effort than the Baillies to smooth out her Scotticisms. Maria Edgeworth reports in a letter to her mother in 1822 that Mary Somerville had a "remarkably soft voice though speaking with a strong Scottish pronunciation – yet it is a well bred Scotch not like the Baillies" (Edgeworth 1971: 321). Mary Somerville, again with that obsessive attention to the national, remarks in turn that Maria Edgeworth had "all the liveliness and originality of an Irishwoman" (Somerville 2001: 126). Mary Somerville's daughter reports that she was self-conscious about her lack of formal education, on which she blamed her possible "lapses" into vernacular:

> She herself was always diffident about her writings, saying she was only a self-taught, uneducated Scotchwoman, and feared to use Scotch idioms inadvertently. In speaking she had a very decided but pleasant Scotch accent, and when aroused and excited, would often unconsciously use not only native idioms, but quaint old Scotch words.
>
> (Somerville 2001: 97–8)

But mathematics was certainly not then felt to be as national a discipline as literature and Joanna Baillie inevitably had an even more fraught relationship with the meaning and significance of Scotland than her friend. And so just as Baillie, like other Scots living in England, made actual journeys back to her native land, so she made literary trips throughout her writing life.

Apart from her lyrics, her Scotch songs in particular, Joanna Baillie turned to Scotland on three significant occasions at roughly ten year intervals. In 1810 her *Family Legend* was produced at the Theatre Royal in Edinburgh; in 1821 her *Metrical Legends* included the exemplary domestic heroine Lady Griseld Baillie and the national martial hero William Wallace; and in 1836 her three volume *Dramas* included the musical play *The Phantom* and, more importantly, the prose drama *Witchcraft* – both plays had been written previously, *Witchcraft* having, Baillie says, been prompted by her reading of Scott's *Bride of*

Lammermoor (1819) and she had given the manuscript of the play to
Scott in April 1828 (Scott 1950: 524). Baillie's relationship to Scotland
and her sense of that country's relationship to Britishness inevitably
underwent a series of shifts during her writing life. After all there were,
over these years, a series of Scotlands and a variety of ways of being
Scottish.

One of the most enduring ways of understanding and representing
Scotland, and the one which underpinned Baillie's first major Scottish
work, *The Family Legend* was, of course, the Ossianic. Remarking on Lady
Jane Wilde's explanation of her son's name – "He is to be called Oscar
Fingal Wilde. Is not that grand, misty and Ossianic?" – Fiona Stafford
points out that what is sometimes regarded as "a curious phenomenon of
the later eighteenth century" had an "enduring appeal," as is clear "from
the steady stream of reprints, selections and new editions that continued
to appear for the next hundred-and-fifty years" (Macpherson 1996: v). It
is, of course, true that a Scotland with a misty, heroic past, presented in a
fashionably melancholy manner, was a much less threatening Scotland
than one sending the wild descendants of these heroes across the border
to rout the English, or assertively claiming its political rights. Scotland
(and Ireland and Wales) could be encouraged to enjoy their romantic
pasts, provided that their people increasingly committed themselves to a
British present and future.

While the Ossian poems had a European currency, it was often the
Scots themselves who were fervently committed to the whole Ossian
package; Mary Somerville remembers enthusiastically reading Ossian and
enjoying the Highland scenery the more for her experience of the poems
(Somerville 2001: 55). But enthusiasm was not confined to those lowland
Scots who had little actual experience of Highland traditions. For a
number of commentators, Highland society was becoming a paradigm for
values that had been insufficiently understood before they were destroyed
or undermined. Some kind of appreciation of Highland culture can be
said to inform much of the understanding of other more distant cultures
during the early nineteenth century. Probably no-one writing in Scotland
in the Romantic period worked harder to make Highland culture valued
and understood before it was swept away or corrupted than Anne Grant,
Mrs. Grant of Laggan, and she was to some extent an insider to that
culture as well as a commentator on it.

Anne Macvicar was born in Glasgow of parents with Highland
connections, but from the age of 3 she spent ten years in America in and
around Albany on the River Hudson, her father having a commission in
the regiment of the Earl of Eglinton. After the end of the war in Canada
the Macvicars returned to Scotland, where at 24 Anne married the Rev.
James Grant, a former army chaplain who had been settled for some years
in the parish of Laggan in Inverness-shire. Anne Grant became the loving,
although not uncritical, interpreter to the wider world of the culture she

found in Laggan: she herself learned Gaelic to promote cultural understanding. She subsequently published both on Highland culture and on the societies she remembered in America. She generally praises Highland society at the expense of Southern sophistication on both sides of the border: "I know nothing so silly," she writes from Fort William to her Glasgow friend Harriet Reid, "as the disgust and wonder your cockney misses show at any custom or dress they are not used to. I now think plaids and faltans [fillets] just as becoming as I once did the furs and wampum of the Mohawks, whom I always remember with kindness" (Grant 1806: I, 48). In her first volume, *Poems on Various Subjects*, Anne Grant includes translations from the Gaelic and publishes a defence of the authenticity of Macpherson's *Ossian*.[1] Her *Essays on the Superstitions of the Highlanders* is committed to a view of Highland culture and society which supports and is supported by the Ossianic. If anyone in the period might have been trusted on Gaelic culture, it was Anne Grant: the contemporary attractiveness of Macpherson's *Ossian* is made clear by her commitment to it.

The Ossianic view of Scotland's heroic past may seem now like the kind of reductive packaging of the country that we deplore when we encounter the clichés of the tourist shops or the heritage industry, and it is certain that the appeal of this version of Scottishness was generally conservative. But there is no doubt that the relationship with their native places of the Scottish Romantic writers, especially those who had elected or been obliged to live out of them, was a much more serious matter than can be covered by any notion of incipient *kitsch*. There is considerable evidence that even among those Scots that had become most English or at least most British, and who would have been horrified by any notion that they were disloyal to the country south of the border, there developed a tie to Scotland which gives the land and its landscapes something of the status in moral and emotional terms that the Lakes have for Wordsworth, with a significance perhaps beyond that, since Scottish landscapes and the life associated with them could be more readily enlisted in support of larger than local values. Similarly, Edinburgh was not simply the focus of the intellectual life of North Britain but, it could be argued, rivalled London itself as the great British center of the life of the mind.

Even Scots who stayed in Scotland usually made some kind of tour of the Highlands and a visit to Edinburgh was obligatory for anyone claiming intellectual status. Elizabeth Hamilton (1758–1816), born in Ireland, brought up by her aunt in Stirlingshire, began her prolific and varied writing career with a journal of a Highland tour. The novelist Mary Brunton remarks a little ruefully in a letter to her brother that her own special relationship with the Highlands is disappearing into mere fashion: "As for the Highlands, you know they are quite the rage. All the novel-reading Misses have seen and admired them in the verdure and sunshine of July" (Brunton 1992: lxvii). Scott himself made a number of excursions to the north while providing, of course, the fodder for the "novel-reading misses." Scott's friend and collaborator, Lady Louisa Stuart, a Scot who was obliged to live in London, records how restorative an early journey to Scotland was for her; she stresses places and people, Scotland's tourist attractions.

> The journey and every other novelty delighted me – Dalkeith and it's environs, Rosline castle, Hawthornden, Leith races, Edinburgh, Holyrood, Dr Robertson, Dr Blair, all the places and all the people I had been many a day longing to behold.
>
> (Stuart, 1985: 65)

These are only a few examples of the way in which tourism by native and non-native helped shape Scotland, as Scotland helped to shape the tourists. But there remained problems about the Ossianic version of Scotland's heroic past which Anne Grant's treatment of Highland culture highlights: Lowlanders could only feel themselves part of it by adoption; they were in some senses as much outsiders to the places and meanings of the North of Scotland as were the English, and the simplicity of the culture of one half of Scotland could be used, as Anne Grant uses it, to reprove the affected manners of the other. And so one of the problems that confronts any writer looking for a national subject is that it may be difficult to compliment one section of the Scots without alienating another.

Joanna Baillie made the obligatory visit to Scotland before she wrote *The Family Legend*. In the spring of 1808 she visited the West Highlands and Glasgow, her native area; from there she "proceeded to Edinburgh, and took up her abode for a week or two under Scott's roof" (Lockhart 1842: 161 – 2). While she was still in Glasgow, Scott wrote that he hoped her Scottish trip would spur her writing: "Nothing will give me more pleasure than to hear that you have found the northern breezes fraught with inspiration" (Lockhart 1842: 161). Apparently they were, since Scott writes to Joanna Baillie in August 1809 that Henry Siddons, the manager of the Theatre Royal in Edinburgh, "is delighted with the piece, determined to bring it out with as much force as he can possibly muster" (Scott 1894: I, 143). *The Family Legend*, unlike Baillie's earlier plays, was performed before it was printed.

The Family Legend was a co-operatively Scottish effort: Lockhart confirms that Scott "exerted himself most indefatigably in its behalf. He was consulted about all the *Minutiae* of costume, attended every rehearsal, and supplied the prologue" (Lockhart 1842: 186). From Scott's letters we derive most of the detail about performances and audience reaction. *The Dublin University Magazine*, confirming the success of the play, marks it as a national event: "The Edinburgh public were pleased and flattered by a national story, given to them by a countrywoman; it was received with warm applause for fourteen consecutive nights, frequently repeated afterwards, and remained long on the stock list of the theatre" (*Dublin University Magazine* 1851: 531). But this rather glosses over some of the problems of the production.

The play was published in 1810. In her prefatory Address to the Reader Joanna Baillie unreservedly identified herself with Scotland, her "native land," which so affectionately received her play. Her pleasure at the kindness of the audience "who willingly and cordially felt that I belonged to them" seems as unaffected as it is gracious: "I have truly felt, upon this occasion, the kindliness of kin to kin, and I would exchange it for no other feeling" (J. Baillie 2002: 131). Walter Scott's "Prologue" concludes by asking "Caledon" to "approve / the filial token of a daughter's love" and the Prologue is also addressed to Scottish exiles, expatriates on "India's burning coasts" or "Acadia's winter-fetter'd soil" (J. Baillie 2002: 132).

Both Prologue and Address admit something of the anxiety of exiles who still feel their deepest ties with the country which they have elected to leave, and, by Scott on one side of the border and Joanna Baillie on the other, Scotland is claimed for the Scots wherever they live. Scott's Prologue turns Scotland into "romantic Caledon," providing a vision of Scotland that will make the "wanderer" a "denizen of Scotland once again," but Joanna Baillie's Address a little ruefully admits some of the problems that have to be overcome to achieve a suitably romantic and heroic vision of the country for present denizen and exile alike. For it has proved, she admits, very difficult to provide a version of the character of the chieftain of the Macleans that would be at all acceptable, and although she defends her dramatic practice, she feels that the character may not have been "very skilfully executed" (J. Baillie 2002: 130). Scott's Prologue speaks of those physical features of the Scottish landscape that were, as I have suggested, crystallizing into a marketable version of the land:

> his native dell,
> the woods wild-waving, and the water's swell;
> Tradition's theme, the tower that threats the plain,
> The mossy cairn that hides the hero slain;
> The cot, beneath whose simple porch was told
> By grey-hair'd patriarch, the tales of old.
>   (J. Baillie 2002: 132)

But as Baillie's Address makes clear, the story upon which the play is based shows a coward rather than a hero in hiding and reveals the untellable within "the tales of old." Baillie's explanations of her shaping of Maclean into something not heroic but at least representable betrays the awkwardness of accommodating "family legends" to contemporary tastes. Offering Caledon to India and Canada and Edinburgh was, after all, a delicate packaging job; and it is because *The Family Legend* was conceived of as a wholly Scottish play that it caused these embarrassments.

The Family Legend is a simple enough tale: Helen, the daughter of the Earl of Argyll, has married the chief of the clan Maclean: the marriage is intended to heal the ancient enmity between the two clans and Helen refuses the love of an English gentleman, Sir Hubert De Grey, to make it. But the followers of the Maclean do not wish amity and eventually by threatening to withdraw their loyalty wear down the resistance of the pusillanimous chief and persuade him to get rid of his wife by exposing her upon a rock which is submerged at high tide. The plan fails because Helen's brother, John of Lorne, and Sir Hubert, who have been making a clandestine but innocent visit to Helen, pass the rock and rescue her. Maclean is tricked into coming to the stronghold of the Argylls in mourning for his wife, who has allegedly died naturally. He is killed in single combat by John of Lorne (Helen, of course, begs for his life); his followers are led off to punishment after Sir Hubert enters with Helen's baby, whom he has rescued from being held hostage by the Macleans.

Joanna Baillie gets the story, she says, from Mrs Damer, and it presumably came to her with the inevitable biases of its origin, for the Campbells of Argyll are certainly the injured parties. Anne Damer was the daughter of Field-Marshall Henry Seymour Conway, soldier and politician, and Caroline Campbell, daughter of Lieutenant-General John Campbell, later Fourth Duke of Argyll. The Third Duke, Archibald, John Campbell's cousin, was famously one of the architects of the Union of 1707. You could not say that the Campbells were not Scottish and you could not say that they were not British.

The Macleans, who are the villains of the story, could not so comfortably make these claims. The Macleans of Duart fought on the Jacobite side at Culloden and their property was confiscated after 1745. If any family had to be offended by Joanna Baillie's Scottish play, then obviously it would be better to offend the Macleans than the Campbells, but more desirable would be not to offend anyone at all. Thus in two ways Joanna Baillie plays down the guilt of the Macleans: in the first place the chief is represented as being under peculiar pressure from his followers and the special relationship of clan and chief is stressed to make this plausible; secondly, the names were changed in performance to protect the guilty. Maclean becomes Clangillian and the clan's head becomes Duart, from the seat of the chief, although since that had been confiscated after Culloden, there must have been raw wounds here too.[2] In other words, as much as possible was done to enable Scottish audiences at home and abroad to identify with the virtues of Helen and the dashing courage of her brother, John of Lorne, without their being too upset by the behavior of the dastard, Duart. Whether it was a wise move to make the gentle Sir Hubert De Grey an Englishman, I cannot say.[3]

In spite of name changes and the sheer spectacle of the be-tartaned clans, which does seem to have been generally approved of, Lucy Aikin reports from Edinburgh in a letter to Mrs Barbauld on November 1811 that a Highland minister had told her "that the clan McLeod [presumably a mistake for McLean] are offended with Miss Baillie's representation of their ancestor, and that *Their Poet* has written a long Erse ballad giving himself well acquainted with the traditions about it" (Aikin 1864: 84–5). But Joanna Baillie's play proved more powerful than Maclean *ripostes*. An account of the clan Maclean "by a Seneachie," a Highland transmitter of family lore, in 1838 accepts that *The Family Legend* had made Lachlan Cattanach Maclean notorious and admits that his character "both private and public is not such as to admit of a single palliative" (*Historical . . . Account* 1838: 28). But the author succeeds in making his admission a validation of the integrity and heroism of all other Maclean chiefs: thus the black sheep enables a whitewash and everyone is presumably happy.

There is no doubt that *The Family Legend* was intended to be, and was on the whole received as, a distinctively Scottish production. It consolidated Joanna Baillie's claim to be *the* Scottish female writer of the period. Even at this high point in the celebration of a national subject on the Edinburgh stage, there was much that was uncomfortable, but on the whole Joanna Baillie's feelings "not of triumph, but of something much better" (J. Baillie 2002: 131) seem fully justified. But I suspect that Joanna Baillie still felt from time to time that her Scottishness was under attack. A letter in 1813 from the novelist Mary Brunton suggests ways in which Joanna Baillie's friends might still be able to make her feel guilty about settling out of her native land. That value that I have proposed the Scots found in the scenery of their native land is invoked by Mary Brunton against her friend Joanna Baillie, the length of whose stay in England is likely to have been to the detriment of her commitment to her own place:

> I suppose you are now returned from your Devonshire excursion and I trust you have brought with you a stock of health and strength for the winter [. . .] However I hope you will be so national as to let me say that a pretty little English knowle is not half so exhilarating as the top of a Scotch hill. Perhaps my feeling on this subject is partly prejudice but it is not quite so; therefore, though you should not join in it do not hold it in utter derision! I have jumped with joy when from the top of one of our own mountains I have unexpecting seen as it were just at my feet some well known object which I thought far beyond my sight – but in the middle of a wide prospect where all is new and strange; one feels emphatically a stranger with all a stranger's cheerless unconcern in the objects round him. However England is no strange land to you, so some winding avenue or some smoke curling above its woods may carry your imagination as

pleasantly away as mine follows a burn dancing in the sun or a glen
that shelters the house of a friend.

(Brunton 1992: lx)

Mary Brunton follows this friendly dig at the corruption of her friend's
taste with lengthy descriptions of Highland scenery and a story in which
a pawky Highlander gets the better of a snooty and impercipient
Englishman, but she ends at least by saluting Joanna Baillie as a "true-
hearted Scotchwoman" (Brunton 1992: lxi–iv).

Autumn 1820, unsurprisingly then, found Joanna Baillie back in
Edinburgh and Abbotsford for her last restorative draught of Scotland
and, if we are to believe Lucy Aikin's memoir of Joanna Baillie, the Baillies
might have felt themselves to be among the last Scots, their nationality
preserved in aspic during their life in England:

> It appeared practicable in her to love Scotch things and persons
> more, without loving the English less. Yet in many respects she never
> Anglicised in the least degree. Whether she and her sister actually
> took pains to keep up their native dialect, I know not, but it is certain
> that on their revisiting Glasgow twenty or thirty years after they first
> quitted it, their friends were surprised to find them speaking with a
> broader accent than themselves, by whom the English pronunciation
> had long been anxiously cultivated as a genteel accomplishment.
>
> (Aikin 1864: 9)

The problem, of course, is that to be more Scottish than the Scots is
perhaps not to be really Scottish at all, and Joanna Baillie may have begun
to think herself not quite of either country.

At this stage, however, Joanna Baillie seems to have decided to play safe
in her latest literary raid into Scotland, for her metrical legends on Lady
Griseld Baillie and William Wallace are among her most cautious and
conservative works, the former, indeed, seemingly attacking her own
craft. The pressure of Scott's poems on these legends scarcely needs to be
proved, although more than Scott she privileges character over incident
and atmosphere. But the Scottish characters that Baillie chooses are
unproblematic in terms of the nature of their heroism and its
appropriateness to gender. Wallace had recently been the subject of Jane
Porter's novel *The Scottish Chiefs* and of a poem by Miss Holford. Joanna
Baillie is quite clear about the nature of his qualifications for national
heroism: "The hero of my first legend is one, at the sound of whose name
some sensation of pride and of gratitude passes over every Scottish heart"
(J. Baillie 1851: 707). Wallace is incontrovertibly a Scottish hero, but he is
equally, Baillie goes on to claim, a universal one. Nor is there any
inconsistency in celebrating his instrumentality in securing Scotland's
independent freedoms, while at the same supporting the Union of the

northern and southern kingdoms. Scotland is fortunate, unlike Ireland, to have joined with England as an equal nation. Indeed, Wallace may be said to have protected Scotland from subordination and England from becoming a despotic power (J. Baillie 1851: 707 – 8). There seems little likelihood, then, that Baillie's historical hero will be a threat to Scottish, English or British feeling. Nor does she feel the need to soften Wallace into the "man of feeling" that he becomes in Jane Porter's version in her *The Scottish Chiefs*. Baillie offers a quite sophisticated justification for writing narrative history and she supports all her legends by copious quotations from her sources; but she does not have to combat likely dissenting voices from her general sense of Wallace as a true, disinterested patriot, fighting for country only, unlike Bruce who fought also for the crown (J. Baillie 1851: 708).

Lady Griseld Baillie is, if anything, an even more conservative choice and can easily be invoked to enlist Baillie on the Hannah Moreish side of gender relations: Griseld Baillie operates within her proper sphere and is the perfect national, domestic heroine. The crucial events of Griseld Baillie's life are derived by her remote descendant, Joanna, from the manuscript version of her life by her daughter, Lady Murray. The salient characteristic of that life is loving devotion to duty, to her father and his associates, to her siblings and then to her husband and children: her heroism is wholly private, yet it is not without its adventurous touches. Joanna Baillie follows Lady Murray's narrative of her mother's childhood heroism during the troubles of Charles the Second's time, when at 12 years old she passed a message to her father's friend, Baillie of Jerviswood, then in prison, and she later ministered to her father who was in hiding in a vault of Polwarth church. Baillie does not comment, except in the historical footnotes, on the wider political scene which necessitated Griseld's heroism: this is a wholly personal narrative. Yet the social and political pressures on Lady Griseld and her unfailing subordination of self to country and family do emerge in a manner that makes her peculiarly unself-pitying. Lady Griseld Baillie's commitment to the family from her earliest days is largely the reason why her most substantial literary monument is her Household Book and not her songs. Lady Murray describes the interruption of her compositions during the family's exile in Utrecht: 'I have now a book of songs of her writing when there; many of them interrupted, half writ, some broke off in the middle of a sentence' (Murray 1824: 49). Joanna Baillie quotes Lady Griseld's claim that these days were 'the happiest and most delightful of her life' but slips over the abortive attempts at composition. Indeed, in the moralistic conclusion to her poem Joanna Baillie stamps on the literary ambitions of her heroine more firmly than either family or duty had done: Lady Griseld's dutifulness is used to reprove recalcitrant female scribblers, "Whose finger, white and small, with ink-stain tipt, / Still scorns with vulgar thimble to be clipt" (J. Baillie 2002: lvi, 247).

Joanna Baillie writes to Miss Berry in 1821 that she is told that the *Metrical Legends* "are pretty well received in Scotland, but I don't think they are much liked in this Southern part of the Kingdom" (Hunter-Baillie papers: 9, 17). The conservatism of her poems had not really, it seems, paid off. And the approval which the poems were given in Scotland is actually rather damaging since it now seems to rest on national feeling rather than poetic merit. *The Edinburgh [Scots] Magazine* gushes, "With great pleasure, exalted by a degree of national pride, we again recognise Miss Baillie in her last and not least meritorious production" (*Edinburgh Scots Magazine* 1821: 260). The whole spirit of the review is distressingly different from the generous reception of Mrs. Hemans in 1809. English writers are told that they should have kept their hands off Scottish heroes:

> We would beseech those ladies besouth the Tweed to content themselves with celebrating King Arthur and all the numerous train of English warriors who well deserve celebration; and we, in return, can assure them, that our Scottish muses will never sing the praises of the first Edward or the eighth Henry. What horrible pleasure can these fair and ingenious Saxons find in singing the crimes, the perfidy, and cruelty, of their own countrymen?
>
> (*Edinburgh [Scots] Magazine* 1821: 261)

After this Baillie went back to Scotland twice in her drama: in the musical drama *The Phantom*, which was usually at least mentioned in reviews of the published volumes in 1836 and which has some lightweight virtues; and in *Witchcraft*, which is a much more serious piece of work. It was, Baillie explains in her Preface, suggested by a scene in Scott's *The Bride of Lammermoor*.

I am inclined to agree with Lockhart that *The Bride of Lammermoor* is perhaps the most intense tragedy that Scott wrote. It is, I think, written in a spirit of depression about the subordination of human values to self-interest and greed. It is also, in the view of a number of its critics, written in a spirit of profound antipathy to Whiggism, and the narrator displays some dissatisfaction with the current state and status of Scotland. Certainly, Scott by this stage did not have an uncomplicated love affair with his own country or with its Union with England. By 1822, to be sure, Scott was enthusiastically acting as stage manager for the visit of George IV to Scotland, and the "tartan frenzy" that transformed Highland dress into Scottish national dress was at its height and unquestionably formed largely by Scott, but Scott's confidence in Britain deteriorated again shortly afterwards. In 1826 Scott published, first in the *Edinburgh Weekly Journal* and then as a pamphlet, his equivalent of Swift's *Drapier's Letters*, *The Letters of Malachi Malagrowther*. The ostensible subject of the letters is the currency question – the government was proposing to stop the Scottish banks from issuing their own bank-notes – but the tone of the letters is aggressively and proudly nationalist. Scott makes it clear through Malachi that he resents the erosion of Scottish traditions and the way in which the Government seems prepared to ride roughshod over Scottish sensibilities:

> I am old, sir, poor, and peevish, and, therefore, I may be wrong; but when I look back on the last fifteen or twenty years, and more especially on the last ten, I think I see my native country of Scotland, if it is yet to be called by a title so discriminative, falling, so far as its national, or rather, perhaps, I ought to say its *provincial*, interests are concerned, daily into more absolute contempt.[4]

> (Scott 1981: 4)

Assuming that Baillie was writing *Witchcraft* round about 1827–28, then she was doing so after an awkward episode in the relationship between Scotland and central government and one in which Scott had been intensely involved. It seems an odd time, then, to invoke Scotland's bad witchcraft record. Interest in the black arts and the supernatural in general was still, of course, running high but Joanna Baillie might well have thought that this was not the best time to let those south of the border think that the sooner the relics of darker days in Scotland were smoothed away in the interests of British uniformity the better. Is this just a case of Joanna Baillie being naive about the possible readings of a play about Scottish witchcraft, or is it that her undoubted fascination with the psychological implications of a genuine belief in the possibility of consorting with the Devil overbore any sense she might have had of the social and political implications of what she was writing? I believe there are signs that Baillie, now in her late sixties, was far from naive about the political implications of her play and that she was also involved in a tense examination of class and gender structures.

In the first place Baillie had given the play a lot of thought.[5] She was determined that some work focusing on witchcraft should get written, and, since she unsurprisingly could not persuade Scott to write it, she decided to take it on board herself. This, of course, merely reinforces the second of my options that she found the subject compelling. But she could have taken the course of most of her other dramas and situated the play in another time and a place far from Scotland; there is no scarcity of European witch-burning. Baillie makes, then, a quite conscious decision to locate the play in Scotland and in a Scotland not all that far removed from the present: the abrogation of the laws against witchcraft happens in the course of the play, which places it in 1734. The actual events of the play are based not on Scott's story but on the last major Scottish witchcraft trial in Renfrewshire in 1697, five years after Salem. Joanna Baillie had certainly read about the trials, although she is vague in her note to the play about where she found her account. The accuser in the

Renfrewshire trials was an 11-year-old girl, Christian Shaw, daughter of the laird of Bargarron in the parish of Erskine; the similarity of the name to Dungarren, the setting of the play in Renfrewshire and the business which surrounds a piece of cloth torn from the gown of the alleged witch, which was an issue in the Renfrewshire trials, make it clear, as the *Athenaeum* reviewer suggests, that it was these late seventeenth century trials that provided the material for the play.

If the unacceptable aspects of *The Family Legend* can be swathed in tartan, no similarly spectacular distractions aid the presentation of evil in *Witchcraft*. Joanna Baillie seems to have decided in this last Scottish play to take a full look at the worst, and when we see what values she plucks out of this courageous and clear-sighted presentation of superstition and evil, we shall surely feel her experiment justified. The Scotland that emerges from *Witchcraft* lacks the misty heroism and colorful pageantry of Baillie's previous versions, but it faces up to the problem and power of evil and, in admitting the oppressions of class and gender, goes some way to aiding their removal. If *The Family Legend* was Baillie's "Highland play," which contributed to the packaging of Scotland into a manageable idea, then *Witchcraft* is her Lowland nightmare. Indeed, to set a play at all in Paisley in the late twenties and publish it in the thirties might in itself seem a political statement. For Paisley was no misty glen but a rapidly expanding textile town which was developing a serious problem with the urban poor. It is twice remarked in *Witchcraft*, once indeed by the villainess and "real" witch, that witches are always old and miserable and poor (Act I, scene i; Act III, scene ii); to remark this kind of demonization of the poor and the dispossessed in the history of a town which was lurching towards its actual bankruptcy in the 1840s might well seem dangerously radical.[6]

And the poor witches are not the real villains of the play. The plot of *Witchcraft* is complicated, although coherent: Violet Murrey, the daughter of a man condemned as a murderer and believed dead, loves and is loved by Robert Kennedy of Dungarren. His mother, Lady Dungarren, is superstitious and has been induced to believe that her sick daughter is being cursed by three old witches. The old women are led by Griseld Bane, an enigmatic figure of unknown origins, who does believe that she has congress with Satan, but who wishes the child no harm. A rich and class-conscious relative of Lady Dungarren, Lady Annabella, loves Dungarren and resents his attachment to Violet. She contrives to have Violet accused as a witch and arranges for a piece torn from Violet's gown to be planted in the child's bedroom. This would probably not in itself work but Violet's father is not dead: the body believed to be his was that of a servant dressed in his clothes after Murrey had escaped from prison. Murrey is not guilty of murder since he struck in self-defence, but the only witness who can clear him has disappeared. Violet is meeting her father in secret in the wood at the same time as the witches are consorting. The local minister, going to comfort Lady Dungarren and the sick child, sees Violet talking to a "dead" man and this overcomes his previous scepticism. Violet is unable to answer the charge of witchcraft without betraying her father, and she and one of the poor, distracted witches, Mary McMurren, are condemned to burn at the stake. At the eleventh hour an Officer of the Crown arrives to proclaim the repeal of the laws against witchcraft. With the Officer is Fatheringham, Murrey's needed witness who had been captured by pirates, and had in any case believed Murrey to be dead. Meanwhile, Annabella, who had procured a view of the execution from the upper storey of a nearby house, has been strangled in this upper chamber by Griseld Bane. Fatheringham identifies Griseld Bane as an Inverness woman who went mad after the execution of her husband for murder. Griseld is led off and Violet and Dungarren, who had throughout believed in her innocence, are reunited.

The play is written entirely in prose, except for a few verse incantations made by Griseld, and Joanna Baillie makes it clear in her prefatory note that she intends the language to be a realistic version of the contemporary speech of high and low at the time. The *Athenaeum* reviewer is unhappy with Baillie's choice of prose throughout, feeling that "the beauty and the innocence, and the distress of Violet Murrey and the pure affections of Dungarren, would, we apprehend, be more effective in verse. We are willing to permit the conversations of the Westland hags, and the murderous envy of Annabella, to remain in humble prose" (*Athenaeum* 1836: 5).

But it is Baillie's refusal to make Violet Murrey linguistically different not just from the villainous Annabella but from the strange, seemingly mad Griseld Bane that makes *Witchcraft* such an interesting play. Drama is full of Violet Murreys, loyal, loving and lovely; it is equally full of vengeful Annabellas, but Griseld Bane is a most unusual witch and it is she in the end who is the agent of justice. Violet Murrey, who is like Griseld Baillie in her succoring of her father, finally needs Griseld Bane to achieve the domestic bliss to which she aspires; the flower garden round Violet Murrey's cottage is actually preserved rather than threatened by the dark "other" that Griseld Bane seems to represent. It cannot be an accident that Joanna Baillie chose the name Griseld for her principal witch, nor that the second name is so darkly reminiscent of Lady Griseld's and, indeed, her own.[7] Joanna Baillie seems to be recognizing in Griseld Bane the demonic other that she has in her Metrical Legends cast out of her picture of Scottish ideal womanhood: Griseld Bane may actually be one of the first of these persistent nineteenth-century "madwomen in the attic" (Gilbert and Gubar 1979: *passim*).

There is no doubt, too, that Griseld Bane is given a number of most impressive speeches during her delusive congress with the Devil. Anne Grant makes superstition the underpinning of real belief in her explanations of Highland customs (Grant 1811: *passim*). Joanna Baillie, belonging as she does both north and south of the border, allows us to cross with her between them in *Witchcraft*. We are permitted the perspective of English rationality, which diminishes Griseld at the end of the play into a mad old wife from Inverness, but we have also been allowed to glimpse Griseld's power, to feel ourselves in the grip of something other, certainly dark, but paradoxically a force for good.[8]

With unperformed theatre, which is also not much commented upon by author or reviewer or readers, there is relatively little that we can speak of securely. By the time that Joanna Baillie was writing *Witchcraft*, she was probably too much a known phenomenon for the difference of *Witchcraft* to be noticed; after all, it appeared in print with a lot of other plays. The sad result is that an unusual play has slipped away from us and can never really have the variety of meanings that it might have had, had Joanna Baillie written it as a younger woman; yet ironically, it is perhaps more astonishing as the production of an ageing woman. Whatever, it is probably unfortunate that the National Drama of Scotland subsequently went the way of *The Family Legend* rather than that of *Witchcraft*; the marketability of mist and tartan and ladies clinging to rocks is obviously greater than the appeal of a mad old agent of justice from Inverness. Nor is Griseld Bane convertible into a quaint peasant, even though her strange charisma is reduced at the end of the play.[9] But lest Joanna Baillie ever again be proffered as conservative and inoffensive, it is as well to have *Witchcraft* up one's sleeve as proof that her affinities are as much with the demonic as the dutiful.

Baillie seems to have been aware of her play's radical potential. Writing to Scott shortly after putting the last touches to *Witchcraft*, she imagines that it might *épater les bourgeois*:

> I have nothing to say but that I finished my prose tragedy on Witchcraft which I mentioned to you a great while ago, and after having let it lye by & reading it again at a considerable distance of time, I am inclined to think well of it. Renfrew Witches upon a polite stage! Will such a thing ever be endorsed!
>
> (Slagle 1999: I, 440–1)

The polite stage was never tested but it may be yet. I have noticed among my students a general feeling that *Witchcraft* is performable and the poet Edwin Morgan recently confessed that *Witchcraft* was the play that convinced him that Baillie's plays were "more than fustian." Griseld Bane may yet challenge the admittedly now rather less polite audiences of her native theatre.

Notes

1   A contemporary remarked that had Anne Grant been obliged to relinquish belief in either Ossian or the Lord, it would have been a near run thing. Given her well-known piety, this is a strong comment.

2   Henry Siddons writes to Joanna Baillie on 19 December 1809: "A great deal will depend on the Actor who performs McLean of Duart . . . By the way I think the fear of giving offence to that Clan by the character of the Chief was a false fear; but this notwithstanding, if the lines be accommodated to the pronunciation of <u>Duart</u>, the name more heroic and poetical than the everyday surname of <u>McLean</u>, the actor may infuse a dignity into the yielding which may in good measure remove any objection" (Hunter-Baillie papers: 9, 50).

3   The fuss about potential offence is highlighted by the fact that Thomas Holcroft had already, apparently unknown to Baillie or Scott, had a version of the story performed as *The Lady of the Rock* in Drury Lane in 1805, without any withers being wrung. Holcroft's version of the story, which he takes, he says, from the Honourable Mrs Murray's Guide to the Western Isles of Scotland, gives Maclean the excuse of his wife's barrenness; Holcroft feels he has to add jealousy, not to protect the Macleans, of course, but to convince a modern audience.

4   It can be argued that Scott's is an anti-radical stance and that he is afraid that a Scotland deprived of dignity and pride in its own traditions will become a dangerously radical place (cf. Lockhart 1842: 614).

5   Lucy Aikin, writing to the Rev. Dr. Channing in Boston in 1836, speaks of Joanna Baillie's own preference for *Witchcraft* among the three volumes of dramas she published that year: "She tells me that her own favourite is 'Witchcraft,' and I think it perhaps goes deeper into human nature than any of the rest"(Aikin 1864: 337).

6   See Lynch (1991: 391) for a discussion of this phase of Paisley's life.

7   Lady Murray's *Memoirs* of her mother were printed in 1824. I have not seen the manuscript version which Baillie uses for her Metrical Legend but in the printed version Lady Murray gives the commonly accepted version of her mother's name, i.e. "Grisell." What is important, however, is not whether the Lady was Grisell or Griseld but that Joanna Baillie names *her* heroine "<u>Griseld</u> Baillie" and the chief witch in *Witchcraft* "<u>Griseld</u> Bane." That the exemplary daughter is called Violet Murrey might not be a coincidence either.

8   Scott found Griseld Bane a 'sublime' creation (Scott 1932–37: x, 425).

9   Adrienne Scullion (1997) discusses these features of *The Family Legend*, which are expected in the developing Scottish National Drama; Scullion also briefly discusses *Witchcraft* and recognizes the difference and power of the play.

6 Joanna Baillie's theatre of cruelty

Victoria Myers

Although she has been neglected for close to two hundred years, Joanna Baillie is fortunate in the timing of her re-emergence, when scholars are bringing to light eighteenth- and nineteenth-century feminist thought, the operation and control of the public sphere, and the rhetoric of revolutionary politics, as well as rewriting theatre history under the influence of such studies. Because of the rich scholarship that can be brought to bear upon her drama and dramatic theory, even her apparently simple and conventional tenets can reveal their considerable resonance and range. Her classification of drama as a "species of moral writings" in her "Introductory Discourse" to *A Series of Plays* counts as one of these conventional tenets (1798: 2), falling in with the demand in eighteenth-century treatises on aesthetics for a literature that will both "delight and instruct" and recalling the prevalence of examples from drama in treatises on human nature and morals.

Perhaps because of its conventionality, Baillie's classification of drama as moral discourse has been thrown into the background in most recent commentary on her writing. To be sure, the spectatorial language with which she connects morals with drama, tracing the traits of human nature to which drama appeals, has not been overlooked, but rather has stimulated creative and revealing commentary. Yet the discussion of spectatorial language has generally served other purposes than an analysis of Baillie's moral theory. Catherine Burroughs, while recognizing Baillie's didactic intention in portraying the workings of the "passions" (1997: 112), has cited this language mainly in order to emphasize Baillie's invitation to spectators to penetrate the feelings of the character, "to 'trace [the passions] in their rise and progress in the heart'" (1997: 86). This emphasis allows Burroughs to raise the question how "the drama of the closet" was to be brought "into public view" (1997: 129), given the massive theatres of Covent Garden and Drury Lane and the consequently "exaggerated" performance styles of the actors (1997: 87). Likewise, while Jeffrey Cox observes that "her plays participate in the confusion of psychological analysis with moral judgement that led Coleridge to condemn the Gothic drama" (1992: 52), he mainly argues that in *De*

Monfort Baillie changes the valence of the fascinated gaze usually directed toward the female (the moral center) in Gothic drama and thus "reveals the play's revisionary stance towards its Gothic tradition" (1992: 54). In her ingenious analysis of Baillie's "Introductory Discourse" in relation to fashion and consumerism, Andrea Henderson also remarks on Baillie's claims on moral knowledge through the portrayal of the passions, but implies that these claims belong to a strategy for competing with other spectatorial fashions of the day, like the interest in reading physiognomies and the passion for the picturesque (1997: 200–1).

In all of these observations and approaches, there are hints for relating Baillie's understanding of drama as "a species of moral writing" to problems raised by her spectatorial language, although none directly addresses that task. It is the intention of this chapter to take up the challenge by placing her claim under close scrutiny. In the "Introductory Discourse" to *A Series of Plays* (1798), Baillie's language shows an affinity with that of eighteenth-century theorists of sympathy, yet Baillie elicits from their studies not so much potential lessons in morality – or even means of conveying moral knowledge from the private to the public sphere – as disturbing ambiguities in the moral role of the spectator/judge. Baillie describes the dark side of that role through her predilection for a language of voyeurism, invasion, and inquisition and through her examples of primitive torture and contemporary hangings. Seeming to discern in the psychology of sympathy the potential for reversal into exploitation and emotional cruelty, Baillie uses her theatre theory to explicate this threat in a manner bordering on subversion of authority, both critical and political.

I

In language which puts into wider historical perspective Baillie's recommendations for a more intimate theatre and acting style, Clifford Siskin describes the late eighteenth-century movement from sensibility to Romanticism as paradoxically "constitut[ing] the self as isolated and thus establish[ing] the ability to communicate as the condition for dwelling with others" (1988: 82). Participation in community was both desired and valorized, but the individual mind, especially that of the reader or spectator, had to become the focus of attention, had to be evaluated, educated, and opened to sympathy in order to participate.

> In terms of the politics of feeling, the moral imperatives to which human behavior had been subject until the late eighteenth century were rewritten and psychologized as aesthetic imperatives – "make us feel" – and their normative content was naturalized as simple medical matters of good mental and physical hygiene and taking the cure.
>
> (1988: 84)

These imperatives, characterizing the new institutionalization of "Literature," demoted sensibility because sensibility prescribed a subordination of the emotional details of "the truly accurate" to truth abstracted and personified (1988: 88); in short, it obscured the subjective "I" in universals and classes that covertly imposed community. In the new context, the literature of sensibility was perceived as making "us learn from feelings rather than insisting that we learn to feel" (1988: 89). I would suggest, however, that effecting the transition entailed moments when the imperative – "make us feel" – was infused with a covert aggression that had been implicit in the earlier thinking about community, but now became explicit in the era of revolutions. As Siskin reveals, "[i]n order to be open . . . man first had to be opened up, and the cutting was done with (a) 'style'" (1988: 83).

Baillie evidently occupies such a moment of covert aggression in this move from sensibility to Romanticism when she considers the style and techniques appropriate to drama in her "Introductory Discourse." This aggression comes to light in relation to two key terms: "sympathy" and "curiosity." At first she describes them as two different but related propensities in human nature: "From that strong sympathy which most creatures, but the human above all, feel for others of their kind, nothing has become so much an object of man's curiosity as man himself" (1798: 2). Here "sympathy" seems akin to the fellow-feeling, the predisposition to benevolence which Francis Hutcheson identifies as an innate sixth sense in humankind (1726: 123–4). While (in Baillie's formulation) sympathy *instigates* curiosity, a desire for knowledge about hidden human feelings, it does not describe the *same movement* as curiosity, which is impersonal and analytical by comparison.[1] "Every person, who is not deficient in intellect, is more or less occupied in tracing, amongst the individuals he converses with, the varieties of understanding and temper which constitute the characters of men" (1798: 2). This analytical endeavor informs the feeling of pleasure associated with it, a pleasure in detecting traits and classifying characters (1798: 2). The predilection for classifying the varieties of human character seems to recapitulate the penchant for generalizing human psychology into classes of traits and qualities, virtues and vices, deployed, as Siskin says, in eighteenth-century poetry as personified agents, but replaced by the subjective "I" in Romantic poetry (1988: 68–77). In Baillie's representation, there is a barely concealed aggression in the language describing this endeavor: one desires "[t]o lift up the roof of his dungeon . . . and look upon a criminal the night before he suffers" (1798: 6); upon the angry person "[e]very eye is directed" (1798: 10); and every person whom we suspect of concealing a passion "from the world's eye" is the object of its avid pursuit (1798: 11). In this eighteenth-century line of thought, "sympathy" comes in as a check and counter-force to "curiosity": "Delicacy and respect for the afflicted will, indeed, make us turn ourselves

aside from observing him, and cast down our eyes in his presence"
(1798: 9).

Baillie, however, also conflates her terms: not "sympathy" and
"curiosity," but "sympathetick curiosity" is the "implanted" propensity,
found among the uneducated and trivial gossips as well as the refined and
discriminating observers of human kind. Moreover, for Baillie the act of
identifying in the scrutinized individual traits that belong to classes of
passions mutates into the study of something more mobile, something
with far more indeterminate boundaries: "the discovery of concealed
passion . . . the tracing the varieties and progress of a perturbed soul"
(1798: 11).[2] Instead of studying varieties in the sense of kinds, the
observer turns to varieties in the sense of variations. Hence, Baillie
corrects the aim of modern tragedy. She recommends that it restore the
"less obtrusive, but not less discriminating traits, which mark [the
passions] in their actual operation," rather than treating them as kinds
which "mark [the] several characters" of a drama. Likewise, she
introduces process and movement when she advises playwrights "[t]o
trace [the passions] in their rise and progress in the heart" rather than
simply "introduc[ing] [them] to our notice in the very height of their fury"
(1798: 38–9). This emphasis on process in effect replaces the abstract
personifications with the human agent, much as (according to Siskin)
Wordsworth detailed the growth of the poet's mind and the new novel
portrayed an "endlessly *developing* self" (Siskin 1988: 92). In addition,
sympathy now fuses with curiosity and becomes a mode of knowing, by
which the spectator assimilates herself to the other and the other to
herself: "In examining others we know ourselves" (J. Baillie 1798: 12).

The two usages – sympathy and curiosity, sympathetic curiosity – are
not as separate as I have represented them here, but occur in frequent
juxtaposition; and intertwining the language of classes with the language
of processes raises fundamental questions about the means and ends of
Baillie's moral project. Will her training of the moral being occur by
teaching about the feelings, by displaying the passions in operation and
in their dire consequences; or will it occur by *teaching the feelings*, by
bringing the observer to participate in the passions and to feel their
consequences? If she hesitates on the brink of the latter choice, if she runs
the one language into the other, it may be because she senses problems
adhering to the view of sympathetic curiosity as a kind of knowing which
are strikingly similar to those afflicting curiosity as a relentless pursuit.
Her convergent term "sympathetick curiosity" shows signs that she was
directly engaged with an important, though at times subtextual, issue in
moral philosophy: namely, whether for all its benevolent resonance in the
literature and propaganda of the period, "sympathy" harbors a potential
for dominance and aggression. In Moral Sense theory, this potential
emerges precisely in moments when the author discusses spectators'
knowing the object of their gaze through sympathy. I would like to take

some time to detail this issue in Baillie's predecessors in Scottish moral philosophy so as to urge the view that Baillie is sensitive to the ideological ambiguity of sympathy.[3]

The move that marks Baillie's usage of "sympathetick curiosity" – the identification of sympathy as a kind of knowing – appeared with the most varied valences in the early work of David Hume. Hume himself occupies an ambiguous place in literary history – credited both with fostering the sentiment movement (linking it with defense of authority) and with unleashing the destructive power of skepticism against reason and religion (thus birthing revolution and its continuation/reaction in Romanticism). Remarking, in his *Treatise of Human Nature*, upon the human susceptibility to adopt the opinions and participate in the emotions of others, Hume defines the operation of sympathy as the propensity "to receive by communication their inclinations and sentiments, however different from, or even contrary to our own" (1978: 316). Unlike Francis Hutcheson, who makes sympathy an instinctive, potentially benevolent countervailing force against self-interest, he specifies this propensity merely as a perceptual-imaginative process or mechanism. At first we see only the external effects or signs of another person's emotion "in the countenance and conversation." These signs "convey an idea" of the emotion to our minds, which (simultaneously harboring an impression of ourselves always intimately and vividly present to us) use whatever similarities or relations can be found between ourselves and the other person to endow the idea of that person's emotion with the intimacy and vividness of ideas of ourselves. "This idea is presently converted into an impression, and acquires such a degree of force and vivacity, as to become the very passion itself" (1978: 317). It is clear that Hume considers this mechanism as a form of knowing, for he draws parallels between it and the operations of the understanding. Like the understanding, these operations also follow the force-lines of resemblance and contiguity and endow ideas with the vivacity of present impressions, or rather infer (in a nonrational way) their actual existence (1978: 318–20; 98–106). In this process, spectators give their own reality to what they see, find in themselves a portion of what supposedly exists outside themselves, and only thus validate exterior reality. This involvement of spectators through lending their own ideas of themselves supplies the psychological rationale for the convergence of sympathy and curiosity in Baillie's term and suggests why she can characterize the mental movement as a cognitive act at some times, and at other times (in the Hutchesonian manner) as a potentially moral act.

Although for Hume sympathy (to begin with) is neither equivalent to benevolence nor a direct determinant of action to the good of society, it does eventually play a key role in his moral theory, but the fact that it is initially a mechanical communication of the emotions grounds a moral ambiguity important for Baillie's dramaturgy.[4] In order to function in

Hume's system of morals, the mechanism of sympathy requires the additional premise that in humankind the contemplation of virtuous action causes pleasure and the contemplation of vicious action causes pain (Hume 1978: 295). On this premise he builds the assertion that human beings, naturally seeking pleasure and avoiding pain, will seek or at least not avoid the pleasure of doing good, whether the pleasure is sympathetically communicated from the recipient of good or arises from self-approbation in seeing themselves as objects of approval. Hume, however, also tries to situate in his system the asocial passions, such as envy and malice. Instead of denying their naturalness, he shows that they arise from comparing our own condition with that of others, comparison being a secondary but intrinsic movement of mind in judging. Since an idea of ourselves accompanies every perception, using ourselves as the reference point for comparisons occurs automatically. What Hume describes is then a virtually involuntary reversal of the social feelings: "[T]he direct survey of another's pleasure naturally gives us pleasure, and therefore produces pain when compar'd with our own. His pain, consider'd in itself, is painful to us, but augments the idea of our own happiness, and gives us pleasure" (1978: 376). Hume, in short, discerns two contrary movements. In the first, knowing the other is lending the self to the other. In the second, judging the other is opposing the self to the other; it is turning sympathy back onto the self and refusing to know the other. Baillie will later adopt this reversal in sympathy itself and yet reintroduce the possibility that one may identify with malice.

What is particularly noteworthy – because of its evidence of ideological struggles that Baillie too may have participated in – is that this reversal does not occur in relation to others who have no resemblance or proximity to us, for in these cases one can conceive no relation to them (1978: 377). This means that the common folk naturally feel no envy against the very wealthy or those exalted in rank. Hume is at some pains to show that people naturally enter sympathetically into the pleasures of the rich and powerful and therefore pose no threat to them (1978: 360). The reversal of sympathy (operative in other instances) refuses to operate here. Added to this natural protection of the powerful, Hume's thumbnail description of remorse as "a kind of malice against ourselves," often felt by the criminal (1978: 376), suggests a masochistic violence in the psychological mechanism. Although Hume thus makes room for a more trusting political environment, in this move he has not completely escaped the dilemma posed by Bernard Mandeville's ironic description of the origin of civilized morality.[5] Mandeville portrays humankind with a strong predilection for violence. Indeed, easily moved by passions such as envy, "[t]hey rail at their Betters, rip up their Faults, and take Paines to misconstrue their most commendable Actions" (1970: 159). They will go so far, says Mandeville, "that if they were not withheld by the Fear of the Laws, they would go directly and beat those their Envy is levell'd at"

(1970: 160). Civilization was achieved, according to Mandeville, only by inducing individuals to turn their violence upon themselves by repressing the satisfaction of their appetites in return for an "imaginary" moral superiority (1970: 82). It was, then, the "Interest" of the most ambitious and unscrupulous to foster moralistic propaganda so that "they might reap the Fruits of the Labour and Self-denial of others" (1970: 86). When in his reflexive mechanism of sympathy Hume depicts the poor spectator as entering into rather than envying the joys of the rich, therefore, he attempts to deny Mandeville's key assumption that human nature is intrinsically violent. Yet in Hume's scheme the "malice" against oneself remains as the factor controlling aggression in general, and the next logical step for Hume as for Mandeville is that the rich and powerful can activate self-directed malice to foster their own ends. Hume's inadvertent convergence with Mandeville points to the dangerous function of the sympathy mechanism within an ideology of morality, an ideology which Baillie will engage from a post-revolutionary (though equally ambivalent) standpoint.

Baillie's psychological treatment of justice in the 1798 plays promotes this supposition by reviving a dilemma with which Hume engages in the *Treatise*, namely the treatment of individuals in terms of general classes. Sympathy so far in the *Treatise* has operated only in relations of individual to individual; when Hume attempts to apply it to the good of society, he runs into problems.[6] For the good of society requires virtues, such as justice, which must ignore short-term pain to particular individuals (arising from restrictive rules concerning property) for long-term good to the whole (the stability of property relations) (1978: 489–98). For Hume (and here he does not differ from Mandeville), passion motivates moral behavior, indeed all behavior, but this attenuation of reason threatens to develop into a hedonism or relativism dangerous to property and political stability. To save his system from this instability he invokes a standpoint for his spectator: "In order, therefore, to prevent those continual contradictions, and arrive at a more stable judgment of things, we fix on some steady and general points of view; and always, in our thoughts, place ourselves in them, whatever may be our present situation" (1978: 579–80). This spectator operates by "general rules," customs or prejudices concerning the interest of society, which direct the seemingly natural movement of approbation and disapprobation through the natural propensities to take pleasure in virtue and feel pain in vice. The operation of general rules, however, is like the thinking in classes seen behind what Siskin identifies as personification; it short-circuits and redirects the operation of complex subjectivity. The consequence of this move from epistemology to morals, in other words, is that Hume must write in protections to the existing social system by setting limitations to sympathy, by refusing to "know" the discrepant details of individuality or refusing to let all that one "knows" enter into judgments. This solution raises the question whether sympathy is compatible with judgment, a question Baillie evidently wrestles with inasmuch as her plays make the very persons who impose moral rules also the most sympathetic to the transgressors and her theory argues that magistrates must attempt to achieve a congruity between sympathy and justice. In short, she attempts to recover the complex subjectivity Hume places at risk.

The need to limit and control sympathy which arose in Hume's *Treatise* makes a parallel appearance in his theory of tragic pleasure, where the requirement of repressive violence becomes more apparent – and more available for Baillie to develop theoretically in the "Introductory Discourse," as she does when she reveals the sadism invested in "sympathetick curiosity," particularly in the context of trials and executions. In his essay "Of Tragedy," Hume takes up an aesthetic problem especially difficult for the Moral Sense School: why do spectators take pleasure in watching the performance of tragedies where virtue is constantly under threat and does not unequivocally win out in the end?

> It seems an unaccountable pleasure, which the spectators of a well-written tragedy receive from sorrow, terror, anxiety, and other passions, that are in themselves disagreeable and uneasy. The more they are touched and affected, the more are they delighted with the spectacle; and as soon as the uneasy passions cease to operate, the piece is at an end.
>
> (1987: 216)

Recalling his explanation of sympathy in the *Treatise*, Hume implies that the mind of the viewer actively contributes something to the production of its pleasure. Here again, however, Hume defends against the possibility that one desires to see pain, that there is a brooding menace in the mind looking for an opportunity to contemplate itself; hence, he delineates a more active means of opposing this threat by proposing that awareness of the art with which the story is represented engages a countervailing pleasure of a more conscious and reflective sort than pleasure in depictions of pain. This additional pleasure is a maker of aesthetic judgments, a cool emotion which, like the general rules in morals, sidetracks the immediate motion of sympathy.

> The impulse or vehemence, arising from sorrow, compassion, indignation, receives a new direction from the sentiments of beauty. The latter, being the predominant emotion, *seize* the whole mind, and convert the former into themselves, at least tincture them so strongly as totally to alter their nature.
>
> (1987: 220, my emphasis)

By a salutary violence, the aesthetic perception takes over the mind and redirects its energies. Just at this moment of violence Hume sets up the movement by which both a rational authority is reinstated over hedonism and subjectivity is universalized (the movement of Kant's *Critique of Judgment*). Baillie, by contrast, will argue that drama can educate the responses of the audience, yet she will also maintain that tragic pleasure arises from primitive emotions. Rather than subsuming the latter in the former, she creates a tension in the aesthetic experience.

By the last quarter of the century, when Baillie was composing her "Introductory Discourse," Adam Smith's *Theory of Moral Sentiments* had brought the aggression in sympathy to new prominence, explicitly asserting (while Hume only implies) the power exercised by the spectator in such a system. He agrees with Hume in basing moral judgment on the sympathetic imagination, but (significantly) denies that an observer can access another's feelings directly or instantaneously through the senses. In most cases, he needs to be informed of the other person's situation, and he responds to the situation with his own feelings rather than those communicated by the other person. As a result, the fit between his feelings and those of the person observed is imperfect, and the movement of sympathy is marked by hesitation and doubt (1984: 9–12). The spectator's power becomes apparent when Smith also considers the reverse direction of the operation of sympathy. The observed takes pleasure in noticing the observer's "fellow-feeling" with his emotions and is "shocked" by its absence (1984: 13–15). Although the spectator desires to sympathize with the other, he cannot of course enter into his feelings with the same intensity and detail. The other knows this, yet "passionately desires a more complete sympathy. He longs for that *relief* which nothing can afford him but the entire concord of the affections of the spectators with his own" (1984: 22, my emphasis). Like Hume, Smith demonstrates that the unsocial passions do not immediately arouse sympathy because unbridled passions are threatening. In consequence, the spectator more readily sympathizes with the person threatened, whose dire situation arouses a counter-force to the demands of the threatener, and the threatener therefore must cool his emotions to make their justness apparent to the spectator (1984: 34–40). The spectator thus has the capacity to control the behavior of those he observes by withholding approval, in Smith's system the same as withholding sympathy.

> For as to be the object of hatred and indignation gives more pain than all the evil which a brave man can fear from his enemies; so there is a satisfaction in the consciousness of being beloved, which to a person of delicacy and sensibility, is of more importance to happiness, than all the advantage which he can expect to derive from it.
>
> (1984: 39)

By conflating sympathy with approval, Smith shows the way to a more deeply manipulative imposition of moral rules – through the granting and withholding of love – than Hume had envisioned. It is clear in the 1798 plays that Baillie has discerned this potential, for the granting and withholding of love appear in her depiction of Jane de Monfort's influence on her brother, as well as in her evocation of Rosinberg's influence on his friend Count Basil. Smith's hints may thus have fueled Baillie's conflation of sympathy with curiosity in her dramatic theory as well, for her scrutinizing judges exercise the standards of public opinion. Yet while Baillie follows Smith in describing the operation of sympathy in judgment, she is more profoundly disturbed by its aggressive implications.

Possibly anticipating the aggression implied in this system, Smith attempts to put moral judgments beyond self-interest by introducing a distinction among spectators: it is not "every wandering eye" which is so discriminating as "the most studious and careful observer" (1984: 62). Smith invokes the "impartial spectator," "the inhabitant of the breast [which] calls to us, with a voice capable of astonishing the most presumptuous of our passions" (1984: 137). Sensing that his distinction between the casual and the careful observer undermines the sufficiency of sympathy as the foundation for morals by suggesting there is a standard of judgment outside the movement of sympathy, he shows how an operation of sympathy itself generates the corrective power of "general rules." The "impartial spectator" is formed when a person compares his behavior with the expectations of those around him – with whom he would naturally sympathize – and, based on this comparison, infers underlying principles of approbation (1984: 157–63). Yet putting this process into the hands of public opinion does not release Smith from the trap of emotional manipulation in the interests of authority, but only (as Baillie seems aware) broadens its operation.[7] Smith is not wholly unaware of the problem entailed by this move: he has already noticed the public's "disposition to admire, and almost to worship, the rich and powerful, and to despise, or, at least, to neglect persons of poor and mean condition." Although Smith grants that the poor might nonetheless possess the real talents for governing, his judgment on this situation is equivocal. The penchant to admire the rich is "necessary both to establish and maintain the distinction of ranks and the order of society," yet he cannot help but call this predilection "the great and most universal cause of the corruption of our moral sentiment" (1984: 61). Nonetheless, his realization of the threat emerging through the formation of "general rules" does not lure him into political radicalism, and sympathy preserves an ambiguous suspension of liberty in authority.

Baillie had witnessed profound shifts in public opinion during the 1790s and could perceive a general corroboration of Smith's fears concerning the manipulability of sympathy, above all its corruption by authority (no matter whether that authority was traditional or usurped) and the consequent instability of its meaning. Perhaps for this reason Baillie partly rewrites Aristotelian dramatic theory along lines suggested by Smith's moral theory. The object of Smith's fellow-feeling, as of Aristotle's tragedy, is relief. In tragedy, however, it is the display of and sympathy with excess that allows relief (the catharsis); in life (by Smith's lights) it is the display of and sympathy with moderation that allows relief. In tragedy it is the observer who feels relief, in real life it is the observed. Although the spectator feels some gratification from being able to feel with the other, in the primary moral movement the other achieves relief by projecting himself into the view of the spectator and acting to his standards. Transferring the moral terms to tragedy (as Hume does) inadvertently reveals the fault lines in the moral system: the spectator who judges in the moral system changes into the observer who sympathizes in the dramatic system. When Baillie argues that drama is a moral education, she makes spectators identify with culprits, an experience they can, if they will, transfer to the responsibilities of their public lives. As the following section will argue, sentiment as a philosophical inheritance and a school of literature is an instrument both for exercising power and for defending against the guilt associated with the exercise of power. The penchant for finding in the operation of sympathy the explanation for both ethical and aesthetic response, however, exposes the dual face of sentiment as benevolence and as cruelty. This duality incidentally explains why sentiment could be seen as both cause of and defense against the terrors of the French Revolution. When Romanticism, in turn, adopts the language of sympathy, turning the subjective "I" upon itself, as in Wordsworth's Revolution passages of *The Prelude*, these two faces begin to merge in Robespierrian self-exaltation and self-martyrdom. But in Baillie's adaptation of the spectatorial theme into a dramaturgical rationale these two faces confront each other.

II

In the context of the Revolution spectacle, the language of cruelty with which Baillie explores the "curiosity" displayed by both the vulgar and the refined marks an important cultural turn. At first she adopts the strategy of Hume, of denying that curiosity about the passions and sufferings of fellow beings is linked with cruelty.

> It *cannot be* any pleasure we receive from the sufferings of a fellow-creature which attracts such multitudes of people to a publick execution . . . To see a human being bearing himself up under such circumstances, or struggling with the terrible apprehensions which such a situation impresses, *must be* the powerful incentive, which

makes us press forward to behold what we shrink from, and wait with trembling expectation for what we dread.

(1798: 5, my emphases)

Baillie's phrasing suggests that she holds at arm's length the possibility that the spectator has a cruel motive in his eagerness to study the countenance of the condemned person. There is a strong resemblance to Hutcheson's claim that "People are hurry'd by a *natural, kind Instinct*, to see Objects of *Compassion* . . . as in the Instance of *publick Executions*" (1726: 217) and even more to James Boswell's defense of his interest in executions: "'But I cannot but mention in justification of myself, from a charge of cruelty in having gone so much formerly to see executions, that the curiosity which impels people to be present at such affecting scenes, is certainly a proof of sensibility not of callousness'" (qtd. in Van Sant 1993: 57). There is, however, also a strong resemblance between Baillie's description of the spectator's eagerness to get close enough to mark the step, the expression, the motion of the body and Boswell's confession of "horrid eagerness to be there," of his having "got upon a scaffold very near the fatal tree, so that we could clearly see all the dismal scene" (1950: 252). The resemblance suggests that, like Boswell, Baillie reluctantly reveals a shameful secret. Describing Boswell's affinity to sentiment, Ann Van Sant recurs to a distinction earlier seen with respect to Hume and repeated in Baillie:

> The union of drama and investigation in these scenes shows Boswell's simultaneous exploitation of the potentially antithetical meanings of sensibility. Scenes of suffering pierce the sensibility, causing pity and leading to sympathetic identification. At the same time the observable sensibility invites curiosity.
>
> (1993: 56)

Thus, sympathy with the culprit vies with, but is controlled by, the inquisitive pleasure of observing his suffering. That Baillie, Hutcheson, and Boswell all focus on executions, the most obvious manifestation of contemporary justice, furthermore, points not only to the link between cruelty and sentiment in the common person, but also to the more subtle connection between these paradoxical passions in the common person and the operation of public authority.

Van Sant uncovers another dimension to spectatorial curiosity when she interprets Boswell's behavior as indicating his penchant for considering "experience as experiment" and says it "should be seen as part of a wider, cultural pattern of experimentation, one which the idea of sensibility encourages" (1993: 56). Van Sant's observations reverberate with R. F. Brissenden's earlier analysis of the links between the fiction of sensibility and the emergent experimental science:

The social, economic, legal and familial substructure of the situation with which [*Clarissa*] deals is firmly and meticulously established: and on this foundation Richardson is able to develop a narrative which is both a novel of ideas and something like a programmed experiment. The situation which he has built up enables him to *test to destruction* certain notions – such as man's innate humanity – which are basic to sentimental morality.

(Brissenden 1974: 34–5, my emphasis)

Given Lovelace's intention to "bring [Clarissa] to the strictest test" and to "try her virtue" (Richardson 1985: 427), the often-noted moral ambiguity of the novel, particularly the readers' predilection for sympathizing with Lovelace in addition to – or instead of – Clarissa, suggests the reader's identification with the investigator as aggressor, a predilection which shadows the novel of sentiment throughout the eighteenth century. Baillie's possible affinities with the experimental approach arise not only because her father was a doctor, and because her uncles John and William Hunter were physicians deeply immersed in experimental research (Carhart 1923: 9–10),[8] but also because the investigations of the moralists of sympathy, from whom she took her theoretical departure, resounded with the language of "experiment" and "specimens." While Baillie's reference to her own "experimental efforts . . . to enlarge the sources of pleasure and instruction amongst men" (1798: 61) sounds relatively innocuous, the terms of invasion with which she describes her endeavor to uncover the secret passions evoke a picture of psychological vivisection. By borrowing such language, Baillie suggests her affinity with the disapproved of, defended against voyeuristic and aggressive side of both sensibility and the experimental method in morals. This dimension to her project is revealed in her exploration of curiosity as a natural human trait shared with primitive cultures. The behavior which vividly enforces this point is the custom among North American tribes of slowly torturing captives taken in battle.

But the perpetration of such hideous cruelty could never have become a permanent national custom, but for this universal desire in the human mind to behold man in every situation, putting forth his strength against the current of adversity, scorning all bodily anguish, or struggling with those feelings of nature, which, like a beating stream, will oft'times burst through the artificial barriers of pride.

(1798: 7)

Although she again rejects the implication that the cruel aspect comprises the essence of the behavior she discusses, what makes the custom "permanent" is rather a "curiosity" about the moral strength of man; the savages, in other words, conduct moral experiments. Something of this emerges in the language with which Baillie describes the tortures as "a grand and terrible game"; like Lovelace's tortures, these "try . . . the fortitude of the soul" (1798: 7).

In spite of these considerable similarities to writers of and about sensibility, there are some subtle differences, evident when Baillie's language is compared with Adam Smith's description of the custom of torture among North American tribes. Rather than bringing together, as Baillie does, common traits from among a diversity of customs, he attempts to divide and classify the "different characters" arising from "different situations," thereby distinguishing European society from that of the Indians: "Among civilized nations, the virtues which are founded upon humanity, are more cultivated than those which are founded upon self-denial and the command of the passions" (1984: 204–5). Hence, when he describes instances of torture, he emphasizes the stoicism with which the tortured individual accepts his pains and thus points up the greater sensibility of Europeans. More important, especially in view of the place of the spectator in Smith's moral theory, he describes in the savage spectators "the same insensibility" that the tortured simulate: "[T]hey scarce look at the prisoner, except when they lend a hand to torment him. At other times they smoke tobacco, and amuse themselves with any common object, as if no such matter was going on" (1984: 206).

Baillie also asserts the victim's glorying in his heroic fortitude, for which (echoing Smith) he "has prepared himself . . . from his childhood" (1798: 8), but her spectators, far from indifferent, are actively engaged in torturing and closely scrutinizing the reactions of their victim: "every hand is described as ready to inflict its portion of pain, and every head ingenious in the contrivance of it" (1798: 8). Smith does describe in more graphic detail the ingenious tortures of his savages, but he renders them all in passive voice and from the victim's point of view. Baillie, however, enters into the view of the spectator. Although this move requires more strenuous effort to justify the apparent cruelty of the tormentors – the victim is complicit in his torture, and this is a species of "justice" his tormentors do him – it also brings the action closer to her readers and (in so doing) obscures the boundary between civilized and savage. She generalizes: "What human creature is there, who can behold a being like himself under the violent agitation of those passions which all have, in some degree, experienced, without feeling himself most powerfully excited by the sight?" (1798: 9–10) The common trait Baillie hypothesizes between civilized and barbaric justice is precisely this penchant for inquisitive cruelty. Her entering into the view of the cruel spectator hints that Baillie's cultural agenda is quite different from Smith's, namely to uncover the dimension of cruelty in governmental power and the collusion of the public in that cruelty, rather than to obscure it in a picture of achieved civilization.

This interpretation of Baillie's turn on the language she shares with the theorists of sympathy and the writers of sentiment, however, is complicated by instances where she seems to share their denial of cruelty. The question arises whether she shares their denial in any fundamental way. At first, it appears that she does. While she asserts that the innate, universal curiosity she has been describing tempts children "to be guilty of tricks, vexations and cruelty," she pleads that if it is an innate propensity, it is "implanted" by God "for wise and good purposes" and particularly that, by means of it, human beings may come to know themselves (1798: 12). Rather than being a malevolent propensity, it may be only sometimes "accompanied with passions of the dark and malevolent kind," and only the presence of these produces cruelty; otherwise, this curiosity produces "more deeds – O many more! Of kindness than of cruelty," holds up "a standard of excellence," and teaches the spectator to "dwell upon the noble view of human nature rather than the mean" (1798: 12–13). Contrary to this view of Baillie as naïve optimist, however, cruelty comes to play an essential, albeit ambiguous, part in her theatre theory. The innate goodness of curiosity gives way to a contest between two contrary positions. On the one hand, the drama controls, disciplines, even eradicates the potentiality for cruelty in viewers. On the other hand, the drama allows, elicits, and fosters the experience of cruelty in order to open spectators to sympathies which move them away from simple obedience to the moral givens of their particular time and make them radically self-conscious about those givens.

In support of the first position, Baillie asserts that it is superficial curiosity which is aggressive and cruel, as in gossip and satire and the mischievousness of children. Her concession that "with the generality of mankind [curiosity] occupies itself in a passing and superficial way" (1798: 13) allows her to define the task of the drama as inducing the spectator to relinquish superficial for deeper engagement, to "reason and reflect" upon the various characters of human beings (1798: 14). Hence, she recommends that the drama show the passions in their "less obtrusive, but not less discriminating traits," "trace them in their rise and progress in the heart," and depict the operation of the passions in a connected and gradual manner (1798: 38–9). But in thus changing the aspect of the drama, she leaves ambiguous the precise effect she expects this exhibit to have on the spectator: does she intend just to redirect the spectator's attention, or does she hope to affect how curiosity works? Does she plan for drama only to reveal a more complex reality or actually to raise mental operations to a capacity for complexity? She admits that not everyone possesses "[d]iscrimination of character" and restricts her ambitions to "checking and subduing those visitations of the soul, whose causes and effects we are aware of" (1798: 43). She implies that drama should teach by example rather than by activating dormant faculties. This approach is more consistent with the view of drama as disciplining and controlling the potential for cruelty than with the view of drama as eliciting that potential. When one inquires who will be the target of this teaching, Baillie also seems to take the less risky line. The group of persons she anticipates being most benefited by the instruction of drama belong to the ruling and professional classes: "Above all, to be well exercised in this study will fit a man more particularly for the important situations of life. He will prove for it the better Judge, the better Magistrate, the better Advocate; and as a ruler or conductor of other men . . . he will find himself the better enabled to fulfil his duty, and accomplish his designs" (1798: 15). Baillie does not let her reader forget that she is writing at a time when mob actions were widely considered an immediate threat: "[Drama's] lessons reach not, indeed, to the lowest classes of the labouring people, who are the broad foundation of society, which can never be generally moved without endangering every thing that is constructed upon it" (1798: 58).

Yet in support of the second position, a closer scrutiny of her text, particularly her combining sympathy with curiosity, suggests equally that she recognizes the violence contained in the literate classes. The passage where she invites the ruler and judge to become the audience of drama can be reinterpreted when she promises that "[h]e will perceive the natural effect of every order that he issues upon the minds of his soldiers, his subjects, or his followers; and he will deal to others judgment tempered with mercy; that is to say truly just; for justice appears to us severe only when it is imperfect" (1798: 15). This promise implies a practice of justice more discriminating, individualized, and merciful than that held out by Hume's and Smith's "general rules." It further implies that justice will be accomplished not simply by showing the audience examples, but by transforming their mode of observation. From sympathy with the victim or even with the culprit as victim, the man of authority will recognize his sympathy with characters enacting the same passions which have motivated him in the exercise of his authority.

If Baillie intended an essentially conservative message, then, one might fairly ask why she gives such extensive play to the attractiveness of cruelty, why weave into the fabric of the "Introductory Discourse" the threads of contrariness brought out above. As Gary Kelly suggests with regard to Wollstonecraft and others, this may be a case of giving prominence to transgressive material that allows or encourages a reader to construct a message counter to the apparent message (1990: 121–2).[9] This suggestion has the more force in that Baillie clearly inscribes her theory upon the terms and arguments of Hume and Smith in such a way as to rewrite them significantly. When, for instance, she argues for a natural and probable depiction of character and action, she transfers Smith's terms from an explicitly moral context to an explicitly aesthetic one, yet in such a manner as to raise the question about the moral implications of her aesthetic choices. "He who made us hath *placed within our breast a judge* that judges instantaneously of every thing [the characters] say. We expect to find them creatures like ourselves; and if they are untrue to nature, we feel that we are imposed upon" (J. Baillie 1798: 24–5, my emphasis). Smith's "impartial spectator" here becomes a drama critic, whose standard of naturalness echoes the impartial spectator's expectation of moderate behavior in morals. But with Baillie the direction of fit is different: Smith's "impartial spectator" expects the observed to come up to his standard of behavior; Baillie's judge expects the observed to come down to her standard, to divulge "the passions, the humours, the weaknesses, the prejudices of men" (1798: 30). Smith, as noted before, depicts sympathy as a reward to be withheld from those recalcitrant to the general standard of society. So does Baillie, but her standard emphasizes the traits which make one's behavior less than the civilized standard, while true to the human norm. Borrowing Smith's language, she says: "To a being perfectly free from all human infirmity *our sympathy refuses to extend*" (1798: 33n, my emphasis). In drama, the "effect" is "proportionably feeble, as the hero is made to exceed in courage and fire what *the standard of humanity* will agree to" (1798: 34, my emphasis). When she delves into the character, moreover, she turns up not only "the smaller frailties and imperfections which enable us to glory in and claim kindred to his virtues," but also "those strong and fixed passions" (1798: 30–1) which civilized man shares with the savage.

Some motivation for Baillie's invoking the cruelty of primitive societies in a key different from Smith's may be found in the language of contemporary propaganda. Alan Liu shows that British newspapers described the events of the French Revolution using the terms "savagery," "barbarism," "bestiality," "cannibalism" and "parricide" (1989: 140). Although the terms were shared by reporters in French newspapers as well, the British used them (says Liu) "with an entirely different intonation": "such language from 1792 on described a realm of 'natural' event whose sole significance was that it was not 'civilized'" (1989: 140–1). The British used it, that is to say, as a means of classifying the French "on a static table divided vertically between high culture and low nature" (1989: 141). On the one hand, it is possible that, if Baillie has such usage in mind (and it would be difficult to avoid knowledge of such a widespread phenomenon), she may be commenting on the defense against the common enemy by significantly deepening the anti-radical ministerial propaganda, which locates the enemy without and (by reflection) within – within British lower classes, more tellingly within the individual psyche.[10] In this version of her project, Baillie consciously discerns and approves the connection between Boswell's sensibility experiment and Hume's property-based justice.

On the other hand, this language has a still more complicated history, particularly in relation to sentiment. This history suggests that Baillie's usage of sentiment harbors a counter-move, which does not so much undermine drama's disciplinary function as reveal the covert operation of discipline. For one thing, the language of barbarism was launched in the 1790s as accusation against the British establishment as well as the French. A common retrospective criticism of the British government's behavior in the American War cited its use of savages to perpetrate brutal acts in its attempt to discipline and punish the colonists.[11] For another thing, this language appeared throughout the century in connection with male aggression against women. As Raymond Hilliard shows in his study of the language of cannibalism in *Clarissa*, oral aggression against the female is manifested "most typically in cultures making a transition from a social system based on close kinship ties to one based on insurgent forms of individualism and accompanied, paradoxically, by a powerful attraction to tyrannical male authority" (1990: 1087). Baillie's identification of "sympathetick curiosity" as universal, her insistent association of it with civilized and savage societies alike, may point to her perception of such aggression against women as the middle class European male's discomfort with the demands of his own independence, such as is evidenced in the works of Hume and Smith. The project of eighteenth-century sentiment, as Barker-Benfield has suggested, was to transform just such cultural aggression (1992: Ch. 2), but these examples assert that, as Baillie discerns, sentiment itself nurtures such threats.

Yet if Baillie recognizes the presence of cruelty in her society, it is not in order to reject the savage component in contemporary life, but to identify and release it in art. This possibility arises particularly with regard to her consideration of the origins of drama and her demand for "natural" portrayal of the passions in drama. Although Baillie credits the ancient Greeks with the origin of Western drama, she asserts that "[t]he progress of society would soon have brought it forth; and men in the whimsical decorations of fancy would have displayed the characters and actions of their heroes, the folly and absurdity of their fellow-citizens, had no Priests of Bacchus ever existed" (1798: 27). Far from finding it deplorable that the drama was connected with brutal rites, she rather traces the impetus to the drama once again to universal "sympathetick propensities" best exhibited in the example of savages, who "will, in the wild contortions of a dance, shape out some rude story expressive of character or passion" (1798: 26). Her footnote to the "Priests of Bacchus," moreover, rather deplores Greece's "high state of cultivation when [its dramatists] began to write," observing that

> their style, the construction of their pieces, and the characters of their heroes were different from what they would have been, had theatrical exhibitions been the invention of an earlier age or a ruder people . . . Had the Drama been the invention of a less cultivated nation, more of action and of passion would have been introduced into it. It would have been more irregular, more imperfect, more varied, more

interesting. From poor beginnings it would have advanced in a progressive state; and succeeding poets, not having those polished and admired originals to look back upon, would have presented their respective contemporaries with the produce of a free and unbridled imagination.

(1798: 27–8)

Although she invokes the eighteenth-century belief in progress in the various arts and in civilization, Baillie puts greater emphasis on rudeness as an important stage in that progress and suggests that the "free and unbridled imagination" would be an important inheritance from that past which has been all but lost because of the modern domination of the drama by critics referring to the polished model of the later Greeks. In the context of her other references to savages, she seems to suggest that the polished dramas of her day have obscured the brutal impulse behind the drama.

To some extent, Baillie participates in the eighteenth-century revival of primitivism, which, as Lois Whitney points out, was paradoxically yoked to progressivism in the literature and philosophy of sentiment (1973: 137). Hugh Blair, who may have been a source for Baillie, offers an instructive comparison. Blair discovers the effectiveness of oratory and tragic drama in the arousal of the passions and, describing early societies as "under the domination of imagination and passion" (1783: 113), he seems to give them the superiority in these arts. But, like Lord Kames and others in the latter half of the century, he still insists that taste must be improved by cultivation. Thus, when he judges Shakespeare's plays as "irregular," he adds that they succeed not because of this trait, but in spite of it (1783: 40). Blair still depicts tragedy as purposing the improvement of morals through the exercise of the social passions, like pity, and, though allowing that poetic justice is not absolutely necessary for tragedy to teach virtue, still warns against shocking spectators with horror or the defeat of virtue. Baillie evidently is negotiating a position within the same paradox of primitivism and progressivism as Blair, valorizing the primitive as passionate and imaginative, but maintaining the progress of civilization in terms of control of the passions and discipline of the imagination. But in Baillie's language one may perceive that the primitive emerges more prominently than the progressive, nor is it subsumed to a sentimental assimilation of the savage to civilized sociability.[12] It emerges with its dangers and threats intact. The "free and unbridled imagination" which Baillie wants to bring forward into modern drama entails the spectators' not only watching the unveiling of the minute gradations, and therefore enforcing the pre-eminent believability, of threatening passions, but also imagining their commonalty with the person of strong and secret passions. Baillie's revelation of the cruelty of sentiment simultaneously disturbs the categories and abstractions of complacent sentiment and recommends cutting with a style, teaching to feel rather than only teaching about feeling, thus opening spectators to frightening aspects of themselves. If Baillie sees this process as contributing to self-control and moral progress, it is by a movement of identification with cruelty which entails recognition of the role of savagery in civilized society and in the maintenance of authority.

Notes

1 Baillie may have felt it necessary to respond to Hutcheson's ambiguous examples on the subject of compassion and curiosity. For example, he remarks that the ancient Romans flocked to gladiatorial combats to see there depicted the moral qualities of the participants. "In the mean time they were inadvertent to this, that their crouding to such Sights, and favouring the Persons who presented them with such Spectacles of Courage, and with Opportunitys of following their *natural Instinct* to *Compassion*, was the true occasion of all the real Distress, or Assaults which they were sorry for" (1726: 218–19).

2 This position is contrary to that of Andrea Henderson, who says that Baillie invites the reader to subscribe only to a better way of classifying physiognomies (1997: 203).

3 In his introduction to the Broadview edition of Baillie's *Plays on the Passions*, Peter Duthie remarks: "Critics of Baillie, both contemporary and modern, have been reluctant to place Baillie and the overall architecture of her 1798 edition within the philosophical and psychological context of her day" (2001: 29). Duthie begins to remedy this oversight by identifying salient ideas in the works of Locke and Hartley, Hutcheson, Hume, and Smith, as well as Reid and Stewart, though he leaves to later critics the opportunity to explore the issues generated by the dialogues and disagreements among these works, particularly issues concerning the relation of morality to spectatorial language which are explored in the present essay.

4 John Mullan (1990: Ch. 1) explores the difficulties Hume encounters in his project of finding a ground for social cohesion. In the *Treatise*, Hume makes the passions, rather than reason, the source of sociability, but he does this by an equivocation which expropriates reason's traditional function to what he calls the "calm passions." As Mullan comments, "[t]he mobility of passions permits the communication upon which society is founded, the 'agreeable movements' which bind its members together" (1990: 24). However, the trouble arises when Hume attempts to make this merely "anatomical" process account for the institution of justice: at this point "[s]ympathy with 'another' is made congruent with sympathy with 'the interest of society'" (1990: 34; qtg. Hume 1978: 579). This elision is closely related to the difficulty discussed in this essay, though I locate the problem earlier, in the mechanism of sympathy itself.

5 Schneider observes, "in the total work of Adam Smith and David Hume one can find unacknowledged elements of agreement with Mandeville despite avowed disagreements" (1987: 101). Duncan Forbes (1985: Ch. 5, esp. 175–9) shows how difficult it is to decide Hume's political leanings. Attempting to assess the precise degree of liberty consistent with stability, Hume looks to the "middling classes" as the pressure which pulls government toward liberty, yet his usage, fluctuating as it is, tends to locate liberty at the upper end of the scale with gentry and merchant classes.

6　These problems have been identified by Mullan (1990: 34). Refer especially to Hume (1978: 577–81).

7　For a different view, see Haakonssen, who describes Smith's justification of law not as dependent on public opinion, but as derived from natural law by the impartial spectator and only accessed by public opinion (1989: 139–51).

8　Frederick Burwick's and Alan Richardson's chapters in this volume provide further discussion of the influence of the medical careers of Baillie's male relatives on her writing.

9　Also see Mellor (1994: 560). A related issue, not yet given much attention by Baillie scholars, is the precise configuration of her political inclinations. Jeffrey Cox warns that while Baillie may present admirable credentials in gender issues, we ought not to assume that her views on other ideological questions are equally challenging to custom. Cox's speculative association of Baillie with Toryism (2000: 31), made before he could have access to Judith Slagle's edition of Baillie's letters, has now been corrected by those volumes. See especially Slagle (1999, vol. 1: 258, 324, 380, 510–11, and vol. 2: 592 and 649), where Baillie claims to be a Whig. Yet Cox's article still provides a salutary reminder to those interpreters who incline to identify Baillie with radical views or who tend to obscure the tensions in her writing. We have yet to clarify in what sense she was a Whig – consider Pocock's discussion of the varieties of Whiggism (1985: Ch. 2) – and we should inquire for what reasons she claimed that allegiance.

10　See, for example, Young (1995: 80–5), especially his terms of "experiment."

11　See, for example, Gerrald (1995: 170–1).

12　Whitney discusses such assimilation (1973: 103–18).

7 Joanna Baillie and the re-staging of history and gender

Greg Kucich

Widely acclaimed as a towering genius in her own time – one of "the brightest luminaries of the present period," according to *The British Critic* ("Miss J. Baillie's" 1802: 194) – Joanna Baillie has just begun to command due attention in recent critical work on Romantic era women writers. Her innovative engagements with a broad range of contemporary theatrical, medical, religious, and political contexts have inspired a number of new scholarly inquiries, among which debates about her drama's relationship to Romantic gender ideology have become particularly compelling. Anne Mellor argues, for instance, that Baillie constructs through her dramas of the mind a unique "counter-public sphere" of female subjectivity, anticipating the projects of current feminist epistemologists, in order to "re-stage and revise" her era's "social construction[s] of gender" (1994: 560–61). Catherine Burroughs expands on that argument with a sustained analysis of the ways in which Baillie's theatre theory and dramatic procedures "clear . . . public spaces for the foregrounding of women's realities" while critiquing established modes of gendering identity and power (1994: 274; 1997).[1] Yet Burroughs complicates this assessment by noting Baillie's inclination, in letters and nonfiction prose, to cultivate a "conservative perspective on women's rights" (1997: 115). Terence Hoagwood has elaborated on that insight in a recent MLA presentation, emphasizing the overall conservatism of Baillie's politics and warning against hasty critical impositions of a putative feminism in her art.

Such disputes about Baillie's gender politics are likely to intensify as one of the more stimulating features of the ongoing reconsideration of her achievement, and I do not intend, or even find it desirable, to resolve the matter here. I would like to broaden the debate, however, by following Burroughs's useful method of examining Baillie's gender positions within the specific contexts of her stage practices and innovations. More particularly, I wish to demonstrate how Baillie's experimental technique of freezing stage action in tableau displays of communal sympathies incorporates an early form of feminist historiography that, notwithstanding its political and dramaturgical limits, adds considerable force to the emancipatory dimension of her approach to the gender systems of her age.

Like many of her contemporary female writers, Baillie felt powerfully drawn not only to historical reading and writing but also to the prospect of reformulating the gender patterns of traditional historiography and their bearing on current social relations. She begins her major theoretical essay on her revolutionary form of drama, the "Introductory Discourse" to her "Plays on the Passions," with a deep consideration of the relationship between dramatic and historical writing. She develops substantial historical frameworks for many of her strongest tragedies, such as *Basil*, *Constantine Paleologus*, and the *Ethwald* series, inspiring contemporary reviewers to encourage her "to go forward vigorously in that path" of writing dramas based on "subjects from history" ("Miss Baillie's Plays," 1813: 170). And she infuses a formidable amount of historical reading into the composition of her own poetic volume of historical narratives, *Metrical Legends of Exalted Characters*. This ongoing cultivation of historical grounds partakes of what Stuart Curran characterizes as a "pervasive engagement with history" among women writers of Baillie's era (1993: 191). Several recent studies of the historical imaginations of Baillie's female contemporaries have shown how this "engagement," despite its various manifestations and political trajectories, derives in large part from a widely shared desire to rewrite traditional history in the service of multiple challenges to contemporary gender practice and ideology (Kelly 1993; Sweet 1994; Burton 1995; Newey 2000).[2] Baillie's declared purpose in *Metrical Legends of Exalted Characters* to recover the poignant experience of a woman "unknown in history," Lady Griseld Baillie (708), reveals her own inclination toward such a revisionary historicism that promotes women's concerns.[3] To understand how her theatrical innovations similarly re-engender the past as a means of altering gender relations in the present, it will be useful to examine how and why so many of her female contemporaries sought to rewrite the gender politics of their own day by imagining what was hitherto "unknown" in history.

History became in the later eighteenth century, as Stephan Bann puts it in a recent study of Romantic era historiography, "the paradigmatic form of knowledge to which all others aspired" (1995: 4).[4] That such a dominant system of knowledge gained its explanatory strength from acts of imaginative and literary construction, rather than from unmediated reflections of empirical "facts," has been well established by Hayden White's pioneering work on "metahistory." Bann and Benedict Anderson (1991) show, moreover, how the cultural force of these historical constructions accrued from their growing capacity to locate competing political, national, economic, and ethnic groups within or without centers of power based on the shared traditions of "imagined communities." The narrative ground of history thus became one of the principal discursive sites of contestation where Romantic era ideologies of class, empire, and nation clashed. With the march of official or mainstream history normally recording the outlook of triumphant groups, as Walter Benjamin adds, the act of rewriting traditional accounts of the past, brushing history "against the grain" (1968: 257), developed into a critical form of resistance to hegemonic regimes of power and truth. Volney's *The Ruins of Empire* (1793), to cite an influential example adapted for sustained social criticism by Shelley in *Queen Mab* (1813), rewrites the history of civilization in service of a radical attack on established religious, racial, and political opinion. A different though not completely unrelated trend in eighteenth-century historiography – the new cultivation of sentimental discourse by Hume's generation of historians – made this form of social critique particularly compelling for women writers of Baillie's generation.

Mark Salber Phillips has demonstrated how the increasing sway of middle-class commercialism in eighteenth-century British society inspired Hume and contemporaries like Smith, Robertson, and Kames to augment the exclusive plots of military conquest and monarchial power struggles in conventional historiography with a new emphasis on mercantile growth, industry, the arts, social relations, domestic life and its affective components. This realignment, intensified by the rise of sentimentality across later-eighteenth-century narrative genres, created an unprecedented historical interest in the social, the inward, and particularly the realm of affect. As Phillips points out, Hume features many "sentimental scenes of suffering and farewell" (2000: 62) in his famous *History of England* (1754–63) while generating sympathy for historical sufferers like "poor King Charles."[5] This increasing domestication of history opened up important new possibilities for women readers and writers, many of whose social experiences and discursive practices now began to converge with the priorities of the new history. Recognizing this alignment, Hume specifically urged women to read history in his 1758 essay "On the Study of History." Not to say that all of women's discursive interests in the later eighteenth century revolved around affective narrative, but, as Phillips persuasively argues, this innovative way of socializing the past gave historical reading and writing a tremendous new appeal for a rising generation of middle-class women authors. The immediate result was, as Devoney Looser explains, a surge of women's historical writing in various genres – memoirs, biography, fiction, poetry, drama, travel narratives, as well as mainstream political history – which has gone largely unrecorded until recently.[6] One of the most compelling and still relatively unexamined features of this large body of work, especially in Baillie's case, remains its deep function as social criticism.

The focal points of this social critique vary widely according to the class backgrounds and political priorities of individual writers – Helen Maria Williams indicts Spanish imperialism in her historical poem *Peru* (1784); Ann Yearsley condemns the tyranny of church policy in her historical drama, *Earl Goodwin* (1791), and attacks the financial greediness of Bristol's merchant class in her abolitionist work *A Poem on the Inhumanity of the Slave-Trade* (1788), which features vignettes of African history; Hester Piozzi defends royalist causes in her unique prose history of civilization, *Retrospection* (1801); Catharine Macaulay passionately decries monarchial oppression in her republican *History of England* (1763–83). Despite these significant differences and the overall indebtedness of women writers to the new innovations in mainstream history, most of those women now entering the historical field shared a substantial level of dissatisfaction with the persisting masculine biases of standard history. Catherine Moreland's notorious pronouncement in Jane Austen's *Northanger Abbey* about the "tiresome" nature of "solemn history," with "the men all so good for nothing, and hardly any women at all" (1985: 123), echoes throughout the historical experiments of contemporary women writers. Lucy Aikin aims to wrest the historical "pencil" from man's grasp, for instance, in her 1810 *Epistles* on the untold "Fate of Woman" (Epistle I, ll. 31, 3). Anna Jameson begins her *Characteristics of Women* (1832) with a protest that "history . . . disdains to speak of [women]" (vol. 1, p. xvii). Such charges cut to the core of a distorted politics of gender in the new history, which notwithstanding its affective and domestic innovations failed to go far enough in revivifying the past with affect and social life inclusive of women's experience.

Although Hume focuses considerable attention on the sentimental and the social, he ultimately subordinates these concerns to the overriding imperatives of political and military history. Moreover, the new enlightenment historiography often sequesters private life from predominant efforts to narrate abstract teleologies of human progress – such as the progressive stages of human civilization in the Scottish stadial theory of Smith, Ferguson, and Robertson; the millennial advances of Priestly, Godwin, and the early advocates of the French Revolution; the dire reversals of gain and loss in Malthus's population theory. However much this new history opened doors for women writers, it also relegated many of their social priorities and discursive practices to a private, feminized zone separated from the main stuff of public and philosophical history. Many of those women who seized the historical pencil thus assumed the challenge with strategic adjustments in mind, specifically aimed toward materializing women's experience in history as a fundamental means of promoting their intellectual, moral, and social equality in the present. That goal of establishing what Aikin terms "likeness . . . between the two partners of human life" constitutes the "Great Truth" and "chief moral" of her historical epistles on women (1996: 817). Mary Hays similarly directs her recovery of women's lives in *Female Biography* (1803) toward the "advancement . . . of my sex . . . [in] the generous contention between the sexes for intellectual equality" (iv).

This type of social intervention entailed not simply inserting more women into the historical record, much as that effort continued. A still more important move, anticipating the practices of feminist historiographers today,[7] altered the basic epistemological structures of mainstream history, not so much by repudiating its philosophical and public concerns but rather by escalating its affective and private elements into the center of historical consciousness. Mary Wollstonecraft thus pauses in her *Historical and Moral View of the French Revolution* (1795) to "shed tears" over the individual victims of revolutionary violence, no matter what their political persuasions (163). Catharine Macaulay declares in her *History of England* that "sympathising tenderness" for "the particular sufferings of . . . individuals," especially within the sphere of "family affection," makes up the essence of "historical knowledge" (1763–83: vol. VI, pp. 21, 23, 28, 130). To position sentiment and domesticity at this higher level did not mean relegating history to a stereotypically feminine realm of private feeling. Quite the opposite, Macaulay rationally contests the major political historians of her time and simultaneously infuses her mode of "sympathising tenderness" into the core of national debate. This complex way of brushing against the grain of mainstream history put the subjectivities and the rights of women – as well as other marginalized groups, such as African slaves and the poor – at the center of historical consciousness and attendant political rights debates in the present. Even more specifically, it countered the visionary and universalizing tendencies in literary Romanticism that feminist critics now find inflected in Romantic era codes of knowledge that were antagonistic toward women. As an early form of what we now call "feminist historiography," this new, more sympathetic story of the past thus entered into the centers of political discourse and vied against the masculine gender ideologies that infiltrate much of Romanticism's writing practices.

The strength of Baillie's attraction to the social benefits of this deepened form of affective history registers most obviously in both the theory and practice of her *Metrical Legends of Exalted Characters* (1821). Her prefatory remarks on the function of legendary narrative present what seems at first like a rather conventional approach to historical composition as an educational device for promoting social models of "real worth and noble heroism," particularly in order to "awaken high and generous feelings in a youthful mind" (706). Baillie clarifies her aim to innovate on this traditional design, however, when she announces her dissatisfaction both with mainstream history, which is too impersonal, and with standard biography, which she finds undiscriminating in its overabundance of anecdotes. Both ways of recording the past strike her as insufficiently emphasizing what really counts in history, moving her to "venture . . . upon what may be considered, in some degree, as a new attempt" (705). The specific originality of this "new attempt," Baillie explains, centers on her special concern with the interior conditions and personal situations of her legendary characters as they negotiate their way through difficult experiences. Where the traditional historian will concentrate on heroic actions, her focus centers on the emotional state, the "beating heart" (706), of the individual struggling to act nobly. This "new" way of seeing the past thus relocates historical value, or "noble heroism," in terms of inner subjectivity, the emotions behind the deed, which Baillie finds most demonstrably realized within the context of family and communal relations. Teaching her readers to sympathize with these domestic affections and thereby strengthen their own empathic powers constitutes the main educational goal of Baillie's "new" history.

Such an affective – Baillie even calls it "sentimental" (706) – approach to history conditions her narratives of famous characters like William Wallace, whose virtue she identifies in his "Big scalding tears" shed for the "piteous case" of his dear friends and fellow soldiers (725), as well as those "unknown in history" like Lady Griseld, whom Baillie honors primarily for the "tender pains" and "heart's affection" that inspires her heroic attendance on her politically oppressed father during the Scottish upheavals of the 1680s (708, 751, 756). This retrospective mode of "dear remembrance" (748), as Baillie characterizes it, shares fundamentally in Macaulay's attitude of "sympathising tenderness" toward the past. It thus inflects the important educational role of Baillie's "new attempt" at historical writing with the specific gender politics of Macaulay's early model of feminist historiography, not simply through the recovered narratives of forgotten women like Lady Griseld, but more significantly through the epistemological recentering of historical vision or "truth" on the "unknown" interior lives of those suffering subjects who people a very particularized "history of human misery."

Given Baillie's strong investment in the social value of this alternative, interiorized historicism, it should come as no surprise to find her incorporating its principles into her innovative theorizing of a new kind of socially reformative drama focused on the complexity of human passion and suffering. Her primary emphasis in the "Introductory Discourse" on "sympathetic curiosity" toward great emotional turmoil – the "wild tossings of despair; the gnashing of hatred and revenge; the yearnings of affection, and the softened mien of love" (3) – grounds her dramatic vision in the mode of "sympathising tenderness" for the suffering heart that also conditions her historical outlook. Baillie's ultimate goal of promoting social "instruction" through this "sympathetic" dramaturgy, which seeks to render the many societal leaders present in theatrical audiences "more just, more merciful, more compassionate" (4), also corresponds with the main educational object of teaching sympathy through her "sentimental" historicism. Moreover, the reformative gender politics that Mellor locates at the center of Baillie's dramaturgical "instruction," specifically operative in her aim to infuse a "women's realm" of "feelings" into public sphere politics (563), relies upon a revisioning of social outlook similar to the internalizing of historical vision that drives the alternative gender politics of Baillie's historiography.

These fundamental links between her modes of re-engendering drama and history explain why she regularly conceptualizes the experimental interiority of the "Plays on the Passions" in terms of her affective historicism: her plays seek to fulfill a deep "desire" for the inner lives of historical figures, which "real history . . . very imperfectly gratifie[s]" (5); they follow history's "great man" into his "secret closet," highly attentive to "those exclamations of the soul" poured from "his nightly couch," in an interiorized trajectory that the traditional "historian can but imperfectly attempt" (8); they seek to evoke the true "dispositions and tempers of men" according to the method of that alternative kind of "historian" who has eschewed abstract facts and deeds in order to "examine . . . human nature" in "minute details," particularly as manifested in the "misfortunes . . . of the more familiar and domestic kind" (5, 9). For Baillie to conceptualize her dramatic theory within this alternative framework of domestic historicism was thus to align her overall creative project with one of her age's most advanced discursive programs of gender reform.

Such a maneuver, as remarkably original as it may have been in a theoretical sense, actually followed a growing tendency among contemporary female playwrights to forge similar connections between alternative forms of interiorized history and drama.[8] As early as 1791, for instance, Ann Yearsley introduces her historical play *Earl Goodwin* with a theoretical preface emphasizing the importance of recovering domestic pathos and, especially, women's sufferings from the more generalized annals of political history. While Yearsley supports the politics of Goodwin's populist rebellion against Edward the Confessor in 1042, she ultimately subordinates political considerations to the personal trauma endured by Goodwin's family, particularly the sorrows of his wife, Emma, when she is falsely accused of infidelity by the king's faction. The "private woe" of "a mother's suffering" and the struggle among Goodwin's family members to regain "dear domestic bliss" thus center the action in Yearsley's domestic mode of dramatizing history (1791: 4, 31). With the same intention of personalizing historical drama, Mary Devrell prefaces her 1792 play *Mary, Queen of Scots* by promoting the act of women rewriting history, "bold[ly]" using "the pen," in order to elevate affective experience, particularly women's suffering, over the militaristic emphases and political intrigues that still dominate traditional historiography (i). This alternative history minimizes the political complexities of Queen Mary's situation while giving center stage to her personal sorrows, what Devrell features as "female woes" (i), extensively rendered in sustained evocations of Mary's "tender heart," her "poor suffering," her "poignant grief," her "[p]oignant misery" (10, 17, 48, 77). Frances Burney's historical tragedy *Edwy and Elgiva*, performed at Drury Lane in 1795, similarly foregrounds "domestic" pathos and women's suffering – Elgiva, a "Sweet Sufferer," is abducted and murdered by the clerical enemies of her new husband, King Edwy (15, 67) – within the more general context of historical struggles between monarchy and clergy.

In thus staging "female woes" and domestic sorrow recovered from the grand abstractions of "real history," all of these works present vivid stage realizations of the epistemological revisionings and contestatory gender politics central to the period's emerging forms of feminist historiography. That pattern of uniting alternative modes of drama and history for the purposes of gender critique, perhaps most vigorously manifested in the diatribe of Yearsley's *Earl Goodwin* against the tyranny of men's "despotic rule over woman" (1791: 20), governs some of the most innovative dramatic experiments of British women writers over the next several decades, including Felicia Hemans's *The Siege of Valencia* (1823), Elizabeth Macauley's *Mary Stuart* (1823), and Mary Russell Mitford's *Charles the First, an Historical Tragedy* (1834). Baillie's various experiments with affective historical drama throughout this period, theorized in the "Introductory Discourse" and given creative shape in such works as *Basil*, the *Ethwald* plays, and *Constantine Paleologus*, thus extended one of the more complex manifestations of the re-engendered historicism developed by so many women writers of the Romantic era.

The major innovation Baillie brought to the theatrical branch of this new historical project entails her unique stage deployment of a specific pictorial mode of representation, tableaux vivants, to highlight the pathos of domestic history. Among the many advanced technological concepts that Burroughs traces in Baillie's theories of dramatizing passion, one of the most intriguing formulations is Baillie's vision of theatrical action in terms of what Burroughs calls "stage pictures" (1997: 93; 1994: 286). In a preface to the third volume of the "Plays on the Passions," Baillie compares the arrangement of stage scenes to the work of a painter and imagines a new kind of smaller stage construction that would project the action of a play as a series of pictures within a frame. By narrowing the width of the stage, removing private boxes on the sides, and "bringing forward the roof of the stage as far as its boards or floor," she suggests the "front-piece at the top . . . the boundary of the stage from the orchestra at the bottom . . . and the pilasters on each side, would then represent the frame of a great moving picture" (235). This view of stage action as a dynamic series of framed pictures draws on the enormously popular new pictorial technologies in London, richly documented by Richard Altick (1978), for mounting theatrical image shows – the stage spectacle, panorama, diorama, magic lantern, shadow show or "schattenspiel," and, perhaps most famous of all, Phillipe Jacques de Loutherbourg's "Eidophusikon," an early type of motion picture device used to project moving images of nature scenes, battles, shipwrecks, and even literary episodes such as the spectacular action in Milton's "Pandemonium" sequence. Altick finds that the main source for this teeming variety of theatrical pictures consisted of historical events, a trend reinforced by popular interest in recent Napoleonic history and by a new fashionable vogue, as Michael Wilson and Martin Meisel explain, to integrate theatrical productions with historical painting. When Baillie began conceptualizing stage representation as what Meisel calls "pictorial dramaturgy" (1983: 41), she was thus specifically engaging with new technologies and theories of how to depict history in "stage pictures."

The most compelling of these pictorial innovations for the special kind of interiorized history Baillie wished to cultivate involved a range of new techniques for arresting stage motion – in posed acting gestures, attitudes, and tableaux vivants – so as to freeze historical action in suspended moments of emotional intensity. Experiments with halting stage action to highlight strong emotional displays became increasingly popular in the later eighteenth century as a dramaturgical outgrowth of deepening emphases in British acting theory on the value of emotive performance.[9] Eighteenth-century theories of staging passion specifically called for actors to hold a range of affective stances or poses for different emotional states, each posture carefully outlined in an elaborate taxonomy or "grammar of attitudes" (Wilson 1987: 210). These frozen gestures were compared directly to paintings and represented with detailed illustrations in acting manuals from the first English version of Charles Le Brun's influential essay on performing the passions, translated in 1702 as *A Method to Learn to Design the Passions*, to Henry Siddons's important treatise of 1807, *Practical Illustrations of Rhetorical Gestures and Actions, Adapted to the English Drama*.[10] Such an interest in pictures of the passions on stage, arrested moments sometimes referred to as "hits," gained momentum later in the eighteenth century with the size expansion of London's patent theatres. The cavernous houses at Drury Lane and Covent Garden, capable of seating thousands, required extravagant stage gesture, a practice further encouraged by the star acting system and its motivation for leading players like John Kemble and Edmund Kean to heighten their box office appeal by striking signatory poses or "points" after an intense scene in expectation of roaring audience approval.

This vogue of performative stage pictures of the passions emerged from the outset as an important mode of historical representation, partly because of its frequent reliance on historical drama and partly because of its specific link to historical painting. Henry Siddons, for instance, urges actors to base their affective poses on a "perusal of history" (1968: 10) and cites numerous historical paintings as models for stage pictures.[11] William Hazlitt, praising these effects in Sheridan Knowles's *Virginius* (1820), describes the play as a "sound historical painting" that features a "succession of pictures" (1930–34: 345–46). By stopping narrative or "real" history to illuminate moments of intense subjectivity, this practice of performing passions as a gallery of historical pictures provided an important new stage technology for just the kind of interiorized history of the closet Baillie was advocating by 1798.[12]

Such an intriguing link between affective stage pictures and interiorized historical representation acquired a special appeal from the sensational new vogue for performing historical "attitudes" developed by Emma Hamilton in Naples. Former actress and portrait model of dubious repute and current vivacious wife to Sir William Hamilton, England's chief envoy to the Kingdom of Naples, Emma Hamilton developed with Sir William by 1787 a new mode of performance art known as "attitudes" that spectacularly expanded the current theatrical fashion for staging history as pictures of the passions.[13] The earliest phase of this performance mode assumed the dynamics of a small theatre, featuring Emma posing for a small courtly audience within a large, blacked out chest, lighted by Sir William himself, in imitation of various well-known statues and paintings from classical mythology, literature, and history. Wearing a simple Greek costume and using only shawls and handkerchiefs as props, Emma would shift rapidly through a variety of poses, intensely arresting a different emotional state in the look or stance of each pose yet fluidly moving through the entire range with stunning rapidity. As the fame of this remarkable innovation spread, Emma became the biggest tourist attraction in Naples after Vesuvius and eventually took her show on the road, becoming the entertainment rage throughout continental capitals and, finally, London in 1791. This huge success inspired numerous pictorial representations of Emma's historical "attitudes" – including Friedrich Rehberg's famous collection of engravings that appeared in 1794 and went through multiple editions – and it spawned numerous British and continental imitators, as a recent British Museum catalogue on Sir William Hamilton explains, "in private and public parlors for the next thirty years" (Jenkins and Sloan 1996: 253). Whatever the pious Joanna Baillie may have thought about the suspect morals of these frankly erotic displays, she was so attracted to the practice of performing historical "attitudes" as to indulge happily in the parlor game inspired largely by Emma Hamilton of dressing up to pose as "different characters" (Carhart 1923: 47).

Baillie's interest in these public and private modes of freezing affective moments in history converged with her attraction to a related development in late-eighteenth-century theatrical practice – the growing vogue of mounting historical tableaux vivants on stage. The practice of arresting a group of actors in expressive poses can be traced to Renaissance masque, medieval theatre, and classical Greek tragedy, but it began to acquire a particularly strong popularity in European theatres and social circles of the late eighteenth and early nineteenth centuries. Diderot experimented with the technique extensively in his own plays and published an important theoretical argument for staging "une succession de tableaux" in the preface to *Le Père de famille* (1758) (qtd. in Meisel 1983: 42).[14] These stage practices developed into popular forms of private entertainment at aristocratic gatherings in Naples, Paris, and St. Petersburg toward the end of the eighteenth century, with dinner guests customarily donning period costumes and arranging themselves in group imitations of famous historical paintings.[15] Altick notes that such fashions, combined with a new rage for waxwork groupings of historical tableaux as well as the enormous impact of Emma Hamilton's historical "attitudes," fostered a widespread interest in similar groupings on the late-eighteenth-century European stage (1978: 342–4). By the first decade of the nineteenth century, Altick explains, "[l]iving tableaux" began to appear frequently in English as well as German plays, sometimes as interludes between acts and frequently at curtain drops (1978: 342). Baillie's early and keen interest in the dramaturgical possibilities of this device for the new affective history can be traced in her sustained use of tableaux vivants to highlight the sympathetic historicism of her plays around the turn of the nineteenth century.

Her key modification was to combine the tremendous emotive force of "attitudes" like Emma Hamilton's with the group dynamics characteristic of staged tableaux vivants. Hamilton's "attitudes" foregrounded the affective display Baillie wished to highlight in her own historical drama, but they also tended to promote an elitist kind of egotism inimical to Baillie's concept of the theatre as a public school dedicated to fostering harmonious social communities. Staged forms of tableaux vivants, in contrast, featured group scenes usually representing characters linked together in various domestic, social, and political situations. Much as these groupings displayed communities, however, they also tended to project a formal rigidity, with characters isolated from one another like statues on a pedestal, that also resisted Baillie's ideal of staging intense emotional interactions.[16] By integrating the group scenario of tableaux vivants with the emotive force of Hamilton-like "attitudes," Baillie developed a unique stage mechanism for highlighting not only the intensity of human passion but also the significance of affective domestic and communal relations. This method of performing tableaux vivants specifically arranges characters in close emotional and physical proximity, frequently reaching out to and even physically supporting one another. Instead of following the customary fashion of placing tableaux at curtain drops, moreover, Baillie mounts these affective tableaux throughout her plays in pictorial sequences of increasing emotional and social complexity. Her stage becomes, to adapt the metaphor of her own theatre theory, a "great moving picture" that dramatically stops its developments of plot and action at key moments to feature an alternative pictorial series of intensifying communal intimacies.

This sequential tableau of living affect particularly forwards the progressive elements of Baillie's gender politics in its recurrent display of equalizing sympathies between the sexes and in its overall promotion of a "woman's realm" of "feelings" suffused throughout the social school of the public theatre. That transformative function becomes specifically pronounced when Baillie inserts such affective tableaux at critical moments in her historical plays, where they physically stop the march of general history on stage, the pageantry of wars and the intrigues of national politics, to punctuate a re-engendered historical outlook on the inner life of sympathetic human relations. Thus vividly re-imagining the past in a sequence of interiorized stage pictures, Baillie's tableaux perform one of the most dramatic and, given her concept of theatre space as a public school, socially persuasive forms of the revisionary historiography applied by so many of her female contemporaries toward "the generous contention between the sexes for intellectual equality." The significance Baillie attached to this strategy registers in her sustained deployment of affective tableaux throughout the climactic scenes of her most accomplished historical plays, *Basil* and *Constantine Paleologus*.[17]

Baillie presents in the opening moments of *Basil*, Mellor argues, a series of gendered divisions between homosocial militarism and feminine domestic sympathy that expose the destructive gender hierarchies of her own time (1994: 563–4). She dissolves those binaries and reimagines public sphere gender dynamics, Mellor elaborates, by dramatizing the infusion of feminine sympathies into a transformed "counter-public sphere" (1994: 560). Baillie specifically illustrates that transformation in a sequence of climactic group tableaux or stage pictures that arrest the play's martial history of Basil's involvement in the sixteenth-century wars of Charles the Fifth to feature, instead, a range of emotional expressions uniting his community of followers and changing their militaristic world into a social sphere of sympathy.

The detailed stage directions for Basil's death scene precisely orchestrate character positioning and gesture for this transformative staging of affective tableaux. Just before Basil's death, for instance, Baillie's directions call for a group of soldiers to "gather round [him,] and look mournfully upon him." Within the center of this tableau, Basil "holds out his hand to them with a faint smile" (47). If staged effectively, the actors will remain briefly arrested in these displays of their exchanged affections until they reassemble a few lines later in several emotionally intensified configurations. Now one soldier "endeavours [unsuccessfully] to speak . . . and kneeling down by Basil, covers his face with his cloak." Simultaneously, Rosinberg "turns his face to the wall and weeps" (47). The emotional force and affective ties of this scene then deepen in a slightly modified tableau picturing Rosinberg "hanging" in a suspended state of grief "over the body" while Valtomer "endeavours to draw him away" in what amounts to a sustained physical embrace (47). Their embrace spreads outwardly to the entire community of soldiers in the next tableau scene, when Rosinberg "Spread[s] out his arms as if he would embrace the soldiers" in a picture of group lamentation designed to be held as a featured pose. Valtomer actually directs such a staging of suspended group sympathy in his command to several soldiers who begin to break the picture by removing Basil's body: "Nay, stop a while, we will not move it now" (47). That injunction, in holding the affective display on stage, also "stops" the course of martial history, the movement in this case toward a state funeral procession, and punctuates the play's shift to a more compassionate historical outlook with a distinctive stage picture of a re-engendered public sphere conditioned by affectionate embraces, tears, and the spread of communal sympathies.

Baillie similarly uses this technique of mounting alternative historical pictures to reinforce her special emphasis on the emancipatory gender dynamics of such a transformed public sphere. To highlight the transformative social effects of feminine sympathies within the play's martial community, for instance, Baillie inserts female characters into the soldierly tableaux in a way that illustrates the spread of sympathies across gender lines and the consequent equalizing of gender relations. Immediately following Valtomer's command to pause over Basil's fallen body, Victoria and Isabella enter the masculine group. Baillie's stage directions first call for Rosinberg to point silently to the body while Victoria collapses "into the arms of Isabella" (47), which momentarily pictures a tableau of conventional gender division – a rigid masculine pose of military decorum contrasted with a fluid feminine grouping of extreme emotional gestures. Baillie quickly reconfigures that picture of separated gendered behaviors, however, into a new tableau featuring male and female characters united, physically and emotionally, in shared grief over Basil's death. The stage directions position Victoria mourning over the body of Basil in an affective stance supported by the arms of both Valtomer *and* Isabella. That picture of gender unity, featuring the mutual expression of sympathy within a transformed public sphere, then receives a final punctuation in the play's last tableau scene, which depicts Rosinberg – formerly the aristocratic misogynist – now supportively holding the hand of Isabella – the female servant – before declaring the superiority of pity, gentleness, and love over military fame. In this remarkably condensed arrangement of stage pictures, Baillie thus displays contrasting historical visions and gender codes in order to realize her ultimate goal of imagining, for the present, a new social order liberated from the constrictive gender ideologies and practices of historical tradition.

Constantine Paleologus – published in 1804, first performed in 1808, and soon thereafter to become one of Baillie's more successful stage plays – goes even further in testing the possibilities *and* limitations of this new technology for revisioning history and the social lessons it teaches. During the exact period when Baillie was publishing and staging this play about the fifteenth-century fall of Constantinople, a series of intensifying

political and military crises in Constantinople directly connected to
Britain's anti-Napoleonic campaigns brought the city's current peril and
its tragic past to the forefront of British historical consciousness.[18]
Comparisons proliferated between "the present critical situation," as one
periodical writer put it, and the catastrophic fall of Constantinople in
1453 (qtd. in Altick 1978: 179). Such historical associations inspired a
spate of panoramic representations of the fall of Constantinople
beginning in 1801, which attracted huge London audiences. These
widespread historical and theatrical preoccupations with a dramatic shift
in history furnished Baillie with just the right conditions for a play on the
same topic, equally rich in theatrical spectacle, that also modifies the
traditional Constantinople narrative of degenerative historical change
into an original performance of the sympathetic transformation of
historical vision that encourages social reform. This redemptive approach
to the topic of historical change emerges as a central concern in the play's
initial scenes.

The opening lines, spoken by Othus the Greek scholar, actually deliver
a philosophical meditation on the sorrows of mainstream history, which
is understood solely from the perspective of military endeavor and
collapse:

> Ah, see how sadly changed the prospect is
> Since from our high station we beheld
> This dismal siege begin! 'Midst level ruin,
> Our city now shows but its batter'd towers,
> Like the jagged bones of some huge animal,
> Whose other parts the mould'ring hand of time
> To dust resolves. . . .
> O, Paleologus! how art thou left,
> Thou and thy little band of valiant friends,
> To set your manly bosoms 'gainst the tide!
> Ye are the last sparks of a wasted pyre
> Which shall soon be trodd'n out. –
> Ye are the last green bough of an old oak,
> Blasted and bare: the lovelier do ye seem
> For its wan barrenness; but to its root
> The axe is brought, and with it ye must fall. –
>   (446–47)

Constantine's wife, Valeria, punctuates this negative view of historical
change with a similarly grim view of the "dark progression" of a historical tradition "mould'ring" within such a military framework:

> Ah! whereunto do all these turmoils tend –
> The wild contention of these fearful times?

Each day comes bearing on its weight of ills,
With a to-morrow shadow'd at its back,
More fearful than itself. – A dark progression –
And the dark end of all, what will it be?

(452)

Valeria's fearful uncertainty about the "dark end" of traditional history
also raises a question, however, of whether a different type of history
might ensue – "what will it be?" And if the "dark progression" of "solemn"
history seems utterly fallen, Constantine, himself the last emperor of
Constantinople and principal upholder of martial history, finds this dual
collapse of city and history clearing the way for a new, potentially
redemptive understanding of time. A "fallen state," he declares, has no
official annals, its "fame" and monumental "acts" buried in its ruins. What
counts in history, instead, consists of private deeds of sympathy and
generosity inspired by the heart's compassion for human suffering.
"[F]ame I look not for," Constantine tells Othus. "Before my fellow men .
. . I will do all / That man may do, and I will suffer all – / My heart within
me cries that man can suffer" (457). It is precisely this alternative record
of private suffering and what Constantine calls "dear domestic ties" (458)
that Baillie's play seeks to rescue from the ashes of Constantinople and
fallen history, thus revisioning a cataclysmic rift in the traditional progress
of time as an imaginative opportunity for new ways of seeing social
relations in the past and present.

  Baillie specifically highlights this shift in historical vision by suffusing
the numerous military scenarios to be expected in a play on such a topic
with the emotional energy of "dear domestic ties." The very invention of
Valeria as a major protagonist in this famous event – Baillie's source
material, Gibbon's *The Decline and Fall of the Roman Empire*, makes no
mention of Constantine's wife – gives such "domestic ties" a new
centrality in the historical record. Baillie's stage directions in the opening
scene reinforce this change of focus, calling for the immediate insertion
of an affective female presence into the center of military conflict. Ella and
her female attendant stand on a balcony as the curtain rises, overlooking
a spectacle of war ravages – ruins, broken roofs, smoke, artillery sound,
and a Shakespearean meeting of subordinate military figures surveying
the devastated prospect. This staged division of masculine and feminine
spheres quickly dissolves when Ella rushes down from the balcony and
interrupts the martial discourse of the male figures to express her deep
concern for the fate of her beloved, Rodrigo, one of Constantine's
principal officers. The stage directions for this interruptive moment direct
Ella to turn "the shoulder" of the "surprised" scholar-soldier Othus, that
pointed change of attitude signaling the fundamental shift of historical
and social outlook conditioning the entire play.

Similar swings of perspective recur with such increasing prominence throughout *Constantine Paleologus* that contemporary reviewers, noting the play's unexpected emphasis on "fond" domestic priorities over military valor, specifically called attention to Baillie's intriguing departure from the strictness of traditional "historian[s]" ("Miss Baillie's Plays" 1805: 62). Constantine's old servant, Heugho, actually flags this new direction early in the play, remarking that his master has discarded the severity of military decorum to adopt "soft domestic habits" and "kindliest feelings" (449). Above and beyond his commitments to his community of soldiers, Constantine pays his "dear devotions . . . first of all" to his wife, Valeria (449). Constantine demonstrates that such devotion to domestic ties does not constitute, as Heugho at first suspects, an irresponsible shirking of his public duties or an overzealous infatuation with his wife's female charms. Instead, he regards Valeria's inner qualities of rationality, sympathy, and loving dedication to her domestic circle as virtues of "noblest worth" (470), which he in turn strives to transmit into his military community. Confessing to Othus his fears for the well-being of his men, he "put[s] off / All form and seeming" and reveals himself as a "heart-rent man" who "in truth must weep" (457). Constantine draws upon that well of sympathy, moreover, in his public sphere activities, allowing Ella to plead in public for her traitorous father, Petronius, and then pardoning the father out of concern for the daughter. Such a dramatic renunciation of stern justice for affective sympathy, symbolically represented in stage directions for Constantine to cast his sword and scabbard aside, enacts just the kind of redemptive domestication of history and public sphere dynamics that Baillie recommends in her "Introductory Discourse" as theatre's best mechanism for reforming social and gender relations in the present – teaching, by example, the judge, the lawyer, the lawmaker to exert sympathy in their public duties.

It is once again the tableau display of group sympathy that Baillie relies upon most heavily, though now with even greater complexity and a new kind of ambiguity, to emphasize the educational significance of these transformative moments. Because *Constantine Paleologus* bustles with military action and spectacle, Baillie's technique of arresting stage motion and freezing the "dark progression" of traditional history to represent an alternative way of seeing past and present becomes even more strikingly effective.[19] When Constantine meets with his soldiers to praise their bravery after a day of heated combat, for instance, he twice interrupts the scene's conventional trajectory of military valorization: first to lament Othus's decision to join the battle as a soldier instead of recording it as a historian; and next to imagine for Othus a new kind of historical work, characterized as "gentle service" in its divergence from the norms of military chronicles toward a different emphasis on human suffering (450). Baillie then emphasizes such a theorized shift in historical outlook by freezing stage action, and even stopping the flow of her blank verse in mid-line, to highlight Constantine's physical gesture of "[t]urning aside" in a suspended indulgence of his overwhelming "emotion" as his men stand by in silence (450). This stage picture of a literal turn to the realm of sympathy, in a metahistorical moment about reimagining the past situated within a play about profound historical change, graphically illustrates the pivotal center of that form of revisionary historiography that Baillie cultivated along with so many of her female contemporaries.

The gender dynamics at the core of this historical turn become increasingly apparent in Baillie's frequent tableaux of female interventions in the military sphere, which feature as in *Basil* the subversion of gender hierarchies through an equal exchange of sympathies across gender lines. As Constantine buckles on his armor and gathers his soldiers sturdily round him to prepare for imminent combat, Valeria hurries on stage accompanied by Lucia, her attendant, and "several ladies." This flowing feminine group stands at first pointedly split off from the severe military assembly, but the division of gendered behavior dissolves when Valeria moves forward to grasp Constantine's hand and plead for the priority of his "domestic ties." Echoing Baillie's own exhortations in the "Introductory Discourse" for the playwright/historian to trace the inner life of great rulers within the closet, by the hearth, Valeria refocuses Constantine's attention from military duty to their private moments of mutually exchanged sympathies:

> I have also shared
> The hour of thy heart's sorrow, still and silent,
> The hour of thy heart's joy. I have supported
> Thine aching head, like the poor wand'rer's wife,
> Who, on his seat of turf, beneath heaven's roof,
> Rests on his way.
>
> (451)

Imploring Constantine not to resign those cherished intimacies for the lure of bloody combat, Valeria is then depicted "Twining her arms round him" in a sympathetic group tableau that physically displays an ideal of gender integration and arrests, at least momentarily, the progression of military history. Constantine, still embracing Valeria, next moves "some distance" from his men and waves at them to go on without him (451).

Baillie's most powerful arrangement of such a historically and socially transformative stage picture occurs at the climax of *Constantine Paleologus*, when Valeria, following the death of Constantine, commits suicide rather than falling into the clutches of the Turkish sultan, Mahomet. Dramatically inserting an anguished feminine presence in the midst of Mahomet's triumphant military court, Baillie brings Valeria on to the stage and has her open her robe to reveal a self-inflicted knife wound "in her breast" (477). This stunning inscription of female suffering within the play's concluding spectacle of historical change – the shift of imperial power from West to East – then develops into Baillie's most elaborate tableau picturing an alternative history of group sympathies across gender lines. As Valeria collapses, a small band of Constantine's surviving followers, male and female, gather round her in loving support. The soldiers Rodrigo and Othus, whose "sheathed sword" marks his final rejection of militarism, join Ella and Lucia in holding Valeria as she expires. Baillie's stage direction calls for this literal embodiment of group sympathy, which dissolves the conventional regulations of military and gender behavior, to be held motionless as the culminating tableau in her succession of alternative historical pictures: a "solemn pause" ensues (478). The educational impact of this arrested scene, characterized by Othus as a "lesson of such high ennobling power" (478), affects even the tyrannical sultan, who exclaims: "Prophet of God, be there such ties as these!" (477). A direct cue to Baillie's theatrical audience of makers and shakers, that announcement declares the potential reformative power of stopping history on stage to reimagine its affective priorities and their particular impact on the social and gender regulations of the present.

Recognizing the elaborate contribution of these stage pictures to Baillie's revisionary historiography, and their specific educational function, can deepen our overall appreciation of the extent to which she does creatively advance, notwithstanding her more conservative biases, some of her era's most significant discursive and theatrical strategies for enacting social and gender reform. To trace the complexity of these transformative moments on Baillie's historical stage, however, is also to grasp her substantial doubts about their practical efficacy in realizing the goal of social change. The tableaux of group sympathies in *Constantine Paleologus*, for instance, repeatedly buckle under the intrusive pressure of military force and conventional codes of gendered behavior. Hints emerge throughout the play that Constantine's devotion to domestic ties has actually precipitated the crisis of Constantinople and must be replaced by his resumption of bold militarism if he is to save the city. Even Valeria accepts this reasoning, insisting with an air of conventional "dignity" that Constantine return to lead his troops just moments after she leads him away from combat into that stage picture of intertwined closet sympathies (451). When the couple literally enter a private closet, Valeria's apartment, to exchange intimate feelings of "joy and grief" in yet another sympathetic tableau – "They weep on one another's necks without speaking" (470) – their suspended embrace is shattered by the iron call of war: "an alarm bell is heard at a distance and CONSTANTINE breaks suddenly from her" (470). These subversive energies compromise the play's climactic tableau of group sympathy as well, for Valeria's very act of suicide constitutes, as Mahomet observes, a triumph of military heroism or "manly state" that actually reverses the process of domesticating public sphere behavior and consumes female subjectivity in a reinscription of separate sphere ideology. Valeria's only access to affairs of state comes through such an adoption of "manly" identity, which simultaneously requires her self-destruction.

If Baillie thus questions the ameliorative impact of her social drama, she also seems aware of the counter-theatrical stasis that her tableau technology could impose on stage, particularly in the cavernous patent houses where the intricate gestures and dramatic effect of tableau scenes would be lost on most audience members.[20] She acknowledges in her preface to the third volume of her "Plays on the Passions" the impossibility of mounting her various theatrical innovations successfully under the "present circumstances" of the London stage (231). And though she does frequently imagine in her theatre theory the rich creative possibilities of a smaller house, where the intimate arrangements of her tableaux would achieve their desired effects, she fully recognizes how the material demands of the patent theatres for the kind of spectacle she offers in *Constantine Paleologus* will continue to "prevent" the successful realization of her alternative tableaux and their affective priorities (390).[21] These reservations and felt inadequacies should not be taken, however, as markers of Baillie's aesthetic failure on stage or her repudiation of a socially reformative theatre. Her innovative mounting of stage pictures anticipated by decades the heyday of theatrical tableaux on the mid-Victorian stage and arguably produced, in their revisionings of history and social relations, the most complex manifestation of the form at any point in the century. Moreover, her pictorial staging of a reimagined sympathetic history did not fail to influence those many observers of *Constantine Paleologus* who remarked upon her unique illustration of Constantine's "domestic affections" (Jeffrey 1805: 414). Such a new historical focus even inspired Thomas Dibdin's 1817 melodramatic adaptation of the play at the Surrey Theatre, retitled *Constantine and Valeria* to exploit the sentimental appeal of Baillie's affective emphasis. Her embedded questions about her new mode of theatrical representation and its social impact ultimately reveal the great degree to which she both extended the possibilities and tested the limits of her period's efforts to brush against the grain of history and gender.

Notes

1   For related discussions of Baillie's critical resistance to entrenched forms of Romantic gender ideology, see Purinton (1994) and Watkins (1993).
2   See also Devoney Looser's important new study (2000) *British Women Writers and the Writing of History, 1670–1820* for the most comprehensive treatment to date of women's historical writing in the eighteenth and early nineteenth centuries. Looser is more concerned, however, with women's substantial and complicated participation in established modes of historical writing during this period (1–27).

3   All citations of Joanna Baillie's works are taken from the Georg Olms Verlag 1976 reprint of *Joanna Baillie: The Dramatic and Poetical Works*, originally published in 1851.

4   For recent studies of major innovations in enlightenment and Romantic era historiography, see also Karen O'Brien, *Narratives of Enlightenment: Cosmopolitan History from Voltaire to Gibbon*, and Mark Salber Phillips, *Society and Sentiment: Genres of Historical Writing in Britain: 1740–1820*.

5   Phillips quotes Hume on Charles I (2000: 60).

6   Looser notes that "women were much more involved in the burgeoning genre of history than we have formerly thought. The way women writers drew on historical discourse in their texts varied enormously, from direct engagement with political history, to the use of historical forms in letters or travel writings, to manipulations of historical material in fictional works" (2000: 2).

7   For recent examples of the theory and practice of feminist historiography, see Joan Wallach Scott (1988, 1996), Ann Louise Shapiro (1994), and Bonnie Smith (1998).

8   Katherine Newey (2000) provides an excellent study of the political imperatives of historical drama by women during the Romantic era. Although Newey's arguments about this political groundwork to women's historical drama certainly apply to Baillie, she does not directly address Baillie's plays.

9   For extensive discussions of eighteenth- and early-nineteenth-century debates about the theory and practice of affective stage performance, see Booth *et al.* (1975), Cheeke (1998), Donohue (1970), Downer (1943, 1946), Flaherty (1990), Wasserman (1947), and Wilson (1987).

10 Drawing on this long tradition of associating staged poses with paintings, William Hazlitt characterizes Sheridan Knowles's *Virginius* as a "living picture" (1930–34: 346). Wilson comments on Siddons's influential comparison of painting and stage gesture: "Actor, amateur painter, and son of the celebrated actress, Henry Siddons published his *Practical Illustrations of Rhetorical Gestures and Actions, Adapted to the English Drama* (1807) as a systematic, if laboured, attempt to render the painter's traditional expressive norms more accessible to the actor for practical application on the stage. Itself an adaptation of a similar guide by a J. Engle of the Berlin Royal Academy, and replete with reference to Le Brun's and Pairesse's works, Siddons's taxonomy proffers in sixty-eight plates a grammar of attitudes whose references to specific plays and roles clearly derive in large measure from the performances of his mother [Sarah Siddons] and John Kemble" (1987: 210).

11 "By [the mid-eighteenth] century," Wilson explains, "John Hill could plainly state in *The Actor* that a performer's 'looks and gestures are so many paintings made to be seen at a distance . . .' The revival of interest in history painting during the last half of the century encouraged applications of the analogy in numerous treatises on acting" (1987: 206).

12 For discussions of Baillie's engagement with the acting theories and manuals of her time, see Curran (1970: 164) and Burroughs (1997: 113–28).

13 Holmström emphasizes the unique originality of Hamilton's attitudes: "It is quite clear that it is a question of a new art form. . . . [S]pectators, whether they came from England, Germany or France, speak of the attitudes as a completely new and unique experience" (1967: 126).

14 Voltaire also experimented with a related form of pantomimic acting style that became popular, according to Holmström, in mid-eighteenth-century French theatres (1967: 21–7).

15 Holmström discusses these aristocratic entertainments (1967: 209–32) and also mentions Goethe's monodrama *Proserpina* (1778) and novel *Die Wahlverwandtschaften* (1809) as significant influences on the developing stage history of tableaux vivants (1967: 78, 209–32).

16 Handbills for mid-nineteenth-century tableaux vivants, reproduced by Altick (1978: 346), depict characters in highly formal poses all separated from one another.

17 Beth H. Friedman-Romell (1999) conducts an illuminating analysis of the performance methods in the four different productions of *Constantine Paleologus* between 1808 and 1825, though she does not directly address Baillie's use of tableaux vivants.

18 As the Ottoman Empire declined in the later eighteenth century, it became increasingly subject to manipulation and coercion by the major European powers. During the Napoleonic wars, the Ottoman leadership based in Constantinople was repeatedly forced to juggle shifting alliances with France, Britain, and Russia while resisting at different times military threats from each power. This balancing act became acutely perilous with the collapse of the Peace of Amiens in 1803, when intense diplomatic and military pressure was applied by Britain and France to forge countering alliances with the Sultan, Selim III. Selim's precarious situation reached a crisis point in 1804 with Napoleon's demand, on threat of invasion, for recognition as Emperor in a move to consolidate his European power base. Russia and Britain simultaneously threatened attacks if Selim granted Napoleon that recognition. In 1804, the year Baillie published *Constantine Paleologus*, the monumental power struggles of the European nations thus converged on Constantinople. While parrying these external threats on all sides, Selim also faced mounting internal resistance within the Ottoman domains from conservative factions opposed to his Westernizing military and economic reforms. This volatile mixture of external and internal strife finally exploded in 1807, when Britain and Russia declared war on the Ottoman Empire and Selim's conservative enemies openly revolted in Constantinople. Selim was deposed, and the streets of Constantinople flared with revolution, counter-revolution, executions, and massacres until both Selim and his deposer, Mustafa IV, were assassinated in 1808, the year that *Constantine Paleologus* was first performed.

19 Many reviewers of the print version of *Constantine Paleologus,* like Francis Jeffrey, were astonished by the elaborateness of the military spectacles that Baillie designed in her stage directions and wondered openly if so much military action could ever be represented "to the eye, within the walls of a theatre" (Jeffrey 1805: 417). Baillie defended her spectacular staging in a preface to her *Miscellaneous Plays*, arguing that she was deliberately appealing to theatrical as well as historical convention in her spectacular military scenes: "Perhaps in the conduct of this Tragedy I have sometimes weakened the interest of it by attending too much to magnificence and show. But it was intended for a large theatre, where a play is rather looked at than listened to, and where, indeed, by a great proportion of the audience, it cannot be heard" (390). Friedman-Romell records that Baillie's attempt at grand spectacle worked effectively in at least two productions of *Constantine Paleologus*, in an 1817 adaptation at the Surrey Theatre retitled *Constantine and Valeria* and in the 1825 performance at the Theatre Royal, Dublin (1999: 154–8).

20 Joseph Donohue stresses the negative theatrical impact of nineteenth-century strategies of freezing stage action in group tableaux: "The crux of the situation . . . is that the notion of *ut pictura poesis*, while an important agent

of imaginative creation in Romantic lyric and narrative verse, became an ultimately devitalizing one for Romantic drama. . . . The moment 'frozen' out of time and set down as a kind of speaking sculpture ultimately and inevitably succumbed to the influence of the 'Laocoön' theory of passion imprisoned, with its stultifying implication of process uneventuating in action" (1970: 185). Wilson elaborates on the fundamental conflict between the active requirements of staged drama in nineteenth-century British theatres and the arrested motion of tableaux vivants: "After all, the forward momentum of the action on stage is a temporal phenomenon that militates against . . . static, spatial perception" (1987: 211).

21 Friedman-Romell demonstrates, moreover, how the intervention of stage managers led to cuts and adjustments in performances of *Constantine Paleologus* that actually diminished the play's more progressive social elements (1999: 158–71).

8 A neural theatre

Joanna Baillie's "Plays on the Passions"

Alan Richardson

There was a time when not only Joanna Baillie's drama, but British Romantic drama altogether was seen as a dismal subject, a forsaken byroad of literary history, one best left untraveled. Among the few scholarly studies to explore this unlikely terrain, the most successful were those that took a dour or even morbid approach, as titles like *The Death of Tragedy* (Steiner 1961) and *The Deserted Stage* (Otten 1972) attest. The dismissive label "closet drama" lent an aura of futility or generic perversity to the works of those who, like Baillie, wished to write for the stage but felt alienated from it, as well as those who, like Byron in *Cain* or Shelley in *Prometheus Unbound*, wrote deliberately (and radically) unstageable poetic dramas. That many regarded *Prometheus Unbound* as one of the great examples of British Romanticism somehow failed to disturb the consensus that Romantic drama did not merit serious attention. Those who wished to challenge the critical status quo, however, could begin from the very contradiction between viewing works like *Manfred*, *Cain*, *The Cenci*, *Prometheus Unbound*, and (sometimes) *The Borderers* and *Death's Jest-Book* as considerable works of poetry, while condemning the category to which they all belonged – Romantic verse drama – to third-rate status.

Byron's term "mental theatre" suggested itself as a kinder alternative to "closet drama," promoting a view of Romantic verse drama as experimental poetry, fusing lyrical and dramatic modes, rather than as stage-poetry manqué (Richardson 1988: 2). In place of the then dominant view of Romantic drama as "monodrama," ironically devoid of dramatic exchange, Romantic mental theatre was reinterpreted as centrally featuring dialogic relations, all the more dramatically charged in their troubling inequalities, moments of incomprehension, and ultimate breakdown. In this view, mental theatre posited a socially constituted self, pursuing a delusory and therefore tragically empty autonomy. The sympathetic imagination – the capacity to overcome the boundaries of the self by imaginative projection to the space of the other – became crucial either in its spectacular failure (as in *Cain* or *The Cenci*) or its hard-won victory (as in *Prometheus Unbound*). According to a newer wave of revisionist critics, however, this conception of mental theatre became itself doubly suspect, retaining a traditional valuation of poetry over drama within Romantic studies and harboring elements of a long-standing "antitheatrical prejudice" within anglophone culture (Carlson 1994: 14–15).

Critics who wanted to underscore rather than downplay the contradictions of Romantic drama – its reliance on theatrical conventions despite its ambivalence toward stage production, its evident preference for reflection over action despite its avowedly dramatic character – rightly emphasized a further problem, a profound ambivalence regarding the body. Neatly summarizing Romantic-era debates on the staging of Shakespeare, Julie Carlson pointed out that while the "stage's dependence on physical 'reality'" renders its portrayal of abstract subjects more "accessible and engaging," its "special relation to the body is also its chief danger, since the body's appeal can block out the less palpable and immediate workings of the mind" (1988: 425). For critics like Carlson, mental theatre promotes a Romantic idealization of mind and imagination at the expense of the body, and its turn from the stage reflects a contempt for the flesh (and for the players who give flesh to dramatic words) with a long and unsavory pedigree. Romantic drama remains interesting, for these critics, not least because its retreat from the stage is never complete and its ambivalence towards bodies, sensuousness, and performativity leaves traces throughout the very texts that would leave the physical world unseen.

Recognizing the vexed status of the body in Romantic drama not only helped restore interest in Romantic theatricality, but provoked new questions regarding the relation of gender to stage performance (and male Romantic "stage fright") as well. It also provided a basis for the renewed interest in the politics of Romantic drama: the suppressed body in the verse plays of the canonical Romantic poets could be read as a performer's body, a female body, the body politic, or (often) all three at once. Significantly, however, the neo-revisionist approach to Romantic drama proved little more hospitable to the works of Joanna Baillie – widely regarded in her own time as the most successful dramatic poet of the age – than had the older "mental theatre" approach. As Catherine Burroughs argues in her groundbreaking study of Baillie's dramatic theory, the standard oppositions of earlier criticism – closet and theatre, mind and body – fail to square off as expected in the signal case of Baillie (1997: 8). Rather than choosing between reading and performance, a private theatre of the mind and the cavernous Drury Lane, Baillie wrote for a "small experimental theatre" attuned to women's daily experience of performing femininity in a domestic interior, a "closet stage" in Burroughs' clever new twist on the once invidious label (1997: 11). Baillie's smaller, more intimate theatre of the future, anticipated in the makeshift stages of private theatricals, could support a style of acting (and dramatic writing) closely attuned to the subtleties of bodily expression, the "variety of fine fleeting emotion which nature in moments of agitation assumes" as Baillie herself put it. Rather than giving the lie to the mind, the body could give, well, body to even the "finer and more delicate indications" of thought and feeling in a theatre that brought actors and auditors in closer physical proximity (J. Baillie 1853: 232). The interpenetration and mutual interaction of mind and body, as a reading of the "Introductory Discourse" to "Plays on the Passions" will show, forms the cornerstone of Baillie's dramatic theory and practice.

If her holistic approach to mind–body relations put her at odds with one strong current within canonical Romanticism, however, it by no means rendered Baillie eccentric or untimely. Anti-dualistic psychologies, grounding the mind in the body and seeking to account for the pervasiveness of mind–body interaction, in fact represented the cutting edge of Romantic-era scientific and medical thought. Herder in Germany, Gall in Austria, Cabanis in France, and Erasmus Darwin and Charles Bell in England all produced accounts of mental life that demanded a central role for the body (especially the central nervous system) in giving form and expression to the mind, all stopping just short, however, of outright materialism (Richardson 2001: 1–38). By the early 1820s basic tenets of the new biological psychologies had been widely disseminated throughout Britain by the phrenology movement and by the materialist–vitalist debates sparked by the notorious lectures of William Lawrence (who *did* advance an openly materialist account of mind). Baillie, however, was uniquely well positioned to follow the development of the new psychologies from their beginnings in the early 1790s, as a member of the "most famous medical family" of the age (McMillan 1998: 70). It was over her uncle John Hunter's intellectual legacy, in fact, that the materialist–vitalist controversy was initially waged. Baillie's brother, Matthew, brought key notions from the new corporeal psychologies – including the greatly enhanced role given to unconscious mental processes (conducted by means of the nervous system) and the "natural" links between psychological events and their (universal) physiological manifestations – into his Gulstonian lectures, as Frederick Burwick's chapter in this volume attests. The co-executor (with Matthew Baillie) of John Hunter's estate was Hunter's disciple (and brother-in-law) Everard Home, who contributed several important essays on the nervous system to the *Philosophical Transactions* of the Royal Society. It is hardly surprising, then, to find a number of correspondences between Baillie's guiding "ideas concerning human nature" in the "Introductory Discourse" and the emergent biological psychologies of the time (J. Baillie 1853: 1).

To begin with, Baillie shares Herder's interest in the "innate, organical, genetic" aspects of mind (Herder 1800: 179), departing implicitly (as Gall and Cabanis do explicitly) from the Lockean "tabula rasa" model (cf. Mellor 1994: 562). Baillie attributes several universal features of mind to a common human developmental process, one that involves extensive interaction with the social environment but is impelled by certain drives and characteristics that are innate or "implanted within us" (J. Baillie 1853: 2). At least some of these features characterize other animal species as well, rather than belonging exclusively to humans. The most important shared feature concerns that "strong sympathy which most creatures, but the human above all, feel for others of their kind," a sympathetic "curiosity" that emerges early in life and is found in all those "not deficient in intellect" (1853: 1). "This propensity is universal," Baillie writes: "Children begin to show it very early . . . GOD ALMIGHTY has implanted it within us, as well as our other propensities and passions" (1853: 4). Baillie's language of universals, propensities, and "implanted" characteristics owes not a little to the "common sense" philosophy of Thomas Reid, a leading Scottish philosopher connected with Baillie's family. Significantly, however, it overlaps as well with the discourse of phrenology and anticipates by a few years the physiological esthetics of Charles Bell, another Scotsman, a student of Reid, a pioneer in neurology and biological psychology, and an acquaintance of Matthew Baillie.

As do Reid, Darwin, Gall, and Bell, Baillie posits a natural, bodily "language" of expression that conveys the passions in a manner that "every age and nation understand" (1853: 3). These passions are themselves largely invariant – the "great original distinctions of nature" (1853: 13) – and their physiological expression takes universally recognizable forms. Interpreting the full range of "native" passions and character traits – especially in their flickerings and nuances and in despite of attempts to conceal them – demands, however, "constant" practice beginning in early childhood. An innate human drive impels such practice in order to increase one's knowledge of the "species," and apparently barbaric practices like public executions or the ritual torture attributed to American "savages" reflect the "universal desire in the human mind" to study how fellow humans react under varied and extreme conditions (1853: 2, 7). (Tragic drama appeals to this same desire in a more artificial manner [1853: 4].) Again in keeping with the nascent biological psychology of the era, much of this cognitive practice takes place beneath conscious awareness – "without being conscious of it" – and can be put to use intuitively (1853: 2). For Baillie, reading other minds through their embodied manifestations is an innately driven, experientially developed, species-wide human practice.

The exercise of sympathetic curiosity does not only give us insight regarding other minds, however; it also gives us insight into our own minds. "In examining others, we know ourselves" (J. Baillie 1853: 4). Building on the sympathy theory of Hume, Rousseau, and Adam Smith, Baillie underscores the limits of introspection and the need to "look into the thoughts, and observe the behaviour of others" in order to gain "knowledge . . . of our own minds" (1853: 9). Her interest in sympathetic projection and its relation to self-knowledge (and to moral life generally) links Baillie's project with the "mental theatre" of the canonical Romantic poets (Richardson 1988: 134–7). But her emphasis on the embodied character of sympathetic exchange, along with her nativist theory of its origin, distinguishes her theory of mind from that informing mental theatre and makes common cause instead with the physiological psychologies of the time. For Herder, the complexity and unique responsiveness of the human nervous system make sympathetic identification possible in the first place: "The structure of his fibres is so fine, delicate, and elastic, his nerves are so diffused over every part of his vibrating frame, that, like an image of the allsentient deity, he can put himself almost in the place of every creature, and can share its feelings" (1800: 99). But the nervous system enables sympathetic identification in a different and equally fundamental manner, registering mental events in bodily actions and expressions in ways that are regular and predictable enough to give rise to a specialized, largely unconscious knowledge system.

The basic commonalties in the structure and functioning of the nerves, and in their commerce with the musculature and with the respiratory and circulatory systems, guarantees that we can transfer knowledge gained from observing one human being to another – or to ourselves. One of the first clear expressions of this idea can be found in Matthew Baillie's Gulstonian lectures, given in 1794, four years before the first volume of the "Plays on the Passions." In the third of his three prescient lectures on the nervous system, Matthew states that the "different emotions of the mind are also conveyed along nerves to different muscles of the body . . . Each emotion . . . sets in action its appropriate muscles, producing a change in the countenance and attitude, which is expressive of emotion. This becomes a natural language, and is not connected with any arbitrary customs of society" (M. Baillie 1825a: 146). Human beings are innately drawn to studying this "natural language," often unconsciously, and will even unknowingly imitate "singular" gestures or expressions which have "called up the attention of the mind" (1825a: 147). As Bell writes, developing these hints in his *Essays on the Anatomy of Expression*, the "expression of emotion and passion, whether by gesture or in countenance," manifests "sufficient uniformity to be the object of art and reasoning" (1806: 1). Darwin versifies this notion in *The Temple of Nature*:

> When strong desires or soft sensations move
> The astonished Intellect to rage or love;
> Associate tribes of fibrous motions rise,
> Flush the red cheek, or Light the laughing eyes.
> Whence ever-active Imitation finds
> The ideal trains, that pass in kindred minds;

Her mimic arts associate thoughts excite
And the first LANGUAGE enters at the sight.
(1806: III, 335–42)

We recognize such signs in others "by having observed the effects" of various passions "on our own bodies," Darwin explains in a note (Darwin 1806: III, 123–4). Joanna Baillie adds that we also learn from observing the bodies of others to better understand the relation between our own mental states and the physical manifestations that accompany them, tracing the subtler windings of the mind through attending to physiological clues. Baillie's interest in expression has sometimes been compared to the pseudo-science of "physiognomy" (Burroughs 1997: 117; Henderson 1997: 203), but contemporary physiological psychology provides a closer analog. Like the pioneering brain scientists of her time, Baillie looks not to fixed peculiarities of the countenance but to living expression, what Bell calls the "expressions, attitudes, and *movements* of the human figure," manifestations of mental "energy" expressed in physical "changes" that can only be grasped with "intuitive quickness" (Bell 1806: vi–viii, my italics). Or as Baillie puts it, "irregular bursts, abrupt transitions, sudden pauses," as well as such subtler indications as the "restless eye, the muttering lip, the half-checked exclamation and hasty start" (1853: 3, 8).

Baillie's presiding interest in capturing the nuances of emotion and character, registering their flights and starts, in fact accounts for her disappointment with the cavernous theatres of official (London) drama. If the practice of public executions yields insight into the birth of tragedy, it also points up the limitations of a "spectacle" staged beyond a certain distance from its audience. Although few "can get near enough to distinguish the expression of a face, or the minuter parts of a criminal's behavior, yet from a considerable distance will they remark whether he steps firmly; whether the motions of his body denote agitation or calmness" (J. Baillie 1853: 2). Theatrical exhibition – "the grand and favorite amusement of every nation into which it has been introduced" – should do better, especially if crafted by a playwright schooled in observing and representing each "native trait of a character or a passion" (J. Baillie 1853: 4). Two obstacles, however, face Baillie at the outset of her projected series of "plays on the passions." First, she has no "likely channel" to the stage and therefore must content herself, for a time, with publication rather than production. Second, as her preface to the third volume of the "Plays on the Passions" makes clear, the "over-sized buildings" housing contemporary stages make it hard for actors to be "distinctly heard and seen," and nearly impossible to convey the "finer and more delicate indications of feeling" (1853: 232–3). As Burroughs points out, Baillie responds to this dilemma in part by considering alternative theatrical venues: smaller country theatres and amateur or private theatricals (1997: 105–6, 113, 143–68). Another aspect of Baillie's response, however, becomes manifest in her dramaturgy, most notably in her extensive use of meta-theatre – pageants, processions, and masks within the play, on-stage spectators, self-conscious role-playing and performance before actor-audiences – in order to convey, through words, the effects that the playgoer – not to mention reader – might otherwise miss.

Count Basil, the first of the "Plays on the Passions," opens with the question "what tidings of the grand procession?" and includes not one but two on-stage processions in the first scene (J. Baillie 1853: 19). The "*military procession*" headed by Basil, "*with colours flying, and martial music*," crosses the "*long procession of ladies*," led by Victoria, with a "*soft music*" of its own, visually announcing the tensions between duty and desire, masculine and feminine spheres, and the personalities of Basil and Victoria that the play will develop (1853: 20). This sounds like a stock Drury Lane spectacle, but Baillie has already suggested the advantages of a closer look through Geoffrey, one of the play's more sympathetic characters, who bluntly declares, "I came not for the show" (1853: 19). Geoffrey desires instead to look at a face – from near enough that an officer tries to push him back – and to study its expression more than its countenance. He recalls the face of Victoria's mother, wishing to compare it with Victoria's, but dwells mainly on her animated "smile – / 'Twas a heart-kindling smile, – a smile of praise." Baillie includes "heart-kindling" not as an abstract metaphor, but rather in an attempt to convey the quick series of physiological changes – the rush of blood to the heart, the surge of blood to the skin, the accompanying sense of warmth – manifesting the combined sense of pride, embarrassment, and arousal that Geoffrey evidently felt at that moment. A more overt example of how mental and physiological reactions intertwine occurs a bit later in the same scene, as Geoffrey, upon hearing Basil's "martial" music, "*walks up and down with a military triumphant step*," causing a bystander to ask, "What moves thee thus?" This is not an old soldier's affectation but rather his spontaneous and seemingly unconscious response – his bodily response – to a stimulus charged with emotional associations: "I've marched to this same tune in glorious days. / My very limbs catch motion from the sound" (1853: 20). Geoffrey's character and history are manifest in his body, not only in the scars he will reveal later in the play, but in his involuntary movements.

The first scene of the first of the "Plays on the Passions," then, urges the reader (or playgoer) to look past the grand spectacle and attempt, instead, to trace the "varieties of understanding and temper" in the subtler physiological responses displayed, or reported, by the dramatic characters. A good part of the drama itself, however, concerns the characters' attempts to read one another's bodily as well as verbal behaviors, and most of the dramatic complications arise from various attempts to screen, contradict, or falsify those behaviors. Although facial expressions, gestures, and physiological reactions like trembling or blushing may together constitute a "natural language," this language, however universal, remains subject to imperfect expression and to misinterpretation, willful or otherwise. It can also be imitated, although the "natural and genuine" acting style called for by Baillie does entail a degree of felt emotional involvement (J. Baillie 1853: 233). Count Basil's tragedy stems in part from his lack of experience in reading women's bodies: long immersed in a military life, he scarcely can begin to discriminate Victoria's affected from her genuine emotional displays. That Victoria appears profoundly confused and ambivalent regarding her own emotions doesn't help matters. Whether the audience can, in turn, discriminate passions barely acknowledged by the characters manifesting them becomes a test of Baillie's dramatic art and an advanced exercise in the "sympathetic" observation theorized in her "Introductory Discourse."

The importance of physical interaction in this play can be seen in the way that Basil falls for Victoria, literally at first sight. Without any verbal exchange whatsoever, Basil becomes deeply – almost madly – enamored. Other critics who have placed Baillie in the context of contemporary medical discourse have usefully emphasized her interest in abnormal psychology, reading the "Plays on the Passions" as an exercise in "mental pathology" that parallels her brother's work in "morbid" anatomy (Burwick this volume; McMillan 1998: 76). Erotic love, however, the "passion" illustrated by *Basil*, notoriously renders normal subjects abnormal, promoting a temporary mental derangement no less naturalistic for causing unnatural behavior in lovers. Basil's love originates in bare physical attraction, a key aspect of Baillie's original design, and one she restored in the third edition of the play after modifying it in deference to her critics (J. Baillie 1853: 22). But the nonverbal and irrational beginnings of Basil's passion do not render it altogether superficial or invalid. It is not just a pretty face that captures Basil's heart, though the effect of Victoria's beauty plays its part, but more crucially the revelation of one uniquely embodied sensibility through a series of movements, looks, and reactions. Again, it is not the spectacle of Victoria in high station and rich clothing, but rather the nearer view of quick, subtle, but telling glances, gestures, and motions of the blood through the skin that catches Basil off-guard.

> But when approaching near, she tow'rds us turn'd,
> Kind mercy! what a countenance was there!
> And when to our salute she gently bow'd,
> Didst mark the smile rise from her parting lips?
> Soft swell'd her glowing cheek, her eyes smil'd too,
> O how they smil'd! 'twas like the beams of heav'n!

> I felt my roused soul within me start,
> Like something wak'd from sleep.

The very power of Basil's emotive response to Victoria assures him that he has correctly read her mind and character in her body, that he has found the perfect mate. But Basil, whose "mistress" has been war from "early youth," reads women as ineptly as he manages his new-found erotic desires. That's his tragedy.

Like the typical protagonist of Romantic mental theatre, Basil boasts a "fixed mind" (J. Baillie 1853: 22), a phrase that evokes Satan's wishful autonomy ("that fixt mind") in *Paradise Lost* (Book I, line 97). Basil's illusory mental transcendence, however, is undone not – as in mental theatre – by the rhetorical onslaughts of a cunning tempter (Richardson 1988: 21–3), but rather by the suddenly insistent claims of the body that cannot be disentangled from his mind. Framing the contrast another way, the protagonist of Romantic theatre learns (or tragically fails to learn) that the mind is not autonomous but socially constituted and upheld. Basil's seemingly impregnable ("unshaken") mind proves vulnerable both because it is "constructed only in relation to other selves" (Mellor 1994: 561) *and* because it is materially instantiated in an organic body. The body does not serve merely to reveal the mind; the body also informs the mind, and can provoke behaviors and feelings without the consent of – sometimes at the expense of – the conscious self or ego. As Herder writes of the "sensibility," his term for the neural energy that runs from the brain throughout the body and provides the basis of mental life: "Its vibrating fibres, its sympathizing nerves, need not the call of Reason: they run before her, they often disobediently and forcibly oppose her" (1800: 100). Darwin develops an analogous conception of the "sensorium" in *Zoonomia* (1794–96: I, 10), as does Cabanis (who uses the term "*sensibilité*") in his treatise *On the Relations Between the Physical and Moral Aspects of Man* (277, 547, 553). All three writers, like Baillie, grant a large role to the unconscious and involuntary aspects of mental life. Contrary to a longstanding critical tradition, the Romantic poets did not "discover" the unconscious in isolation (Trilling 1950: 34–5).

Basil's erotic passion for Victoria manifests itself bodily for all to see – and in on-stage comments for the benefit of readers or auditors who would otherwise miss its subtler signs. Basil himself cannot help but recognize his body's newly insistent claims as the physiological manifestations of passion disrupt his conscious thought processes and vex his willed behaviors. In the scene (II.i) that portrays his second meeting with Victoria, Basil flushes when she enters the room, "*changes countenance*," a stage direction reiterated by the Duke (Victoria's father), who comments, "your colour changes" (1853: 23). Basil momentarily loses the ability to understand spoken language – "I crave your pardon – / I somewhat have mistaken of your words" – as his speech becomes fragmented and he all but faints from a surge of passion. "A dizzy mist that swims before my sight – / A ringing in my ears – 'tis strange enough." Rosinberg, Basil's cousin and confidant, remarks to him (and us) that Basil's "hand shakes." Nearly all of Basil's speeches to Victoria falter; at one point, he finds himself merely repeating her, a lovesick automaton (1853: 42). Like old Geoffrey mechanically marching to familiar music, Basil barely registers his own words and actions, governed more by his body, emotions, and involuntary reactions than by anything like conscious volition.

Not that love renders Basil altogether dysfunctional. At a critical moment in the plot, when his soldiers have mutinied and threaten to murder him, Basil reasserts his command as much through sheer physical charisma as through a critically understated verbal harangue. Basil's military ascendancy has rested from the beginning on an innate capacity (Rosinberg contrasts it with the lesser "native pow'rs" of the other officers) for inspiring his men on the field through a unique presence of mind and an imposing physical demeanor (1853: 20). These qualities go on display in Act IV, scene two, as Basil faces his rebellious soldiers alone, "*looking at them very steadfastly*" and speaking in a loud and confident voice (1853: 36). Brushing off their threats of physical violence, he "*walks up to the front of his soldiers*," both to show his fearlessness and to enable them to see at close range that his courage and command remain unshaken and unfeigned. Basil restores order with his body; he counts on his men to read his authority in his demeanor, his movements, and his tone of voice.

This is not the play's most striking moment of bodily inspiration, however. In an earlier scene, Basil animates his soldiers by honoring the legendary old campaigner Geoffrey before them: "The sight of thee will fire my soldiers' breasts" (1853: 30). Again, the metaphor has a physiological basis, the soldiers' emotion making itself felt through supercharging the circulatory system; the men are, as we might say, "pumped" by these displays of embodied valor. Valtomer's description of Geoffrey reacting to Basil's "heart-moving words" (off-stage) provides an especially rich and extended example of Baillie's physiological esthetic.

> his count'nance chang'd;
> High-heav'd his manly breast, as it had been
> By inward strong emotions half-convuls'd;
> Trembled his nether lip; he shed some tears.
> The gen'ral paus'd; the soldiers shouted loud;
> Then hastily he brush'd the drops away,
> And wav'd his hand, and clear'd his tear-chok'd voice,
> As though he would some grateful answer make;
> When back with double force the whelming tide
> Of passion came; high o'er his hoary head

His arm he toss'd, and heedless of respect,
In Basil's bosom hid his aged face,
Sobbing aloud.

Valtomer continues by describing his own physiological reaction:

I felt a sudden tightness grasp my throat
As it would strangle me; such as I felt,
I knew it well, some twenty years ago,
When my good father shed his blessing on me:
I hate to weep, and so I came away.

(1853: 30)

Baillie's understanding of how cognition and emotion, anatomy and physiology, interact in complex but broadly consistent ways can be readily aligned with the emergent biological psychologies of her day. Her additional insight into how certain physiological states link up with and can trigger emotionally salient memories, however, may well be unprecedented. Such moments of original psychological insight underscore how literary writers like Baillie, Austen, and Keats not only adapted but significantly extended the embodied approach to mind being worked out in Romantic brain science (Richardson 2001: 93–150).

Against this masculine world of heroism and fealty – and, less predictably, of bodily knowledge and hot passions – Baillie sets the feminine world of Victoria and her train. Although *Basil* places masculine and feminine spheres in opposition, however, there is no clean divide, in the play or in Baillie's theory of mind, between male and female subjectivities. By insisting throughout the play on the embodied and emotive character of *male* subjectivity, Baillie has already departed from the traditional alignment of male with mind (and culture) and female with body (and nature), found throughout the Western tradition and thrown into question by the emergent biological psychologies of Baillie's time. As Anne Mellor argues, "Baillie implicitly asserts that a hitherto marginalized 'women's realm,' the realm of feelings, sympathy, and curiosity, is in fact the basis of all human culture" (1994: 563) – a statement that applies as well to the corporeal accounts of mind and culture then being advanced by Darwin, Cabanis, Bell, and other early brain scientists. Baillie again goes further, however, in insisting that mind and temperament are not gendered – that there is no character trait or mental capacity that cannot be found among both men and women. In *Basil*, the most "magnanimous" character (a supposedly male-coded trait, according to Baillie herself [1853: 9]) is the Countess Albini, Victoria's companion and duenna. Yet Victoria, in her flirtatiousness and coyness, makes use of what Albini herself calls "woman's wiles" – "studied" to be sure and not innately feminine (1853: 33). Denied access to real social power, Victoria takes pleasure instead in the exercise of erotic mastery (or, in Albini's phrase, "tyranny" [1853: 27]). Despite her distrust of conventional or "hegemonic" notions of gender (Mellor 1994: 561), Baillie saddles Victoria with a stock feminine failing.

Basil's ineptness at "courtship ritual" – part and parcel of what Burroughs calls his "rigid style of performing masculinity" – accounts only in part for the spectacular futility of his attempts to interpret Victoria's feelings (1997: 131, 139). Victoria helps engineer the failure of Basil's mindreading by means of her contrastingly artful social style, alternately masking and counterfeiting feelings with her considerable "talent for performing hyperfemininity" (Burroughs 1997: 136). Baillie highlights this emotional artificiality by associating Victoria both with literal masking and with the precocious Mirando, Victoria's *"favourite"* (1853: 18). Mirando, plucked by Victoria from lower-class squalor to serve as a kind of human pet, delights in mimicking the erotic behavior of Victoria's suitors, manifesting the childish bent for imitation noted by Baillie in the "Introductory Discourse" but in a way that suggests that the "natural" language of feeling can be artfully (if imperfectly) reproduced. "How did he look?" Victoria asks of one of her former conquests, and Mirando replies in a manner that both mocks the unfortunate Count Wolvar and starkly contrasts with the genuine emotional displays described elsewhere in the drama.

Give me your hand: he held his body thus:
(*putting himself in a ridiculous bowing posture.*)
And then he whisper'd softly; then look'd so;
(*ogling with his eyes affectedly.*)
Then she look'd so, and smil'd to him again.
(*throwing down his eyes affectedly.*)
(1853: 28)

The parody of Wolvar becomes a parody of Victoria's habitual mimicry of erotic desire. The scene serves at once to parody the "exaggerated expression" endemic to London theatre (1853: 232) and to underscore Victoria's more effective imitation of the physical signs of passion – effective, at least, with fools like Wolvar and naifs like Basil.

Victoria hides as well as counterfeits her feelings, a risky (if perhaps unavoidable) practice that finds its most overt expression in the masked ball represented in the third scene of Act II. It follows closely upon Valtomer's speech recounting the moving exchange between Basil and Geoffrey, the scenic juxtaposition between open and hidden feelings and countenances underscored by Basil's costume – a *"wounded soldier"* (1853: 31). The scene also connects social masking to the politically motivated dissembling of the Duke and his minister Gaurechio, would-be Machiavels who take advantage of Basil's infatuation to stall and ultimately ruin him. It is an atmosphere that Albini, a woman of reason skilled in social behavior, can negotiate and even exploit, but its effect on Basil is maddening. With faces obscured, gestures contrived, and even voices disguised, Basil, his own "flutt'ring heart roused like a startled hare," fails to recognize Victoria even when speaking with her (1853: 33). The scene underscores the limits of verbal exchange stripped of nonverbal cues, Victoria's dubious preference for disguise, and Basil's fatal combination of rigid integrity, emotional instability, and social ineptitude.

The hunt scene (the fifth scene of Act IV), describing the last interview between Basil and Victoria, brings out these same motifs in quite a different manner. Here Basil can speak with Victoria face to face, and spoken language becomes only one element of a richer form of embodied communicative exchange. When Victoria asks him not to speak of love, Basil replies:

> Ah! wherefore should my tongue alone be mute?
> When every look and every motion tell,
> So plainly tell, and will not be forbid,
> That I adore thee, love thee, worship thee?
> (1853: 42–3)

Victoria, however, manipulates the ambiguities of verbal language to torment Basil, rousing his jealousy by letting him believe she has a more favored lover (when in fact she is speaking of her absent brother). When she then corrects his mistake, seemingly in order to plague him further, Basil is so overwhelmed with relief that he becomes forcibly animated (recalling old Geoffrey in Act I) and "*walks up and down with a hurried step, tossing about his arms in transport*" (1853: 43). Such involuntary, emotionally charged physical "transport" may be endearing in the old soldier, but it renders Basil ridiculous and a little scary, and Victoria shortly sends him away. Cruel as she appears in such scenes, Victoria has proved sympathetic to recent critics like Burroughs, who admires the "theatrical skills" that allow her to "create a social performance through which she can self-consciously assess herself in relation to her culture" – a patriarchal culture that will inexorably curtail her opportunities for self-discovery (1853: 137). This line of argument persuades up to a point, yet the performative notion of subjectivity that underwrites it runs athwart of Baillie's own preference for "natural and genuine" forms of expression (1853: 233). Victoria, after all, has a "*true voice*" that contrasts with her variety of assumed poses (1853: 34). Even actors, according to Baillie, depend on a history of genuine emotional experience in order to imitate it convincingly, reliving passion as they represent it. Criticizing the "false" expression characteristic of London theatre, Baillie writes that "we are enabled to assume the outward signs of passion, not by mimicking what we have beheld in others, but by internally assuming, in some degree, the passion itself" (1853: 232). (This explains why Mirando's childish mimicry of passion is so patently ridiculous.) Is Victoria's deception of Basil as effective as it proves because, at least in part, she does feel something akin to love for him? The conclusion, in which she throws herself on Basil's corpse and promises to love him in "horror and decay," seems to imply something more than guilt and remorse (1853: 48). In playing on Basil's feelings, Victoria has been playing with her own.

I would not want to argue, however, that Victoria is solely or even primarily responsible for the play's tragic ending: Victoria, the Duke, Gaurechio, and others may have helped lead Basil to despair, but Basil himself pulls the trigger. He has all along courted tragedy for a reason that resembles Victoria's obsession with erotic conquest: namely, his own obsession with military reputation. Baillie posits both a self thoroughly intertwined with (if not inextricable from) the body and a subjectivity that can develop only through social experience, even if innate "predispositions" bias and constrain subjective development in turn. Hence her emphasis, in theory and dramatic practice, on human interaction that is both embodied *and* social. To the degree that subjectivity is socially constituted, however, it remains dependent upon the acknowledgment of others (including internalized "others" within the self) for its very continuation. (This self-splitting in sympathy theory has been discussed in terms of the theatrical model it implies – an other within the self observing the actions of the self – by David Marshall [1986: 167–92].) Baillie has Gaurechio (the Duke's duplicitous henchman) almost stumble upon this truth in Act III:

> he who teaches men to think, though nobly,
> Doth raise within their minds a busy judge
> To scan his actions.
>
> (1853: 31)

More clever than wise, Gaurechio externalizes a process that is in fact internal: each human subject already has a representative of social law and order within, witnessing and judging his or her *own* actions. Basil and, in parallel fashion, Victoria externalize the process in a different manner, seeking constant validation from others in ways that can never appease the other within the self. Albini makes just this point in her critique of Victoria's pursuit of "ideal tyranny":

> For she who only finds her self-esteem
> In others' admiration, begs an alms;
> Depends on others for her daily food,
> And is the very servant of her slaves.
>
> (1853: 27)

Basil, too, requires constant "admiration" in order to maintain his sense of self, rendering him the creature of the soldiers he claims to command.

Basil's dependence on others for his sense of self comes out most starkly, of course, in the mutiny scenes – "What! think they vilely of me? threaten too!" – where his sense of palpable threat remains secondary to anxieties that his social image has become debased (1853: 35). Far from resisting this bondage to men's opinions, Basil endorses it as an unbreakable law:

> Stern honour's laws, the fair report of men,
> These are the fetters that enchain the mind,
> But such as must not, cannot be unloos'd.
>   (1853: 24)

For a critic raised on Romantic Prometheanism, the "fiery" Basil's unquestioning acceptance of his mind-forged manacles can only seem perverse (1853: 25). More to the point, however, is that, in a play that insists throughout on the richness of nonverbal communication ("he who feels is silent" [1853: 24]), reputation or "fair report" is notoriously unstable precisely because of its purely verbal character. To an extent, Basil can control his reputation locally, even in the face of betrayal and mutiny. But when the appearance of cowardice undermines his wider name for valor, after the battle described to him as imminent has in fact been fought and won without him, a "fallen, fameless" Basil can envision no other option than suicide (1853: 45). Hell and damnation trump infamy:

> I can bear scorpions' stings, tread fields of fire,
> In frozen gulfs of cold eternal lie,
> Be toss'd aloft through tracts of endless void,
> But cannot live in shame.
>   (1853: 45)

It's not a very convincing speech and isn't intended to be. Boasting of a Titanic stoicism even while whining with self-pity, Basil can no longer be taken seriously, dying without dignity and martyring himself to a skewed notion of public image.

Count Basil, then, not only illustrates Baillie's guiding theory of the innate "sympathetic propensity of our minds," but shows how readily "sympathetic curiosity" can be perverted into an obsession with social reputation (1853: 2). In subjecting himself to the vagaries of a purely verbal form of social construction – "fame" – Basil forgets the lesson he himself articulates in making light of the Machiavellian attempts to turn his men against him.

The nature of man's mind too well thou knowst,
To judge as vulgar hoodwink'd statesmen do;
Who, ever with their own poor wiles misled,
Believe each popular tumult or commotion
Must be the work of deep-laid policy.
Poor, mean, mechanic souls, who little know
A few short words of energetic force,
Some powerful passion on the sudden rous'd,
The animating sight of something noble,
Some fond trait of the mem'ry finely wak'd,
A sound, a simple song without design,
In revolutions, tumults, wars, rebellions,
All grand events, have oft effected more
Than deepest cunning of their paltry art.

(1853: 39)

Basil's theory of mind recapitulates a number of points made by Baillie in tandem with the emergent biological psychologies of her time: a preference for organic over "mechanic" models, the salient role of emotion in mental life, the importance placed on tonal "force" and other nonverbal or extrasemantic aspects of human communication, the fine or subtle (rather than mechanically associationist) links among perception, memory, "passion," and volition, and the power of spontaneous or intuitive appeals over conscious "policy" in affecting the mind. In other words, Basil, like Baillie, shares the key assumptions of an embodied psychology. He also implicitly criticizes the "paltry art" of the contemporary stage, which relies primarily on an unnaturally heightened speaking style and a contrived system of pose and gesture to reach its distant audience. Ironically, however, it is the imagined reaction of a removed, virtually disembodied audience that impel Basil toward suicide at the play's close. Having played the lead role in a drama that throughout underscores the importance of "flesh and blood" interaction (1853: 21), Basil ends by isolating himself in a theatre of the mind, filled with the imagined voices of others but with no living body to sustain him. Victoria is left to claim the "cold corse" she spurned when it was all too warm (1853: 48). Basil's inanimate body provides a grisly emblem, as the action closes, of the corporeality that the play has insisted upon all along.

9   Staging Baillie

Jeffrey N. Cox

I

How should one imagine Joanna Baillie's plays being staged? Of course, for the most part, her dramatic texts are simply analyzed apart from the stage. A strong critical tradition insists upon separating her dramas – and, in fact, Romantic literary drama as a whole – from the theatre of the late eighteenth and early nineteenth centuries.[1] While some see this divorce between stage and page arising from Baillie's inability to write stageable plays, the most interesting recent work on her plays has argued that Baillie faced a hopelessly degraded theatre and was thus forced to seek to reform the stage through a turn to the "closet," where she could create an experimental drama.[2] While we have learned much from this fine work on Baillie as a dramatic reformer, I think we misconstrue her art when we see her reforms as expressing either a generalized anti-theatrical prejudice or even a rejection of the contemporary stage; rather, her reforms seek to use the theatrical means available on the London stage of her day to create a contemporary form of tragedy. Put simply, Baillie finds in the spectacular effects of the stage of her day the dramaturgical strategies she needs to create her drama of the passions (see section II below).

This is not to say, however, that Baillie managed completely to overcome the tensions between the literary and the theatrical that marked her cultural moment as much as our commentary on it. Her simultaneous commitment to a rational, moral drama and reliance upon violent spectacle reiterate the tension between page and stage, authoritative text and theatrical performance (section III). Moreover, actual performances of Baillie's plays indicate that for all her desire for rational authorial control, on the one hand, and her willingness to contend with the messiness of the theatre, on the other, her plays on stage can indeed suggest that the contingencies of performance undo authorial control and a unified moral message (section IV). In the revolutionary climate of her day, this uncontrollable stage might seem to mirror the threat of an unruly commonwealth beyond the theatre's walls. While Baillie, with her drama of spectacular moralism, can be seen to offer an alliance with the popular melodrama in an attempt to forge an authoritative moral drama both theatrically powerful and ideologically safe, finally I will argue that Baillie's plays return from melodrama to tragedy exactly when they are performed (section V). For her plays to retain their tragic richness, they must be staged.

II

The critical story of the opposition during the Romantic period between the literary drama and the stage is almost so familiar as to obviate its retelling: poets with no knowledge of the stage stand alienated from theatres too large for an audience to hear their words clearly, while star actors, music, and special effects dominate theatrical practice. In simple terms, the drama of the period has split into poetry unfit for the stage and a theatre designed to present not words but spectacle. Then and now, we read of the destructive power of spectacle. It is telling that it was exactly at this moment, at the end of the eighteenth century, when, according to the *OED*, the meaning of "spectacle" comes to be "a piece of stage-display or pageantry, as contrasted with *real* drama" (my emphasis). Ironically, as the theatre acquired the means to provide ever more impressive special effects, such as those created by Jacques de Loutherbourg (1740–1812), that increased its ability to present both the realistic and the marvelous, the theatre was seen to threaten both the "real" drama and an "imaginative" response to the play text. While this rejection of spectacle is complex – linked to changing attitudes towards gender in the theatre as Julie Carlson (1994) has shown, to concerns about the spectacular fêtes of the French Revolution, to worries about a mass art capable of reaching the illiterate, to the changing relationships between theatre, fiction and painting tracked by Martin Meisel (1983) – it could rapidly translate into a wholesale renunciation of the theatre's powers of sight and sound.[3] The theatre, for some critics of the period, no longer stands as the proper home for the drama, as we see most famously in Lamb's "On the Tragedies of Shakspeare, Considered with Reference to their Fitness for Stage Representation" (1811).

Yet, the literary women and men of the period – from Wordsworth to Byron, from Hannah More to Hemans – invested an enormous amount of energy into plays that they hoped to have performed, and I would argue that there are successes for a merger of literary art and theatrical means – in the works of Elizabeth Inchbald, for example, in Coleridge's *Remorse*, in plays by Matthew Lewis such as *Alfonso, King of Castille* and even the much maligned *Castle Spectre*, in Maturin's *Bertram*, in a number of plays by Colman the Younger and Thomas Morton, and in the plays of Joanna Baillie. While there were clearly some plays in the period that turned from the theatre of the day – Shelley's *Prometheus Unbound*, for example, or

Byron's *Cain* – we err when we try to read all the plays of the period through an anti-theatrical lens.

While there is a general tendency to isolate Romantic drama from the theatre, I believe there is a more specific cause within Baillie criticism for this split. The separation of Baillie's plays from contemporary popular theatre relies in large part on a pervasive move to analogize her dramatic theory, set forth in the "Introductory Discourse" to the first volume of *A Series of Plays: in which it is attempted to delineate the stronger passions of the mind each passion being the subject of a tragedy and a comedy* (usually referred to as the "Plays on the Passions"),[4] with the poetic theory set forth by Wordsworth in the preface to the 1800 edition of *Lyrical Ballads*. One finds the parallel drawn throughout Baillie criticism, from Margaret Carhart's 1923 biography to Burroughs' 1997 account of Baillie's theatre theory. Both Jonathan Wordsworth's introduction (1990) to his reprint of Baillie's 1798 volume and Donald Reiman's preface (1977) to his reproductions of her "Plays on the Passions" highlight the connections between Baillie and Wordsworth, and both William D. Brewer (1991) and Mary F. Yudin (1994) have written essays devoted to tracking the connections between the two prefaces. This argument is made in order to praise Baillie, to find a woman who had already outlined key ideas of Romanticism's most famous theoretical manifesto. However, while this comparison helps us to see Baillie's commitment before Wordsworth to modified diction and her celebration of the lives of "the middling and lower classes of society, where it [human nature] is to be discovered by stronger and more unequivocal marks" (20), it leads scholars to move beyond finding similarities in Wordsworth's and Baillie's treatment of diction and subject matter to making an assumption that they shared views on genre: that is, tying Baillie's "Introductory Discourse" to Wordsworth's preface, which among other things is an argument for poetry over against the drama and the novel and other modes of discourse, ends up allying her argument with an anti-theatrical prejudice or at least with an antipathy to the "popular" theatre, filled with "sickly and stupid German Tragedies."

Baillie, however, did not share Wordsworth's distaste for the London theatres. In fact, the *Eclectic Review* ("Miss Baillie's Plays" 1813: 186) went so far as to criticize her for a "partiality for *the boards*," "making her address the senses rather than the imagination, and in placing before her the mimic representations of things rather than the realities themselves." When she wrote her "Introductory Discourse," she was presenting plays she hoped would be staged at Drury Lane or Covent Garden, unlike Wordsworth who wrote his preface after he (and Coleridge) had seen their dramatic efforts rejected by the patent theatres royal.[5] Her goal was to capture the major London stages.

Towards the end of her "Introductory Discourse," Baillie notes that her readers may feel that, because she published her plays before seeing them performed, she was writing for the closet, but she makes it clear she wants to see her plays on the stage: "A play, but of small poetical merit, that is suited to strike and interest the spectator, to catch the attention of him who will not, and of him who cannot read, is a more valuable and useful production than one whose elegant and harmonious pages are admired in the libraries of the tasteful and refined" (66). Desiring the applause and tears of the theatrical public, Baillie "should, therefore, have been better pleased to have introduced them [her plays] to the world from the stage than from the press" (66). When she published her *Miscellaneous Plays* in 1804, Baillie again expressed her "strongest desire to add a few pieces to the stock of what may be called our national or permanent acting plays," plays which "might have a chance of continuing to be acted even in our canvass theatres and barns" (387). Baillie sought popular theatrical success – even in a barn – over the approval of the "tasteful" and the "refined."

It is, of course, true that Baillie urged a reform of the theatre in her preface to the third volume of her series (published in 1812); Burroughs has shown how Baillie argues for a kind of new, experimental "closet" theatre that called for "a smaller stage to permit the subtler dramatization of both public and private realms; a more emotionally expressive, less exaggerated acting style to counter the stasis of neoclassicism; and a lighting design that would allow audiences to read the psychological shifts being performed by actors" (Burroughs 1997: 87). However, while Baillie desires theatrical reform, she never turns against the stage, not even against stage spectacle. It is worth quoting her balanced account of contemporary stage practice from her 1812 volume (reprinted in her 1851 collected works) at length:

> But when I say, present circumstances are unfavourable for the reception of these plays upon the stage, let it not be supposed that I mean to throw any reflection upon the prevailing taste for dramatic amusements. The Public have now to choose between what we shall suppose are well-written and well-acted plays, the words of which are not heard, or heard but imperfectly by two-thirds of the audience, while the finer and more pleasing traits of the acting are by a still greater proportion lost altogether; and splendid pantomime, or pieces whose chief object is to produce striking scenic effect, which can be seen and comprehended by the whole. So situated, it would argue, methinks, a very pedantic love indeed for what is called legitimate drama, were we to prefer the former. A love for active, varied movement, in the objects before us; for striking contrasts of light and shadow; for splendid decorations and magnificent scenery; is as inherent in us as the interest we take in the representation of the natural passions and characters of men: and the most cultivated minds may relish such exhibitions, if they do not, when both are fairly

offered to their choice, prefer them. Did our ears and eyes permit us
to hear and see distinctly in a theatre so large as to admit of chariots
and horsemen,[6] and all the "pomp and circumstance of war," I see no
reason why we should reject them.

(231–2)

While she is concerned about the difficulties in being heard in London's
vast theatres (in a sense, all she desires is an amplification system), she is
not opposed to the spectacular effects that succeeded in filling them.
Rather, she sees spectacle as an essential ingredient of a fully realized
drama, and she finds the desire for spectacle as natural as our interest in
the passions which lie at the heart of her dramas. In the earlier
"Introductory Discourse," in speaking of Greek tragedy, she notes that
Athenian audiences had long been accustomed to hearing Homeric epics
recited and were thus quite willing to sit through plays dominated by
language: "whole scenes frequently passed, without giving the actor any
thing to do but to speak" (27n.). While such a play might seem to be
Baillie's ideal, she goes on to say: "Had the Drama been the invention of
a less cultivated nation, more of action and of passion would have
been introduced into it. It would have been more irregular, more
imperfect, *more varied, more interesting*" (27–28n. my emphasis). Baillie
does not embrace a chaste, classicizing, regular, "legitimate" drama
but the "varied," "irregular," "interesting" tactics of the so-called
illegitimate theatre.

Baillie finally sees theatrical effect as essential to the success of her plays
in particular. It is important to realize that Baillie's design for a series of
tragedies set forth in her "Introductory Discourse" is offered in
opposition not to the popular plays of the 1790s (as often seems to be the
assumption) but to the tradition of heroic drama that ran from Beaumont
and Fletcher through Dryden and on into the nineteenth century.[7] If we
reread Baillie's criticism of conventional drama, we find her attacking not
the contemporary Gothic drama nor the incipient melodrama, but instead
the tradition of the heroic drama with its "great and magnanimous heroes,
who bear with majestick equanimity every vicissitude of fortune" (32) and
who are "made to exceed in courage and fire what the standard of
humanity will agree to" (34); she objects to the "pompous and solemn
gravity" of these plays (32), and she finds that these works are more
concerned with imitating tradition – the "works of the great Dramatists
who have gone before them" (32) – than with dealing with nature. She
dislikes the heroic drama because it is aristocratic, rhetorical, and
artificial. Most importantly, she contends that in such plays the psychology
of the tragic hero is lost because, in their focus on action, they are not
concerned with investigating his or her inner struggles: "it is events more
frequently than opposite affections which are opposed to them; and those
often of such force and magnitude that the passions themselves are

almost obscured by the splendour and importance of the transactions to which they are attached" (39). Simply put, she rejects the heroic drama's emphasis upon plot.

However, she realizes that any turn against the plot threatens the power of a play – after all, Aristotle had proclaimed that tragedy was an imitation of an action not of persons. Baillie was at times accused of writing plays that lacked sufficient action, as when the *Scots Magazine and Edinburgh Literary Miscellany* criticized the *Family Legend* for lacking suspense and surprise, "two of the most powerful instruments in the production of stage effect" ("Review of *The Family Legend*" 1810: 104). Arguing that in order to present passion naturally the drama should adopt simple plots, Baillie admits that "there is a very great danger of making a piece appear bare and unvaried"; but in a note, she then adds, "To make up for the simplicity of plot, the shew and decorations of the theatre ought to be allowed, to plays written upon this plan, in their full extent. How fastidious soever some poets may be in regard to these matters, it is much better to relieve our tired-out attention with a battle, a banquet, or a procession, than an accumulation of incidents. . . . The shew of a splendid procession will afford to a person of a best understanding, a pleasure in kind, though not in degree, with that which a child would receive from it" (60 and n.). At least for plays written upon her plan, she argues that the pleasures offered by heroic tragedy's operatic plots must be replaced with the thrills provided by stage spectacle. Far from sharing Wordsworth's disdain for the stage practices of the day, she embraces the spectacular effects possible on the late eighteenth-century stage as a means for re-forming the drama by breaking the domination of the intricate plots that were the hallmark of the heroic tradition. The display of passionate character over against plot requires spectacle.

III

Baillie also needs spectacle to resolve a tension in her theory of the drama between her repeated assertion that the drama is an instrument of moral instruction and her location of the birth and continuing vigor of performance in the voyeuristic appeal of rituals of violence.[8] Since moral instruction must be clearly heard and since rituals of violence lend themselves to spectacular display, we see here again a playing out of the relationship between the verbal drama and a theatre of sights and sounds, but spectacle for Baillie is finally not in opposition to a moral message but a way of insuring its impact. If spectacle can interest an audience even in a play that lacks a strong plot, it is because spectacle connects with what for Baillie is a primal scene of watching others face terror, suffering, and death: we are enthralled by scenes of violence to the other. However, in that Baillie seeks to offer moral instruction, the exhibition of violence itself cannot be sufficient; we must not take pleasure in violence but learn from it.[9] Spectacle provides Baillie not only with the means by which to exhibit violence – moments of execution, torture, and supernatural threat require spectacular staging – but also with a way to contain our engagement with theatrical violence. The very spectacular nature of these staged moments of violence reminds us that we are, after all, only watching a play, and as we are detached from our powerful emotional engagement in these moments, we are released into moral judgement.

Baillie is clearly interested in reaffirming the moral power of tragedy, but she realizes that tragedy poses a challenge to the simple moralizing evoked by the notions of poetic justice embodied in much conventional tragedy as represented by the tradition of heroic drama. As she opens her "Introductory Discourse," she rapidly moves to take up an issue often raised in discussions of tragedy: how can we take pleasure in watching on stage a series of horrors? She confronts the issue more generally: "If man is an object of so much attention to man, engaged in the ordinary occurrences of life, how much more does he excite his curiosity and interest when placed in extraordinary situations of difficulty and distress" (5). The *Eclectic Review*, in a wide-ranging account of the "Plays on the Passions" and the *Family Legend*, also sees this issue as central to Baillie's project: "Before we enter upon the consideration of the plays themselves, however, we must detain our readers a little upon an old question, which Miss Baillie has brought forward anew in the preface to her first volume; viz. how it comes to pass that tragedy can be agreeable? – that a composition, the very glory of which it is to draw tears, should be the source of the most exquisite pleasure" ("Miss Baillie's Plays" 1813: 21).

In dealing with this paradox, Baillie posits a universal human curiosity, but the question then becomes why we should be curious to see others in distress. That is, Baillie wants to ground our interest in the drama in an inherent "strong sympathy" (2) with others that should be the foundation of a moral response, but the examples of curious engagement she adduces – spectators watching an execution in order to witness firmness of spirit, Native Americans sacrificing prisoners of war with "hideous cruelty" so that they can view "man in every situation putting forth his strength against the current of adversity" (7), people dressing up "hideous apparitions to frighten the timid and superstitious," risking "destroying their happiness or understanding for ever" (8) – do not seem so much moments of identification or sympathy with the other as controlled, collective enactments of violence against the other.

They are also moments calling for spectacular stage effects, for they engage moments of mass violence – executions, battles – or eruptions of the supernatural into the everyday world. The theatre of the day was well equipped to present supernatural terrors or the violence of war, as we can see in the efforts in Lewis's *Castle Spectre* and elsewhere to put ghosts on stage or in the impressive depictions of battles offered in theatres from Drury Lane to Sadler's Wells.[10] Spectacular drama shares with moments of collective violence an almost irresistible appeal, as we feel forced to watch what we might be expected to shun. As Baillie describes watching an actual execution, her language links that experience to sitting in the huge London theatres with their reliance upon spectacle. She notes that at an execution "few at such a spectacle can get near enough to distinguish the expression of face, or the minuter parts of a criminal's behaviour, yet from a considerable distance will they eagerly mark whether he steps firmly; whether the motions of his body denote agitation or calmness; and if the wind does but ruffle his garment, they will, even from that change upon the outline of his distant figure, read some expression connected with his dreadful situation" (5–6). While Baillie clearly has reservations about large theatre spaces and the spectacles that filled them, she proves herself here to be a master semiotician of such productions, reading a meaning into each gesture that can be seen on the huge stage of the scaffold. She would use exactly the appeal of such moments in *Rayner* (1804), where Act III, scene i, opens on a "spacious court with a magnificent building in front; a great concourse of people are discovered as if waiting in expectation of some sight" (402), that sight being the possible execution of Rayner; members of the crowd exchange stories about various executions they have previously witnessed.[11] Again in *Witchcraft* (1836), Act V, scene ii, opens upon "the Market-place prepared for execution . . . a great crowd of people are discovered."

Baillie gives further evidence of her sense of the importance of ritual violence to theatrical appeal in her account of Native Americans' "dreadful custom of sacrificing prisoners of war":

> But the perpetration of such hideous cruelty could never have become a permanent national custom, but for this universal desire in the human mind to behold man in every situation, putting forth his strength against the current of adversity . . . . This custom, therefore, must be considered as a grand and terrible game, which every tribe plays against another; where they try not the strength of the arm, the swiftness of the feet, nor the acuteness of the eye, but the fortitude of the soul.
>
> (7–8)

While she believes such practices may have begun in revenge against one's enemies, they have evolved into something more complex and more palatable. What looks like revenge becomes, in fact, an opportunity for the "victim" to demonstrate his strength of soul. This "grand and terrible game" is like dramatic tragedy in that it offers in the guise of play an opportunity to witness extreme moments of suffering and incredible examples of endurance. Like the drama, torture allows us to experience vicariously the most intense and excessive emotional states. *De Monfort*, with its detailed, excruciating analysis of inveterate hatred, is an example of drama that derives its power from our interest in watching the title character struggle through the tortures imposed upon him by his passionate antipathy to Rezenvelt. Throughout her plays – from *Rayner* with its evocation of an execution to *Orra* with its apparent appearance of a ghost, from *The Family Legend* where a woman is left to drown upon an isolated rock to *Witchcraft* where throughout the final scene Mary MacMurren remains bound to the stake before a crowd eager to see her burn – Baillie relies upon spectacles of violence and dread. Baillie's sense that our love of spectacle is "as inherent in us as the interest we take in the representation of the natural passions" arises from spectacle's link to the ur-drama that Baillie locates in executions, hauntings, torture. For Baillie, tragedy would seem to offer an amoral celebration of gross and violent stimulants.

Yet Baillie's commitment to the moral power of the drama is quite clear. She places the drama amidst other "species of moral writing":

> The Drama improves us by the knowledge we acquire of our own minds, from the natural desire we have to look into the thoughts and observe the behaviour of others. . . . it is only from the enlargement of our ideas in regard to human nature, from that admiration of virtue, and abhorrence of vice which they excite, that we can expect to be improved by them.
>
> (37)

Or more succinctly, she writes: "The theatre is a school in which much good or evil may be learned" (58). When Baillie comes to summarize her project (41), her major claim for a series of plays on the passions is "that tragedy, written upon this plan, is fitted to produce stronger moral effect than upon any other" (41–2).

Baillie's sense of the moral efficacy of tragedy is in apparent tension with her contention that tragedy invites us to witness horrible deeds and even to empathize with evil individuals. Baillie claims that her plays appeal to the moral mind, and thus they should engage a reflective, analytic, moralizing mode, a mode that Shelley in his "Preface" to *The Cenci* gave the provocative label of "restless and anatomizing casuistry" (1977: 24), but which we might identify with a kind of Shavian theatre of rational analysis. At times, she seems to be calling for an intimate theatre of subtle psychological exchanges that would lead to a reasoned, moral response. However, in that her tragedies are filled with hatred, murder, ritual violence, witchcraft, and supernatural fears, they at times seem closer to Artaud's theatre of cruelty. Artaud might seem to sum up Baillie's engagement with a theatre of violence, when he states: "Without an element of cruelty at the root of every spectacle, the theater is not possible" (Artaud 1958: 99).[12]

Artaud goes on to suggest an essential link between spectacular cruelty and conscious reflection that can help us see Baillie's attempted resolution of the tension in her theory: "Cruelty is above all lucid, a kind of rigid control and submission to necessity. There is no cruelty without consciousness and without the application of consciousness. It is consciousness that gives to the exercise of every act of life its blood-red color, its cruel nuance, since it is understood that life is always someone's death" (102). This can be seen to implicate consciousness in cruelty; rational analysis and judgement itself can be violent. When we experience violence towards another in the theatre of cruelty, we are aware the other experiences pain so that we may take some sort of theatrical pleasure in that pain. In its most drastic formulation, Artaud suggests that when we are conscious of another dying on stage, we feel more alive. However, Artaud's formulation also suggests that the goal of the theatre of cruelty is not an unexamined immersion in scenes of torture and death but instead a self-conscious reflection upon our living dependence upon the death of something else. What the theatre gives us – and what cannot be gained through watching an execution, participating in a battle, confronting a ghost – is both immersion and distance, both enthrallment and ironic detachment. The power of spectacular theatre is that it allows us both to enjoy and to understand monstrous, horrible situations.

We can perhaps see more clearly how Baillie uses violence in the service of moral instruction if we examine our relationship with her violently passionate characters. Time and again, Baillie puts on stage characters who are dominated by destructive passions – hate, fear, irrational love. If we identify with them to the point that they escape judgement, the drama would seem to undermine moral evaluation. We would then have only an immersion in gross stimulation. However, if we simply condemn these characters, if we cannot see the greatness in titanic men of passion, the audience will not sympathize with them sufficiently to engage in the process of moral education Baillie proposes – we must see ourselves in these passionate criminals. In her "Introductory Discourse," Baillie attempts to resolve this tension in the formula, "it is the passion and not the man which is held up to our execration" (65). This variation on hating the sin and not the sinner, however, poses problems in staging her plays, as we will see most clearly in John Philip Kemble's production of *De Monfort*. Still, in spectacle Baillie finds the kind of moment of simultaneous engagement and reflection she needs. As Gamer puts it, Baillie "argues for supernatural and psychological spectacle as a potential tool for moral and intellectual instruction" (1997: 60). As we watch theatrical spectacle, we are overwhelmed by stage effect, swept up in the moment as if we were actually experiencing it. While this may be most directly clear in the kind of "jumping-out-from-dark-places" shock tactics we find in the Gothic drama (and film) – where we are scared along with the characters – it occurs whenever the realism or wonder of the special effects forces us into a temporary un-willing suspension of disbelief. For Baillie's purposes, the spectacular moment allows us to glimpse a human experiencing extreme emotional states – facing death, undergoing torture, losing rational control in the face of the supernatural. This is essential if we, living ordinary, humdrum lives, are to experience and thus understand the passions in their most virulent and violent forms. Thus, the *Eclectic Review* ("Miss Baillie's Plays" 1813: 23) finds Baillie instructing the rational man in madness: "The figures and images of a man under the dominion of violent passions, seem insanity to him whose mind is calm and unagitated. He must be made to sympathize with the sufferer, must feel in a measure the agonies of grief, and the palpitations of terror, and the madness of rage; and then he may enter into the higher and grander beauties of the tragic strain."

However, as *Orra* (with its depiction of a woman driven mad by her lover's appearance in the guise of a ghost) demonstrates, there is a fine line between a theatrical experience of such extreme states that enables one to analyze the passions displayed and a sympathetic identification that leads the viewer to experience the unmediated passions, the terror and madness, being offered on stage. That audiences sometimes crossed that line can be seen in the reactions to Baillie's favorite actress, Sarah Siddons, who often evoked tears, screams, and even fainting fits from spectators too involved in what they were observing.[13] Baillie needs spectacle to create sympathy with terror and madness, but she needs to move us beyond this sympathy if she is going to evoke the moral lesson she seeks. Here, spectacle does double duty for it both vividly engages us in the action and yet, through its very power that renders us passive absorbers of what occurs on stage, reminds us that we are only spectators, that we are safely watching a show not undergoing the passions. Spectacle, as the most theatrical of moments, has the capacity to evoke a metatheatrical response, a recognition of the staginess of the most powerful moments of stage craft. Unlike plot, which for Baillie involves us in headlong action that keeps us looking forward and thus prevents us from reflecting, spectacle provides free-standing moments of engagement and reflection, violence and moral consciousness. The shared moment of engagement with violence provides the ground upon which we can arrive at a communal moral judgement.

IV

Critics of spectacle feel that it reduces the power of drama by offering a simplified experience. As opposed to a supposedly infinitely rich response to a dramatic text, spectacle is seen as evoking a crude, restricted, one-dimensional reaction. Spectacle is seen as deadening the powers of the imagination, perhaps because it seems to dictate a unified response from the audience – everyone jumps when startled, nearly everyone turns from scenes of violence, most are impressed with wondrous effects, many react directly to stage eroticism. Spectacular effects – which in one sense are a perfection of stage craft – are resisted exactly because they offer moments when we feel controlled by the play before us. In response to such objections, Baillie seeks in spectacle a stage tactic that does produce a unified response but one that is rational, that goes beyond a shared gut-wrenching experience to a collective moral judgement. For her, spectacle should unite us in both sympathy and judgement.

Witchcraft demonstrates how Baillie would like spectacle to function within her plays.[14] There is no doubt the play is driven by spectacle. In addition to various scenes around the impressive Tower of Dungarren and striking natural settings – such as Act III, scene i, where we are presented with a "half-formed cave" with a brook running in front of it and "precipitous rocks" functional enough that Dungarren can climb down them – there is the execution scene mentioned before and the scene on a "wild moor" where, to the sounds and sights of thunder and lightning, we witness the gathering of the women who believe they are witches. This spectacular storm, coupled with the appearance of the mysterious Murrey, is seen by Grizeld Bane as proof that Satan has appeared to them, and we might also be swept away by the force of the scene to believe that the supernatural has appeared, as Coleridge (1983, II: 222) complained was the case with the storm that opened Maturin's *Bertram*. Baillie works against such a reaction, however, as we know that Murrey is forced by circumstance to play the part of Satan. Rutherford also watches the scene, as Violet enters to meet her father, whom everyone believes is dead; seeing Violet with what he believes to be a ghost, Rutherford is convinced that she is involved in witchcraft. This moment provides a metatheatrical commentary on our experience of spectacle: when we are swept up by what we *see* but do not *hear* or *understand*, we can fall into error; what seems so real may only be an illusion or play-acting.

The play in fact revolves around errors in perception: Rutherford's mistake about Murrey, Dungarren's error about Violet's involvement with another man, and most centrally the "witches'" self-imposed error in believing themselves "to have had intercourse with the Evil One," as Baillie puts it in her preface (613). Visual evidence, the evidence of spectacle, leads all of these characters to believe they have seen the face of evil, whether supernatural or sexual. But evil comes disguised in the play. The truly destructive figure is the beautiful, cultured Annabella. While she is in some ways a conventional stage seductress, Dungarren identifies her as the true "witch" in the play: "I will stay and contest with the termagant, as I would with an evil spirit" (I, ii).

To clinch her point, Baillie has the climax of her play again hinge upon a metatheatrical moment that reveals the way spectacle works. Annabella joins us as the audience for the play's ultimate spectacle, the execution scene. Hoping to watch Violet's burning from a room above the market place, Annabella believes she has arranged the spectacle of violence towards the other that Baillie identified as the true source of dramatic interest. Only this spectacle does not unfold as Annabella has written it. Fatheringham arrives as a kind of governmental *deus ex machina* to proclaim that the laws against witchcraft have been overturned. An enlightened parliament will no longer believe in false images. Fatheringham also enables the truth about Murrey to be revealed, so that good and evil can be sorted out at the play's close by reason not by mistaken sight. Moreover, the violence of the witch burning we expected to see spectacularly in the theatre is displaced off stage, as Grizeld Bane murders Annabella. Where Annabella wished to watch violent spectacle, she instead becomes the victim of unseen violence. Throughout the play, Baillie uses spectacle to capture our interest, but in the end she sets aside spectacle and its violent heart. She can thus return to her moral vision, as Dungarren closes the play, saying of Annabella: "Those who have felt the tyranny of uncontrolled passion will think, with conscious awe, of her end" (V, ii). The collective desire for violent spectacle is replaced by a communal assertion of a rational moral order. Dungarren's "conscious awe" – a self-conscious deployment of spectacle, of the awe-ful, that allows us to see through the spectacle, to disenchant the awe – might be the motto of Baillie's moral theatre.

Spectacle, however, was not so easily controlled when Baillie's plays were put on stage. When we examine, for example, the famous stage production of *De Monfort* at Drury Lane in 1800 by John Phillip Kemble and Sarah Siddons, we find a play that we as readers might think of as an example of a spare, stripped down dramatic style offered instead as grand spectacle. As Genest recorded, Drury Lane was committed that year to splendid, daring staging: "Besides *Pizarro*, the *Egyptian Festival*, and the *Tragedy of Montford*, are to be *Grand Spectacles*, and aided by the charms of music."[15] The *Morning Post* complained that Baillie and her adapter Kemble did not have the "confidence sufficient to renounce the popular charms of spectacle" (*Morning Post* 1800: n. pg.). Audiences responded to such showy moments as the "gaudy show" of the ball in Act II, i,[16] the banquet in Act III, and the procession in Act V. They were overwhelmed by the recreation of a fourteenth-century church on stage in Act V, one of the earliest examples of three dimensional set scenery as opposed to backdrops.[17] While we tend to care only about Baillie's words, we need to remember that the play was filled with the music of Michael Kelly and Thomas Shaw.[18]

As Baillie's theory suggested, such spectacle was necessary to engage the audience in her analysis of the passions in a way that would both enthrall them and allow for moral reflection. As Baillie's design required, the plot was simple. As the *Times* puts it: "The plot is told in a sentence. *De Monfort*, sensible of the superiority of *Rasenberg* [sic], in the accomplishments of mind and body, entertains a marked detestation of him from their earliest acquaintance, which is wound up as to induce him to assassinate the man he hates" (*Times* 1800: n. pg.). Spectacle was needed to make up for the absence of action. The difficulties in achieving the balance between engagement and judgement that Baillie seeks, however, are revealed in one particular piece of stage action that Kemble deleted.

In the original 1798 version of the play, Baillie offered in Act III, scene iii, a key moment of violence and of humiliation for De Monfort. De Monfort and Rezenvelt engage in a sword fight which results in De Monfort being disarmed and disgraced: *"They fight: Rezenvelt parries his thrusts with great skill, and at last disarms him"*; when De Monfort calls upon his enemy to take his life, Rezenvelt instead decides to "take away your sword . . . for your safety"; *"De Monfort stands for some time quite motionless, like one stupified."* Apparently, Kemble felt that this scene, in which De Monfort is both churlish and incompetent, diminished too severely the character he was going to play. The copy of the play sent by the theatre for licensing to the Examiner of Plays, John Larpent, which represents what the theatre intended to put on stage (LA 1287), eliminates Rezenvelt and the confrontation from this scene. However, the detailed review of the performance by Thomas Dutton in the *Dramatic Censor* (1801) indicates that Rezenvelt was present in the performed scene but that the two men did not fight. There is a version of the play matching Dutton's description, a manuscript in the hand of Thomas Campbell prepared for Sarah Siddons who has annotated the text (Huntington MS 32693).[19] It is this final version that seems to record what was actually done in performance: De Monfort challenges Rezenvelt to a duel, but Rezenvelt – in consideration of Jane and of his vow to end the enmity between De Monfort and himself – refuses. Violence is threatened – interest is raised – but De Monfort is not humiliated.

What this series of alterations suggests is the difficulty Baillie and her adapters had in staging the tension between the sympathy for De Monfort that is necessary if he is going to appear as the hero of the play and our condemnation of his passion and the violence it leads him to. As in all of her "Plays on the Passions," Baillie must both make her audience sympathize with the central passionate character and allow them to judge him. A double vision of De Monfort is present in the very first scene of the play, as the servants discuss how "difficult, capricious, and distrustful" he can be: "Yet I know not how, / A secret kindness binds me to him still" (I, i); it is still present as the play reaches its climax, as De Monfort leaves with a grand gesture, leading out the sister he loves (V, ii), and as she praises him as one "Who, but for one dark passion, one dire deed, / Had claim'd a record of as noble worth, / As e'er enrich'd the sculptur'd pedestal," only to have Baillie in a note reassert that De Monfort "notwithstanding his other good qualities, [is] proud, suspicious, and susceptible of envy" (V, iv).

Baillie chose not to stage the ultimate moment of violence, the murder of Rezenvelt, but in the much contested scene in Act III she reveals De Monfort's vicious hatred in perhaps an even less appealing way, for here he can appear both violent and inept, perhaps even cowardly. As Kemble and the Drury Lane company reworked this scene, they revealed how difficult it was to achieve the kind of unified, balanced, rational response that Baillie sought. Baillie wished to calibrate our emotional responses exactly, so that we would remain sympathetic to a figure who is offered in one sense as a tragic hero while remaining able to condemn his or her actions. She had hoped that the spectacle of the duel would both capture our interest and release us into a collective moral judgement. Finally, however, as Baillie's own willingness to alter the play for performances by Kemble or later Kean suggests, the contingencies of performance prevent the kind of emotional closure that Baillie's theory required. Baillie – embracing the stage and opening her plays to the revisions of others and to the variability of performance – cannot be the Author of a stable, definitive text.

V

Closure was simply not a feature of the theatre of Romanticism, with its multiple-item play bills, with its performance style which emphasized not only spectacular moments but various "points" made by star actors, with its frequent interruptions from the audience that could range from friendly responses to riots. We still do not have a full grasp of this theatre that was multiple and fragmentary, that was so unlike any notion of "organic" unity; and spectacle in particular offers a moment that is experienced at least as much for itself as for its contribution to the work as a whole.

Moreover, Baillie – like her fellow playwrights of the 1790s and early 1800s – faced a series of interlocked crises that made it even less likely that one could present a unified cultural object. First, many perceived a crisis within the institution of literature, a crisis we might usefully follow Michael Gamer (2000) in linking to the Gothic,[20] the crisis which Wordsworth's preface to *Lyrical Ballads* addressed with its attempt to protect poetry from the incursions of novel reading and the popularity of "sickly and stupid German tragedies." This was a crisis of both genre and mode or style. Within the drama, this crisis can be seen through the influence of a Gothic mode or style in plays ranging from tragedies to burlesques and through the proliferation of new forms – burletta, pantomime, various hybrids such as "grand operatic romance," and most importantly the melodrama. Within the theatre itself, there was in addition a crisis of representational means, usually identified with the enlargement of the theatres at Covent Garden and Drury Lane; as Baillie's own reaction suggests, there was a fear that the new, larger houses – holding over 3,000 people each – offered, in Richard Cumberland's words, "theatres for spectators rather than playhouses for hearers" (1807, II: 384). Competing with the non-verbal theatrical fare of the "minor" theatres, struggling to find the means to command and to fill their enlarged spaces, the theatrical companies at the patent theatres royal resorted increasingly to stage spectacle, special effects, non-verbal communication, and a new, passionate acting style identified with Sarah Siddons and then Edmund Kean. In a sense, the "majors" adopted the theatrical means of the "minors," just as Baillie was willing to use spectacular means to rejuvenate tragedy.

These threats to literary and theatrical tradition might have seemed harmless enough had they not appeared to echo the larger crisis we refer to by the short-hand phrase of the French Revolution debate. Here, Baillie appears as divided as many of her contemporaries. With her turns to the "middling" ranks in her plays, she might seem to be a "leveler" in literature. We should be careful, however, in how far we push the notion of Baillie as embracing "democratic" principles. While she repeatedly asks that tragedy stop dealing only with aristocrats and with "heroic heroes," while she wants the drama to appeal to the "middling" ranks, she does not extend the appeal of her plays to those below that middle: the drama's "lessons reach not, indeed, to the lowest classes of the labouring people, who are the broad foundation of society, which can never be generally moved without endangering every thing that is constructed upon it" (57–8). Baillie shares with many of her contemporaries a fear that the power of the drama will move the people not only to emotional response but to political action, a real possibility in the day of theatrical riots such as the "Old Price" Riots that beset Covent Garden for sixty-seven nights in 1809.

One feared the political impact of the drama because, as we can see in the Edinburgh staging of Baillie's *The Family Legend* (29 January 1810), her "Highland Play" as she called it (J. Baillie 1851: 480), which treats the struggles between the Campbells and the Macleans and the legend of the lady rock, it was as difficult to achieve ideological clarity in the theatre as it was to ensure emotional closure. Despite repeated assertions about Baillie's inability to command the stage, this was again a successful production: the play had an initial strong run of thirteen consecutive performances (it was successful enough to spark a revival of *De Monfort*)[21] and long remained part of the theatre's repertoire. In discussing the ideological uses to which Baillie's plays could be put, we need first to see how strongly Baillie was supported by the theatrical and cultural establishment. If the production of Baillie's *De Monfort* was undertaken by John Philip Kemble and Sarah Siddons, the king and queen of the London theatre, the staging of her *Family Legend* was organized by the Edinburgh theatre's manager Henry Siddons, Sarah's son, and Sir Walter Scott, who also supplied the prologue for the play. The epilogue was written by Scotland's "Man of Feeling," Henry Mackensie, as Scott wanted to be sure that the evening would be "entirely of Scotch manufacture" in order to offer "every chance of succeeding before a national audience" (1932–37: II, 286).

To insure this success and in keeping with Baillie's design, *The Family Legend*, like *De Monfort*, received a spectacular production, even if it was within the smaller confines of the Edinburgh Theatre Royal.[22] Scott (1932–37: II, 218–29) wrote to Baillie of the work being done on the costumes, with the rival clans being given contrasting colors to provide a striking visual effect. Scott, finding the scenery "very good," was particularly pleased with spectacular scenes such as the banquet scene and the combat. He makes special note of how the scene of exposing Helen on the rock "was so contrived as to place Mrs. Siddons [Henry's wife], in a very precarious situation to all appearance" (1932–37: II, 290–91). The *Scots Magazine* also praised this scene and the play's spectacle in general: "The situation of Helen, left alone on this desolate rock, with the waves roaring around her, and venting her despair at the view of her rapidly approaching fate, is one of the wildest and most singular that was ever presented to an audience" (1810: 105); "The scenery was very fine and striking, so far as the too limited extent of the theatre would admit," which, of course, suggests that this reviewer at least would have liked a larger theatre and more spectacle. While having some reservations about the play, the reviewer found "that there were beauties, even in point of stage effect – , which might well establish its character as a popular and pleasing addition to our stock of acting plays" (104). In addition to praising the language of the play, the review lauds the "constant succession of detached scenes, striking from the situations which they present" and which provide an "excellence . . . altogether appropriate to the theatre" (104). The reviewer finds that: "The appearance of this piece may fairly be considered as forming an era in the literary history of this metropolis" (103). In Adrienne Scullion's view, "spectacular and energetic" staging saved the "exaggerated drama" of this verse tragedy "through the —*lan* of production" (1997: 161).

As with *De Monfort*, one piece of stage business is particularly telling. As noted above, Scott was anxious to make sure there was a clear visual contrast between the two opposed clans. However, Scott and Siddons in the end masked the identity of the clans in order to prevent any uproar in the theatre: "Knowing the strong feelings of pride and clanship which had existed amongst Highlanders" (1932–37: II, 253–4), Scott substituted fictitious clan names so that the Macleans would not take offense. However, Scott was not always so sensitive to the feelings of Highlanders; in order to supplement a scene in which troops gathered (V, iv), "I got," he told the author, "my brother's highland recruiting party to reinforce the garrison of Inverary and as they appeard beneath the porch of the castle and seemd to fill the courtyard behind the combat scene had really an appearance of reality" (1932–37: II, 292). While Scott is concerned here with spectacle and realism, he has not apparently thought about the ideological implications of his bit of staging; that is, he put on stage one of the groups of men who since the passage of the extremely unpopular Scottish Militia Act of 1797 had been used to coerce the Highland poor into the army. While there has been good work done to show how this play fulfills the kind of Edinburgh Tory ideology that Scott espoused,[23] even so precise a manager of theatrical effects as Scott could not control all of the ideological readings the audience might give the performance. While he desired a play of "Scotch manufacture" capable of pleasing a national audience and while there is evidence that he at least pleased the Edinburgh establishment (see, for example, the *Correspondent*, 12 March 1810), his spectacular display of troops was almost surely viewed differently by the Highland portion of his audience than he would have had them view it. Scott desired a unified ideological response from a crowd that could thus be forged into a "national audience," but he like Baillie herself runs up against the vagaries, the variability of performance.

It is when we note this ideological precariousness that we can identify the dangers some saw in the inherent instabilities of theatrical performance. It is against a background of threats to political, cultural, and literary traditions that we can understand that the desire for an Author as a source of authority appeared as an attempt to shore up power. If we think of the Romantic author seeking to project a unified, purposeful, authoritative voice, then the contingent, unpredictable, necessarily collaborative world of the theatre appears as a threat. The oppositions that appear in commentaries then and now – between single authorship and collective theatrical performance, between unified text and variable spectacle, between literary genres worthy of authorship such as tragedy and those theatrical forms left anonymous such as the pantomime – presuppose that a writer interested in the drama creates her- or himself as an author, rather than a hack or scribbler, by penning a unified text of a print tragedy rather than the multivoiced creation that is a performed play.[24]

For some, for Wordsworth perhaps or Coleridge attacking Maturin's *Bertram*, the popular theatre was a dangerous place where moral, cultural, and political power is threatened by a mob that in desiring theatrical novelty perhaps signals a longing for political innovation. What is interesting about Baillie is that – as both her theory and actual performances suggest – she and her collaborators were fully willing to embrace the period's "revolution" in theatrical means in order to shore up the traditional dramatic genre of tragedy as a high cultural defense against the dangers posed when the "labouring people" are "generally moved." In a sense, Baillie – who desired to free the British theatre from the controlling aristocratic dramatic tradition that stretched back to Beaumont and Fletcher but who worried about the people in the theatre – was happy to embrace the theatrical tactics we identify with the newly forged melodrama.[25] It is perhaps telling that a third play of Baillie's that reached the stage, *Constantine Paleologus* (Theatre Royal, Liverpool, 7 November 1808), was reworked by a member of a key theatrical family, Charles Isaac Mungo Dibdin, as *Constantine and Valeria; or, The Last of the Caesars* (Surrey, 23 June 1817), a "melodramatic spectacle."[26] Baillie at times seems to have understood that tragedy was not susceptible to the kind of final moral judgement she embraced in her theoretical pronouncements, but, as Peter Brooks (1976) has argued powerfully, such ambiguity could seem quite threatening, even subversive, in a period of revolutionary destabilization of the order of things. For Brooks, it is the melodrama that provided a form through which the moral order could be reasserted – and reasserted exactly through the spectacular display of violence central to Baillie. Baillie's desired theoretical reform of the stage – with its turn to spectacle and violent effects in pursuit of morality – has more to do finally with the melodrama that would triumph on the nineteenth-century stage than with the differing attempts to restore tragedy undertaken by, say, Shelley or Byron. However, on stage, the aesthetic, moral, and ideological closure she sought was subverted by the very fact of performance: in the contingencies of performance, in the uncertainty and messiness of the theatre, the tragic ambiguities at the heart of Baillie's plays rather than her theory were in fact restored. However we imagine staging Baillie, her plays must be staged.

Notes

1   During Baillie's own lifetime, the *Edinburgh Magazine and Literary Miscellany*, for example, praises the poetry of her plays but argues that they cannot hold the stage ("Remarks" 1818: 517–20). Watkins (1993) summarizes the feelings of many when he accuses Baillie of "writing plays that were utter failures on stage in her own day and that continue to baffle (and often bore) would-be sympathizers today" (39). The turn from the theatre in discussions of Romantic drama can also be seen in Jewett (1997): "I have chosen not to emphasize the relations between this largely unperformed canon of plays and the theatrical world of early nineteenth-century London" (4).

2   See, for example, Burroughs (1997: 87). Thomas Crochunis's chapter in this volume sees the closet as a venue through which Baillie's ambivalences about theatre and publication could be negotiated.

3   As Gamer (1997: 49–50) notes, there is a "general tendency within dramatic criticism of separating closet from performed drama, which, in the case of criticism of Romantic drama, often entails ignoring, altogether, what was performed."

4   In general, I have consulted Baillie (1851). For her "Introductory Discourse," I have used the first edition (1798). For *De Monfort*, I have used my edited text in Cox (1992). Citations will be given in the text.

5   For Wordsworth's attempt to have *The Borderers* staged, see Osborne (1982: 3–7). Wordsworth's antipathy to the drama of the day is also revealed in his response to the success of Lewis's *Castle Spectre*; see his March 1798 letter to James Tobin, in Wordsworth (1967: 210). Coleridge shared this distaste for Lewis's successful play.

6   Baillie's embrace of horses and chariots on stage is quite striking, given that she published this remark around the time of the uproar over the introduction of live horses into productions of Colman's *Bluebeard* (Covent Garden, 18 February 1811) and Lewis's *Timour the Tartar* (Covent Garden, 29 April 1811).

7   For an account of this tradition's importance to Romantic drama, see Donohue (1970).

8   See Victoria Myers' chapter in this volume for further discussion of Baillie's use of violent spectacles for political and pedagogical purposes.

9   Baillie immediately denies that pleasure can be the key to our interest in, for example, a public execution: "It cannot be any pleasure we receive from the sufferings of a fellow-creature which attracts such multitudes of people to a publick execution" (5). The "powerful incentive" which draws us to executions is our desire to "see a human being bearing himself up under such circumstances, or struggling with the terrible apprehensions which such a situation impresses" (5).

10 On the representation of war in the theatre of the day, see Russell (1995).

11 As the *Eclectic Review* notes, Burke too had linked theatrical performance to the staging of executions; the reviewer quotes from the first part, paragraph 15 of Burke's essay on the sublime and beautiful: "Choose a day on which to represent the most sublime and affecting tragedy we have; appoint the most favourite actors; spare not cost upon the scenes and decorations; unite the greatest efforts of poetry, painting, and music; and when you have collected your audience, just at the moment when their minds are erect with expectation, let it be reported that a state criminal of high rank is on the point of being executed in the adjoining square; in a moment the emptiness of the theatre would demonstrate the comparative weakness of the imitative arts, and proclaim the triumph of real sympathy" ("Miss Baillie's Plays" 1813: 26–7). The *Eclectic Review* usefully places Baillie's comments on tragedy in the context of discussions by Burke, Hurd, and especially Hume, a more appropriate theoretical milieu for Baillie, it strikes me, than that of Wordsworth and his preface. Victoria Myers' chapter in this volume explores Hume's relevance to Baillie's dramatic and moral theory.

12 Of course, at times, Artaud would seem to be utterly opposed to Baillie with her desire to follow the great man into his closet; after all, it was he who proclaimed: "An idea of theater has been lost. And as long as the theater limits itself to showing us intimate scenes from the lives of a few puppets, transforming the public into Peeping Toms, it is no wonder the elite abandon it and the great public looks to the movies, the music hall or the circus for violent satisfactions, whose intentions do not deceive them" (1958: 84). The resort to spectacle here is, of course, relevant to my sense of what Baillie is up to.

13 On the power of Siddons' appearances on stage, see Backscheider (1993: 204–17), Cox (2000: 23–47), and Pascoe (1997: 12–32).

14 I want to thank the faculty and students of the University of Bari and the University of Bologna for focusing my attention on *Witchcraft*; in particular, since I am interested in the staging of Baillie, I want to thank the students at Bologna who allowed me to watch rehearsals for a performance of *Witchcraft* they were preparing under the supervision of Lilla Maria Crisafulli.

15   Carhart (1923: 115) cites this as from "Genest's scrap-book," presumably cuttings from periodicals; I have not been able to locate the original source.

16   In a Philadelphia production of the play (Chestnut Street Theatre, 8 February 1811), a band was placed on the stage for this scene and a masquerade ball was presented. See Carhart (1923: 138), who draws upon the prompt book of the performance held in the New York Public Library.

17   See Fitzgerald (1871: II, 19). Thomas Campbell and James Boaden both spent considerable effort in describing the set for the later scenes where the audience was presented with "a church of the 14th century, with its nave, choir, and side aisles, magnificently decorated, consisting of seven planes in succession. In width this extraordinary elevation was about 56 feet, 52 in depth, and 37 feet in height. It was positively a building" (Campbell 1834: II, 251-2). See also Boaden (1827: II, 257). The *Monthly Magazine* indicates how impressive the scenery was: "The scenery of this play deserves unqualified praise. A scene representing the inside of an abbey, is one of the most beautiful and magnificent on the English stage" (1800: 487).

18   The key theatrical composer Michael Kelly wrote the music for the second and fourth acts of Baillie's play, while Drury Lane's band leader, Thomas Shaw, provided the score for the music in the third act. We are told that a song – not in Baillie's text but mentioned in the Larpent licensing copy (Cox 1992: 257n.) – was added in the second act and was received with applause; a glee was offered in the third act (cut in later editions but present in the first); and in the fourth act Mrs. Crouch backed by a chorus of nuns sang a kind of requiem.

19   Both the licensing manuscript and the Campbell/Siddons manuscript are held at the Huntington Library, San Marino, California. I have detailed the various versions of this scene in Cox (1992: 232, 280-9). The scene in question is III.iii in the 1798 version, III.v in the Larpent version, and IV.ii in the 1851 edition.

20   On the Gothic drama in particular, see Backscheider (1993) and "Introduction" in Cox (1992).

21   Carhart dates the production of *De Monfort* between March 24 and March 30, 1810, but this seems to be a special performance of the play with Sarah Siddons reprising her 1800 role; see Scott, letter to Joanna Baillie, 30 March 1810: "I have I understand missd the very finest performance ever seen in Edinburgh Mrs. Siddons (the elder) in Jane de Monfort" (Scott 1932-37: II, 319). However, in a 20 February letter to Sophia Baillie, Joanna's sister-in-law, Scott wrote: "De Monfort last night was acted with deep and powerful effect to a crouded audience" (1932-37: II, 297). This production was with the younger Mrs. Siddons, wife to the theatre's manager, Henry Siddons, who performed with his mother when she came to Edinburgh in March. The play seems to have received a series of performances that spring following upon the success of the *Family Legend*.

22   The production is recounted in Dibdin (1888: 261-2), and in Scott's letters to Joanna Baillie of 13 June 1809 (Scott 1932-37: II, 196-7), 15 August 1809 (II, 217-21), 13 October 1809 (II, 253-5), 27 October 1809 (II, 257-60), 22 January 1810 (II, 287-9), 30 January 1810 (II, 290-2), 31 January 1810 (II, 293-4), 6 February 1810 (II, 295-6), and 20 February 1810 (II, 300-4). A good account of the play is found in Scullion (1997).

23   See Friedman-Romell (1998). For a fine account of the efforts of Scott and other Edinburgh Tories to negotiate the tensions between a Scottish national identity and membership in the United Kingdom, see Snodgrass (1999). See, also, Scullion (1997: 164-5).

24   As Moody (1999) argues, dramatic authorship – the identification of a play with a single text owned by an individual – was not "invented" until the Dramatic Copyright Act of 1834.

25   Dowd is also interested in the interplay in Baillie's commitment to both tragedy and melodrama; as she puts it, "Baillie works to attract and to instruct both a middle-class and a mass theater audience by exploiting German melodramatic techniques, while simultaneously promoting British nationalism and 'legitimate' tragedy by positioning herself as a 'female Shakespeare' " (1998: 469).

26   On productions of *Constantine Paleologus*, see Friedman-Romell (1999). Other Romantic dramas were converted into melodramas, with Dibdin converting Milman's *Fazio* into the melodramatic *Italian Wife* (Royal Circus, 26 December 1816) and Coleridge's *Zapolya* into *Zapolya; or, the War Wolf* (Royal Circus, 9 February 1818). To get a better sense of the move to "melodramatize" Romanticism, one would want to look at dramatizations of Byron's poems and Scott's novels.

10 Joanna Baillie's ambivalent dramaturgy

Thomas C. Crochunis

Count Basil, the first of Joanna Baillie's plays to appear in her 1798 first volume of the *Series of Plays [on the] Passions*, opens to a Mantuan street "crowded with people, who seem to be waiting in expectation of some show." Members of the crowd anticipate the arrival of a "grand procession" of the princess Victoria's train of ladies on their way to the shrine of Saint Francis. A citizen in the crowd discovers the old soldier Geoffry among the crowd. Asked why he has come to see "this courtly show," Geoffry tells of his memory of returning from battle and receiving favor from his prince and a gracious smile from the prince's consort, Princess Victoria's mother. Having heard of the anticipated procession in town, the old soldier has come to see "some semblance of her mother" in Victoria. A public scene, anticipated procession, and an old soldier with an amputated arm who is on the scene because he desires to compare one generation of female beauty to another all accentuate the embodied theatricality of this bustling opening exposition. Theatricality is further heightened when, unexpected by the citizens on stage, there is the sound of "martial music heard at a distance." Another arriving citizen reveals that Count Basil's troops are marching through town by way of this very street. The old soldier, who has a good opinion of Basil based on the Count's reputation for strict discipline, is so moved by the music and the anticipation of the military's entry that he begins to "walk up and down with a military triumphant step," his body propelled into action by a theatrical *mise en scène* that revivifies the old and wounded by evoking memories and stirring old passions.[1]

Baillie's play invites its reader to simulate its theatre. But then, with the theatrical spectacle and situation thus imaginatively established through character dialogue and descriptions of closely integrated movement and sound, the processions finally arrive. At this point in reading Baillie's text, a crucial shift takes place; the anticipated first encounter between Basil and Victoria is conveyed entirely through a stage direction:

> *Enter Count* BASIL, *Officers and Soldiers in Procession, with Colours flying, and martial musick. When they have marched half-way over*

the Stage, an Officer of the Duke's enters from the opposite side, and speaks to Count BASIL, *upon which he gives a sign with his hand, and the martial musick ceases; soft musick is heard at a little distance, and* VICTORIA, *with a long procession of Ladies, enters from the opposite side.*

(J. Baillie 1798: Ii 102–10)[2]

After all the imagined theatrical vividness of the play's opening, my own silent, private, embodied reading confronts me as I read Baillie's stage direction: *"The General &c. pay obeisance to her, as she passes; she stops to return it, and then goes off with her train. After which the military moves on, and Exeunt."* The two lines of dialogue that close the opening scene, reasserting the play's theatrical conceit, only serve to underscore the peculiar interplay between projected theatricality and silent reading. Baillie's tragedy on the passion of love uses mixed media to stage its fateful meeting. The impassioned ambivalence of Baillie's dramaturgy places textuality and theatricality in dialogue, inviting us to read silently the theatrical enactment of Basil's meeting with Victoria.[3]

Baillie uses mixed media – stage and page – to give complex performances for the public.[4] Baillie's passionate ambivalence for dramatic writing – sustained even while she understood the limited success she could hope for in the theatres of her time – deserves to be considered as the motive for a lifelong artistic campaign that it was, not seen as a coincidental feature of a series of distinct dramaturgical performances by a playwright who learned little from her plays' reception. Though I would not argue that Baillie's dramatic writing pursued a unifying purpose, followed a developmental progression, or even employed a consistent strategy, her dramaturgical career reveals that both publication and theatrical production were venues that offered her something of what she desired as an author.

Dramaturgical and literary history can gain by viewing ambivalently closeted drama such as Baillie's as a significant psychological and cultural formation that illuminates the context from which modern dramatic writing emerged. Authors of "closet dramas" are sometimes dismissed as though they had failed as stage dramatists, while in many cases the adjective "closet" is applied to a play of uncertain stageworthiness to indicate the writer's intention that the text be read (in a reader's "closet") rather than staged publicly.[5] In the case of plays that gesture toward both production and reading, the "closet" dramatist is seen as lingering, dramaturgically speaking, at the place where the paths towards published text and stage performance diverge. However, it is seldom noted that this ambivalence might have some relationship to the literary marketplace in the late-eighteenth and early-nineteenth centuries – an important historical moment for closet drama – when writers had opportunities to publish dramatic texts either before, after, or instead of performance.[6]

With dramatists like Baillie shuttling between closet and stage – both practically and imaginatively – the era's dramatic texts include elements of both performance script and book. So while many plays of the era have features characteristic of closet dramas, writers like Baillie explored dramatic forms that call into question the naturalness of a play's orientation toward the public stage.

Baillie, writing in an important historical moment for the relations between print and theatrical culture, negotiates formal and thematic ambivalence that we need to study rather than resolve. Like Baillie, I want to mix the public and the personal in rethinking the terms of dramaturgical history, discussing sexuality theory's analysis of the rhetoric of identity because doing so reveals how Baillie's dramatic forms complicate British literary and theatrical culture in the years around 1800 and the histories we might write of them.

Closet drama's orientation

While Baillie's dramas have been positioned at various points on a continuum between dramas written for performance and for reading, ambivalent dramaturgy such as Baillie's occupies a psychological and historical moment of split object venues and rhetorical desires that has largely gone unaccounted for in the social history of drama and theatrical culture.[7] Many questions remain about why Baillie – like other important writers of her era such as Lord Byron and Percy Shelley – would have chosen seemingly marginal dramatic strategies for addressing the public.[8]

Historiographically, there tend to be two basic critical approaches to plays that have been positioned as "closet dramas." Either they are viewed as failing the theatre – that is, they were never written for performance or are not practical theatrically – or the theatre failed them due to limiting technologies, social assumptions, or political agendas that made these (from this perspective) visionary dramas "unstageable." The first viewpoint has tended to dominate study of the plays of writers such as Lord Byron because of his conflicted relationship with the idea of writing for the public theatre. The second view often underlies study of Baillie's plays and seems well justified by Baillie's prefatory remarks, which explicitly state her interest in writing for a new kind of aesthetically disciplined theatrical performance. Critics often insist that plays that may well have been written for both page *and* stage must have been intended more for one medium than the other. By contesting a dramatist's true orientation, criticism fails to study the multivalent forms of many crucial documents in the history of British dramatic writing in the Romantic era. Baillie, in particular, suffers from this limiting critical strategy.

While Jeffrey Cox in his chapter for this volume sees Baillie as a writer who employs spectacular techniques from the theatre of her era to enhance her instructive intent, Catherine Burroughs, acknowledging

Baillie's close critical attention to the theatre practice of the day, views Baillie as a dramatist who looked beyond the limited stagecraft of Britain's late-eighteenth and early-nineteenth centuries (Burroughs 1997: 86–94). For Burroughs, Baillie's dramaturgy, influenced by the traditions of women's writing and staging of private theatricals, envisions a more intimate theatre than the one that existed in the patent houses of her day. Ellen Donkin's *Getting into the Act* suggests that we might interpret the arc of Baillie's development as a playwright by investigating her career sociologically and historically. For Donkin, Baillie's interest in stage dramaturgy and gradual acceptance that the difficulties of a playwriting career might be insurmountable can be understood through studying public critical response to her plays, their staging, and Baillie's own remarks about involvement in the business of theatre (Donkin 1995: 159–83).

For historians of women's writing like Donkin or Burroughs, Baillie has much in common with other women of the era who sought a public for their dramatic writing through publication, thereby supplementing the possibilities for theatrical production, which were often uncertain for women. Feminist historians identify many reasons why some women wrote plays "for the closet." The class and gender inflected parameters of literary professionalism and theatre practice certainly played a role in how dramatic works were constructed and eventually delivered to the public. Also, a woman writer's aesthetic and psychological choices often reflected both her cultural background (education, class, and regional context) and the available aesthetics of her time (London stage drama, private theatricals, published poetic dramas). An even more complex set of issues are those introduced by considering how historiographic ideology has led to the omission from the historical record of women's playwriting in the late-eighteenth and early-nineteenth centuries.[9] Baillie's long, prolific career certainly has as complex a relationship to the historiographic dramatic closet as that of any writer of the period.[10] Not enough has been said about the authorial *passion* of someone who pursues a lifetime commitment to dramatic writing even when her plays receive little stage production.

Of course, Baillie's introductory remarks to the first published volume of the *Series of Plays* foreground her ambivalence when she asserts that her goal is to write plays that will be produced on the public stage but also outlines her plan to write (and publish) a *series* of plays on the passions. Whether her plays were, in fact, stageworthy is difficult to determine in retrospect since a play can be "unsuited to the stage" for any combination of aesthetic, political, financial, and even psychological or personal reasons.[11] We may know whether a play was (or was not) staged, but determining whether it could have been staged is much more complex. In some cases, a play is called a "closet" drama today when critics retrospectively judge that it failed practically or aesthetically as stage drama, but this assessment is often influenced by the play's stage history in its time. As Donkin and others have shown, however, for women playwrights of the era, getting plays performed in the public theatre of the day was understood at the time to involve complex social and ideological negotiation.[12] By considering both the stage and social conditions and alternative forms of publication and performance that influenced dramatists in the British Romantic era, we can easily imagine why women playwrights in particular wrote dramas at odds with contemporary theatre practice. And yet, the mixture of strategies employed in dramatic texts by writers like Baillie has only begun to be interpreted as complex gestures within public discourse.[13]

Determining the *orientation* of a late-eighteenth or early-nineteenth century dramatist's writing is complex, for in that era the relationship between textuality and theatricality that structures dramatic writing's history had become troubled and denaturalized. Romantic period dramas like Baillie's remind us that dramatic form developed in relation to both expansions of the reading public and increasingly spectacular theatrical productions. In comments on her dramatic writing, Baillie expressed mixed feelings about both the stage and page as venues. Seeming to suggest that neither venue's reception structures could requite her multiple dramaturgical desires, she claims – in texts presented first through publication – that she privileges the stage as medium. Recent discussions of Baillie's plays have tended to accept that the stage was her one true dramaturgical orientation, but resolving Baillie's ambivalence oversimplifies her authorial gestures and prevents us from seeing in Baillie the ambivalent impulses toward writing for readers and for performance that form much modern dramatic writing, but are often viewed as natural to drama. By studying Baillie's ambivalence closely, we might, harking back to Freud, say that bi-dramaturgy is a part of all dramaturgy after the eighteenth century, a constituting orientation of dramas that our scholarly practices have helped to naturalize.

Sexuality and ambivalence

Baillie's mixed dramaturgical gestures claim a public venue for her authorial performances amidst political, social, psychological constraints that were as much within Baillie as part of her cultural *mise en scène*. Her dramatic writing is ambivalent not in the sense of "lacking passion or desire," but in the sense of "unsure of which desire is most compelling." She wants her plays to influence the public morally through the stage and to engage the growing reading public psychologically through intense, closeted reading experiences. She also aspires to both public reputation and continuation of her own familiar domestic life.[14] Baillie's plays exemplify the complex ways in which an author with ambivalent desires engages with the cultural *mise en scène* in relation to which she performs.

There are interesting parallels between the issues raised by dramatic closets (such as the one Baillie strategically occupied) and those that have emerged in recent scholarship on the cultural history and theorization of bisexuality. While it has become almost common to speak of the uncertain visibility of the bisexual body and its always-not-exclusively-here desire enacted at multiple sites, some have questioned the fetishization of bisexuality's invisibility. Marjorie Garber, in her cultural history of bisexuality, *Vice Versa*, suggests that many commentators, faced with bisexuality's evasiveness, settle for seeing it as a transitional (or in-between or compromised) sexuality.[15] However, closet drama (like bisexuality) might more resourcefully be seen as the product of a meta-orientation toward the not-here – toward the "both/and" – that always keeps part of its apparel offstage (or in the closet), and is best understood through the particulars of its practices rather than through the various objects of its desires. Like bisexuality, the unreadable social complexity of dramatic closets often gets reworked to fit within familiar historical narratives, thereby concealing what makes ambivalent drama significant within dramaturgical history.[16]

Recent literary and cultural criticism has identified ways in which the rhetorical structures of sexuality complicated interpretation of literary history. Terry Castle, in *The Apparitional Lesbian*, cites Freud's remarks on the rhetoric of the analysand's narration of dreams in order to explain the trope of the apparitional lesbian. Castle notes that Freud argued in "Negation" that repressed thoughts enter consciousness through disavowal; therefore, Freud writes, when the analysand says that an unknown person in a dream "was not my mother,"

> We emend this: so it *was* his mother. In our interpretation we take the liberty of disregarding the negation and of simply picking out the subject-matter of the association. It is just as though the patient had said: "It is true that I thought of my mother in connection with this person, but I don't feel at all inclined to allow the association to count."
>
> (Freud's "Negation," cited in Castle 1993: 61)

While Castle adapts Freud's remark to explain the rhetoric underlying her book's central trope, we can adapt Freud's example of "authorial ambivalence" to inform our reading of Baillie's dramaturgy if we adapt it carefully. For example, Baillie's plays – both in their rhetoric of publication and their local dramaturgical strategies – make statements ("this play is *not* just written to be read") that their forms complicate. We need to study how Baillie uses both revelation and negation as significant – if ambivalent – gestures.

I find another suggestive clue to interpreting dramatic writing and its ambivalence toward theatrical bodies in Judith Butler's discussion of Lacan's reading of female homosexuality:

> If every refusal is, finally, a loyalty to some other bond in the present or the past, refusal is simultaneously preservation as well. The mask . . . [consider substituting "dramatic text" for mask] thus conceals this loss, but preserves (and negates) this loss through its concealment. The mask has a double function, which is the function of melancholy. The mask is taken on through the process of incorporation which is a way of inscribing and then wearing a melancholic identification in and on the body; in effect, it is the signification of the body in the mold of the Other who has been refused.
>
> (Butler 1990: 49–50)

Though Butler (and Lacan) are referring here to gendered bodily performances, Baillie uses the bodies of stage drama as a kind of authorial "mask," thus "signif[ying] . . . the body in the mold of the Other [that] has been refused." And so, when dramatic writing preserves its textual status – when it addresses itself to readers even as it also cites the discourses of stagecraft – it refuses to articulate its desire solely in terms of embodied theatrical production. It keeps one foot in each of two places while signaling its mixed desires, but the integrity of its form is necessarily compromised by this straddling act – in Baillie's case by identification with the refused theatrical venue. While Baillie's plays seem naturally enough to project embodiment on stage as their medium, we can problematize the nature of her dramatic desires by noticing how her rhetorical address to the public – her authorial performance – uses references to bodily gestures and styles, and narrative framing of these "acts." Freud, Castle, and Butler, then, suggest ways in which sexuality theory might provide not a biographical explanation but rather a suggestive strategy for interpreting the psychological and cultural syntax of Baillie's ambivalent closet drama.

Plays like Baillie's that have often been placed in proximity to "closet drama" have intimate relationships with plays more tailored to the theatrical venues of the era. The rhetorical use of bodies in closet dramas, even when not particularly sexualized, provides a revealing site for interpreting closet drama's ambivalent dramaturgical desires. While gendered bodies might or might not seem to be products of an author's personal identification or desire, textualized dramatic forms and potential bodily enactments can be highly charged authorial gestures when presented to the public – as both Baillie and Byron understood.[17] Bodies are an important part of the psychological structure of Baillie's dramatic writing, for she bases her plays' moral instruction on the embodied passion of a central protagonist to whom audience/reader response is complicated by the projection of theatrical performance and by the juxtaposition of the character with other (virtually) embodied characters. While these strategies resemble standard dramaturgical practice, Baillie's use of both page and stage invites the public to interpret the complex rhetoric of embodiment in her plays as a gendered performance of dramatic authorship.[18]

Baillie's own remarks on her aspirations as a dramatist invite comparison to structures of desire:

> So strong is my attachment to the drama of my native country, at the head of which stands one whom every British heart thinks of with pride, that a distant and uncertain hope of having even but a very few of the pieces I offer to the public represented to it with approbation, when some partiality for them as plays that have been frequently read shall have put it into the power of future managers to bring them upon the stage with less risk of loss than would be at present incurred, is sufficient to animate me to every exertion that I am capable of making.
>
> (1851: 388)[19]

Both pragmatic in her understanding of the relationship between publication and theatrical production and yet asserting a sustained commitment, a faithfulness grounded in "attachment," Baillie's remarks on her purposes as a dramatist both here and elsewhere foreground the complex forms of her desires and performances as dramatist. By studying the syntax of Baillie's ambivalent dramaturgy, we can see how a woman's authorial passion expressed publicly might have operated within the cultural *mise en scène* of her time, a time when desire to improve "the national drama" had become symbolically important.

The ambivalent desires underlying Baillie's dramaturgy are public and private, professional and personal and their structures resemble those described in recent theories of sexuality. To see in Baillie's dramaturgical performances a self-performance as personal (and yet public) as sexuality is to reconsider how we think about dramatic form. Rather than attempting to uncover Baillie's true desires – either dramaturgical or sexual – we learn more by studying the syntax of her dramaturgical utterances.[20] Bisexuality and dramatic closets trouble categories and complicate visibility – of sexual and dramaturgical orientations, respectively. Bisexuality calls into question the teleologies of emergence on which unified sexual identities are based, offering instead of a consistent orientation a meta-orientation that can intensify awareness of shifting feelings and desires. By considering bisexuality theory, historians of drama that was written with readers in mind can resist the either/or arguments that conceal from view the mixed desires and performances of those authors who wrote, at least in part, for the closet.[21]

The rhetoric of Baillie's dramaturgy

Baillie exploits the rhetorical possibility of onstage bodies by describing dramatic embodiment explicitly in her plays, making use of elements that are pointedly theatrical – movement within stage space, styles of inflection or gesture, descriptions of bodily gesture rather than character thought.[22] *Count Basil*, the first of Baillie's plays to appear in her 1798 first volume of the *Series of Plays*, demonstrates her skilled use of both reference to theatrical practices and dramatic enactment of a protagonist's passion. As I have shown, it is through a stage direction that Baillie introduces the play's central dilemma through a spectacle of encounter in which the music and procession of Basil's army gives way, allowing Victoria's train to pass and its music to be heard. First Basil, then Victoria, offer brief gestures of "obeisance." In further scenes, temporal/spatial passing and asynchrony are exploited further to heighten the sense of Basil's desire. In Act II, tension about Basil's staying longer in the court begins to mount. After a brief flirtatious conversation between Victoria, the ladies of the court, Rosinberg, and Basil, Victoria points the way to a passage that offers an exit by way of some "famous paintings" that "strangers love to see." The men follow this new route, giving the lure of love a spatial representation, and this "alternative passage" leads Basil into increasingly passionate feelings for Victoria. The play's opening and its subsequent uses of the spatio/temporal enactment of Basil's passion anticipate the play's plot. The play builds its crisis through time pressures related to staying or going, a more abstract and internalized version of the passing exchange of looks that the play's opening physically enacts as an intersection of two different passionate parades. Baillie's exploitation of space as an affective medium enhances her reader's desire for staging, using the not-here (theatre) to align the rhetoric of her series of plays with the psychological experience of her texts.

If Baillie sometimes uses gestures toward theatrical *mise en scène* to influence the public's experience of her drama, she also uses fundamental elements of dramatic form such as characterization, dialogue, exposition, and dramatic action to simulate for her reading public psychological situations that are both more intimate than the theatre and more conflicted than the fully private reading closet. The rhetoric of Baillie's instruction involves her putting forward a central protagonist and then complicating the reader's response through reframing that character as a theatrical performance (using explicit references to staging) and as a single figure within a social milieu (using emotionally linked characters to pressure the reader's experience of the protagonist's perspective).[23] While Baillie's dramaturgical rhetoric might seem to anticipate standard realist practice, its ambivalence about matters of professional purpose (page or stage?) invites us to read her writing as a complex gendered performance of dramatic authorship.

In *Basil*, Baillie surrounds her central character with an array of male interlocutors, each of whom applies psychological pressure to the Count's identity while also creating the simulated social scene in which Baillie's reader is invited imaginatively to make his or her knowledge of the passions. Geoffry, the "old soldier very much maimed in the wars," who in the opening scene has come to town to see both Victoria and Basil, is identified with "old school" values of soldierly duty and honor. Later, Basil's officers tell how Geoffry was singled out for note before the soldiers, moving the old soldier to tears, and also moving those who witnessed the event and those who hear it told. The intensity of feeling that circulates through Basil's interactions with Geoffry reveals to us the complex homosocial community relations that inform Basil's psychology. For Baillie's public, the emphatic embodied traits of Geoffry – his war injury, his enactment of his moods – counterpoint his psychological significance for Basil. Baillie keeps both page and stage in play as part of the drama's expressive potential.

In contrast, Basil's actions in response to the rebellious soldiers and to his mutinous officer Frederic further intensify the emotion within the community of men. In one of the most startlingly raw emotional scenes in the play, Basil, confronted in act IV, scene ii, by his unruly soldiers, grabs one particularly vocal member of the group, "drags him out from the ranks, and wrests his arms from him; then takes a pistol from his side, and holds it to his head." Baillie's dramaturgy here has such a shocking sense of theatrical immediacy that the scene is hard to imagine on the stage of her era in a play that aims at psychological realism. Through challenging dramaturgical categories, the scene enriches the reader's psychological experience of Basil and, in particular, of his passionate social identity as leader. Later in this scene, once Basil has quashed the mutiny, Frederic, the officer who has fomented the rebellion, arrives, surprised to find that his rebellion is already ended. He admits what he has done, and awaits Basil's punishment. Basil, however, shocks his colleague by offering Frederic another chance to be "an honest man" and "my friend." Again, Basil's gesture toward one of his fellow soldiers seems to enact their shared homosocial code so pointedly that Frederic is momentarily speechless. The effect again is to simultaneously stage theatrically the range of feelings within the male social group, and to draw the reader into Basil's affective state. In numerous instances, Baillie's manipulation of her public's sensitivity to the cultural dynamics of public enactment informs psychological meaning. Drawing on her own awareness of what bold manipulation by a woman playwright of actions such as Basil's on a public stage might signify, Baillie injects characterization with startling colors, again drawing on the mixed media of her authorial performance to intensify the play's simulation of passion.

From an entirely different perspective, Baillie uses the bit part of Victoria's favorite, the boy Mirando, to further intensify the experience of

Basil's character through staging alternative versions of masculine feeling. After Basil's impassioned pronouncement in act II, scene ii, of his feeling for Victoria, in scene iv Baillie offers a playful travesty of Basil's passion in the boyish affection of Mirando. Later, in act IV, scene i, in the midst of the masked ball, Basil encounters the boy, who is dressed as Cupid. Hearing from the boy of his closeness to Victoria, Basil himself feels a kind of intense affection for someone so close to Victoria and grasps and kisses the boy. But Mirando resists, saying "[T]hy kisses are so rough / So furious rough – she doth not kiss me so." Through introducing this young man's affectionate bond with Victoria, Baillie further stages Basil's ill suitedness for the role of lover, something also revealed by his vehement pronouncements and protestations to Victoria herself. Looking past the literal role definition for Mirando, we can see that Baillie employs cross-gender play, giving the boy a position in relation to Victoria and Basil that makes him an object of mixed affection and thus using the boy as a kind of liminal figure between female and male in this highly gender-conscious play. Baillie again exploits the potential enactment of Mirando's scenes on stage (where they would offer comic relief) while also making use of his unusual psychological placement as a figure with psychological significance in the read text in order to complicate the reader's experience of the play's central passion.

The most richly drawn male counterpart to Basil in the play is Rosinberg. Basil and his friend and fellow soldier share an intense homosocial relationship grounded in a code of soldierly honor, a belief in the importance of brotherly affection and regard, and a shared history. Although Rosinberg serves as the voice most opposed to Basil's fraternization with women, he himself seems quite capable of a masculine performance of playful flirtation and witty interchange, as evidenced by his appearance at the masked ball as a stereotypical poet-lover and by his many sharp interchanges with Victoria and the women of the court. Rosinberg displays the kind of detached self-possession and social finesse when among women that Basil lacks, but the older man's feelings are stirred by Basil's emerging passion for Victoria. Rosinberg's attempts to persuade Basil to leave the court seem to be based both on sound concern about Basil's indulgence of uncontrolled passion and on Rosinberg's fear that he may be supplanted in the affections of his close friend. In act IV, scene iii, the two men have a passionate argument reminiscent of Brutus and Cassius in Shakespeare's *Julius Caesar*. As they snap back and forth at each other, pointing to each other's intimate flaws in an attempt not only to persuade but also to wound, the passion between them almost seems a constituent part of Basil's inability to let go of his obsession with Victoria. Though the two men's argument provokes momentary resolve on Basil's part to break away from the court, as soon as a message comes from Victoria, he tears himself away from his friend to go to her, leaving Rosinberg to rail bitterly against women's "artful snares." Again, struggle within Basil is played out theatrically for readers through scenes with Rosinberg, the most fully developed of Basil's male interlocutors. In Baillie's handling of Rosinberg, she moves closest to direct exploration of the homosocial passion that resists straightforward interpretation in either this or others of her plays. Rosinberg serves as a functional figure through whom Baillie can channel dramaturgical interference to the course of Basil's passion and through whom the public can engage with Basil's increasingly altered state from the perspective of an intimate of his private rooms. Of all Basil's dramatized interlocutors, Rosinberg is the one Baillie uses to draw her readers in closest; he is perhaps her most intimate dramaturgical gesture in the play.

Baillie scripts these male counterparts to engage the public with knowledge of the passions through both playing out and observing scenes in which states of mind are simulated within social contexts. As stage drama, the play surrounds Basil with men whose passions arouse his multiple desires; as closet drama, Basil's thinking is externalized through his dialogue with characters who might be said to reflect aspects of himself. Dramaturgically speaking, it is precisely, however, because these men exert homosocial pressure on Basil that he cannot reconcile his own internal conflicts by suppressing some of his own conflicting voices. His desires are not entirely internal, for they constitute his social position as well as his character. And so, when he confronts these interlocutors he is faced with the potential loss of his social identity – as friend, as leader, as admired soldier. Baillie's reliance both on the distinct characterizations of this array of men and on staging theatrically intense encounters between them and Basil aids the reader in simulating Basil's homosocial crisis. Baillie's mixed dramaturgical performance draws her public into making its own knowledge of the passions.

The struggle of masculine identity in Basil, however, is not entirely played out through parallels of character. Baillie insists that men's histories have complex effects on their passions. Baillie foregrounds offstage history in her note to act I explaining the authorial history of the narrative of the relationship between Basil and Victoria. (See note 2.) The old soldier Geoffry, who appears in the play's first scene, also provides a personal historical reference point because of his past military service, memory of Victoria's mother, and acquaintance with Basil's reputation. In fact, in the first scene, before the processions arrive, a small moment of dramatic tension is based on lack of recognition when an officer tries to move Geoffry aside and is "much ashamed" when he is reminded of the old soldier's identity. Other reference is made to the complex histories Basil and his men share with each other, but the most intimate personal history seems to be shared by Rosinberg and Basil, who often reference each other's past actions in the midst of their quarrels.

For Baillie, the conflict between past and present is also a conflict within her chosen aesthetic medium. Offstage is history; onstage is the present. What is told onstage, what is narrated in the language of the text comes into conflict with what is embodied and enacted. The testimony is not always consistent, and when characters – particularly men – are confronted with the discrepancy between what they are in the dramatic present and what they were in the narrated past, their passions become inflamed, they feel beset, and they take risky actions to realign their discrepant selves. While, in one sense, this conflict occurs between two parts of a character within a closeted version of Baillie's drama, the conflict is also enacted through two distinct media within the proposed staging of the play – between what is said to have been and what takes place in the stage present. No wonder then that in the central relationships – between Rosinberg and Basil, and Victoria and Basil – promises and pronouncements about what will be done are a key site of duress. Will Basil depart as planned, or will he succumb to his desire to stay? Is his pronouncement of love for Victoria a wish or a fact of his character? By contrasting gaps in narrated histories to those between what is told and what is done, Baillie heightens the crises of her drama, showing that Basil faces not only uncomfortable changes in his self-narration, but a crisis of his own bodily enactment of identity. The passions that tear at Basil resonate with those of the play's author. Because ambivalent dramaturgical rhetoric both performs and negates Baillie's desire to author theatre, the play's public witnesses both Basil's and Baillie's ambivalence. Most importantly, the reading public of Baillie's plays is drawn into the performance of theatrical authorship, reminded again and again of the concerns of the writer whose compelling voice addressed them – at first anonymously, without an identified gender – in the "Introductory Discourse" to the first volume of the *Series of Plays*.

*

The ambivalence at the heart of Baillie's dramaturgy places the public of her plays in an intimate relationship with the complexity of their author's desire for these plays' enactment. It is precisely because Baillie's plays engage with the discourses of staging of her era that their texts draw their reading public both into and out of the dramatic closet, intensifying the intimacy of imagined passions and projecting possible enactment not just within simulated lives but as public displays. The psychological action Baillie's ambivalent dramaturgy created in the public deserves further investigation through attention to published reviews and private correspondence and journals of her contemporaries, but this further inquiry needs to look beyond the defensive dead end of arguments over whether her plays were meant for, or effective on, the stages and pages of her era. More important is the question of how these plays worked on the public and what their effects reveal about both Baillie's authorial strategies and the emergence of newly hybrid forms of dramaturgical performance, by women writers in particular, in Baillie's time.

If Baillie had not been deeply engaged by the expressive potential of the movement between stage and closet, her entire playwriting career would not have walked the fine line between dramaturgical strategies suited to publication and to production.[24] Because her commitments were thoroughly mixed, her dramaturgy displays a peculiarly ambivalent mixture of strategies, fully suited neither to reading nor to staging. While it may be misleading to describe as ambivalence what for Baillie seems to have been a fierce mixture of strategies, devices, and modes of address to her public, to understand Baillie's dramaturgy we need to respond to its multi-directionality and play the multitude of roles it requires of us. When we choose sides on whether Baillie wrote for stage or page, we diminish the complexity of her writing. But if we consider her ambivalence carefully, we can find that her peculiar ways of not just portraying but simulating the desire to dramatize passions are historically important signs of the emergence of multi-directional aesthetics that engage many different publics and marketplaces at once. To reposition Baillie historically with her split authorial orientation in mind, we may need to read the aesthetics of her dramatic writing receptionally, interpreting both how her texts were structured to anticipate various modes of reception and how they were received by both individual readers and institutions (including more recent scholarship and pedagogy).

The significance of Baillie's ambivalent dramaturgy does not lie in its implications for her private sexuality, but rather in how it leads her to perform dramatic authorship for the public. Her dramatic career is notably "odd" – not quite like anyone else's in her era. Whatever we might think of where a playwright's desires ought to have been directed, we will serve Baillie best if we read her dramas on their own shifting terms, remembering that it is Baillie's oddness that makes her important to any revision of dramaturgical history and to the history of women's writing in the Romantic era. Baillie's dramaturgical ambivalence prompts us to re-examine the limits of a univalent view of dramatic authorship, particularly in the British Romantic period and particularly for women writers. Like allowing ourselves to register the complex patterns of desire that inform the actions of those who resist hetero- or homo-characterizations on indices of sexuality, observing closely the movement in Baillie's dramatic authorship between page and stage does two significant things. It allows us to see her authorial practices as complex negotiations – socially and psychologically – of the world her writing inhabited. Perhaps even more significant, noticing Baillie's ambivalence causes us to rethink the limiting paradigms of Romantic dramatic criticism that would seek to choose the "true" orientation of a dramatist or play text in order to discipline any ambivalent gestures toward theatre production or publication and thereby hold fast to the integrity of authorial purpose at the expense of negotiated social process.

Writers of drama in the British Romantic era enacted socially complex desires. Much past historiography and criticism has made it too easy to tell integrated stories of authorial orientation – about Cowley, More, Wordsworth, Coleridge, Sheridan, Inchbald, Byron, Percy Shelley, and others. The historical reality of dramatic authorship is much more complex and the author who more than any other lived in relationship to this complex social process was Joanna Baillie, the epitome of a British (woman) dramatist of her era.

Notes

1 Anne Mellor has noted how production of this opening scene stages the play's gendered systems of value (Mellor 1994: 563). Baillie's public likely interpreted the gestures toward theatrical production that these processions make in relation to their own knowledge about the gendered social spaces of page and stage.

2 I quote this stage direction from Peter Duthie's 2001 edition of the 1798 "Plays on the Passions." Baillie made only minor changes of wording and capitalization to this scene in later editions. Whether Basil and Victoria have or have not met before is addressed in a note at the end of the first act in the version of *Basil* included in Baillie's 1851 collected works: "My first idea when I wrote this play was to represent Basil as having seen Victoria for the first time in the procession, that I might show more perfectly the passion from its first beginning, and also its sudden power over the mind; but I was induced, from the criticism of one whose judgement I very much respect, to alter it, and represent him as having formerly seen and loved her. The first review that took notice of this work objected to Basil's having seen her before as a defect; and, as we are all easily determined to follow our own opinion, I have, upon after-consideration, given the play in this edition [*third*], as far as this is concerned, exactly in its original state. Strong internal evidence of this will be discovered by any one who will take the trouble of reading attentively the second scenes of the first and second acts in the present and former editions of this book." It is interesting to note that Baillie made no significant changes to the play's first scene, however, even when making this substantial adjustment in character history. Except as otherwise noted, my citations refer to the text of *Basil: A Tragedy* in Baillie's *Works* (1851).

3 When I write of Baillie's "ambivalence," I do not mean to suggest that she was indifferent to either publication or theatrical production. In fact, she seems to have been highly invested in using both as authorial venues.

4 Elsewhere, I have examined Baillie's theatre criticism as part of her public performance of authorship (Crochunis 2000).

5 Dramatists are sometimes viewed as sharing the preference of Romantic critics for reading dramas (such as those of Shakespeare) rather than seeing them performed; the critical preference is most famously expressed in Charles Lamb's "On the Tragedies of Shakspeare, Considered with Reference to their Fitness for Stage Representation" (1903–05; orig. 1811). For a consideration of the Romantic male critics' penchant for claiming a preference for reading literary drama rather than seeing it staged, see Heller (1990).

6   The broad picture of the discourses of periodical publishing and reviewing in Britain, discussed in Klancher (1987), has some bearing on dramatic publishing. For historical overviews of issues related to publication and playwriting in the Romantic era, see Stephens (1992) and Conolly (1976). Donkin (1995) and Davis and Donkin's edited volume (1999) focus on women and playwriting in relation to publication and staging.

7   Catherine Burroughs (1997) investigates the social history of British Romantic closet drama. Previous critical discussions of this era's plays for readers (Otten 1972, Richardson 1988, Wang 1990, Jewett 1997, and Simpson 1998) have only occasionally addressed the sociology of British Romantic closet dramatic form.

8   The most influential examination of Byron's dramatic ambivalence is David Erdman's 1939 essay "Byron's Stage Fright: The History of His Ambition and Fear of Writing for the Stage." The 1997 collection of reprinted essays, *The Plays of Lord Byron: Critical Essays,* takes Erdman as one of its anchors and arrays around his work a number of essays that endorse and complicate Erdman's biographical argument. The most thorough historical account of Byron's involvement in the management subcommittee of Drury Lane is Richard Lansdown's "Drury Lane" (1992: 11–58), Chapter 1 of *Byron's Historical Dramas.* Louis Crompton's *Byron and Greek Love* (1985) provides the fundamental starting point for discussion of Byron's complex sexual history, but Crompton has little to say about Byron's drama. In recent books, both William Jewett and Michael Simpson argue that both Byron and Shelley chose to write poetic drama for readers for complex political reasons. See in particular Jewett's "Introduction" (1997: 1–19) and Simpson's "Introduction: Casting and Rehearsals" (1998: 1–24).

9   Tracy C. Davis and Ellen Donkin's introduction (1999: 1–12) to their edited volume of essays considers the need for new historiographic approaches to *Women and Playwriting in Nineteenth-Century Britain*; also Davis's essay "The Sociable Playwright and Representative Citizen" (Davis 1999: 15–34) examines the problematics of the omission of women's role as playwrights from the historiographic record. My essay "The Function of the Dramatic Closet at the Present Time," included in a special issue of *Romanticism on the Net* on "British Women Playwrights around 1800," examines the historiographic assumptions that constitute the way "the closet" is used in contemporary critical discussions of drama of the Romantic era (Crochunis 1998). Further discussion of the historiographic questions surrounding women's dramatic writing in this era is a part of both this online journal special issue and of the ongoing work of the *British Women Playwrights around 1800* Web project that Michael Eberle-Sinatra and I co-edit. For broader consideration of how historiographic practices and ideologies shape histories of women's writing, see Margaret J. M. Ezell's *Writing Women's Literary History*, particularly her "Introduction: Patterns of Inquiry" (1993: 1–13).

10 Susan Bennett in her provocatively titled essay "Outing Joanna Baillie" (2000) provides a valuable critique of too-facile placements of Baillie in the dramatic closet, arguing that Baillie is an important figure precisely because of her theatrical intent. My discussion here is a different kind of "outing" than Bennett's, however, for I see significance in Baillie's relationships with both page and stage.

11 Beth Friedman-Romell, in her essay on *Constantine Paleologus* (1999: 151–73), demonstrates the many ways in which Baillie's plays challenged what could be staged, even when they were in fact produced. Also see Ellen

Donkin's discussion of Baillie's reluctance to become involved in theatre business (1995: 159–83).

12   I have argued elsewhere that writers like Baillie and Inchbald seem in fact to use this well-known "difficulty" as part of their public performances of authorship (Crochunis 2000: 228–36).

13   Both William Jewett (1997) and Michael Simpson (1998) see poetic drama of the Romantic era as a provocative choice of form for plays often rife with political content, elaborating on a juxtaposition between form and content that was first described by Alan Richardson (1988). However, each of these studies focuses on the dramatic works of major male Romantic writers. For women writers, the content of dramaturgical form – considering the kind of gendered social space that the theatre of the era was – is an essential part of interpreting dramaturgy as public discursive gesture.

14   Baillie's comments about preparing her 1836 *Dramas* show that she understood private studies to be where public authorship is performed: "I have been much occupied since last June in correcting the proof sheets of my new publication. I thought I had done with all this business, but circumstances arose to make me desirous of leaving all my Dramas in print corrected under my own eye, so I was obliged to throw aside the indolence & desire of quiet & privicy [sic] so natural to old age" (Letter to Anna Carr of 12 December 1835; Slagle 1999: II, 1198). Tracy Davis (1999: 23) first drew my attention to this revealing passage.

15   Garber notes in her discussion of the narratives and depictions of various bisexual lives that commentators on sexual orientations tend to create a plot that "imposes a plausible narrative of continuity and logic over the heterogeneity of thoughts – and desires" (1995: 324). Ki Namaste sees Derrida's notion of "citationality" and DeMan's examination of "misreading," both of which complicate J. L. Austin's speech act theory, as significant theoretical predecessors when analyzing the rhetoric of bisexuality (Namaste 1996: 73–6). Like bisexuality, dramatic form's duality – both advocating for performance and seeming to cite performance – can provide a key rhetorical site in interpreting Baillie's authorial performances.

16   Garber's comments on the rhetorical effects of stating one's bisexuality while in a relationship – doing so acknowledges the limitations on full fusion with another person, as if to say "I am here, but no structure or institution guarantees that I will stay here" (1995: 451–2) – remind me of Lord Byron's comments on his plays and their status as performance or reading texts. When Byron heard that his works were not (or when he anticipated that they would not be) well received, he retaliated against presumed judgements against him; it was as if, anxious of failure in popular venues (Erdman's "stage fright"), he struck preemptively, warning all around him that he had *other* literary desires or, rather, that any desire he expressed would always withhold something. Ultimately, it is hard to say whether Byron's dramaturgical anxiety originates with the reception of his plays or with his own sense of his multiple dramaturgical orientations and desires. Similarly, Baillie's cautiously strategic self-deprecation in the midst of explaining her avowedly ambitious plan to create a body of dramatic work preemptively reminds readers of both her limitations as a stage dramatist and her belief in the importance of writing plays for the theatre. While, as Donkin explains, it would have been understandable for Baillie to have limited knowledge of stage practice (1995: 168–75), Baillie's comments serve to articulate her own inability either to be fully present in the form of her works or to anticipate being fully received.

17   Michael Evenden (1993) discusses the complex use of bodies in Byron's dramatization of subjectivity in several of his plays – *Manfred*, *Cain*, and *The*

Deformed Transformed. Both Jewett (1997) and Simpson (1998) see the poetic, textual evocation of bodies in writers such as Byron and Shelley to be politically suggestive gestures within British society of the era. Alan Richardson's chapter in this volume provides a thorough analysis of the way in which Baillie writes about passions through exploring their bodily causes and effects. Richardson's explanation for Baillie's use of bodies, related as it is to Baillie's intellectual relationships with her uncle and brother, provides an interesting and enriching counterpoint to my examination of the ambivalent desires that Baillie's authorial performances enact.

18   Donkin notes that when women playwrights "took control of the authorship of human action . . . the authoring of action . . . created a ripple of anxiety" (1995: 38). Beth Friedman-Romell observes that critics noticed the "oddness" of Baillie's homosocial subject matter but avoided discussing the playwright's sexuality (1998: 41–3). In interpreting the reception of Baillie's plays, it is important to read discussions of her plays' suitability for stage production, of her subject matter, and of her reputation as a cultural figure in relation to one another. Often, speculations about her "oddness" that could not be publicly articulated in relation to her life became possible when displaced onto observations about her dramaturgy or her personal style. For another critical discussion that touches upon different aspects of Baillie's enactment of "ambivalence," see Dorothy McMillan's chapter on Baillie's mixture of Scottish and British styles and political values in this volume.

19   Susan Bennett draws attention to this particular passage in the remarks "To the Reader" from Baillie's first volume of the *Miscellaneous Plays*, citing them to underscore Baillie's "sheer determination in getting her plays to the attention of potential producers" (2000: 167). Bennett challenges the view of Baillie as a "closet dramatist and literary aristocrat," arguing that "Baillie demonstrates a deft understanding of how the theatre works – as a craft and as an institution. Her response is not, most definitely not, a retreat into the closet" (172). But Baillie's invocation of Shakespeare, the central figure in her time in the formulation of drama as published literature, seems highly significant and helps us begin to see in cultural perspective the paths that her desire for public performance led her to follow.

20   Slavoj Žižek, characterizing Lacan's view, writes that "interpretation is in its most fundamental dimension an act of scansion, of establishing the proper syntax, not an act of bringing to light the 'repressed' meaning" (1996: 248n37).

21   Of course, closet drama neither began nor ended in the British Romantic period; however, the peculiar dilemmas faced by authors within the literary and theatrical marketplace of the British Romantic era make the strategies of this period's closet drama particularly worth examining. For an article that provides an overview of recent scholarship on closet drama of a number of different periods, see Straznicky (1998).

22   See Burroughs (1997: 110–42) for discussion of the contrasting gendered performance styles employed by Baillie.

23   See the chapters by Jeffrey Cox and Victoria Myers in this volume for fuller consideration of Baillie's instructional intent and its relationship to her dramaturgical strategies.

24   As Cox notes in his chapter in this volume, different positions have been taken regarding Baillie's real purposes as a dramatist. While Cox, Gamer, and others have demonstrated Baillie's commitment to writing for the stage of her own era, Burroughs and Bennett allow for some flexibility in interpreting Baillie's desire for theatrical production – Burroughs (1997) through seeing Baillie's dramaturgy as experimental and Bennett (2000) by registering

Baillie's appreciation of the cultural challenge of achieving performance of plays like hers on the stage of her era. The challenge for historiography, it seems, is not settling this ultimately insoluble question, but rather finding a theoretical framework that will allow a number of these well-supported positions to inform each other and dramaturgical history generally.

11 "A reasonable woman's desire"

The private theatrical and Joanna Baillie's *The Tryal*

Catherine B. Burroughs

Designed primarily to amuse those who had enough money to buy off boredom, late eighteenth-century British private theatricals were often unabashedly elitist projects not only in the sense that many took place in exclusive environments but because they required – in addition to time – a great deal of money to arrange. Sybil Rosenfeld writes that Lord Barrymore's expenses for cake alone at the opening night reception of his private theater at Wargrave in 1789 were "rumoured" to be £20, small change after the £60,000 that was spent on the theater building itself.[1] To overcome the luxury of boredom is the impetus behind the staging of Elizabeth Inchbald's 1798 translation of August von Kotzebue's *Lovers' Vows* (1791) in Jane Austen's *Mansfield* Park (1814), perhaps the best-known work of literature that features the late eighteenth-century phenomenon of amateur acting. The eagerness with which most of Mansfield's youthful residents embrace John Yates's proposal to put on a play is not only indicative of "a love of the theatre," which the narrative labels "so general."[2] Yates arrives onto an already indolent scene embodied by the frequently supine Lady Bertram, and his proposal to do a private theatrical follows on a painfully aimless visit to Mr. Rushworth's country house during which each person's "spirits were in general exhausted."[3]

From the perspective of a feminist theater historian, however, the exclusivity of private theatricals was important for providing certain women (and sometimes their servants) with a forum for experimenting with the theater arts.[4] It would be misleading to suggest that British private theatricals constituted some sort of avant-garde movement at the height of their vogue (1780–1810).[5] Even though new works were performed on private stages, they often derived from the canonical plays[6] that dominated eighteenth-century patent theaters and which comprised

From *Texas Studies in Literature and Language*, Vol. 38, No. 3/4, Fall/Winter 1996, pp. 265–84. Copyright © 1996 by the University of Texas Press, P.O. Box 7819, Austin, TX 78713–7819. All rights reserved.

the bulk of private theatrical offerings.[7] Yet because private entertainments were usually produced in isolated settings – making theatrical activity accessible to a group of people who were not necessarily theatergoers – they inevitably deviated from London productions in spirit; they were certainly more conducive to spontaneity. Often rehearsed in the context of a house party that could go on for several weeks and in small spaces that rendered more permeable the customary barriers between spectator and actor, the private theatrical could offer its participants a deeply personal and imaginative experience, not only allowing for a great deal of playfulness and delight in the act of improvisation but also encouraging a serious self-consciousness about the performative features of social acting.

Because scholars have been preoccupied with debating the degree to which the turn to the closet in the period's canonized theater criticism does – or does not – express an "antitheatrical prejudice," the actual theater that was produced in the closeted spaces of the private sphere during the romantic period has often been overlooked. This theater of the closet, while not exclusive to women, was particularly friendly to women's creative endeavors, and it is this theatrical context that Joanna Baillie's earliest comedy, *The Tryal* (1798), explores. Written during the British private theater movement and considered for a private theatrical production at Bentley Priory in 1803, *The Tryal* probes some of the tensions caused by the trend among certain aristocratic women to write and direct improvisational performances in domestic space. Through the character of Agnes Withrington, an heiress who directs two women in a plot designed to determine the motives of the men who would marry her, *The Tryal* looks closely at those "ordinary" and "familiar" circumstances that comprised "Characteristic Comedy," Baillie's term for plays like her own that featured emotional trials on domestic stages.

Defined as "performance wholly or mainly by amateurs [presented] to selected or invited audiences, as opposed to the general public,"[8] private theatricals are usually distinguished in narratives of theater history from those plays that were acted privately by professionals.[9] Therefore, as Sybil Rosenfeld notes, the first amateur actors in England may be considered the priests and guild members who performed church-sponsored mystery and morality plays.[10] By contrast, because the performers of early Tudor "household revels" were on retainer as specialists of acting, they conform to a position that we would today refer to with the label "professional."[11] As Keith Sturgess has written, by 1620 the word "private" in reference to theater meant that a play was to be performed "indoors,"[12] and these private theaters – conceived along the lines of "a club, an academy, and an arthouse"[13] – were attended largely by aristocratic audiences looking to distance themselves from the rowdier playgoers of outdoor stages. The associations of aristocracy with theater in an exclusive setting were reinforced by seventeenth-century masques and "aristocratic entertainments," such as John Milton's *Arcades* performed at Harefield in the early 1630s. Yet the rage for private theaters in England did not take off until the eighteenth century, when this mostly aristocratic pastime was encouraged by developments in France, which had more than sixty private theaters by 1750 in Paris alone[14] and during the latter quarter of the century boasted variations on the private theatrical, such as the pornographic dramas often featured in "clandestine theatres."[15]

These "clandestine theatres" require a brief mention here, since the fact that French women "assumed great importance in the development of this theatre culture"[16] points to some parallels in Great Britain. Neither England, Scotland, Ireland, nor Wales produced a figure comparable to France's Duchess de Villeroi, who – in a move forecasting certain aspects of feminist theater in the 1980s[17] – sometimes excluded men from the audience for the purpose of featuring "plays glorifying lesbian love and setting the scene for huge sapphic orgies involving women from the opera and the Comedie Francaise."[18] But just as the private theater scene in mid-eighteenth-century France had its Marie Antoinette and Marie-Madeleine Guimard, and the German court theater Charlotte von Stein in the 1770s,[19] so the British private theatrical community enjoyed the passionate commitment to private entertainment of many (primarily aristocratic) women.

By organizing, sponsoring, writing, and performing in private theatricals, eighteenth-century women were following the example set in earlier eras by English aristocrats such as Alice Spenser, Dowager Countess of Derby, who acted in Jacobean masques and attended country-house entertainments,[20] Queen Henrietta Maria, who in the early seventeenth century took the then unusual step of appearing in two court pastorals,[21] and the Princesses Mary and Anne, who performed in Crowne's *Calisto* in 1675. By the dawn of the next century it was not unusual to find wealthy women directing their children, grandchildren, or friends in an evening of theater for which they were the primary organizers, or writing plays for them, as in the case of the Countess of Hardwicke, whose *Court of Oberon* blended together a French piece with her original composition in order to "render it more suitable to her juvenile performers, the youngest of whom was but two years old."[22] An anonymous letter to the editor of the *European Magazine* written in 1788 indicates how firmly the private theater movement had taken hold by century's end:

> The practice of people of distinction and fortune to erect theatres, and commence actors to perform in them, *en famille*, is now so general, and is indeed, under certain restrictions, so very praiseworthy and innocent, that a sort of general account of all the playhouses and players of *ton*, to be continued occasionally, would perhaps be a pleasant, not to say profitable, companion or vade-

mecum to those places of resort: and it might, appositely enough, be called The Fashionable Rosciad.[23]

Among the better-known amateur playwrights and actresses in Great Britain was Elizabeth Cobbold, whose memoirist wrote that not only was she "a very frequent attendant on the theatre," but she "herself also possessed much taste and skill in dramatic composition, and wrote several pieces of great merit."[24] While it was not the case, as the character of Bombast says in Archibald Maclaren's play *The Private Theatre* (1809) that "little theatres furnish actors for the great, as little rivers furnish salmon for the sea,"[25] nevertheless amateur performer Charlotte Twistleton received acting training on the private stage at Adlestrop House sufficient to launch a professional career. Between 1780 and 1805 Elizabeth Berkeley Craven either composed, translated, adapted, or altered nineteen plays.[26] As Lady Craven she organized and appeared in private performances in Warwickshire and, upon relocating with her second husband from Germany to England, as the Margravine of Anspach she supervised the building and operation of a private theater in the 1790s at Brandenburgh House in Hammersmith. Here she alternately performed the functions of actress, playwright, producer, translator, musician, and singer. "My taste for music and poetry, and my style of imagination in writing, chastened by experience, were great sources of delight to me,"[27] she wrote in her memoirs in 1826:

> I wrote *The Princess of Georgia,* and the *Twins of Smyrna,* for the Margrave's theatre, besides *Nourjad* and several other pieces; and for these I composed various airs in music. I invented *fetes* to amuse the Margrave, which afforded me a charming contrast to accounts, bills, and the changes of domestics and chamberlains, and many other things quite odious to me.[28]

Craven's reference to the domestic context in which her comedies, pantomimes, and musical dramas were forged reminds us to pay particular attention to private settings in constructing women's theater history. For it is often in domestic spaces, far away from the traditional stage, that much of women's drama and theatrical art has actually been produced. For instance, Kirsten Gram Holmstrom's study of monodrama, "attitudes," and *tableaux vivants* devotes a large portion of the text to an analysis of a trend among upper-class European women to create "mimoplastic art" in the public spaces of their homes between 1770 and 1815.[29] Whether striking neoclassical poses and manipulating costume pieces as in the case of Lady Emma Hamilton (whose stark gestures framed by special lighting effects anticipated photographers' models in the twentieth century), miming scenes to music as did Ida Brun,[30] or creating "art-historical etudes" as did Henriette Hendel-Schutz (in which academic audiences could discuss with her the intellectual and artistic choices she had made), it is clear that the domestic setting was essential to these women for developing "a new genre on the borderline between pictorial art and theatre."[31]

Conceived and rehearsed on the homefront and attended by a group of acquaintances, friends, and relatives theoretically inclined to tolerate women's ventures into acting and playwriting, the British private theatrical gave those who would otherwise have had no theatrical experience a mode for exploring the theater arts. In the case of professional female actors, private performances also afforded opportunities for participating in theater in ways often unavailable to them on the public stage. Professional actress Harriot Mellon complained that "there never was such a stupid task as drilling fine people!," but an evening of private theater at Strawberry Hill was nevertheless an occasion for her to manage the stage, in addition to occupying the position of "privy-councillor in all matters relative to costume and other little etceteras known only to the initiated in Thespian mysteries."[32] Elizabeth Farren frequently undertook the task of directing the amateur actors at Richmond House's private theatricals in 1787–88, "the most fashionable and exclusive . . . of their time."[33]

Although women who participated in private theatricals did not own their domestic dwellings or necessarily get credit for their contributions to private entertainment, their role as organizers of domestic space gave them at least a measure of control over some of the ways in which their social identity was configured and represented. Reginald Brimsley Johnson has noted how the English bluestocking circle, for example, arranged domestic space in specific ways – from Elizabeth Montagu's semicircle to Elizabeth Vesey's zig-zags to Mrs. Ord's "chairs round a table in the centre of the room"[34] – in order to encourage different approaches to conversational topics. The private theatrical also encouraged audiences to appreciate domestic space for the fact that it allowed them to "indulge in delicacies and subtleties that would be thrown away at Drury Lane or Covent Garden,"[35] a fact that could make social issues more vivid. Anthropologist Victor Turner has written at length about the idea that "theatre is the most forceful, ac*tive* . . . genre of cultural performance, . . . a play society acts about itself."[36] It is "this proximity of theatre to life" – in Turner's view – that "makes of it the form best fitted to comment or 'meta-comment' on conflict."[37] "When we act in everyday life, we do not merely re-act to indicative stimuli, we act in frames we have wrested from the genres of cultural performance." It therefore follows, Turner writes, that stage acting should concentrate on "bring[ing] into the symbolic or fictitious world the urgent problems of our reality."[38]

Those who made theater in their homes between 1770 and 1810 confronted the performative aspects of their actual experience through the process of self-consciously adopting roles for the private stage. Especially for women, whose performance of femininity was tested perhaps most stringently in the semipublic spaces of the domestic sphere, the private theatrical provided often unlooked-for opportunities to analyze how social identities are constructed and represented. As Bruce Wilshire (1982) has observed, "theatre is an aesthetic detachment from daily living that reveals the ways we are involved in daily living – particularly our empathetic and imitative involvements."[39] But it was just this potential to disturb domestic harmony by revealing "the ways we are involved in daily living" that made the private theatrical particularly problematic where women were concerned.

In an essay called "Remarks upon the Present Taste for Acting Private Plays" (1788), playwright Richard Cumberland expressed his anxiety about amateurism by referring specifically to female actors in private theaters: the

> Andromache of the Stage may have an infant Hector at home, whom she more tenderly feels for than the Hector of the scene; he may be sick, he may be supperless; there may be none to nurse him, when his mother is out of sight, and the maternal interest in the divided heart of the actress may preponderate over the Heroine's .[40]

Disturbed by a trend in which the act of playwriting seems demystified, is "thoroughly bottomed and laid open," and is "now done by so many people without any difficulty at all,"[41] Cumberland warned that this fashion "should be narrowly confined to certain ranks, ages, and conditions in the community at large" and that "young women of humble rank and small pretensions should be particularly cautious how a vain ambition of being noticed by their superiors betrays them into an attempt at displaying their unprotected persons on a stage, however dignified and respectable." If they "have both acting talents and charms,"[42] Cumberland continues, "I tremble for their danger."

Because women powerfully influenced the dynamics of domestic space, fictional works from the British romantic period that treated the private theatrical often focused their anxiety on women characters. The issue of women acting on any stage (whether public or private) is throughout British history a source of deep concern for certain segments of the population, and the idea that closet spaces were becoming formally theatricalized during the late eighteenth century often aroused strong responses.

For instance, Richard Brinsley Peake's *Amateurs and Actors* (1818) links private theatricals to disorder and impropriety through a plot in which the two main female characters run amok. It is the lot of a retired manufacturer named Elderberry – "simple in wit and manners, and utterly unacquainted with Theatricals"[43] – to try to retrieve his ward, Mary Hardacre, from an elopement that uses a private performance as a strategy to override parental consent. Mary's lover, David Dulcet, has arranged to announce their marriage to his relatives immediately after he and Mary have participated in a private production of *Romeo and Juliet,* which will be attended by Dulcet's family. The plot also contains the conflict between Wing and his estranged wife, Mary Goneril, a "Strolling Tragedy Actress," who has run off with a manager but who finds herself employed to act Juliet on the same private stage with her former husband.

As the person who perceives Dulcet's house "a receptacle for lunatics,"[44] Elderberry is presented as a ridiculous figure for his ignorance about amateur acting. But amateur performances are also satirized with equal force, especially in the exchanges between O. P. Bustle – the manager of a provincial theater hired to supervise this private production – and Wing, a poor country actor. "We who know something of the matter," says Bustle, "must laugh at private performers. As Garrick observed, one easily sees, when the Amateurs are acting, that there is not an *Actor* among them."[45] This is a theme anticipated by Archibald Maclaren's musical drama, *The Private Theatre* (1809), which ties together private entertainment, domestic disorder, and moral corruption. Modewart chastises his brother for writing private plays by saying, "Let us have no more of your Pantomimical Funerals. Convert your private theatre into a public school, or useful workshop. Mind your own business, and leave the trade of acting to those who make it their profession."[46]

But although private theaters made many uneasy because they brought acting into the home, the idea that amateurism could provide a corrective to professional stage practices was a theme also consistently sounded during this period. In the same essay cited above, Richard Cumberland admits that the aristocracy was usually better suited than the professional actor to perform a variety of theatrical roles, since in

> all scenes of high life they are at home; noble sentiments are natural to them; low-parts they can play by instinct; and as for all the crafts of rakes, gamesters, and fine gentlemen, they can fill them to the life.[47]

Yet the fact that the amateur can narrow the gap between actor and character in the service of greater realism and less artificiality worried those for whom theater was threatening precisely because the medium could blur for audiences the distinction between what was acting and what was not.

This fear lay behind the era's concerns with controlling theatricalized space, and it is one of the central issues in Joanna Baillie's *The Tryal,* which presents amateur acting as the means by which certain women can assert themselves, even if only temporarily, over the plot that shapes their domestic lives. It is interesting to contemplate the fact that Baillie's first comedy was almost performed for the first time on a private stage by amateur actors,[48] since such a mode of representation might have caused its participants to view *The Tryal* metatheatrically, to appreciate some of the ways in which this play investigates amateurism and private entertainment in relation to gender and space. Caught between what she calls "a reasonable woman's desire"[49] to direct her own future and cultural imperatives that require her to marry, for the first part of the play Agnes Withrington attempts to take charge of her destiny by creating, performing in, and directing an improvisational theatrical in the privacy of her uncle's home: the social and closeted spaces of a fashionable English house in Bath become the setting for amateur acting. For a time female laughter reigns as Agnes – using winks and gestures to control the movement of bodies in domestic space – directs her cousin Mariane and her maid Betty in an improvisation designed to expose the greed of Agnes's suitors and determine the true character of Harwood, the man whom Agnes wants to marry.

The frequency and ease with which Agnes and Mariane touch their uncle's body underscore the relaxed atmosphere over which Withrington presides, as well as show how the dynamic of this domestic space encourages the women to use their imaginations. Introduced by the stage directions as "hanging upon [Withrington's] arms, coaxing him in a playful manner as they advance towards the front of the Stage" (I.i, 195), Agnes and Mariane are subsequently described as "clapping his shoulder" (I.i, 196), "stroaking his hand gently" (I.i, 199), resting an "arm on his shoulder" (I.i, 200), leaping round his neck" (I.i, 201), and taking "him by the hands and begin[ning] to play with him" (I.i, 238).

Given this jocular familiarity between uncle and nieces, one might expect that Agnes and Mariane could persuade Withrington temporarily to become an actor in their plot. But he will not participate, foreshadowing Fanny Price's staunch refusal in *Mansfield Park* to perform in a private production given by her cousins. The language with which Withrington refuses suggests that the nexus of amateurism, women, and private performance is central to the dramaturgy of *The Tryal*: "It would be very pleasant, truly," he says teasingly, "to see an old fellow, with a wig upon his bald pate, making one in a holy-day mummery with a couple of mad-caps" (I.i, 195). This comparison between Agnes and Mariane's proposed improvisation and "holy-day mummery" recalls that the origins of English amateur acting were in the Christian church, once the locus of theatrical activity in spite of its anxiety about theater's potential to lure audiences into identifying with and imitating characters represented on stage.

Christianity's historical ambivalence toward British theater is embodied in Withrington's ambivalence about his nieces' amateur acting. As *The Tryal* progresses, Withrington's seeming approval of amateurism gives way to his attempt to regain control of his domicile, which he fears is becoming, under Agnes's direction, the scene of what we might call "street theatre." In Act III, Withrington says that his house seems foreign to him – like "a cabin in Kamschatka,[50] and common to a whole tribe" – because it has been penetrated by entertainers, animals, and indigent children:

> In every corner of it I find some visitor, or showman, or milliner's apprentice, loitering about: my best books are cast upon footstools and window-seats, and my library is littered over with work-bags; dogs, cats, and kittens, take possession of every chair, and refuse to be disturbed: and the very beggar children go hopping before my door with their half-eaten scraps in their hands, as if it were an entry to a workhouse.
>
> (III.i, 60)

Alarmed at the means by which Agnes and Mariane reveal the absurdity of their suitors' performative postures, Withrington expresses his anxiety about the stability of his nieces' gender and class position by saying that "all this playing, and laughing, and hoydening about, is not gentlewomanlike; nay, I might say, is not maidenly."

> A high-bred elegant woman is a creature which man approaches with awe and respect; but nobody would think of accosting you with such impressions, any more than if you were a couple of young *female tinkers.*
>
> (III.i, 240, my emphasis)

Indeed, although he is extremely fond of his nieces and seems at times to enjoy the exuberance of Agnes and Mariane's high-spirited acting, Withrington continually criticizes their jolly improvisations by equating theatricality with foolery, witchery, and madness. It is therefore no surprise when he comes to complain that he "can't approve of every farce you please to play off in my family, nor to have my relations affronted, and driven from my house for your entertainment" (III.i, 239), or when he declares a few lines later, "I am tired of this" (III.i, 240).

The "this" is Agnes's plot, which requires that Mariane pretend to be Agnes in order to "get the men to bow to us, and tremble" (240–41) and that Agnes and her servant Betty produce a feminist variation of *The Taming of the Shrew.*[51] By acting peevishly and staging several tantrums for the sole purpose of discerning how well Harwood can tolerate a woman who expresses herself passionately, Agnes investigates why female anger is so upsetting to many men. She senses that the veneer of tolerance worn by her suitors during the courtship ritual masks their disgruntledness at having to effect such a pose; that such seeming delight in the woman wooed will give way to a desire to control her person. Therefore, much of the fun for Agnes in staging this improvisation rests with exposing the real motives of her suitors, such as Sir Loftus Prettyman who, when treated to a dose of Mariane's affected indifference, vows in a series of asides: "when she is once secured, I'll be revenged! I'll vex her! I'll drive the spirit out of her . . . I'll tame her!" (IV.iii, 271).

Harwood has no difficulty passing Agnes's test. But the play does not allow the lovers to get together so easily, and it is this complication that underscores some of the problems faced by women who would do theater in the privacy of their homes. A monologue in Act V marks the turning point of the play, since it is at this juncture that Agnes abandons the trajectory of her original improvisation in order to devise another plot responsive to her uncle's concerns. Here is Withrington's speech:

> To be the disinterested choice of a worthy man is what every woman, who means to marry at all, would be ambitious of; . . . But there are men whose passions are of such a violent, overbearing nature, that love in them may be considered as a disease of the mind; and the object of it claims no more perfection or pre-eminence among women, than chalk, lime, or oatmeal do among dainties, because some diseased stomachs do prefer them to all things. Such men as these we sometimes see attach themselves even to ugliness and infamy, in defiance of honour and decency. With such men as these, women of sense and refinement can never be happy; nay, to be willingly the object of their love is not respectable.
>
> (V.ii, 276–7)

On the one hand, this monologue reads as the expression of Withrington's concern for Agnes's welfare; but on the other, it seems designed to make her incredulous that any man could actually desire her as his wife. Withrington "withers" Agnes's spirits with the insinuation that Harwood's apparent devotion to her may be something to shun rather than to admire, since "there are men whose passions are of such a violent, overbearing nature, that love in them, may be considered as a disease of the mind." If Harwood is indeed the indiscriminately passionate man that Withrington implies, then the object of his love can be discounted. For such a man – in claiming from women "no more perfection or pre-emininence . . . than chalk, lime, or oatmeal do among dainties" – can be assessed as having a "diseased stomach." This diseased appetite might cause a man to "attach" himself "even to ugliness and infamy," a choice of words that Agnes in all probability hears as a reference to herself, accustomed as she is during the play to having her physicality criticized. Though Withrington implies that Agnes is a woman "of sense and refinement," he goes on to say that if she "willingly" allows herself to be the object of such a diseased person, then she is "naughty." This is a statement the harshness of which Withrington apparently recognizes when he disingenuously trivializes his judgements as "niceties." You are still "respectable," he tries to convey to Agnes after having implied just the opposite.

Agnes is stunned. The young woman who has earlier described herself as "light as an air-ball!" (III.i, 238) in reference to the fun she derives from her private theater now becomes quite somber and quiet, telling Withrington that she has "ventured farther than I ought" (V.ii). She apologizes for her direction of the first plot, through which she has already achieved her goal of proving Harwood genuinely attracted to her character. Mariane, coming onto the stage after Withrington's speech to find Agnes looking glum, immediately asserts that she is "very sure the plot is of [Withrington's] hatching, then, for I never saw Agnes with any thing of this kind in her head, wear such a spiritless face" (V.ii, 279). From this point on in the play Agnes "seems thoughtful" and speaks with "a grave and more dignified air" (V.ii, 277). By contrast – as if to symbolize his regaining control of domestic space – her uncle borrows a gesture that we have come to associate with Agnes and Mariane when they were at their most confident: he "claps" Agnes on "her shoulder affectionately" (V.i, 278).

At the beginning of *The Tryal* – in answer to Withrington's question about "who will fall in love with a little ordinary girl like thee" – Agnes pointedly reminded him that "an old hunks of a father" once prevented his marrying the beautiful rich lady who was in love with him (I.i, 197). Withrington comes dangerously close to activating this kind of patriarchal control when he suggests the insufficiency of Agnes's first plot to determine Harwood's suitability. Indeed, in an apparent gesture toward Rousseau's *La Nouvelle Heloise* (1761) – in which Wolmar, the reigning patriarch at novel's end, devises a two-tiered trial to test the virtue of his wife, Julie, and her former lover, Saint-Preux – Baillie has Withrington contrive a second test that will determine whether Harwood elevates desire for virtue over his desire for Agnes's person. (Agnes's original plot was constructed not to discover whether Harwood would choose virtue over the flawed woman in a quest after some feminine ideal but rather to see how he would deal with imperfections, idiosyncrasies, and mood swings.) In the scenes that follow Agnes designs a new plot, but her contributions as an actor and director are curtailed. Instead, her cousin Royston takes center stage, performing in an improvisation to which Agnes is but a silent witness, sequestered behind a screen. In fact, at several points during this scene, Agnes chafes at her passive position, complaining about Royston's inability to understand what good acting is and about his compulsion to explain to others what is intended as stage illusion.

That it is a serious risk for Agnes to undertake this second plot is confirmed when the scene is later performed. Presented with a letter written by Agnes, Harwood is so undone by the implications of Agnes's impropriety that "his hand trembles" and he has trouble retaining it.

Subsequently "staggering back, [he] throws himself into a chair, . . . and covers his upper face with his hand" (V.ii, 289–90). "See how his lips quiver," Royston exclaims, "and his bosom heaves! Let us unbutton him: I fear he is going into a fit. As Harwood starts to rise to leave the room, "he falls back again in a faint" (V.ii, 290). The potential danger to Harwood's health casts a skeptical light on the merit of what in retrospect can be seen as Withrington's unnecessary interference in Agnes's private improvisation, even though Harwood proves himself to be vitally concerned that Agnes not behave immorally, thus passing the test and satisfying Withrington's concerns.

I want to suggest that Withrington's misgivings about Harwood do not derive simply from Withrington's uneasiness with the dramaturgy of Agnes's plot, which reveals the potential of private theatricals to destabilize domesticity. Withrington's worry over Harwood's virtue may also mask his unease about the way in which Harwood "does" his gender. Described as wearing "a plain brownish coat" (I.i, 204) – Baillie's sartorial signal that Harwood is destined for the physically plain Agnes (whom he recognizes as "the most beautiful native character in the world" [I.ii, 210]) – Harwood the future lawyer is characterized in direct opposition to "your men of fashion" (I.ii, 211), the pretentious Sir Loftus and his sidekick, Jack Opal. Harwood's idealism about his profession, his scholarliness, and his open enthusiasm pair him with Agnes as the "heartwood" of the play. Both are genuinely interested in extending themselves to help others, as Agnes's private staging suggests when she opens up Withrington's fashionable home to poverty-stricken children. Likewise, Harwood is praised for conceiving of the practice of law as more than "a dry treasuring up of facts in the memory," as the profession of one "who pleads the cause of man before fellow-men," who must therefore "know what is in the heart of man as well as what is in the book of records" (II.ii, 228). When Agnes thanks Harwood for promising to marry her at play's end, she predicts that he "shall . . . exert your powers in the profession you have chosen: you shall be the weak one's stay, the poor man's advocate; you shall gain fair fame in recompense, and that will be our nobility" (V.ii, 299). Throughout the play Harwood claims that he is looking for a real partner rather than an idealized paragon: "insipid constitutional good nature is a tiresome thing" (IV.i, 253), he says to himself; "we ought not to expect a faultless woman" (IV.i, 258), he confesses to his friend Colonel Hardy; "I can't bear your insipid passionless women: I would as soon live upon sweet curd all my life, as attach myself to one of them" (V.ii, 288), he exclaims to Royston.

Yet though clearly the hero destined for Baillie's heroine, Harwood is also characterized as a man who often assumes an exaggeratedly expressive gesture and speech typically associated with femininity: he runs breathlessly onto the stage; he hangs around Agnes without apology; he blurts out his feelings. Furthermore, in Act IV, Harwood offers to thread

Agnes's needle, albeit "awkwardly" (IV.ii, 66), and in the final act of the play, like many of the heroines in English romantic drama – who, when confronted with surprising news, sink to the ground – Harwood does something quite unusual for a male character in a play from this period: he swoons. Given Withrington's concerns about Agnes's femininity in the context of her original improvisation, Harwood's characterization seems to require that Uncle Withrington assert his role as patriarch of a fashionable home and propose a further test for the young lawyer, one designed to answer some of the questions that Withrington has about the degree to which Harwood's masculine identity can be regarded as secure and one that requires Agnes to restrict her involvement in private improvisation.

Eleven years before *The Tryal* was published, James Powell's farce about the rage for amateur acting, *Private Theatricals* (1787), also featured a plot in which the head of a household tries to control his family's and servants' enthusiasm for putting on private plays. But unlike Baillie, Powell reserved for his leading female character a subversive moment at play's end. The actress playing Lady Grubb is allowed to advance "to the front of the Stage" where she asserts her love of private theater: "But if my audience do but approve, I shall bless the day when I first commenc'd my PRIVATE THEATRICALS."[52]

By contrast, *The Tryal* charts the process by which the owner of a fashionable home reasserts his control over domestic space, in his view rendered chaotic by amateur performance. As we have seen, Anthony Withrington resembles several other characters in the fiction of the private theatrical movement who function to suggest that amateur acting on private stages is potentially disruptive. While not consistently an antitheatrical force like Austen's Sir Thomas Bertram in *Mansfield Park*, who is so upset by his children's experiment with private theater that he burns "every unbound copy of 'Lovers' Vows' in the house" when he returns from the West Indies,[53] still Withrington closes *The Tryal* with words that evoke Austen's description of how Sir Thomas "reinstates himself" upon his arrival at Mansfield Park: one of the tasks that Sir Thomas performs before he can resume "his seat as master of the house at dinner" is to oversee the dismantling of the little theater in the billiard room.[54] Similarly reestablishing himself as the benevolent host of an orderly domicile, Withrington says to the company gathered on stage at the end of *The Tryal*: "Now, let us take our leave of plots and storytelling, if you please, and all go to my house to supper" (V.ii, 299).

Read in the context of the amateur entertainment vogue, Baillie's first comedy emerges as an exploration of how some women sought to theatricalize domestic space in order to respond to "a reasonable woman's desire" to control the representation of women's social reality. Indeed, Baillie's eight comedies richly reward students of late eighteenth- and early-nineteenth-century culture by attending to some of the more pressing social issues of the period. Yet because Baillie's comedies address topics that would have interested early-nineteenth-century playgoers through a subtle exploration of her characters' emotional trials, critics have generally had difficulty appreciating them. Baillie alluded to this problem in her preface to the second edition of *Miscellaneous Plays* (1805) when she wrote that the comedy *The Country Inn* (1804) "has been generally disliked."[55] Seven years after publishing *The Tryal*, Baillie had come to realize that to

> those who are chiefly accustomed, in works of this kind, to admire quick turns of thought, pointed expression, witty repartee, and the ludicrous display of the transient passing follies and fashions of the world, this play will have but few attractions.[56]

Time has proved her thus far prophetic. In 1930 Allardyce Nicoll wrote that every one of Baillie's comedies "is stilted. Not a laugh rises from a single scene."[57] More recently, in 1974, Terence Tobin overlooked Agnes's dilemma to focus on the subplot – Mariane Withrington's secret engagement – and concluded that a lack of "complications" dooms *The Tryal*,[58] a critique that echoes Margaret Carhart's over fifty years earlier. *The Tryal*'s complications arise from Baillie's characterization of Agnes, whom Alice Meynell summarized in 1922 as "hard to capture."[59] Meynell is almost alone in appreciating Baillie for making

> such pretty eighteenth-century sport of her theme (her hero keeping the fine sensibilities, expressed with impassioned elegance, of Steele's *Conscious Lovers*) that it is not easy to realize that she passed the middle of the nineteenth century, albeit in extreme old age . . . It is the exceeding sweetness of the two good girls bent upon their frolic (which is also a romp) that makes the charm of this happy play. They exchange names upon the wildest impulse consistent with their Georgian manners.[60]

But it was the painter Thomas Lawrence – who proposed *The Tryal* for a private theatrical in 1803 – who praised the play for those very features that Baillie herself advocated in her theory of comedy, natural speech and characterization. In a letter to his sister, Lawrence wrote that he was "for Miss Bailey's Comedy, 'The Trial,' one slightly spoken of by the world, but which I am sure, Mr. Homer would like for its truly natural dialogue and character."[61]

Baillie articulated her theory of comedy at length in her 'Introductory Discourse" – the essay she attached to the 1798 volume of plays in which *The Tryal* first appeared – which suggests that domestic spaces are fruitful sources of theater and drama. Baillie's belief that it is comedy's "task to exhibit" people "engaged in the busy turmoil of ordinary life, . . . and engaged with those smaller *trials* of the mind by which men are most apt to be overcome" caused her to prefer realistic situations that she could have encountered in her own life.[62] In contrast to the "satirical, witty, sentimental, and, above all, busy or circumstantial Comedy," Baillie advocated what she called "Characteristic Comedy," a genre that represents "this motley world of men and women . . . under those circumstances of ordinary and familiar life most favorable to the discovery of the human heart."[63] Eschewing contrivance, artificiality, and self-conscious wit, Baillie's theory argues that the most interesting kind of comedy derives from what we might today be inclined to call "situational" writing in which "even the bold and striking in character, should, to the best of the author's judgment, be kept in due subordination to nature."[64]

But even as Baillie argued for a more subtle kind of dramatic writing – one focused on "the harmonious shades" of character – she wanted to avoid dwelling on "senseless minuteness."[65] Thus, she criticized eccentric characterizations, remarking that: "Above all, it is to be regretted that those adventitious distinctions among men, of age, fortune, rank, profession, and country, are so often brought forward in preference to the great original distinctions of nature,"[66] since such an approach has

> tempted our less skillful dramatists to exaggerate, and step, in further quest of the ludicrous, so much beyond the bounds of nature, that the very effect they are so anxious to produce is thereby destroyed, and all useful application of it entirely cut off, for we never apply to ourselves a false representation of nature.[67]

It is in "ordinary life," Baillie emphasized throughout her theater theory, that "strong passions will foster themselves within the breast; and what are all the evils which vanity, folly, prejudice, or peculiarity of temper lead to, compared with those which such unquiet inmates produce?"[68] By seeking to justify a focus on "unquiet inmates" in domestic settings, Baillie's theory of comedy suggests that we should pay close attention to the drama and theater produced in closet spaces, a theatricality largely controlled by women confined to the private sphere. Thirty-six years old when she published her first plays – which, in addition to *The Tryal,* included *Count Basil* and *De Monfort* – Baillie argued the need for a *mature* comedy, one that featured characters in "the middle stages of life."[69]   Margaret Carhart finds the characterization of Agnes "typical of the busy comedy that Miss Baillie criticized so sweepingly."[70] But Agnes is also nothing if not "thoughtful," and the complexity of her struggle to determine whether her beloved Harwood is morally the best match for her is at the heart of the play's plot. While her uncle eventually restrains Agnes's theatrical experiments, Baillie gives us a play in which the struggle of her heroine to assert "a reasonable woman's desire" centers on her attempt to theatricalize domestic space according to her own design.

Though not generally regarded as a women's movement, the British private theatrical is significant for those scholars trying to fill in the picture of women's history in theater. In addition to affording certain classes of women with increased opportunities for theatrical endeavor, the private theatrical movement anticipated subsequent developments that highlight the achievement of women in theater. For example, Madame Vestris's management of the Olympic theater in the 1830s – conceived as an alternative to the London patent stages – is a logical outgrowth of an eighteenth-century phenomenon in which a number of women had the experience of managing small theaters for the first time.[71] In praising Vestris's management of the theater in the dedication letter he attached to *The Two Figaros* (1836), playwright James Robinson Planché wrote that "the model is not less instructive because it is made on so small a scale and preserved in the cabinet of a lady"[72] Likewise, Frances Maria Kelly's "Little Theatre in Dean Street," which was built in the 1830s "as an extension to her private house,"[73] resembles the private theaters of the previous era in that Kelly planned to feature those fledgling performers whom she trained in the acting school, which she also moved to her house from the Strand.[74] Biographer Basil Francis describes Kelly's "'modern' Little Theatre," as "well-appointed, both from the view of the player and playgoer, with 'modern' machinery, ample entrances and exits, comfortable dressing-rooms and above all a stage that would incorporate every new improvement that the mind of man could devise."[75] Though Kelly's dream went unrealized (as the result of stage machinery that was so noisy that the actors could not be heard), her desire to create a space for actor training and performance within the bounds of her home reminds us that many women's theatrical experiments have originated within domestic settings.

A study of the late eighteenth-century British private theatrical movement reminds us that a particular class of women[76] have had a long history of theatricalizing closet space and helps us more readily appreciate the degree to which some plays from the romantic period – such as Baillie's *The Tryal* – confront the issue of how women have sought to control domestic spaces for both theatrical and nontheatrical purposes. Moreover, the act of opening up British romantic closets in order to expose the variety of theatrical activities that actually took place there can deepen our understanding of how private spaces and domestic settings influenced public stages – before, during, and after the romantic era.

Notes

1 Sybil Rosenfeld (1978: 18–19).
2 Austen (1966 [orig. 1814]: 147).
3 Austen (1966: 133).
4 A partial list of those women who participated in late eighteenth-century private theatricals (through a combination of acting, writing, and organizing)

includes Joanna Baillie, Mary Berry, Frances Burney, Marianne Chambers, Elizabeth Knipe Cobbold, Elizabeth Berkeley Craven (the Margravine of Anspach), Mary Champion Crespigny, Elizabeth Farren, Catherine Galindo, Elizabeth Inchbald, Frances Anne Kemble, Harriot Mellon, Eliza O'Neill, Amelia Opie, Sarah Siddons, Mariana Starke, Peg Woffington.

5   Although the private theatrical movement in England took place primarily between 1780 and 1810, Marvin Carlson notes that as late as 1833 in England a private theater was erected at the castle of Chatsworth (1989: 56).

6   These canonical works included plays by women writers, among them Susanna Centlivre, Hannah Cowley, and Elizabeth Inchbald.

7   For a list of the most popular plays performed on the eighteenth-century private stage, see Rosenfeld (1978: 169–70).

8   Rosenfeld (1978: 9).

9   My information for this history is collected from the following sources: Charles Kendal Bushe's *The Private Theatre of Kilkenny, with Introductory Observations on Other Private Theatres in Ireland, before it was opened* (1825), composed mostly of the information on playbills, along with the prologue and epilogue to each play and reviews of performances; Tom Moore's review of that volume in the *Edinburgh Review* (46 [1827]: 368–90), which after stating – "There is no subject that we would sooner recommend to a male or female author, in distress for a topic, than a History of the Private Theatres of Europe" (368) – discusses British private theatricals in the context of private theaters in ancient Greece, Renaissance Italy, modern Russia, and France; Sybil Rosenfeld's *Temples of Thespis* (1978), which includes two helpful appendices drawn from Rosenfeld's survey of records pertaining to "120 places in which private theatricals were held" (7): one listing the performance of private theatricals by year and the other identifying those English plays "first performed at private theatricals" (180); and Marvin Carlson's chapter "The Jewel in the Casket" in *Places of Performance* (1989). Nina Auerbach's *Private Theatricals: The Lives of the Victorians* (1990), while promisingly titled, is focused not on the private theatrical phenomenon, but rather uses the term to discuss "the source of Victorian fears of performance," which Auerbach argues "lay in the histrionic artifice of ordinary life" (114).

10   Rosenfeld (1978: 8–9).

11   Further information about these players is provided by Suzanne R. Westfall (1990).

12   Keith Sturgess (1987: 3).

13   Sturgess (1987: 4).

14   Carlson (1989: 51).

15   See Karl Toepfer's fascinating account of this phenomenon, including erotic marionette theater, in chapter 2 of *Theatre, Aristocracy, and Pornocracy: The Orgy Calculus* (1991).

16   Toepfer (1991: 66).

17   See chapter 4 of Sue-Ellen Case's *Feminism and Theatre* (1988) for a discussion of this trend, led by theater groups such as Lavendar Cellar Theatre, Medusa's Revenge, and Red Dyke Theatre.

18   Toepfer (1991: 66).

19   For more information on von Stein and her theatrical activity, see Katherine R. Goodman (1992: 71–93).

20   Cedric C. Brown (1985: 15).

21   Sturgess (1987: 57).

22   This quotation is from the preface to the Countess of Hardwicke's play, *The Court of Oberon, or The Three Wishes,* in which the writer explains why it took so long for the play to "see the light." (The play was written in the late

seventeenth century.) On the occasion of Princess Victoria's intent to patronize "a Bazaar, for the succour of the distressed Irish," it was "suggested that among the contributions made by Ladies of their Fancy works for the profit of the Bazaar, this [play] might also find a place. – Yet it could scarcely have been ventured upon without the condescending permission of Her Royal Highness the Duchess of Kent, to dedicate this little work to Her Royal Highness the Princess Victoria" (Anonymous, preface, *The Court of Oberon, or The Three Wishes*, by the Countess of Hardwicke [1831]).

23   Anonymous, "To the Editor of the *European Magazine*. Plan for a Fashionable Rosciad; and some account of Mr. Fector's Private Theatre at Dover," *London Review* 14 (1788): 66.

24   Laetitia Jermyn (1825: 16).

25   Archibald Maclaren (1809: I.ii, 12).

26   Elizabeth Berkeley Craven's original dramas are listed in the introduction to vol. 1 of her memoirs (1826) republished under the title *The Beautiful Lady Craven: The Original Memoirs of Elizabeth Baroness Craven afterwards Margravine of Anspach and Bayreuth and Princess Berkeley of the Holy Roman Empire (1750–1828)*, 2 vols. (1914 [orig. 1826]).

27   The French edition of Craven's memoirs (1828) was republished as *Mémoires* (1991).

28   Craven (1914, vol. 2: 106).

29   Kirsten Gram Holmström (1967: 128).

30   Holmström (1967: 216.

31   Holmström (1967: 139).

32   See vol. 1 of Mrs. [Margaret] Cornwell Baron-Wilson's *Memoirs of Harriot, Duchess of St. Albans* (1839: 280).

33   Rosenfeld (1978: 34).

34   Reginald Brimley Johnson, introduction, *Bluestocking Letters* (1926: 10–11).

35   Rosenfeld (1978: 168).

36   Victor Turner (1982: 104).

37   Turner (1982: 105).

38   Turner (1982: 122).

39   Wilshire (1982: ix).

40   Richard Cumberland (1788: 116).

41   Cumberland (1788: 115).

42   Cumberland (1788: 118).

43   Richard Brinsley Peake (1827 [orig. 1818]: 10).

44   Peake (1827: 30).

45   Peake (1827: 17).

46   Maclaren (1809: II.i, 24).

47   Cumberland, 116.

48   Baillie's associations with private theatricals extend back to her childhood. Sarah Tytler and J. L. Watson noted that at school Baillie became "the chief figure in something like private theatricals" (1871, vol. 2: 193) – school plays figuring as amateur performances. George Barnett Smith wrote that Baillie "was early distinguished for her skill in acting and composition, being especially facile in the improvisation of dialogue in character" ("Joanna Baillie," vol. 1 of *The Dictionary of National Biography*, 22 vols, p. 886). Catherine Jane Hamilton made a similar observation: "at school, by her sister's report, she was principally distinguished in being the ringleader of all pranks and follies, and used to entertain her companions with an endless string of stories of her own invention. She was also addicted to clambering on

the roof of the house to act over her scenes alone and in secret" ("Joanna Baillie," vol. 1 of *Women Writers: Their Works and Ways* (1892–93: 114).

49   My text for *The Tryal* is the 1990 reprint of Baillie's 1798 *Series of Plays* published by Woodstock Books (Oxford), which includes this drama along with *Count Basil* and *De Monfort*. (N.b.: the 1851 edition of this play spells *The Tryal* as *The Trial*). Citations from *The Tryal* appear within the text by reference to act, scene, and page number.

50   "Kamchatka" is a peninsula of northeast Russia between the Bering Sea and the Sea of Okhotsk (Dudley Stamp (ed.) (1966) *Longmans Dictionary of Geography* (London: Longmans, Green and Co. Ltd), 224).

51   Margaret Carhart has observed that "Harwood's railing against Agnes is an echo of the tone of Petruchio in *The Taming of the Shrew*, and Agnes's description of her suitors recalls the similar scene in *The Merchant of Venice*" (1923: 73).

52   James Powell (1787: II.viii, 37).

53   Austen (1966: 206).

54   Austen (1966: 206).

55   Baillie (1976: 386).

56   Baillie (1976: 389).

57   Allardyce Nicoll (1930: 209).

58   Tobin (1974: 195).

59   Meynell (1968 [orig. 1922]: 61).

60   Meynell(1968: 59).

61   Cited in Rosenfeld. Rosenfeld also cites a letter written by Harriet Cavendish concerning the same private theater, which indicates that another Baillie play, *Count Basil*, was also under consideration. Like *The Tryal*, however, it went unperformed (158).

62   Baillie (1976: 11), my emphasis.

63   Baillie (1976: 12).

64   Baillie (1976: 14).

65   Baillie (1976: 13).

66   Baillie (1976: 13).

67   Baillie (1976: 14).

68   Baillie (1976: 14).

69   Baillie (1976: 13).

70   Carhart (1923: 196).

71   See chapter 5 of Sandra Richards (1993).

72   This citation appears in Griffinhoof (1830).

73   Basil Francis (1950: 156).

74   For more information about Kelly's acting career, her theater, and acting school, see Holman (1935).

75   Francis (1950: 155).

76   For a discussion of "the amateur productions of the provincial gentry" as well as those performed by members of the army and the navy, see chapter 6 of Russell (1995).

12 Baillie's *Orra*

Shrinking in fear

Julie A. Carlson

Ghosts are making something of a come-back these days. Long at home in fictional domains, they are reappearing in theoretical texts as non-fictional participants in the daily reality of social exchange. These are not the same ghosts who stalked a pre-enlightened world. They neither replicate any of the five types familiar to medieval Catholicism nor the three that sustained the Reformation until European Enlightenment banished them from consciousness.[1] Nor are they simply projections of psychic realities that undermine the unity of Spirit. Today's ghosts are sociologized, rather than theologized or psychoanalyzed, and they are deeply politicized. Specters of Marx, the enslaved, apparitional lesbians – they haunt this world in its other-ing dimensions. They mourn the loss of justice, the power of power to render others invisible, and thus they manifest the social processes that have made them what they are: repressed, marginalized, liminal, carrying out the death drive within culture.

Recognizing the claims of contemporary ghosts on society makes the apprehension of ghosts an urgent matter for social organization and reform. Historians, sociologists, politicians are being called to reckon with ghosts, to acknowledge their place in human reality, collective mentalities, and histories of oppression.[2] This project not only changes political practice but historiography as we know it. It unsettles rationalist procedures and academic disciplines, making fiction – and thus literary study – indispensable to social inquiry, poetics having long been philosophical about its partiality and particularity. Sociologist Avery Gordon signals the contemporary take-over by using the term "social science fiction" to describe her discipline, and apparently she is not alone in fictionalizing science. Increasingly, titles are advertising, rather than stigmatizing, their content by calling it fable, performance, fantasy, myth.[3] Today's scholars are far more skeptical about Enlightenment reason than about the ghosts that it laid to rest. Not ontology but hauntology describes our being and time.[4]

Today's ghosts, then, occupy our minds, histories, politics in ways that change our conceptions of these categories and their modes of operation in and on the world. Acknowledging them, according to Jacques Derrida, places us in a better conceptual and political space: between a life and a death – indeed, between "all the 'two's' one likes" – that is, necessary for thinking and living "more justly" (Derrida 1994: xviii). Spectrality welcomes a time and a body that is "out of joint" – spirits, too, for that matter (xx; also 39–40). It adjusts our vision by disjoining seeing from believing, from knowing, from be-ing. Such shifts in apprehension, which have been visible for some time, are now seen as crucial to a notion of justice that requires "the principle of some responsibility, beyond all living present, within that which disjoins the living present, before the ghosts of those who are not yet born or who are already dead" (xix). The question remains what share vengeance should have in the justice that the contemporary come-back of ghosts serves, for some ghosts are encouraged to return with a vengeance against wielders of reason who have eliminated them and their political concerns.[5] They speak on behalf of social and sexual minorities who have been ghosted, silenced, rendered invisible for all too long.[6] Other ghosts render justice apart from vengeance, distinguishing the "disadjustments of the unjust" from those that welcome "the infinite asymmetry of the relation to the other" (Derrida 1994: 22). These are the ghosts that move us beyond forms of enlightenment that still want their equality, restitution, individuality but without their reason. These ghosts bear a justice that returns to the living the inhumanity that sets living going in the first place.

Joanna Baillie is making something of a come-back these days. Once an esteemed participant in the early-nineteenth-century British literary scene, she is gaining visibility along with Romantic theatre generally, after having long been ignored by Romantic scholars trained to view that scene as lyrical, transcendent, male, and immaterial. Theatre is to Romanticism what ghosts are to hauntology: a "paradoxical phenomenality" that disturbs dreams and that, until recently, has kept both theatre and ghosts in the closet (Derrida 1994: 7). The visibility of Baillie's theatre is to literary politics what ghosts are to the twin branches of hauntological justice. Her monumental "Plays on the Passions" force Romantic scholars to rethink time and space, unsettling conventional boundaries between external and internal, event and passion, page, stage, and world. It speaks for and to the silenced by a writer whose reception, both then and now, has turned on sexual politics. The original anonymity of the first volume of the "Plays on the Passions" facilitated praise for the masculine strength and vigor of its author which, when her identity was revealed, was then construed as either weakening the volume's appeal or proving that this lady-dramatist had balls.[7] If Baillie's appearance today does not exactly out her as lesbian, it uncovers the queer dimensions of her character(s) and the feminism and performativity that underlie her notions of gender.[8]

Baillie's come-back makes a more dramatic intersection with the contemporary come-back of ghosts through *Orra*, one of the two tragedies Baillie devotes to the passion of fear. *Orra* does not simply dramatize the inherent theatricality of ghosts but stages the come-back of ghosts in ways that are open to otherness. This way lies madness for Orra but also political critique and poetic forms of hauntological justice for her viewers. The play's portrayal of ghosts anticipates the aims of hauntology, in associating ghosts both with histories of oppression and with the dissolutions of category, person, meaning. Too, *Orra* manifests Baillie's prescience in the treatment of ghosts in her day, especially in relation to the two arenas differently invested in denying their reality and visibility: historiography and theatre. Enlightenment historiography charts the progress of mind in proportion to its triumph over superstition, miracles, portents, ghosts.[9] Romantic theatre critics uphold belief in theatre's suspension of disbelief by proscribing the appearance of supernatural beings on stage. As Charles Lamb contends, "[i]t is the solitary taper and the book that generates a faith in these terrors: a ghost by chandelier light, and in good company, deceives no spectators – a ghost that can be measured by the eye, and his human dimensions made out at leisure" (Park 1980: 99). They also keep from view those bodies that hauntologists discern within the ghosts who return with vengeance – women, the masses, rulers of color. Even cannier historical and novelistic projects that raise the dead in order to live with them limit the mobility of ghosts. Godwin's *Essay on Sepulchres* (1809), like Burke's transgenerational social contract, deems only the "illustrious dead" worthy of revival, those whom Coleridge calls the "great living-dead men of our island" and who compose "England."[10] Gothic fictions, like Romantic medievalism, usually raise ghosts in order to keep them and the living in line: designating a "then" from "now," imagining by reading, but not by seeing or staging, ghosts.[11] Baillie's *Orra*, then, in stressing Orra's desire to socialize with ghosts, moves beyond these forms of containment in visible ways. It makes the then now by setting its action and audience in the waning Middle Ages and by placing this disjointed time, and its ghosts, on stage. It syncopates time by featuring a "forward" girl who "shrinks" in fear.

But the value of *Orra* is also linked to the way that its aura keeps its timeliness in the air. The aura of *Orra* is uncanny in the Freudian sense: uncovering the strangeness of home, and woman's estrangement from the familiar, as fundamental to Orra's madness; exposing what subjects have not surmounted, even when they think that they have moved beyond belief in the existence of ghosts. For *Orra* is a disturbing play in itself and to the alleged humanism of Baillie's theatrical projects. Its treatment of fear situates Baillie within longstanding debates on the relation of fear to tragedy and of drama to morality which ends up undermining her characteristic position on these topics.[12] The usual depiction emphasizes the morality of Baillie's theatre and its endorsement of middle-class values, assertions that she makes in her "Introductory Discourse" and subsequent prefaces. In these venues she extends domestic tragedy's critique of (Aristotelian) tradition, lowering the social class of tragic protagonists on the theory that audiences identify with those who are like them and offering theatre as the arena in which human character is best analyzed and reformed.[13] *Orra*, however, tells a different, and less humane, story about fear. It portrays what fear presupposes, why fear is reassuring, and thus what remains behind when ghosts reappear. In this, *Orra* challenges residual beliefs by hauntologists that encounters with ghosts can be understood or withstood. As Orra says even before she loses her mind after her "fearful interview" with a ghost, "I heard thy voice, but not thy words. What saidst thou?" (244)

*

The plot of *Orra* follows the Gothic stories toward which the eponymous heroine is drawn. The ward of her dead father's best friend, Orra has angered Count Aldenberg by refusing his son Glottenbal's offers of marriage. On the advice of Rudigere, a bastard of a branch of the family of Aldenberg who is in love with Orra and who wishes to keep her from Theobald, his most serious competition for Orra's affections, Count Aldenberg banishes Orra to Brunier's castle, which is known to be haunted every St. Michael's Eve by a "noble hunter-knight" murdered by one of Count Aldenberg's and Orra's ancestors. Though Orra respects Theobald, in contrast to the scorn she feels for her other two suitors, she does not wish to marry anyone. Theobald attempts to rescue Orra from the haunted castle on St. Michael's Eve by disguising himself as the hunter-knight and gaining access to her chamber through a secret underground passage. He has alerted Orra to his plan in a letter, but Rudigere throws the letter into the fire before she can read it. The rescue succeeds at the cost of Orra's sanity. Orra no longer recognizes her friends but sees herself surrounded by the living-dead.

Even without its hospitality to ghosts, *Orra* is a recognizable example of Romantic medievalism. The advantage of specifying its "Time, towards the end of the 14th century," is visible from the first scene which has our three contenders for Orra's favor entering fresh "from the lists," or, more precisely, entering in degrees of freshness that indicate the worth of their character: Glottenbal "bare-headed and in disorder, his arms soiled with earth or sand," Rudigere brooding over his defeat, and Theobald sporting a "green sprig stuck in his helmet." *Orra* enlists an array of medieval trappings – a haunted castle, legendary hunter-knights, a patriarchal father, a band of outlaws, feudal law, a theatricality of nobility, belief in magic. The literal and atmospheric setting is chivalry in its characteristic arts of rule.[14] A thematics of "mastery" and "subjection," constellated especially around relations between the sexes but also between men and among social classes, is characterized as "wizardry," "possession," "hauntings."

The wizardry of mastery, however, positions Baillie's readers not within the Middle Ages but within superimposed layers of time. In one sense, this is a structural necessity of theatre that does not separate a past of its content from a present of its show. Theatre is magical timing that transports audiences to a then-now. But Baillie foregrounds the split time of *Orra* in prefatory remarks that disarticulate superstition from days gone by. Fear "of the returning dead," she writes, is "so universal and inherent in our nature, that it can never be eradicated from the mind, let the progress of reason or philosophy be what it may" (228). The project is less to ridicule former belief in ghosts than contemporary belief in the supersession of this belief. "A brave and wise man of the nineteenth century, were he lodged for the night in a lone apartment where murder has been committed, would not so easily believe, as a brave and wise man of the fourteenth century, that the restless spirit from its grave might stalk around his bed and open his curtains in the stillness of midnight: but should circumstances arise to impress him with such a belief, he would feel the emotions of Fear as intensely, though firmly persuaded that such beings have no power to injure him" (228). *Orra* thematizes this split-time in the dispositions of its characters, who run at different speeds, even directions, in relation to enlightenment. Here is where *Orra* begins to manifest Baillie's difference from other Romantic medievalists, for she portrays "medieval" minds that themselves do not believe in ghosts but instead manipulate belief in them to master those few who do, the plot against Orra working because she is more or less alone in her belief.[15] Baillie's advance is in criticizing this manipulation *and* this disbelief through the play's sympathetic treatment of Orra, and in so doing exposing the asymmetric weight that the return of the dead places on specific kinds of person.

The dominant plot, determining Orra's future, displays the multiple times in which these characters are living. Their worlds are characterized by splits between "medieval" and "enlightened" sensibilities and, within these divisions, according to where power positions persons in relation to law. The question of Orra's future distinguishes the genders: men worrying how to win consent without coercion; women how to maintain the right to self-rule. But the nature of consent also differentiates classes of men by displaying the waning of paternal authority in an ostensibly medieval age:

Hugh: I cannot force
          A noble maid entrusted to my care.
Rud: That were indeed unfit; but there are means
          To make her yield consent.

Hugh: Then by my faith, good friend, I'll call thee wizard,
          If thou canst find them out. What means already,
          Short of compulsion, have we left untried?
          And now the term of my authority
          Wears to its close.

                                                    (239–40)

The need for a plot against Orra already challenges paternal authority, since this ward does not receive the father's word as law. The timing and invention of the plot evacuate it, for another man not only devises and enacts it but feels that he must intervene because the Count is worn out, "harass'd" by toiling for "this untoward match" (239). That this other man is Rudigere, with designs of his own in terrorizing Orra, reveals not only the illusion of paternal law but the gullibility that founds, not only sustains, it. The father's lack of inventiveness makes him resemble his son, perceived by everyone, including his doting (and thus again non-authoritarian) father, as a "dolt," a "fool." A "medieval" plot, then, is enlisted to contravene "modern" failures of men, anxious about the grounds on which women might consent to be mastered by them. Neither old nor young men – or any age of women – are confident about where exactly male supremacy resides.

With women, enlightenment resides in their desire to live independently, such efforts at self-mastery being blocked, however, by the ongoing "medieval" nature of men. Orra's forwardness is expressed in her indictment of marriage as slavery ("well I know, / In such a partnership, the share of power / Allotted to the wife" [240]). She is fearless in disobeying her guardian and scornful of her suitors, except Theobald, to whom she offers not a hand in marriage but a plan to be "co-burgher" of Basle with him. The man does not exist who could share in Orra's "generous plan" to live singly and devote herself to "improv[ing] the low condition of my peasants," for men's nature, as even Theobald depicts it, is "fierce, contentious, / Restless and proud, and prone to vengeful feuds [sic]; / The very distant sound of war excites us" (241). Orra's forwardness contrasts with female characters like Eleanora and Cathrina, the nature of whose subjection to men makes male backwardness visible. The Count's wife, Eleanora, is the only person in relation to whom he appears authoritarian.[16] The virtuous Cathrina is under Rudigere's control because of a prior sexual indiscretion.

Ghosts, then, enter a scene in which enlightened time is seriously out of joint between the sexes. Ghosts are the last resort of men who impersonate them in order to terrorize women into subjection or to obtain political or economic gains from society. No man in *Orra* believes in ghosts but their varying uses of them differentiate groups of men according to the "justice" of their claims to live outside the law. Since "[t]he laws have cast me off from every claim / Of house and kindred,"

Rudigere reasons, "I'll cast them off: why should they be to me / A bar and no protection?" (237). His scheme to terrorize Orra by confining her in Brunier's castle is facilitated by the band of outlaws whose livelihood depends on "uphold[ing] the terrors of the place." They haunt the castle in order to keep others away from their property, the "lawless[ness]" of which is justified by "hard necessity" (257). The staging of ghosts as hoax, then, manifests an enlightened sensibility in men who are even granted sympathy for their dissimulations because laws are unfair and times are hard.[17] Theobald's "true" nobility is expressed in his willingness to assume the guise of a ghost to rescue Orra, his consent to which plan ennobles the robber-leader, Franko, who concocted it and happens to be Theobald's lost childhood friend.

Orra's relation to ghosts manifests a more susceptible frame of mind. Her belief is less the sign of woman's medieval mentality or characteristic melancholy than a part of her – and Baillie's – emancipatory ends. Baillie offers as "excuse" for breaking her usual pattern of writing one tragedy and one comedy for each passion an "*esprit de corps*" with her sex that makes her "unwilling to appropriate this passion in a serious form to my own sex entirely" (229). Orra's preference for ghosts expresses a feminist indictment of the inadequacies of living men who are inherently warlike and scheming, and contingently stupid (Glottenbal) and base (Rudigere). In the face of such options, Orra makes a defensible choice: "And let my dull hours by the dead man's watch / Be told; yea, make me too the dead man's mate, / My dwelling place the nailed coffin; still / I would prefer it to the living lord / Your goodness offers me" (244). While comically brutal about the attractiveness of men – "dost thou put [Glottenbal] in thy estimation / With bones and sheeted clay?" (244) – Orra's preference expresses as well a subtle critique of the hubris that sustains faith in enlightenment: truly receptive minds feel the reality of ghosts and their share in composing human reality. But Orra is exceptional in her love for the dead and the extent of her kinship with them. In daily life she hears "the sound of time long past / Still murm'ring o'er" her, invites ghosts to her fireside, and makes "their gloomy home, now . . . mine" (246). She loves stories that tell of living beings who have survived "intercourse" with the dead and is clinical in her analysis of her joy in fear or *jouissance*: "when the cold blood shoots through every vein; / When every pore upon my shrunken skin / A knotted knoll becomes, and to mine ears / Strange inward sounds awake, and to mine eyes / Rush stranger tears" (242).

This joy in fear distinguishes Orra from her companions but undermines her desire to remain single. Indeed, it explains why she prefers a dead man as mate (he is the only thing going) and why her receptivity to the dead will not let them leave her alone. Orra's acceptance of the "awful bond" that links "the living and the dead" is a clear indictment of the delusions of enlightened minds who refuse to recognize their kinship, indeed their (future) identity, with the dead. "Woe's me that we do shudder at ourselves – At that which we must be" (253). But precisely her openness to this identity dims her prospects for the future. Ghosts by definition impede autonomy, and these dead obstruct the forward movement of subjects. The final scene of *Orra* is a chilling depiction of what seeing the living and dead in "horrid neighborship" actually looks like: "See! from all points they come; earth casts them up! . . . Oh! the void / Of hollow unball'd sockets staring grimly, / And lipless jaws that move and clatter round us / In mockery of speech!" (259). The detailing of the sheer numbers and generations of the dead underscores how the dead crowd out the living and take over their space. Perceived by Orra, this view is a further extension of the play's political critique of the patriarchal power articulated by and embodied in Count Aldenberg ("right well thy father . . . vested me with power that might compel thee / To what he will'd should be" [244]). Power is behind the times in both senses: it authorizes certain living-dead men to count as history, and its interest lies in delaying progress. The number of men after Orra is nothing compared to the number before her who control her destiny. Orra's last words, then, voice a precondition of hauntological justice: "Back, back! – Oh, they close upon us. – . . . Back, back, I say! / Back, back!" Reckoning with ghosts, especially by those who have been ghosted by them, means feeling the pressures of their presence and still finding ways to move forward.

Some of the pessimism of this ending can be modified by viewing it as a tragedy in Baillie's understanding of the form. She promotes tragedy as a school of moral instruction whose effectivity resides in rendering visible what is usually impossible for humans to see in others and thus about themselves. By featuring characters who withstand "extraordinary situations of difficulty and distress" and by following them into their closets where they act (ostensibly) without disguise, tragedy satisfies human curiosity regarding the inner workings of passion and, by charting these workings, provides an early warning system in the detection and regulation of passion (11). *Orra* is central to Baillie's overall project, for what occupies humans most intensely, what "makes us press forward to behold what we shrink from," is those who have held "intercourse, real or imaginary, with the world of spirits." In fact, *Orra* thematizes and then cancels the indirection that Baillie specifies as the mode by which humans usually learn about ghosts: "No man wishes to see the Ghost himself, which would certainly procure him the best information on the subject, but every man wishes to see one who believes that he sees it, in all the agitation and wildness of that species of terror" (3). One could say, then, that Orra is sacrificed (twice) for the greater good of those who view her tragedy. She confronts the ghosts that the rest of us prefer to witness through mediation and stages the senselessness of patriarchy's intense pressures on women. The play itself suggests that things did not have to end in tragedy. If Theobald's letter had not gone astray, presumably Orra would not have gone mad. Nor, the play suggests, would Orra be insane if her character had not previously gone astray. Her being terrorized is the "fruits" of her "unconquer'd pride," her uncompromising though capricious nature. Scorn like hers turns men into terrorists, as Rudigere warns her. "Beware lest scorn like this should change me / E'en to the baleful thing your fears have fancied" (247). This censure of Orra, moreover, is consistent with the moderation that characterizes Baillie's emancipatory projects and her characterizations of desirable intelligent women.[18] The extremity of Orra's scorn for men invites, if it does not deserve, the treatment she receives.[19]

Such assertions regarding the need for reform in Orra and thus the reform value of *Orra* are challenged, however, by the play's depiction of fear, the relation of fear to ghosts, and the relation of both to theatricality, theatre, and current stages of history. In effect, and as its tragic effect, *Orra* renders visible the limits to humanist conceptions of fear. Fear's share in sustaining human community is voiced as a leveling of social distinctions both within *Orra* and in the preface to it. "We are all creatures, in the wakeful hour / Of ghastly midnight, form'd to cower together, / Forgetting all distinctions of the day, / Beneath its awful and mysterious power" (247). Hearing ghost stories solidifies community and constitutes group recreation by having folks shut out the cold and assemble around domestic firesides. In the depths of her fear, Orra becomes cognizant of the "something of [her] kind" in ghosts and even in her arch-foe Rudigere, for "welcome is aught that wears a human face" (249, 251). But the capacity of fear to solidify humanity is also qualified by the various ways that ghosts make their appearance in this play.

A double plot line or its convergence in the central character is hardly surprising in a play about ghosts. Still, the oppositions that each strand foregrounds suggest the impossibility of maintaining firm oppositions between the living and the dead and hints at what blocks justice for the oppressed of history. Plans by Theobald to rescue Orra from the plot to terrorize her into marriage run afoul of prior claims on her time, the "fearful interview" having long been scheduled by the hunter-knight with "some true descendent" of his murderer's race on St. Michael's Eve. Besides uniting Orra's past and her future, this convergence pits imposter ghost against real ghost and illegitimate against legitimate claims on her. Sins of the father require redress even if living sons are invested in perpetuating them. Here, too, moral and epistemological distinctions regarding ghosts are drawn only to be blurred. Moral distinctions are obviously troubled when the worthy suitor resorts to imposture; but even the appearance of a "real" ghost does not seem able to maintain its integrity. The "awful form" of Orra's father rises between her and the Count, its "look of anguish" expressing sympathy for the unfair restraints placed on his forward girl. But this sympathy is undercut by the father's clear position on the side of men. Early on Hartman predicts that he will win Orra for Theobald out of her gratitude for his having fought "in the bloody field" by her father's side (237). Later, the Count praises her father's wisdom in perceiving "that all thy sex / Stubborn and headstrong are" (244).

The play's thematization of imposter ghosts emphasizes a deeper concern with legitimacy that, coupled with the implications of Orra's fearful interview, underscore the (mal)function of fear in keeping humans in form. Fear's relation to form is explored in two more suspensions of opposition, Orra's kinship with Rudigere and the (in)difference between hearing ghost stories and seeing a ghost. Orra and Rudigere are linked through their critiques of the claims associated with blood, though initially opposed on the moral ends that their critiques serve. While Rudigere's alleged illegitimacy absolves him from moral law, Orra detaches nobility from blood in order to attach it to heart, less in the sense that nobles should marry for love than that claims to legitimacy are moral, not biological. "But in thy heart, false traitor! What lives / there?" (249). This enlightened ethical distinction, however, is doubly nullified by the claims of blood in *Orra*. On the most basic level, both Orra and Rudigere affirm that "in my veins there runs / A murderer's blood," another basis for Orra's attraction to Rudigere in the depths of her fear. But this recognition is part of a more fundamental struggle in the play over blood's support of life: does it flow in veins or in vain when seen as the source of nobility? The homonym keeps blood circulating apart from living.

The audible, but not visual, indeterminacy of vein/vain foregrounds the status of hearing as a suspension of form. It qualifies initial suggestions regarding the conviviality and domestication achieved by listening to ghost stories, and outlines instead the comforts in seeing ghosts. These are comforts of form, of giving a shape to anxiety. Opposed to them is the play's focus on the means of a story's dissemination – sound, voice. Sound is presented as dissolving meaning in *Orra;* it is said to "hollow out" persons and things. Sound is "swallow'd" by the "cavern'd earth," and, in combination with "mysterious night," itself contrasted to the "enlighten'd earth," "lap[s]" "things unutterable" (249, 251). Compared to such eviscerated locations, any "aught" that "wears a human face" is reassuring. This reassurance is confirmed by the tears that signify Orra's kinship with ghosts and makes the apprehension of them occasion for pity, not fear. "A horrid sympathy jarr'd on my heart, / And forced into mine eyes these icy tears. / A fearful kindredship there is between / The living and the dead – an awful bond! / Woe's me! That we do shudder at ourselves – / At that which we must be!" (253). But what distinguishes Orra from human community is her desire to *shrink* in fear. Her joy in fear arises out of becoming through fear what all living things one day will be – things, unconscious, icy, cold. On such grounds she envies floorboards their insentience and their superior position over women. "Ye happy

216 *Julie A. Carlson*

things of still and lifeless being, / That to the awful steps which tread upon ye / Unconscious are" (252). Reduced to them on St. Michael's Eve, she gets her wish.

This is hardly an auspicious platform on which to campaign for justice for women, but it helps to establish Baillie's credentials as hauntologist. The play's emphasis on Orra's spectral features – her felt neighborship with the dead, desire to shrink, permeated ego – sets the stage for the presentation of a subject who can take responsibility for actions that are in her blood but not of her making. This requires envisioning a subject that is positioned, as Derrida notes, between all the twos that serve oneness and thus violence and vengeance. Baillie goes remarkably far in *Orra* in sketching out what a spectral subject looks like and, in the final scene, what it sees, especially regarding how being surrounded by the living dead impedes one's forward movement. Nor are the a-human dimensions of personhood reserved only for characterizations of Orra. When Count Hughobert eulogizes the now-dead Glottenbal, he describes his "child" as "the thing that from his cradle grew, / And was before me still," suggesting the kinship in thing-ness between our beginning and end (257). But in this striking revision of what counts as self, blood, and community, *Orra* is the exception to, not the rule of, the *Series*. Most of Baillie's plays work to reform rather than deform or dissolve character and are concerned with positioning women more securely in this world. Baillie's credentials as hauntologist, then, are more consistently confirmed by her aesthetics rather than thematics. They are visible in her endorsement of the im/materiality of the stage and her revision of dramatic precedent.

The vocabulary of *Orra* portrays ghosts, and thus one's relation to the returning dead, as a theatrical matter. The apprehension and comprehension of ghosts require the same states of mind and vision as does theatre: suspension of belief in some of the chief oppositions that structure the world – now/then, being/seeming, live/dead, person/thing, this world/the otherworldly. The final scene not only depicts ghosts as theatrical and as upstaging the living but alludes to the properties of theatre in calling the "horrid neighborship" of living and dead "th' uncurtained reach." Baillie's emphasis on the linkage between spectrality and theatre is directed at two targets against which much of her writing is aimed: those who confine representations of the dead to tragedy and tragedy to the illustrious – and therefore male – dead, and those who restrict the appearance of ghosts to processes of imagination, not seeing. In the latter concern, Baillie counters antitheatrical poets and novelists in the spirit of Lessing's endorsement of theatre. "Why build a theatre, disguise men and women, torture their memories, invite the whole town to assemble at one place if I intend to produce nothing more with my work and its representation, than some of those emotions that would be produced as well by any good story that every one could read by his chimney-corner at home?"(Lessing 1962: 198). For that matter, why consider interior processes invisible or dreams antithetical to staging?

Baillie's point is not just that ghosts make good spectacles or that theatres are capable of staging them along with the passions that animate and deform humans. Her point is that spectators should take seriously theatre's special effect of transporting them to the time when lights, shadows, voices had value but no meaning. Baillie champions spectacle precisely for its capacity to transcend plot and character and thus to appeal to the before-human within each of us. "A love for active, varied movement, in the objects before us; for striking contrasts of light and shadow, for splendid decorations and magnificent scenery, is as inherent in us as the interest we take in the representation of the natural passions and characters of men: and the most cultivated minds may relish such exhibitions, if they do not, when both are fairly offered to their choice, prefer them" (232). For similar reasons, she prizes sound as it floats apart from meaning. ("[F]or mingled voices, heard afar / . . . seem wild-goblin sounds" [246]). In this regard, theatre has value in recalling the proximity of humans to things as a hauntological reality with social and moral implications. Who among us does not have "murderer's blood" in our veins? It also restores to us pre-human but theatrical delight in lights, passion, action.

Baillie's endorsement of spectacle distinguishes her from many of her contemporaries, who support drama to the extent that it promotes poetry and denigrates theatre. Her specification of human delight in spectacle puts her in a class by herself. Delight in the lights, colors, materials of theatre arise from, and transport humans to, a different place and time than does the "interest we take in the representation of the natural passions and characters of men." That is, it takes us to the psychic space that we occupied before we were meaning-makers but after we have become captivated by the sights and sounds of the world. This challenge to precedence, especially regarding art's relation to the human, is conducted on a different level by Baillie's attacks on literary precedent. One of her primary aims in composing the "Plays on the Passions" is to reduce the weight of literary precedent on contemporary writers so that literature can encompass more kinds of character and experience. Dramatic writers who rely too exclusively on "the great dramatists who have gone before them" overlook "the varieties of human character that *first* furnished materials for these works" (8; emphasis added). Her *Series* aims at a democratization and domestication of what counts as history: private affairs, ghosts in the closet, passions that determine and undermine events. This requires not only opening the stage to a world of experience until then not deemed part of (literary) history but engineering the machinery of the stage to make passion, interiority, aggression visible. It also means re-engineering human subjectivity to perceive these elements as the stuff of its theatre.

Orra combines both dimensions, and levels, of Baillie's assault on precedent. Its thematic interest in ghosts turns hauntologic in staging the before and after of life as a presence within Orra's subjectivity and current reality. This thematic interest also becomes hauntologic in the way that it revises literary precedent. For *Orra* conjures the aura of Shakespeare through the re-entry of the ghost of the father. On the one hand, it levels an implicit critique against Shakespeare for associating ghosts and their tragedies with illustrious men by directing the ghost to return this time to a daughter who is determined to live independently from men. On the other, it challenges the possibility of independence for any spectral subject on the level of content and the play's treatment of sound. For sound, hearing, voices – and the sound of hearing voices – are portrayed as solidifying community apart from reliance on the individual, the human, or sense. Such sounds compose and reassure us as a community but also leave us defenseless, captivated by echoes and confined by the "so they say" (the most repeated phrase in *Orra*) of communal histories. *Orra* characterizes the "old tunes" that a people know by heart as having their "measure" "beat" by "[t]he bones of murder'd men" (258).

This is a sinister look at literary tradition, precedent, and the difficulties, particularly in drama, of owning one's words. It makes theatre literally into a haunted house, an echo chamber, and, as Baillie writes in her "Introductory Discourse," the author into a medium. "I am frequently sensible, from the manner in which an idea arises to my imagination, and the readiness with which words, also, present themselves to clothe it in, that I am only making use of some dormant part of that hoard of ideas which the most indifferent memories lay up, and not the native suggestions of my own mind" (17). In this regard, the spectral light of *Orra* gives a different cast to Baillie's status as the latest incarnation of Shakespeare in her day. In ours, hauntologic poetic justice is served in acknowledging her again to be the follower-leader of Romantic theatre.

Notes

1 According to Richard Corum, English Catholics before the Reformation recognized five kinds of ghosts: angels and souls of saints sent from heaven to advise, warn, or console the faithful; souls of the ordinary dead returning from purgatory to take care of unfinished business; demons in the shapes, bodies, or clothes of the recent dead coming from hell to lure the weak and gullible to damnation; figments of melancholic imaginations; frauds invented to gain wealth and power. With the elimination of purgatory and the transformation of the holy spirit into conscience, Protestants recognized only three kinds of ghosts, all negative: demons, hallucinatory figments of melancholic imaginations, or frauds (1998: 115). See also Schmitt 1998.

2 Besides the two texts alluded to above, Jacques Derrida's *Specters of Marx* and Terry Castle's *The Apparitional Lesbian: Female Homosexuality and Modern Culture*, I am thinking about the following recent invocations of ghosts in social and political theory: Avery Gordon, *Ghostly Matters* (1997),

Tom Keenan, *Fables of Responsibility* (1997), and Patricia Williams, *Alchemy of Race and Rights* (1991). See Fredric Jameson's discussion of this phenomenon in his review of Derrida's *Specters of Marx* (1995).

3   Gordon does not privilege literature over sociology either; literature has its "own problems, or rather, it has its own business," but it "enable[s] other kinds of sociological information to emerge" (1997: 24–7).

4   Derrida proposes hauntology as an "irreducible" category that "is first of all to everything it makes possible: ontology, theology, positive or negative onto-theology." It is related to spectrality, which signifies the "doubtful contemporaneity of the present to itself." The spectrality effect undoes the opposition between "actual, effective presence and its other" (1994: 51, 39, 40).

5   Given the importance of *Hamlet* to the current sociologizing of ghosts, Corum's remarks regarding the genesis of Hamlet's ghost are intriguing. There was no ghost in the legendary source for *Hamlet*, but one was added "by the author of the no longer extant *Ur-Hamlet*" to cry "Hamlet, revenge" (1998: 113).

6   Terry Castle's *The Apparitional Lesbian* is an example of this line of argument in its efforts to "bring the lesbian back into focus" after having suffered invisibility—or, at best, a ghostly immateriality—for centuries because of patriarchal culture's deep "fear of 'women without men'" (1993: 2, 5). For Castle, however, literature is guilty of perpetrating the work of ghosting "more intensely" than other forms of writing. Since the eighteenth century, the literary history of lesbianism is a "history of derealization" (34). While her argument also depends on making the lesbian's "apparitionality" a paradoxical sign of her "vitality" and "cultural power," her efforts are restorative, not deconstructive, of identity (7, 8, 46). Her formulation, "she is not a nonsense," means that for Castle justice does not need to be rethought, simply attained (13). Comfort with Enlightenment categories is made even clearer in her goal: to affirm the "connection between lesbian experience and human experience" (18).

7   On the reception of the anonymous first volume, see Carhart (1923: 12–18); for Byron's famous description, see letter for 2 April 1817 (Marchand 1975–82: Vol. 5, 203).

8   See Catherine Burroughs's discussion of Baillie's anticipation of tenets of performance theory and the implications for a queer subjectivity (1997). Also see Thomas C. Crochunis's chapter on Baillie's "ambivalent dramaturgy" in this volume.

9   Eighteenth-century and early nineteenth-century literary histories of England are prone to chart this progress of mind, especially the works of Thomas Warton (*History of English Literature*, in 4 volumes), Adam Smith (*Lectures on Rhetoric and Belles Lettres*), Hugh Blair (*Letters on Rhetoric and the Belles Lettres*), Bishop Hurd ("On Chivalry and Romance"), William Godwin ("On History and Romance," *The Lives of the Necromancers*), and Sir Walter Scott ("Essay on Chivalry and Romance").

10 *Essay on Sepulchres* is a "proposal" that Godwin submits to politicians for keeping the dead alive by "erecting some memorial of the illustrious dead in all ages on the spot where their remains have been interred," memorials that serve as "commentaries and illustrations of history" without which "all other records and remains" of illustrious persons are left in a "maimed and imperfect state" (Philp 1993: VI, 7, 27, 30). Burke's social contract, as is well known, is a contract among the dead, the living, and the yet to be born (*Reflections on the Revolution in France*). Coleridge's remarks are in his *Collected Notebooks*, where he proceeds to name names: "Let England be Sir

P. Sidney, Shakespeare, Milton, Bacon, Harrington, Swift, Wordsworth, and never let the names of Darwin, Johnson, Hume <u>furr</u> it over!" (Coburn *et al.* 1961: II, 2598).

11 Margaret Carter emphasizes the frequency with which Gothic novelists use an editorial frame in order to mark their distance from the superstitions that their "found" tale upholds (1987: 9–10).

12 See Carlson (1999) for a fuller discussion of these issues.

13 "Thus, great and magnanimous heroes, who bear with majestic equanimity every vicissitude of fortune . . . have been held forth to our view as objects of imitation and interest: as though [dramatic writers] had entirely forgotten that it is only for creatures like ourselves that we feel, and, therefore, only from creatures like ourselves that we receive the instruction of example" (J. Baillie 1976: 8–9). All subsequent citations of Baillie's works are from this edition with page numbers in parentheses in the text.

14 On the operations of medieval chivalry, see Fradenburg (1992).

15 Rudigere characterizes her love for ghost stories a "secret weakness of her mind" (237).

16 For example, in such undermotivated and winning exchanges as "What, again! / Have I not said thou hast an alien's heart / From me and mine. Learn to respect my will: —Be silent, as becomes a youthful dame" (244). Baillie portrays woman's domestic status as resident alien in a more serious, and thoroughgoing, fashion in her characterization of Helen in *The Family Legend*.

17 Though he is generally a villain, one begins to sympathize even with Rudigere's concern for a haunted Orra in Act III, scene ii ("I deride [your weakness]! No, noble maid! say rather that from thee / I have a kindred weakness caught" [247]).

18 Exemplary women include Jane de Monfort, Countess Albini, Lady Griseld, all characterized by mixtures of courage, gentleness, and intelligence.

19 Though somewhat disingenuous given the frequent brutality of Baillie's depiction of men, this censure seems borne out by Theobald's intensified love for Orra after she has been humbled. "No, rise thou stately flower with rude blasts rent; . . . I've seen thee worshipp'd like a regal dame . . . but now, / No liege-man to his crowned mistress sworn, / Bound and devoted is, as I to thee; / And he who offers to thy alter'd state / The slightest seeming of diminish'd rev'rence, / Must in my blood – " (258). At the same time, Baillie is critiquing the values of chivalry.

13 Pedagogy and passions

Teaching Joanna Baillie's dramas

Marjean D. Purinton

This very title of Joanna Baillie's 1798 volume "Plays on the Passions" gives us a starting point to think about the teaching and presenting of her dramas. Her curious use of the word *passions*, a term frequently invoked in relation to British Romanticism, has been variously interpreted by recent scholars. In *Romantic Ideology Unmasked*, I connected Baillie's references to passions to her political, proto-feminist agenda (Purinton 1994: 125–62). Catherine Burroughs has demonstrated how we might understand passions in relation to the transitional acting styles of the late eighteenth and early nineteenth centuries (Burroughs 1997: 110–42). Jeffrey Cox and Michael Gamer associate Baillie's passions with the legacy of the Gothic upon which many of her dramas draw (Cox 1992: 50–57; Gamer 2000: 127–62). Terence Hoagwood has suggested that passions may have been the marketing strategy that Baillie recognized as essential to sell her dramas to the public (Hoagwood 2001: 293–316). Andrea Henderson has connected Baillie's passions to the period's aesthetic tastes, particularly those of fashion, and Anne Mellor associates Baillie's passions with the "Wise woman" who combines the nation's exemplary characteristics of rational prudence and sympathetic understanding (Henderson 1997: 198–228; Mellor 2000: 40–46). My most recent work on Baillie's dramas (2001) suggests that the passions might be associated with the medical and scientific revolutions of the Romantic period, particularly in their examination of female sexuality and hysteria. Baillie's uncle, Dr. William Hunter, and her brother, Dr. Matthew Baillie, were renowned physicians whose anatomical theatres were the sites of medical experimentation and instruction ("Life of Joanna Baillie" 1853: ix).[1]

We also know that Baillie was passionate about promoting the theatre as a site of education. From her own schoolgirl days at Miss McDonald's boarding school in Glasgow, Baillie experienced educational possibilities for drama and storytelling, often entertaining companions with "an endless string of stories of her own invention" (Carhart 1923: 7). As Margaret Carhart chronicles, Baillie wove stories into dramas, which she and her schoolmates presented. Sometimes, she also acted as a costume designer and stage manager (Carhart 1923: 8).[2] Young Joanna demonstrated skill in adapting dresses and decorations of the poorest kind for theatrical costumes and props, and her powers of acting and composition made audiences forget the deficiencies of her costumes ("Life of Joanna Baillie" 1853: viii). Perhaps her great memory and adeptness with character were generated from her own private readings and tellings of dramatic scenarios. She would have known the period's conduct books with their instructional strategies of stories and scenarios. Lucy Aikin reports how Baillie was "addicted to clambering on the roof of the house, to act over her scenes alone and in secret" (Carhart 1923: 7).[3] Baillie certainly played a part in the educational reforms of her day.

Baillie's father's dramatic soliloquies from his clerical pulpit were another source of performative and didactic storytelling that she regularly witnessed and perhaps appropriated. Her "Introductory Discourse" to the 1798 "Plays on the Passions" asserts that drama should be instructional: "The theatre is a school in which much good or evil may be learned" (1851: 14). She seeks to achieve this moral imperative through dramas that elicit the human propensity of "sympathetic curiosity towards others of our own kind which is so strongly implanted with us" (2). Baillie believes the theatre possesses the special ability to create between characters and audience an enlightening identificatory relationship. Drama, she argues, "improves us by the knowledge we acquire of our own minds, from the natural desire we have to look into the thoughts, and observe the behavior of others" (9), for "in examining others we know ourselves" (4). According to Julie Carlson, Baillie conceives that theatre is a site of education and sociability as a consequence of its moral efficacy, its "capacity to analyze and consequently avert passions that overwhelm the mind" (Carlson 2002: 146).

The passions, therefore, open up numerous possibilities for reading, discussing, and staging Baillie's dramas. The scholarly conversations about the passions at the heart of Baillie's dramas demonstrate how successfully her plays demand cognitive and analytical participation from their audiences. While her dramatic characters often stage the consequences of acting out passions and emulating emotions without critical thought, her dramas empower readers to become critical readers and respondents of the fictional world and conflicts being staged. In our twenty-first century's pedagogical contexts, Baillie's staging of a primary dramatic passion in each play is particularly well suited to audiences fascinated with visual spectacle, hyperbolic emotions, and uncomplicated plots. Like the theatre-going audiences of Baillie's day and like recent Romantic-period scholars, our students will respond to, will engage a "sympathetic curiosity" with, "passions." Baillie's dramas expose the power of internalized patterns of knowing, so deeply woven into the fabric of social interaction that we scarcely recognize them. Baillie's dramas compel us to think about the ways we have been conditioned to think and to feel. This is a formidable assignment, as she remarks in the 1798 "Introductory Discourse": "To hold up for our examples those peculiarities in disposition and modes of thinking which nature has fixed upon us, or which long and early habit has incorporated with our original selves, is almost desiring us to remove the everlasting mountains, to take away the native-land markers of the soul" (11). Baillie's dramas expose the connections between knowledge and the social organization of cognitive authority and the power of ideology. Her plays make tangible the pervasive and ubiquitous social conditioning that shapes patterns of thinking. In seeing and reading her dramas, audiences are invited to acknowledge the ways in which epistemology and ideology silently operate in public spaces, how they profoundly shape private cognition and identity formation. Her dramas perform a radical educational function for her day as well as today, for they seek not to inculcate prevailing socio-political thought but to empower individuals to think for themselves. Is this not what courses in the humanities in our institutions of higher education seek today?

Why teach Joanna Baillie's plays to contemporary college students? Precisely because Baillie's plays are not familiar to contemporary undergraduates, especially in contrast to those of William Shakespeare, George Bernard Shaw, or Tom Stoppard, her dramas invite students to think critically about cultural and cognitive structures that guide behavior and autonomy. Her plays constitute an important stage in our students' cultural memory. For example, we can rely on Baillie's plays to demonstrate the many issues of first-wave feminists that we are still attempting to resolve. Her plays are hauntingly contemporary for feminists, reflecting a fundamentally unchanged ideology operative in the gender relations of Western culture. Baillie's contributions demonstrate the heritage, coherence, but also the incompleteness of feminist activism. Because Baillie stages and contests gender scripts, dramatizing patterns of behavior in the fluid spaces demarcated private and public, she becomes part of the public discourse in her era about the status of women that is a missing link in many of our students' cultural memories. Moreover, critical and analytical readings of Baillie's dramas constitute exercises that can be applied to contemporary public discourse, current literary, legal, cultural scripts for women and men. Baillie's dramas constituted a form of public discourse that had the potential to change the ideological texture of her society. Our undergraduates certainly can have, once they read Baillie, a better understanding of the power of public discourse to reify, to challenge, to change cultural patterns and societal customs.

Beyond our graduate and undergraduate classrooms, why "teach" Baillie's plays to members of those communities surrounding our colleges and universities? What a wonderful vehicle for bringing campus and community together in a collaborative project. On at least two occasions, I have seized community-based opportunities to advance the works of British Romantic women playwrights, particularly Baillie's. (I will detail these productions below.) Both of these highly successful presentations provided optimum conditions for extending public relations, for community members attending these productions could actually see and experience what we do in the humanities, particularly literary studies, an area that remains somewhat mystifying, esoteric, and perhaps even impracticable to the general public and the taxpayers who support public and private education. At a time of increasing accountability for accreditation and for financial support, these productions constitute one way for departments of literature, women's studies programs and performance or feminist theory courses to make their educational contributions visibly valuable. These productions enabled me to historicize first-wave feminism in ways that engaged our conservative community in West Texas, drawing them in through employing "sympathetic curiosity" and raising their consciousness without putting at risk the financial support of our community and key constituents. Our community members delight in discovering women pioneers with whom they feel some affinity, some passion, and, as Misty Anderson has demonstrated, women playwrights of the long eighteenth century were more visible to their audiences as women than present day women screenwriters are to us. Though they fell out of circulation, Romantic women playwrights broke important ground (Anderson 2002: 207).

Despite the sentiment that West Texans have for independent groundbreakers, collaborative university–community productions were truly pioneering projects for Texas Tech University, and, like Baillie, I had to work within the confines of my cultural contexts, recognizing my audiences' comfort zones and conceptual limitations, before launching such performances. In *Geographies of Learning: Theory and Practice, Activism and Performance*, Jill Dolan reminds me why performing and interpreting Baillie for our contemporary campus and community audiences is important when she asserts: "If theatre is engaged in deconstructing epistemology, questioning how we know what we think we know, and who we think we are, its representational apparatus can be pressed into service" (Dolan 2001: 83). The goal of these community-based presentations is to utilize Romantic drama as a site of continuing education, the pedagogical potential that Baillie recognized in theatre. In other words, as Baillie recommends in her 1798 "Introductory Discourse," we can take theatre and performance into public culture, contextualizing it with our scholarly knowledge and our pedagogical expertise, so that it is no longer merely a discrete unit for a limited number of students but is accessible to broad-based audiences, both community and campus. Like our students, community members can participate in the social dimensions of Romantic-period theatre and become critically involved in the meaning-making process that Baillie's dramas encourage.

Because Baillie centered the socializing pedagogy of her "Plays on the Passions" with which she sought to engage readers and spectators, it is with the passions, then, that we begin to teach her plays. It is important for students to realize that "passions" were not unique with Baillie, as they see in the juxtapositions of her plays with other Romantic-period writings with similarly interesting relationships of passions to epistemological and social theory. For example, *Count Basil* (1798) works well in tandem with Mary Wollstonecraft's incomplete novel *Maria, or The Wrongs of Woman* (1798) to provoke students to consider how socially constructed and gendered patterns of knowing might be interrogated. The gender-bending strategies of characterization in both works destabilize perceived and accepted "natural" gendered roles and behaviors. Passions are politicized in both works. Like the multiple stories of women's wrongs embedded in Wollstonecraft's novel, *Count Basil* exposes the relations abuses (father–daughter, mentor–friend, lover–beloved) within a gender system in which women function as currency or objects. In both novel and drama, stereotypical behaviors are exposed as performances analogous to the actual roles assigned to women at the end of the eighteenth century. The fall of tragic characters in both works is connected with the demise of cultural orders (class systems, gender hierarchies, political regimes). Baillie's drama, like Wollstonecraft's novel, seeks to elicit a "sympathetic curiosity" from readers not so much that they may empathize with particular characters but to foster their critical evaluations of the sexual politics in play at the historical moment in which the tragedy is set and in the period of its initial publication and reception. *Maria* and *Count Basil* similarly lend themselves to examinations of the gender-bending Wollstonecraft and Baillie execute in their works and of how this gender-bending blurs the ideological line between public and private gender spaces.

Strategies for teaching Baillie's dramas

Besides reading Baillie's dramas in dialogue with other Romantic-period texts as suggested above, other strategies help students discover various ways the passions operate in Baillie's plays. Students have fun reading scenes aloud in class, and this strategy also helps them to discover the ways in which spoken language emphasizes human passions. Students benefit from being assigned parts in advance of the class reading so that they can practice and interpret the passions they give to Baillie's words. Sometimes students can stage a small segment of dialogue, enlivening the passions with body as well as with voice. They can stage a segment in a way designed to address audiences as we know they were in Romantic-period theatres, and they can then recast that segment for contemporary theatregoers, noting the differences in theatre structures and audience decorum in the meaning-making process of performing the dramatic scene. It helps for students to hear theatre music of the eighteenth and nineteenth centuries, such as James Paisible's "Aires," composed for Colley Cibber's comedy *She Wou'd and She Wou'd Not* (1703), and William Croft's "Aires," composed for David Crauford's comedy *Courtship-a-la-Mode* (1700), or Charles Dibdin's "The Joys of the Country," from *Wags, or The Camp of Pleasure*, performed 18 October 1790 at the Lyceum.[4] The period's theatre music captures and stimulates passions experienced on and off stage. Students might also render a visual representation of a scene or diagram the blocking of a passage to highlight the optical dimensions of passions presented theatrically. The opening processional scene in *Count Basil* and the party scene in *De Monfort*, for example, work well with this strategy.[5] Using PowerPoint, students can create background scenery to complement their stagings.

Students might describe how they would film a scene or direct the staging of an act from Baillie's drama in the theatre of her day, or in their own university theatre. Their descriptive discourse could include verbal and visual representations of costuming, scenery, make-up, blocking, lighting, special effects, and camera positions. Ask students to identify classmates or current media stars they would cast as characters in Baillie's drama and why those selections would help to engage the audience with significant aspects of the characters. Another strategy requires students to rewrite a scene for contemporary staging or film adaptation, including visual and auditory effects. These two strategies require students to think critically about the voices, gesturing, posturing, and blocking that characters would assume as well as the effects or identificatory processes the characters would generate among various audiences. These activities enable students to see Baillie's drama from all angles – playwright, director or stage manager, characters, and audience.

Another position from which students can experience the identificatory process of the passions in Baillie's drama is that of the theatre critic or reviewer. Adopting the persona of a noted reviewer in Romantic periodicals (e.g., Francis Jeffrey), students might write a review of Baillie's play, identifying the publication in which their review will appear and its target audience. As preparation for this activity, students might research and read period-specific reviews of Baillie's plays to discern what literary and theatrical critics of her day thought about her drama. The review of the first volume of "Plays on the Passions" in the *British Critic and Quarterly Theological Review* (March 1799), for example, would give students a basis for speculating about why critics' readings and responses to Baillie's plays frequently did not account for the social purposes of the passions. Like the activities discussed above, this strategy similarly requires students to discover something about the nature of the theatre in which Romantic-period plays were staged and the ways in which theatregoers behaved when they attended theatrical performances. Graduate students might construct an annotated bibliography of nineteenth-century reviews of Baillie's dramas, in both staged and published forms, and then analyze the ways in which those reviewers agree or disagree about the quality of her dramas and about the meanings of their passions – especially those such as Orra's presumed hysteria or Mary McMurren's alleged witchcraft, nefarious passions associated with female weaknesses that Baillie's plays challenge.

An alternative to writing a review of a play or an analysis of reviews of Baillie's dramas would be for students to construct promotional playbills and advertisements for specific plays. Students would need to think about how these promotional documents suggest interpretations and establish expectations for the play – whether they promote Baillie's drama in ways that support the educational theory of theatre presented in her introductory discourses. Students might also play the part of Licenser of Plays who reviewed Baillie's dramas, *De Monfort*, *The Tryal*, and *Count Basil*, for example, previous to their staging at Drury Lane.[6] Baillie's comedy *The Election* is strategically useful for this exercise, for it raises issues of class dissolution, parliamentary redistribution, female disenfranchisement, and women's solidarity that to the Lord Chamberlain might appear likely to stir potentially dangerous passions if enacted in a public forum. Would the Licenser of the Plays recommend production? What segments would be excised or edited? Why? In what ways would those changes alter the educational, social, or political content of the plays? What passions might be considered dangerous, and why? This activity requires students to become familiar with the socio-political nature of Romantic-period theatre and the limitations of gender on performance. Graduate students might explore Baillie's correspondence or correspondence about Baillie, such as that written by Walter Scott, Lord Byron, or William Wordsworth, for example, as evidence of her theatrical and educational interests. In a March 4, 1808 letter to Miss Smith, for instance, Walter Scott remarks: "We have Miss Baillie here at present, who is certainly the best dramatic writer whom Britain has produced since the days of Shakespeare and Massinger. I hope that you have had time to look into her tragedies (the comedies you may [pass] over without any loss), for I am sure you will find much to delight you, and I venture to prophesy you will one day have an excellent opportunity to distinguish yourself in some of her characters" (99). While Scott predicts that the actress will play a character from one of Baillie's tragedies, he also suggests that the strength of Baillie's playwriting lies in the "sympathetic curiosity" that her characters of passion engender in the audience.

Another way for students to interrogate Baillie's dramatic passions asks them to participate in an educational process that simulates what Baillie attempts to achieve in her dramas. Ask students to think back to elementary school experiences or to childhood recollections associated with civic or religious settings in which theatre was used as a teaching device. Students record their memories, and then respond to questions such as what makes the experience and its lesson memorable? How did the performance affect your thinking and/or feeling at the time? What makes spectacle, as Baillie reminds us, a powerful tool of instruction? What role did the passions play in the educational process? In this activity, students replicate a powerful Romantic-period tenet – the recollection of powerful emotions – in a theatricalized setting. They discover the potent legacy of Romantic theatre for contemporary education, a function of drama that Baillie theorized and enacted in her drama.

After students have reconstructed a personal experience that demonstrates the educational potential of theatre, they might read a selection from the conduct-book literature or a political treatise of the late eighteenth century that similarly recognizes the instructional power of spectacle. In *A Vindication of the Rights of Woman* (1792), for example, Wollstonecraft emphasizes the instructional power of spectacle interpreted by a passionate identification between the viewer and the scene:

> When we hear of some daring crime – it comes full on us in the deepest shade of turpitude, and raises indignation; but the eye that gradually saw the darkness thicken, must observe it with more compassionate forbearance. The world cannot be seen by an unmoved spectator, we must mix in the throng, and feel as men feel before we can judge of their feelings. If we mean, in short, to live in the world to grow wiser and better, and not merely to enjoy the good things of life, we must attain a knowledge of others at the same time that we become acquainted with ourselves – knowledge acquired any other way hardens the heart and perplexes the understanding.
>
> (239–40)

Wollstonecraft, like Baillie, asserts that in appealing to viewers' "sympathetic curiosity," to their passions, spectacles teach readers/spectators something about the world, about the human condition, and about themselves. Both writers recognize how the identificatory dynamic between staged characters and spectators contributes to the process of self-actualization, a goal, as we have seen, embraced by humanities courses in undergraduate curricula.

In reconstructing their own theatrical and educational memories, students can test Baillie's theory, one grounded upon pedagogical notions shared by other Romantic women writers, against their own experiences. Students might discuss how theatre functions as school, the importance of various media in collective socializing and instruction. From these discussions, students might synthesize more critical, less personal, observations about the role of theatre in cultural education and public conditioning. In working from the personal experiences toward the more critical assessments, students replicate in their minds the kind of "sympathetic curiosity" that Baillie asserted in her 1798 "Introductory Discourse" as the basis for her "Plays on the Passions." This activity can help students to recognize the powerful reclamation of passions as teacher that Baillie's theory and dramas accomplished for Romantic-period uses.

Cultural contexts for teaching Baillie's dramas

For students to understand the lessons that Baillie's plays might have imparted to late eighteenth- and early nineteenth-century audiences, however, it is helpful to reconstruct some cultural contexts with which the plays were engaged. In this section, I will turn to ways in which specific cultural expositions and critiques when applied to representative plays can demonstrate the pedagogical function of theatre in Baillie's theory and the various ways in which passions signal those contexts.

Because the three plays in the 1798 "Plays on the Passions" occur at a historical moment fraught with political and social revolution, they too participate in the debates about the rights of men and women that followed the French Revolution. *De Monfort, Count Basil*, and *The Tryal* politicize gender and class categories as cultural practices that can, therefore, be analyzed and reconceptualized. The excessive passions of hatred and love are played out by characters who resist conventionally assigned gendered emotions and behaviors. These unexpected characterizations prompt the audience to think about how, by disrupting customary and habitual patterns of gender in private or public spaces, the plays interrogate male and female performances in social systems that commodify women. Similarly, the disguises characters adopt in the plays ironically unmask the performativity of social roles, real and imagined, to the audience who, unlike those onstage, can see what lies behind the masks and costumes. Students might also find themselves puzzled by the seemingly unresolved conclusions of the plays. The discomfort that these endings engender illuminates the cultural conflicts in the plays that cannot be satisfactorily resolved. These plays are thus instructional case studies of how to perceive and negotiate the destabilized social and political dimensions of late eighteenth-century British culture, and they invite audiences to think critically about the structures and institutions shaping their lives and to take an active role in the restructuring of post-revolutionary socio-political order.[7]

Other plays such as *Constantine Paleologus; or, The Last of the Caesars* (1804) and *The Family Legend* (1810) rely on historical moments of political and social turmoil within the plays (a fifteenth-century battle between Greeks and Turks in Constantinople and a fifteenth-century

Highlands feud between the Argyll and Maclean clans) in order to teach their audiences how to cope with the political stresses of their day (Napoleonic Wars and British colonization).[8] *The Bride, The Beacon*, and *The Martyr* (1826) also expose British commercial and imperial activities that cause audiences to question the ethnocentricity of the "civilizing mission" Britain purports to achieve in its actual policies and practices. These plays portray in provocative ways the powerful part that seemingly benevolent religious education plays in the colonizing enterprise, in turn educating British audiences about the political projects that are disguised as humanitarian.

The Gothic provides another avenue of entry into Baillie's plays as educational theatre. *De Monfort* might be approached as a psychological and cultural study in madness – an excess of passion that late eighteenth- and early nineteenth-century audiences found fascinating. Mary Shelley's novella *Mathilda* (written in 1819), Percy Shelley's tragedy *The Cenci* (1820), Matthew Lewis's monodrama *The Captive* (1803), Sophia Lee's tragedy *Almeyda; Queen of Granada* (1796), Charles Robert Maturin's tragedy *Bertram; or, The Castle of St. Aldobrand* (1816), James Boaden's *The Romance of the Forest* (1794) and Baillie's Gothic dramas *Orra* (1812), *The Phantom* and *Witchcraft* (1836) can also be read in relation to *De Monfort* and in the cultural context of Gothic treatments of madness.[9] The tragedy of *Orra* features, as Baillie's Preface to the third volume of "Plays on the Passions" explains, fear of ghosts that cannot be eradicated from the mind. The Gothic was, of course, a way for early nineteenth-century writers to explore psychological responses and socially taboo subjects. Baillie remarks that anyone who can hold intercourse with supernatural beings and be devoid of fear is unnatural and represents "an instance of mental monstrosity" (229). *Orra* is tragically deceived by the legends of ancestral ghosts and the staging of an avenging spectre, and in writing this Gothic tragedy Baillie may have recollected the successful storytelling episodes and impromptu theatricals that were a salient part of her own educational experiences. In examining *Orra*'s hysterical responses to supernatural stories and phenomena, the audience is provoked to question its own uncritical acceptance of superstition as tradition and fiction as fact. Students might consider how the Gothic conceals as well as reveals individual and cultural madness and how that madness – viewed as excessive passion – functions pedagogically.

Like *Orra*, *The Phantom* explores optical and imaginative verifications of the supernatural, but in this play the ghost actually "appears" onstage, horrifyingly delightful to the audience but also pressing the audience into reconceptualizing phantasmagoria against the Gothic tradition of the past and in light of the scientific revolution of the early nineteenth century. *Witchcraft* also plays with a Gothic/past and scientific/present dichotomy in its staging of a woman-demon, a creature ostracized by religious and cultural mores. The grotesquely strangled body displayed onstage impels the audience to read and interpret the body in the context of competing conceptual paradigms – superstition and science. For this play, the theatre has been rendered an anatomical clinic where the body and its passions are examined, an educational arena that Baillie may have remembered from her uncle and brother's medical theatres on Great Windmill Street.

In connection with the Gothic, we can introduce the influence of scientific activities and medical practices that rendered what I term "techno-gothic grotesques and ghosts" – Gothic conventions infused with new significations by scientific and medical discourses and experimentation (technologies) of the late eighteenth and early nineteenth centuries. The spectacular staging of science may, in fact, explain the predominance of the Gothic and melodrama as dramatic genres during the Romantic period. While Gothic drama, including that written by Baillie, is often associated with cultural hysteria in response to the political turbulences of the day, the psychological and pathological responses of Gothic females, like Orra, and effeminate Gothic males, like De Monfort, can be seen as instances of medicine theatricalized. Madness and hysteria reflect ways in which cultural preoccupations about science were being staged. In the works of Franz Anton Mesmer, Thomas Beddoes, Thomas Trotter, George Cheyne, and Jane Marcet, for example, students will discover medical bases for the conditions enacted by Gothic characters in drama. In *Letters on Demonology and Witchcraft* (1831), Walter Scott diagnoses those who claimed to see apparitions as "mad," pathologically unbalanced, deceived by a "lively dream, a waking reverie, the excitation of a powerful imagination, or the misrepresentation of a diseased organ of sight" (344). Baillie's reading public would have been familiar with the powerful and electrifying influence of staged science as itinerant lecturers and "doctors" performed electrocutions of torpedo fish, intoxications by nitrous oxide as well as extravagant displays of magneticism and galvanization.

Baillie's readers would have recognized the historical associations of female healers and midwives with witchery, a connection that reclassified "wise" women as "evil" and "melancholic" and helped to legitimize the male medical profession of the day.[10] It was during this time that theories of hysteria were reintroduced into medical discourses, and physicians linked hysteria causally to female sexuality.[11] Medical discourses re-eroticized madness as a distinctly female disorder and recontextualized witches as neurotic, hysterical, psychotic, and emotionally disturbed women. In other words, women who did not perform the roles assigned by patriarchal culture were diagnosed as mad – techno-gothic grotesques outside the boundaries of "normative" society as classified by the period's scientific revolution. It is in the context of these medical "discoveries" that Baillie's drama *Witchcraft* portrays male figures of legal and ecclesiastical authority in collusion against women believed to be involved in witchery and explores how the seventeenth-century ecclesiastical condemnation of independent women had, during the course of the Romantic period, been replaced with an equally powerful check on female liberation – scientific and medical discoveries that pronounced women inferior in anatomy and in mind. Given the medical and scientific interests of Baillie's uncle and brother, as well as the general public, it is not surprising for her plays to offer revealing readings in this cultural context.[12] Students can research other scientific and medical activities that found their way into Baillie's dramas.

Students interested in feminist readings of Baillie's plays will find her work particularly promising in its portrayal of women's "romantic friendships." In *The Election* (1802), for example, Charlotte Freeman, age 15, and Isabella Baltimore, age 24, develop an engaging relationship despite the fact that Isabella's husband, Squire Baltimore, hates Charlotte's father, both being rivals for the same parliamentary seat of Westown, a small rural village in northern England. Students will discover that Charlotte and Isabella portray an alternative to heteroreality or compulsory heterosexism in how they act (bodies) and by what they say (language) as well as through how other characters read or misread them (performances). Even at a time when the cult of sensibility figured women's friendships as "intimate," Isabella and Charlotte experience an unconventional relationship. Their female connectedness also presents an alternative to the masculinist-driven hatred, the passion Baillie identifies as the focus of the play. Isabella's and Charlotte's pleasures are not limited by the social markers of gender/sex or class, and their relationship confounds meanings conventionally assigned to the female body and to female sexuality, an ambiguity or multivalence that Baillie supports as potentially revolutionary.[13]

Another point of cultural entry approaches these plays through considering theatre practices of the day.[14] Students might explore matters of "legitimate" theatre, stage design, costuming, make-up, special effects, and acting styles.[15] Students could investigate the leading performers of the day, the popular playwrights, and the actual theatres where plays were performed. Students need to ask, who comprised the audiences that attended these theatres? What were the acting conditions (physical, auditory, visual) of these theatres? What contributions did women make to the theatre?[16] Graduate students might research the performance history of a particular play. They could consider how *The Family Legend*, for example, might be performed differently for Scottish, English, and American audiences? How would the location of the performance alter the pedagogy of passions? What interpretative and therefore educational differences would specific performers lend to these productions? What cultural expectations and contexts would diverse audiences bring to the theatre?[17] Students might remember that Baillie's plays suggest metatheatrical discussions as they perform instructional critiques about drama and playacting. Part of Baillie's reclamation of theatre for education involves metatheatrical criticisms of drama, performance, and performativity. While a number of plays include metatheatrical moments, *The Tryal*, *The Election*, and *The Family Legend* are especially good for students to read as metatheatrical and meta-educational stagings.[18]

The Tryal, for example, makes its own pretense as theatre ironically powerful as a teaching strategy when it places women's sovereignty on trial repeatedly in the forms of Agnes's and Mariane's playwriting, directing, and acting, metatheatrics suggesting that the scripts that women perform in life as well as on the stage can be written. Connections between the courtroom and the theatre, like those between theatre and science, were commonplace in Britain's social unconscious by 1798, and Baillie finds pedagogical potential in the public fascination with theatrical trials, which, in *The Tryal*, she resituates as domestic comedy. Baillie adopts the disguise of playacting that had become a familiar female strategy for appearances in public-spaces.[19] The layered performances contained within the domestic space of *The Tryal* open up other safe spaces to subvert pejorative associations of "public" women, women of the theatre and the courtroom, for example, which denied their epistemological sovereignty. The metatheatrics of Baillie's comedy function pedagogically in exposing the fictions that women were, in actual society, forced to perform, drawing aside the curtain of an epistemology constructed to deny women's sovereignty in thinking and learning. Students might explore other forms of mind control that limit critical or innovative thinking and are held in place by social power.

As I have suggested, the pedagogical function that Baillie's theoretical statements connect to theatre is uncovered by readings of her plays in relation to historical contexts (French Revolution, Napoleonic Wars, and emerging imperialism), in relation to genre (Gothic and scientific writing), and in relation to performance practices. Other strategies might situate her plays in relation to gender studies, class analysis, and comparative analysis of other literary texts.[20] In placing Baillie's dramas in these cultural contexts and with specific strategies for teaching Baillie's dramas that I suggested earlier, students can achieve the same kind of critical thinking and knowledge construction that Baillie theorizes. In some ways, Baillie's educational theory anticipates contemporary classroom practices and pedagogical approaches – especially those informed by feminism. Baillie's dramas seek to make passions intellectual, a pedagogical strategy that encourages theatre audiences to repossess themselves and then initiate social change, a predecessor to cognitive therapy. Her dramas unveil partial knowledge masquerading as generalized, universalized "truths" in which power resides. By depicting passions, Baillie's dramas demonstrate that cognition is possible for all women and that experiential knowledge is authoritative and therefore empowering. Her dramas encourage the kinds of reflective thinking and conceptual critiques that influenced the educational revolution of radical women in her day and inform the work of feminist teachers today.[21]

Community stagings of Baillie's plays

Recently, at Texas Tech University, we have experimented with public readings or community stagings of Baillie's dramas to make her work accessible to broader, community-based but campus-connected audiences. The first occasion for performing and interpreting Baillie's dramas occurred in September 2001 for the Women's League of the University Museum Guild, a group of museum benefactors, primarily women, who meet monthly in open forums. My presentation, entitled "The Impassioned British Romantics: Drama, Music, and Women," attempted to broaden my audience's awareness of Romantic-period writers, and particularly the contributions women made to the period's theatre and music. While playing recordings of piano trios by Clara Schumann and Fanny Mendelssohn and showing slides of British landscape and seascape paintings, I read, in character, representative speeches from Baillie's *Count Basil* and *De Monfort* as well as other dramatic selections from plays by Felicia Hemans and Elizabeth Inchbald. The setting for this stage, the University Museum Theatre, enabled me to create a one-person, one-hour show followed by a lively discussion that would be possible in various public spaces. We printed a program, and I prepared a handout indicating the names of the characters in the plays from which I read speeches.

To prepare my audience for my interpretative readings, I provided general biographical backgrounds of the women playwrights and musicians, trying, whenever possible, to tap into life experiences with which my audience could relate, such as writing drama as a respectable way of obtaining financial support for children, or male family members encouraging women to read and write, despite the period's gendered expectations about education. While this approach may not be as complicated theoretically as are our typical explorations of literary works, it is nonetheless important and appropriate for this audience. Next, I provided historical context about the licensing procedure for the legitimate, patent theatre in London – what kind of drama would have been performed and where. Finally, I provided just enough plot background for my audience to understand the representative passages I would be reading. I selected passages that I believed would provide points of connection between characters' and audience's experiences. From *De Monfort*, for example, I read the passage from Act II, Scene ii, in which Jane implores her brother to reveal what is disturbing him.

The role of Jane, I explained, was performed on the Romantic stage by Sarah Siddons, and I showed a slide of *The Tragic Muse* by Sir Joshua

Reynolds and explained something of the stardom of Siddons. To illustrate Siddons's powerful presence on the legitimate stages of Covent Garden and Drury Lane, I read Timothy Testy's comments from *The Miseries of Human Life*, purportedly recorded by James Beresford, from the tenth edition that appeared in 1825. Testy remembers seeing Siddons on the boards and exclaims: "I saw her once, myself; and I must own, she so effectually conjured me away to the supposed scene of action, that as often as she finished her speech, I was within an acre of leaping on the stage, and knocking down all the rest of the Dramatis Personae, for lugging me back again to Covent Garden – no, Drury-lane – it was before she took her last flight from one stage to the other" (I, 93).

The discussion of Romantic female stardom then gave way to an explication of the Romantic theatre, lighting, sound, stage design, audience decorum, and acting styles. Generally, the Women's League was excited to learn about women's contributions to British culture during the Romantic period. They were fascinated by the abilities of women like Baillie to overcome the social and political obstacles that sought to limit their participation in the public sphere. They were grateful to learn that our students were obtaining an understanding of the Romantic period that included women playwrights like Baillie – a much more diverse and complex understanding than what they could recall from their own high school and university courses in Romantic-period literature.

The second occasion for performing and interpreting British Romantic drama by women occurred in March 2002, as part of Women's History Month at Texas Tech University. As her culminating project for a graduate course in "Special Problems in Directing," Ph.D. student Priscilla Anderson directed drama students and faculty members in a performance of a parlour reading of excerpts from Baillie's *Count Basil*, *De Monfort*, and *The Election*, as well as selections from plays by Hemans and Inchbald. We secured an actual parlour from a faculty member's home, a house on the Texas Registry of Historical Homes. As dramaturge for the production, I selected the dramatic excerpts, provided critical background for the performers, attended rehearsals, wrote and read a script of contextual and critical commentary inserted between each scene performed by the parlour readers. We attempted to replicate a parlour reading such as might have been performed by members of the Bluestockings or a private reading of a work in progress, such as one that might have occurred among those in the Shelley Circle.[22] The production was entitled "A Peep into the Parlour: Staging British Romantic Women Playwrights." We gathered a diverse audience of students, faculty, and community members, and we invited them one evening to participate meta-theatrically, to "peep" for one evening into the parlour of such a reading, an "un-closeting" of Romantic drama by women playwrights.

As in my Women's League Museum presentation, I provided cultural, historical, biographical, and plot-line contexts appropriate for each excerpt to be performed. My script suggested specific clues for the audience to listen for, as I guided their reception to the dramatic segment. The clues were sometimes suggested by the printed page itself, but sometimes they reflected the director's interpretative promptings. Thus, audience attention, sometimes focused on my contextual script and sometimes engaged by the players' reading, was directed by the tandem of page and stage. In preparation for Scene iv of Act II in *Count Basil*, for example, I made the following remarks:

> In this scene, we will peep in on a conversation among Victoria, the Countess of Albini, and Isabella, a lady attending upon Victoria. Isabella and Victoria are playing chess, while the Countess of Albini is reading. Notice, however, how Victoria plays with the youth Mirando, who enters the scene, an indication that Victoria is not aware of the power of love. Notice also, how our parlour participants perform the gender-bending that characterizes Baillie's dramas.

The character of Mirando was in fact played by a young woman who cross-dressed for the scene. For the broad-based, community audience, I was deliberate, conscious, and explicit about how I prepared them for the scene they were about to experience. In other words, I allowed my community audience less of an open discovery process in learning about dramas by Baillie and other Romantic women than I do students in my classes.

While my commentary told the community audience what to listen for in the parlour-reading scenes, my concluding summation recapitulated what the audience may have perceived from the evening's performance. I helped the audience synthesize with the following peroration:

> In these excerpts, we have seen the conflation of domestic and cultural politics, of private and public spaces, so as to give woman a newly defined place in the world of the early nineteenth century, a world that was being shaped by political revolutions, British class destabilizations, commercialized imperialism, educational changes, scientific and medical discoveries, redefined familial and sexual identifications, as well as first-wave feminism. We have seen gendered behaviors inverted, disguised, and performative. We have heard passions expressed by women playwrights through strong female characters. We have witnessed meta-dramatic and meta-theatrical scenes exposing the artificiality of social roles. We have perceived that drama could serve as a pedagogical instrument, and these plays dramatically depict the need for restructuring successful leadership, codes of conduct that embrace women's ways of being and feminist thought. As feminist foremother Mary Wollstonecraft maintains in her 1792 treatise *A Vindication of the Rights of Woman*, to change society,

there must first be changes in what and how people think. We have, quite frankly, peeped into a parlour negotiating Romantic-period literary, epistemological, and cultural changes, and as Lord Baltimore's friend Truebridge remarks at the end of Baillie's comedy *The Election*, "Now let us leave this happy nook."

The performers and audience alike thoroughly enjoyed the opportunity to get to know some dramas by Romantic women playwrights like Baillie, and they are anxious to know more, to investigate the possibilities of a full-stage production of a Baillie play.[23]

These public performances of Romantic dramas by women complement classroom explorations of dramatic texts and Romantic-period literature for English majors and graduate students. Playing a part in the productions has enriched my teaching of dramatic texts in class, has helped me to assign reading roles to students, and has helped me to emphasize the ways in which "acting" and "performance" serve as forms of knowledge-making in Romanticism and ways in which the stage was the locus of public education in the Romantic period. One of the immediately discernable consequences of the production of "A Peep into the Parlour" was a stronger connection between literary studies and theatrical performances, a cross-disciplinary connection that is especially important on our college campuses today. Our drama students need the theoretical and cultural contexts for Romantic drama, and our English students need to understand, perhaps even experience, the divergences and convergences of staged and read drama. "A Peep into the Parlour" also provided an occasion for faculty, graduate students, undergraduates, and community members to work and learn together, a leveling of hierarchy that put feminist theory into practice and that replicated class destabilizations engendered by the Romantic theatre.

Teaching texts of Baillie's drama

In closing, I want to comment briefly on the availability of teaching texts for Baillie's dramas. The 1996 edition of *British Literature, 1780–1830*, edited by Anne K. Mellor and Richard E. Matlak, includes the 1798 "Introductory Discourse" and *Count Basil*. Jeffrey N. Cox's 1992 anthology *Seven Gothic Dramas 1789–1825* includes *De Monfort. Joanna Baillie: A Selection of Poems and Plays*, edited by Amanda Gilroy and Keith Hanley in 1997, includes *Basil* and *De Monfort*, but it is an expensive edition. Adrienne Scullion's anthology *Female Playwrights of the Nineteenth Century* includes *The Family Legend*. In 2001 Broadview Press published Peter Duthie's edition of the first volume of "Plays on the Passions" and, in 2003, Jeffrey Cox and Michael Gamer's *The Broadview Anthology of Romantic Drama*, which contains Baillie's *Orra*. The online site for electronically edited plays, *British Women Playwrights around*

1800, will offer a hypertext of *De Monfort*, edited by Michael Eberle-Sinatra in 2003.[24] While I hope that in the next few years, we will see additional editions and anthologies of Romantic drama, especially plays by Baillie, suitable for classroom use, we may be increasingly looking to the technologies of electronic editing and hypertexts as alternatives to printed forms of drama. I have to wonder what the innovative Baillie, who could see so much pedagogical potential in theatre, would think about the possibilities of a virtual theatre of mind and technology. Could she imagine using this new medium to create a "sympathetic curiosity" between characters and participants in dramas staged in cyberspace? If a cyber-closet theatre were technologically engineered to foster an identificatory dynamic between characters and virtual participants, then I think Baillie would embrace the theatrical and educational promise of the simulative cyberstage.

Notes

1   See the chapters by Frederick Burwick and Alan Richardson in this volume.
2   Carhart reports from *Chambers's Edinburgh Journal* N.S. 15: 257.
3   Carhart (1923: 9) records Lucy Aikin's comments from Philip Le Breton's *Memoirs, Miscellanies and Letters of the Late Lucy Aikin* (London, 1864).
4   The excerpts to which I refer can be found on the CD recordings *Playhouse Aires: Eighteenth-Century English Theatre Music* and *Jane Austen Songs*.
5   Both Mellor (1994: 563–5) and I (1994: 35–8) discuss the importance of the opening processional scene in *Count Basil*.
6   For helpful discussions of Romantic theatre censorship and licensing, see L. W. Conolly (1976) and Marilyn Gaull (1988: 81–9).
7   For critical studies relevant to the social and political context of "Plays on the Passions" (1798), see Watkins' Marxist analysis of *De Monfort* (1993: 39–59); Mellor's socialist feminist discussion of *Count Basil* (1994: 559–67); and my historicist and feminist readings of *Count Basil* and *De Monfort* (Purinton 1994: 125–64) and of *The Tryal* (Purinton 2000).
8   Friedman-Romell considers Baillie's refinement of Christian Stoic philosophy and British stereotypes about Muslim barbarism in *Constantine Paleologus* (1999: 165–71). Hoagwood argues that Baillie celebrates the subordination of women in domesticity in *Constantine Paleologus* (2001: 308–11).
9   Cox (1992: 50–57) recognizes that Baillie owes a debt to the Gothic tradition while also reworking its conventions in her own construction of the feminine. Gamer (1997: 49–88) sees Baillie's use of the Gothic as a strategy that divorces her drama from the German novels that were popular and threatening at the end of the eighteenth century. Dowd (1998: 469–500) points to the gap between Baillie's theoretical prefaces and dramatic practices as the locus that reveals her critique of national interests and gender issues through the use of Gothic tropes.
10 See, for example, Ehrenreich and English (1973: 6–20) for their historical analyses of witchery and its connections to midwifery.
11 Micale (1995: 22–23) points to the period's medical association of hysteria and female sexuality. For a developed analysis of the causal links of hysteria to female sexuality, see Veith (1993).
12 I argue elsewhere (Purinton 2001: 139–56) that *Witchcraft*, by staging sixteenth- and seventeenth-century medical practices of domination, control,

and persecution of women, exposes the theoretical and fictive nature of medical science that essentializes sexed bodies.

13 Elsewhere, I read Baillie's *The Election* through the theoretical lens of French feminism and show how the play works against the prevailing phallocentric system of the early nineteenth century (Purinton 1998: 119–43).

14 Burroughs' "Teaching the Theory and Practice of Women's Dramaturgy" (1998) offers alternative pedagogical strategies related to theatre history.

15 For architectural designs and structures of eighteenth- and nineteenth-century theatres, see Leacroft (1988: 118–219). Burroughs' excellent analysis of acting styles in *De Monfort* and *Count Basil* is helpful (1997: 110–42).

16 Donkin (1995: 165–75) exposes the impediments to Baillie's efforts to stage her plays as well as contemporary criticism and reviews of her printed drama. Cox (2000: 23–47) examines the cultural power Baillie possessed and exercised, especially in relation to other women writers of her day. Crochunis (2000: 223–54) also discusses the power theatrical women such as Baillie could exert both on the stage and page of the day's drama.

17 For a discussion of the performance history of *Constantine Paleologus*, see Friedman-Romell (1999: 154–65), Carhart (1923: 154–5), and Nicoll (1927: 159). For a discussion of the performance history of *De Monfort*, see Zall (1982: 17–20), Carhart (1923: 110–42), Nicoll (1927: 225), Genest (1832: VII, 465–7), and Donkin (1995: 169, 173–5).

18 While Burroughs reads *The Tryal* as a private theatrical that celebrates women's cultural worth (1997: 143–68), I see it as a metatheatrical parody of courtroom drama and the portrayal of gender politics (Purinton 2000: 132–57). My analysis of the metadramatic treatment of *The Election* exposes the performative nature of relationships through the play's parody of parliamentary and patriarchal behaviors (1998: 119–30).

19 Ferris, for example, claims that an actress's acting on-stage is merely an extension and exposure of her "acting" off-stage. The "masquerade" gave women temporary immunity from "respectability" and an opportunity to play-act their fantasies and desires (1989: 149–53). Studies by Burroughs (1997: 51–66) and Pascoe (1997: 68–94) demonstrate the problematic relationship between the private and public Sarah Siddons, for example, and Pascoe reveals how Mary Robinson capitalized on her public acting image. Donkin outlines how Elizabeth Inchbald used on-stage/off-stage connections to her personal and professional advantages (1995: 110–31).

20 Brewer explores the mutual influences of Lord Byron and Baillie (1995: 165–81); Ross looks at the interactions between Felicia Hemans and Baillie (1989: 285–89).

21 Among the many discussions of feminist epistemology and pedagogy, those most useful in the context of Baillie's educational program include Minnich (1990), Jaggar (1989), Addelson (1993), Belenky *et al.* (1986), Duran (1991), Jipson and Munro (1999), Code (1993), Collins (1990), and Moylan (1999).

22 Burroughs (1997: 86–94) has discussed the value Baillie placed on a small, intimate theatrical space where public performances could be realistically staged.

23 At the 2002 meeting of the North American Society for the Study of Romanticism in London, Ontario, Frederick Burwick discussed the possibility of a full-stage performance of a Baillie play at Texas Tech University. He has successfully directed Baillie's *The Tryal* at UCLA. I am also encouraged by recent efforts to bring seventeenth- and eighteenth-century women playwrights' works to the stage by Mallory Catlett and Gwynn MacDonald and The Juggernaut Theatre Company in New York City. Their program entitled "The First 100 Years: The Professional Female Playwright" began with a

symposium on women playwrights of the seventeenth- and eighteenth-century English stage on October 26, 2002, a symposium that brought together scholars, playwrights, actors, and community members. Throughout 2002–3, this project featured numerous actors and companies giving readings at a variety of New York venues of plays by Aphra Behn, Susanna Centlivre, Hannah Cowley, Elizabeth Inchbald, and Joanna Baillie.

24 For a comprehensive bibliography of Baillie's dramas and scholarship about her work, see Bugajski's contribution to this volume.

14 Joanna Baillie

An annotated bibliography

Ken A. Bugajski

Notes on methodology and terminology

Although I endeavored to view as many of the sources as possible, limits of time and resources prevented me from examining each source listed here, especially those from the nineteenth century. I have placed an asterisk (*) before any source which I have not seen. In regard to reviews of Baillie's plays, I include references gathered from other resources (such as Carhart's biography and A. S. Ward's *Bibliography of Literature Reviews in British Periodicals*) and list them as reviews based on their date of publication and their proximity to the publication date for one of Baillie's works. In other words, reviews marked with an asterisk have the potential not to be a review of the work under which the review is listed, though this likelihood is small.

Baillie scholars may note that several references listed in the appendix of Margaret Carhart's biography are not included in this bibliography. In some cases, Carhart's citations appear, to the best of my knowledge, to be inaccurate; in others, Carhart notes a publication containing only a passing reference to Baillie. As these sources provide little critical evaluation of Baillie, I have omitted them from my bibliography.

Throughout this bibliography, I define works as "contemporary" if they were published during Baillie's lifetime, while "modern" sources are those published after Baillie's death in 1851. Abbreviations used in this bibliography include:

ADD	American Doctoral Dissertation
DA	Dissertation Abstracts
DAI	Dissertation Abstracts International
n. d.	no date
n. pag.	no pagination
n. pub.	no publisher
ns	new series
os	old series
ser.	series

Acknowledgments

I would like to thank Michael Eberle-Sinatra and *Romanticism on the Net* for permission to republish parts of my bibliography which appeared in a slightly different form in that journal. I would also like to thank the following people for their contributions to this project: Harrison T. Meserole for his annotations for the secondary criticism in German; Jeffrey Cox and Marjean Purinton for their help in an earlier phase of this project; Catherine Burroughs, Michael Gamer, Michael Laplace-Sinatra, Janice Patten, Julie Anderson, and Tricia Bugajski for reading and commenting on an early draft of the secondary criticism section; Judith Slagle for her willingness to share her research on Baillie's letters; James L. Harner for his always good advice and citation format expertise; and Tom Crochunis for his perpetual counsel throughout this project.

Outline

 I. Primary works
  A. Contemporary editions
   1. Dramatic works
    a. Multi-play volumes
    b. Plays published individually
   2. Non-dramatic works
   3. Collected works
   4. Works in anthologies or collections
    a. Complete works
    b. Selected poems and excerpts
   5. Edited works
   6. Adaptations and translations
   7. Miscellaneous
  B. Modern editions
   1. Dramatic works
    a. Individual volumes
    b. Complete dramas in anthologies
   2. Non-dramatic works
    a. Individual volumes
    b. Selected poems and dramatic excerpts
   3. Letters
    a. Letters written by Baillie
    b. Letters written to Baillie
  C. Manuscripts
   1. Published works
   2. Unpublished works
   3. Letters (major collections)
 II. Secondary works
  A. Biography
   1. Nineteenth century
   2. Twentieth century
   3. Biographical dictionaries
  B. Critical interpretations
  C. Dissertations

PART I, SECTION A1 – PRIMARY WORKS/CONTEMPORARY
EDITIONS/DRAMATIC WORKS

Multi-play volumes

Dramas. 3 vols. London: Longman, Hurst, Rees, Orme, and Brown, 1836.
Contains *Romiero*, *The Alienated Manor*, *Henriquez*, *The Martyr* (Vol. 1), *The Separation*, *The Stripling*, *The Phantom*, *Enthusiasm* (Vol. 2), *Witchcraft*, *The Homicide*, *The Bride*, and *The Match* (Vol. 3).
  Reviews:
  Athenæum 427 (2 Jan. 1836): 4–5.
  Blackwood's Edinburgh Magazine 39 (1836): 1–16.
  Edinburgh Review 63 (1836): 73–101.
  Fraser's Magazine 13 (1836): 236–49.
  Gentleman's Magazine ns 6 (1836): 3–15.
  London and Westminster Review 33 (1840): 401–24.
  Museum of Foreign Literature and Science 28 (1836): 458–68.
  (Reprints the review from the *Quarterly Review*, below.)
  Quarterly Review 55 (1835–6): 487–513.
  Performance reviews:
  Rev. of *Henriquez*. *Athenæum* 439 (26 Mar. 1836): 228.
  Rev. of *The Separation*. *Athenæum* 435 (27 Feb. 1836): 164.
  Rev. of *The Separation*. *Mirror of Literature, Amusement, and Instruction* 27 (1836): 155–8.
Miscellaneous Plays. London: Longman, Hurst, Rees, Orme, and Brown, 1804.
  *2nd ed. London: Longman, Hurst, Rees, and Orme, 1805.
  Includes the plays *Rayner*, *The Country Inn*, and *Constantine Paleologus*, or *The Last of the Caesars*.
  Reviews:
  Annual Review 3 (1804): 609–17.
  La Belle Assemblée 1 [Suppl.] (1806): 17–18.
  British Critic 27 (1806): 22–8.
  Critical Review 3rd ser. 4 (1805): 238–54.
  Eclectic Review 10 (1813): 21–32; 167–86.
  Edinburgh Review 5 (1805): 405–21.
  Imperial Review 3 (1805): 252–63.
  Lady's Monthly Museum 16 (1806): 201.
  Literary Journal 5 (1805): 49–64.
  London and Westminster Review 33 (1840): 401–24.
  Monthly Magazine 19 [Suppl.] (1805): 660.
  Monthly Mirror 19 (1805): 327–34; 398–403.
  Monthly Review 49 (1806): 303–10.
  New Annual Register 25 (1804): 351.
  Poetical Register 4 (1804): 506.
Plays. New York: Longworth, 1810.
  Contains *The Beacon*, *The Family Legend*, and *The Siege*.
A Series of Plays: In Which it is Attempted to Delineate the Stronger Passions of the Mind – Each Passion Being the Subject of a Tragedy

and a Comedy. 3 vols. London: Cadell and Davies (vols. 1 and 2); Longman, Hurst, Rees, Orme, and Brown (vol. 3), 1798–1812.

   *New ed. 3 vols. London: Longman, Hurst, Rees, Orme, and Brown, 1821.

*A Series of Plays: In Which it is Attempted to Delineate the Stronger Passions of the Mind – Each Passion Being the Subject of a Tragedy and a Comedy. Volume 1. London: Cadell and Davies, 1798.

   *2nd ed. London: Cadell and Davies, 1799.
   *3rd ed. London: Cadell and Davies, 1800.
   *4th ed. London: Cadell and Davies, 1802.
   *5th ed. London: Longman, Hurst, Rees, and Orme, 1806.

      Contains the "Introductory Discourse," *Count Basil, The Tryal*, and *De Monfort*.

Reviews:

   *Analytical Review 27 (1798): 524–8.
   British Critic 13 (1799): 284–90.
   *Critical Review ns 24 (1798): 13–22.
   *Imperial Magazine 1 (1804): 335–44; 2 (1804): 89–97.
   *Lady's Monthly Museum 13 (1804): 126–7.
   *Literary Leisure 1 (1800): 221–34.
   London and Westminster Review 33 (1840): 401–24.
   Monthly Magazine 5 [Suppl.] (1798): 507–08.
   Monthly Mirror 11 (1801): 112–14; 14 (1802): 258–9.
   Monthly Review 27 (1798): 66–9.
   *New London Review 1 (1799): 72–4.

Performance reviews:

   Dutton, Thomas. Rev. of *De Monfort. Dramatic Censor* 2 (1800): 112–18; 127–33.
   Rev. of *De Monfort. European Magazine* 37 (1800): 384–6.
   Rev. of *De Monfort. Monthly Magazine* 9 (1800): 487.

*A Series of Plays: In Which it is Attempted to Delineate the Stronger Passions of the Mind – Each Passion Being the Subject of a Tragedy and a Comedy. Volume 2. London: Cadell and Davies, 1802.

   *2nd ed. London: Cadell and Davies, 1802.
   *3rd ed. London: Longman, Hurst, Rees, and Orme, 1806.

   Includes *The Election, Ethwald* (parts one and two), and *The Second Marriage*.

Reviews:

   *Annual Review 1 (1802): 680–5.
   British Critic 20 (1802): 184–94.
   Critical Review ns 37 (1803): 200–12.
   Edinburgh Review 2 (1803): 269–86.
   European Magazine 42 (1802): 126.
   London and Westminster Review 33 (1840): 401–24.
   Monthly Review 43 (1804): 31–9.
   New Annual Register 23 (1802): 319.
   Poetical Register 2 (1802): 449–50.

*A Series of Plays: In Which it is Attempted to Delineate the Stronger Passions of the Mind – Each Passion Being the Subject of a Tragedy

and a Comedy. Volume 3. London: Longman, Hurst, Rees, and Orme, 1812.

    Contains *Orra, The Dream, The Siege,* and *The Beacon.*

    Reviews:

        British Critic 40 (1812): 554–9.

        British Review 3 (1812): 172–90.

        *Critical Review 4th ser. 1 (1812): 449–62.

        *Eclectic Review 10 (1813): 21–32; 167–86.

        *Edinburgh Magazine ns 2 (1818): 517–20.

        Edinburgh Review 16 (1811–12): 261–90.

        Monthly Magazine 14 [Suppl.] (1802–03): 600.

        Monthly Review 69 (1812): 382–93.

Plays published individually

*Basil: A Tragedy. Philadelphia: Carey and Lea, 1811.

*The Beacon: A Serious Musical Drama, in Two Acts. New York: Longworth, 1812.

    **London: Strahan and Preston, 1815.

*The Bride: A Drama in Three Acts. London: Colburn, 1828.

    **Philadelphia: Neal, 1828.

    **Philadelphia: Diggens, 1828.

*De Monfort: A Tragedy in Five Acts. London: Longman, Hurst, Rees, and Orme, 1807.

    **New York: Longworth, 1809.

*The Dream: A Tragedy in Prose, in Three Acts. New York: Longworth, 1812.

*The Election: A Comedy in Five Acts. Philadelphia: Carey, 1811.

*The Family Legend: A Tragedy. Edinburgh: John Ballantyne; London: Longman, Hurst, Rees, Orme, and Brown, 1810.

    **New York: Longworth, 1810.

    2nd ed. Edinburgh: Ballantyne, 1810.

    Performance reviews:

        British Critic 38 (1811): 53–9.

        *Eclectic Review 10 (1813): 21–32, 167–86.

        *Edinburgh Monthly Magazine 1 (1810): 47–9.

        *Glasgow Magazine 1 (1810): 140–8.

        *Hibernia Magazine 1 (1810): 336.

        Monthly Mirror ns 7 (1810): 313–14.

        Monthly Review 69 (1812): 382–93.

        Poetical Register 8 (1810–11): 595–6.

        Scots Magazine 72 (1810): 103–07.

*The Martyr: A Drama, in Three Acts. London: Longman, Hurst, Rees, Orme, Brown, and Green, 1826.

    Reviews:

        *La Belle Assemblée 3rd ser. 3 (1826): 267.

        *Inspector 1 (1826): 130.

        *Lady's Magazine ns 7 (1826): 246–8.

        *Literary Gazette 484 (1826): 260–61.

        Monthly Review 3rd ser. 2 (1826): 174–84.

        New Monthly Magazine 18 (1826): 230.

Panoramic Miscellany 1 (1826): 665–68.
Orra: A Tragedy in Five Acts. New York: Longworth, 1812.
The Siege: A Comedy in Five Acts. New York: Longworth, 1812.

PART I, SECTION A2 – PRIMARY WORKS/CONTEMPORARY EDITIONS/NON-DRAMATIC WORKS

Ahalya Baee: A Poem. London: [Printed for private circulation by] Spottiswoode and Shaw, 1849.

*"The Bonny Boat." *Cole's Selection of Scottish Melodies 2*. Baltimore: Cole, 1800.
  *Hartford: Kappel, n. d. [1830–39].

*"Epilogue to the Theatrical Representation at Strawberry-Hill." 1800. An epilogue for Mary Berry's *Fashionable Friends*, published as a broadside. Reprinted in *The Dramatic and Poetical Works of Joanna Baillie: Complete in One Volume*, listed in Primary/Contemporary/Collected, below.

"Epistles to the Literati, No. 9." *Fraser's Magazine* 14 (1836): 748–9. Responds to the *Quarterly Review*'s appraisal of her *Dramas*, specifically the character of Romiero. Argues that Romiero possesses dignity and nobility, and compares her hero to Othello.

Fugitive Verses. London: Moxon, 1840.
  *New ed. London: Moxon, 1842
  *London: Moxon, 1864.
  Reviews:
    Athenæum 691 (23 Jan. 1841): 69–70.
    Quarterly Review 67 (1841): 437–52 (Although a review of *Fugitive Verses*, almost fifty percent of the review discusses the "Plays on the Passions," especially *De Monfort*).

*Metrical Legends of Exalted Characters. London: Longman, Hurst, Rees, Orme, and Brown, 1821.
  *2nd ed. London: Longman, Hurst, Rees, Orme, and Brown, 1821.
  Reviews:
    Eclectic Review ns 16 (1821): 428–42.
    Edinburgh Magazine ns 8 (1821): 260–5.
    European Magazine 79 (1821): 239–42.
    Lady's Monthly Museum ns 13 (1821): 158.
    Literary Chronicle 94 (3 March 1821): 129–32.
    Literary Gazette 214 (1821): 113–15.
    Monthly Review 2nd ser. 96 (1821): 72–81.
    New Edinburgh Review 1 (1821): 393–414.

Poems: Wherein It Is Attempted to Describe Certain Views of Nature and of Rustic Manners; And Also, To Point Out, In Some Instances, the Different Influence Which the Same Circumstances Produce on Different Characters. London: Johnson, 1790.
  While this volume is listed in the *New Cambridge Bibliography of English Literature* and mentioned in several works, including Carhart's biography, as the first edition of *Fugitive Verses*, Roger Lonsdale has correctly identified this title as Baillie's first published volume.

A View of the General Tenour of the New Testament Regarding the Nature and Dignity of Jesus Christ: Including a Collection of the Various Passages in the Gospels, Acts of the Apostles, and the Epistles which Relate to that Subject. London: Longman, Rees, Orme, Brown and Green, 1831.

A View of the General Tenour of the New Testament Regarding the Nature and Dignity of Jesus Christ: Including a Collection of the

Various Passages in the Gospels, Acts of the Apostles, and the Epistles which Relate to that Subject. To Which Are Now Added a Correspondence with the Late Bishop of Salisbury, Together with Remarks on the Pre-Existence of Christ, and on Toleration and Fanaticism. 2nd ed. London: Taylor, 1838.

PART I, SECTION A3 – PRIMARY WORKS/CONTEMPORARY
EDITIONS/COLLECTED WORKS

The Complete Poetical Works. Philadelphia: Carey and Lea, 1832.
The Dramatic and Poetical Works of Joanna Baillie: Complete in One Volume.
   London: Longman, Brown, Green and Longmans, 1851.
      *2nd ed. London: Longman, Brown, Green and Longmans, 1853.
   Reviews:
      Athenæum 1211 (11 Jan. 1851): 41.
      Eclectic Review ns 1 (1851): 407–23.

PART I, SECTION A4 – PRIMARY WORKS/CONTEMPORARY EDITIONS/WORKS IN ANTHOLOGIES OR COLLECTIONS

Complete works

*Baillie, Joanna. *Basil: A Tragedy in Five Acts*. Philadelphia: Palmer, 1823.
   Published with Thomas Otway's *The Orphan, or, The Unhappy Marriage*.
* ——. *The Beacon*. London: Longman, n. d.
   Published with Robert Jephson's *The Count of Narbonne*, Robert Francis
   Jameson's *The Students of Salamanca*, and David Garrick's *The Country Girl*.
*——. *The Beacon. Select Plays*. 2 vols. New York: Longworth, 1813.
   Published with *The Bankrupt, The Liar*, and *The Orators* by Samuel Foote and
   The Peasant Boy by W. Dimond.
——. *De Monfort: A Tragedy in Five Acts. The British Theatre, or, A Collection of
   Plays*. Vol. 24.
   Ed. Elizabeth Inchbald. London: Longman, Hurst, Rees, and Orme, 1808.
   *2nd ed. London: Longman, Hurst, Rees, Orme, and Brown, 1816.
   Published with *The Road to Ruin* and *The Deserted Daughter* by Thomas
   Holcroft, *The Stranger* by Benjamin Thompson, and *Point of Honour* by
   Charles Kemble.
   For Inchbald's introduction, see Secondary/Critical, below.
*Baillie, Joanna, and Joseph Gostick. *Fugitive Verses, with* The Spirit of German
   Poetry: A Series of Translations from the German Poets. London: Smith, 1845.

Selected poems and excerpts

Note: For this section, I have listed the poems as they appear in each volume, including variations in titles and of spelling. However, in cases where the collection titled one of Baillie's lyrics as "Song," I have instead given the first line.

Bethune, George W. , ed. *The British Female Poets: With Biographical and Critical
   Notices*. New York: Hurst, 1848. Essay Index Reprint Series. Freeport: Books for
   Libraries, 1972. 159–80.
   Prints brief excerpts from *Ethwald, Rayner, Orra, The Beacon, The
   Separation* and "The Kitten." Also includes "The Travellers by Night,"
   "Reveille," "The Chough and the Crow" [from *Orra*], "Bridal Song,"
   "Serenade," "Hymn of the Martyr," "Wished-for gales the light vane veering,"
   "Where distant billows meet the sky," and "The gliding fish that takes his
   play."
Chambers, Robert, ed. *Cyclopedia of English Literature: A History, Critical and
   Biographical, of British Authors, from the Earliest to Present Times*. 2 vols.
   Edinburgh: Chambers, 1844. 451–3, 511–14.
   Includes "The Kitten," "Address to Miss Agnes Baillie on Her Birthday," and
   scenes from *De Monfort, Orra*, and *Ethwald*.
Hall, S. C., ed. *The Book of Gems*. 3 vols. London: Bohn, 1849. 3:268–73.

Prints Baillie's "To a Child," "The Kitten," and "O welcome bat and owlet gray."

*Inglis, Robert. *Gleanings from the English Poets, Chaucer to Tennyson.* Edinburgh and London: Gall and Terrace, 1881.

Prints Baillie's "Picture of Country Life."

Rowton, Frederic. *The Female Poets of Great Britain.* London: Longman, Brown, Green, and Longmans; Philadelphia: Carey and Hart, 1849. 287–306.

Reprints "To a Child," "A Mother to Her Waking Infant," "What voice is this, thou evening gale," "The Grave of Columbus," and scenes from *De Monfort* and *Henriquez.* For Rowton's critical assessment, see Secondary/Critical, below.

*Scott, Walter. *English Minstrelsy. Being a selection of fugitive poetry from the best English authors; with some original pieces hitherto unpublished.* 2 vols. Edinburgh: Ballantyne, 1810.

Prints "The Kitten," "The Heathcock," and a song.

PART I, SECTION A5 — PRIMARY WORKS/CONTEMPORARY EDITIONS/EDITED WORKS

Baillie, Joanna, ed. *A Collection of Poems, Chiefly Manuscript, and from Living Authors*. London: Longman, Hurst, Rees, Orme, and Brown, 823.

> Prepared for a Mrs. Stirling, a friend of Baillie's who had fallen into financial straits. Contains poetry from many notable poets of the day, including Anna Barbauld, General Alexander Dirom (see O'Reilly, Primary/Modern/Letters/By Baillie, below), Felicia Hemans, Sir Walter Scott, William Sotheby, Robert Southey, and Baillie herself. Includes Baillie's "A Volunteer Song," "To Mrs. Siddons," "To a Child," "Address to a Steam Vessel," "A November Night's Traveller," and "Sir Maurice."

Reviews:

> *British Critic* ns 19 (1823): 551–5.
>
> *Eclectic Review* ns 20 (1823): 264–76.
>
> *Monthly Review* 2nd ser. 103 (1824): 410–17.

*———. *Occasional Verses: To Which Are Added, Extracts from Letters, &c.* By Sophia Baillie. London: [L. Miller], 1846.

> Contains poems and letters of Baillie's sister-in-law, collected after her death.

PART I, SECTION A6 – PRIMARY WORKS/CONTEMPORARY EDITIONS/ADAPTATIONS AND TRANSLATIONS

*Beethoven, Ludwig van, arr. "O Swiftly Glides the Bonny Boat: A Scotch Air." Baltimore: Cole, 1822.

    *New York: Dubois and Stodart, 1824.

    *New York: Geib and Walker, n. d.

*Cramer, Karl Friedrich, trans. *Ethwald, ein Traurspiel in funf Acten.* [Amsterdam]: Rohloff, 1807.

    A translation of the second volume of *A Series of Plays.*

**The Election: A Comic Opera in Three Acts.* Ms. 1971. Henry E. Huntington Library, Larpent Collection of Plays, California.

    FirstSearch states that the play is "Altered from Joanna Baillie," but gives no information on who altered it.

*Horn, Charles Edward, arr. " 'Tis Love in the Heart: The Admired Rondo [from *The Election*]." Words by Samuel J. Arnold. Philadelphia: Blake, n. d.

    *London: Williams, 1819.

    A song from *The Election* altered by Arnold, FirstSearch states, "with the approbation of the authoress."

*Kemble, John Philip. *De Monfort: A Tragedy in Five Acts.* Ms. 1287. Henry E. Huntington Library, Larpent Collection of Plays, California.

    According to Jeffrey N. Cox in *Seven Gothic Dramas*, this manuscript reworks *De Monfort* by making use of contemporary sources (232).

*Schreiter, H. G. , trans. *Basil: A Tragedy.* Altenberg: n. pub., 1807.

    A translation of *Count Basil* into German.

Thomson, George. *The Select Melodies of Scotland, Interspersed with Those of Ireland and Wales.* 5 vols. London: Preston; Edinburgh: Thomson, 1822.

    Includes "O welcome bat and owlet gray," "The gowan glitters on the sward," "Woo'd and Married and A'," "Poverty Parts Good Company," "The Note of the Black Cock," "The Maid of Llanwellyn," "The morning air plays on my face," "Hooly and Fairly," "Now bar the door, shut out the gale," and "O Swiftly Glides the Bonny Boat." Composers for Baillie's lyrics include Kozeluch, Beethoven, and Haydn.

Review:

Edinburgh Review 39 (1823–24): 67–84.

PART I, SECTION A7 — PRIMARY/CONTEMPORARY/ MISCELLANY

*Baillie, Joanna. *De Monfort*. Huntington Manuscript 32693. Huntington Library. California, United States.

   According to Jeffrey N. Cox in *Seven Gothic Dramas*, this manuscript appears in the hand of Thomas Campbell, who prepared it for Sarah Siddons, Jane De Monfort in the original production (232). Siddons added her own marginal notes to this manuscript.

*Bishop, Henry R. *The Overture, Songs, Duett, Glees and Choruses, in the Musical Play of Guy Mannering*. Additional text by Joanna Baillie. London: Goulding, D'Almaine, and Potter, 1816.

*——. "The Chough and Crow to Roost Are Gone." Additional text by Joanna Baillie. London: Goulding, D'Almaine, and Potter, 1820.

   *2nd ed. Philadelphia: Blake, n. d.

   Originally from *Orra* and then transferred to *Guy Mannering*, this song was published separately after *The Overture, Songs, Duett, Glees and Choruses*.

*Shakespeare, William. *Shakespeare's Tragedy of Macbeth*.

   FirstSearch states that the "Folger Shakespeare Library's copy is Edwin Booth's promptbook for an unspecified production. Manuscript annotations include remarks about the play by Joanna Baillie, portraits of Edwin Booth as Macbeth, Charlotte Cushman as Lady Macbeth, [and] some prompt notes."

**PART I, SECTION B1 — PRIMARY WORKS/MODERN
EDITIONS/DRAMATIC WORKS**

Individual volumes

*The Dramatic and Poetical Works. Anglista and American 177. Hildesheim and
New York: Georg Olms Verlag, 1976. Reprints the 1851 edition of *The Dramatic
and Poetical Works of Joanna Baillie: Complete in One Volume.*
The Family Legend *and* Metrical Legends of Exalted Characters. Ed. and introd.
Donald H. Reiman. Romantic Context: Poetry. Significant Minor Poetry,
1789–1830. New York and London: Garland, 1976.
> Reprints the 1810 first edition of *The Family Legend*. For the annotation of
> the introduction, see Reiman, Secondary/Critical, below.
*Joanna Baillie: A Selection of Poems and Plays. Ed. Keith Hanley and Amanda
Gilroy. Brookfield: Pickering and Chatto, 1997.
Miscellaneous Plays. Ed. and introd. Donald H. Reiman. Romantic Context:
Poetry. Significant Minor Poetry, 1789–1830. New York and London: Garland,
1977.
> Reprints the 1804 first edition. For the annotation of the introduction, see
> Reiman, Secondary/Critical, below.
A Series of Plays. 3 vols. Ed. and introd. Donald H. Reiman. Romantic Context:
Poetry. Significant Minor Poetry, 1789–1830. New York and London: Garland,
1977.
> Reprints the first edition of each volume. For the annotation of the
> introduction, see Reiman, Secondary/Critical, below.
**A Series of Plays: In Which it is Attempted to Delineate the Stronger Passions of
the Mind*. Ed. Caroline Franklin. London: Routledge, 1996.
A Series of Plays, 1798. Ed. and introd. Jonathan Wordsworth. Oxford and New
York: Woodstock, 1990.
> Reprints the first edition of the first volume of *A Series of Plays*. For the
> annotation of the introduction, see Wordsworth, Secondary/Critical, below.

Complete dramas in anthologies

Count Basil. British Literature, 1780–1830. Ed. Anne K. Mellor and Richard E.
Matlak. Fort Worth: Harcourt Brace, 1996. 458–93.
> Prints the first edition of *Count Basil* as it appears in Jonathan Wordsworth's
> Woodstock facsimile edition (see this section, above).
*De Monfort. Romantic Tragedies. British Theatre: Eighteenth-Century English
Drama 20. Frankfurt: Minerva, 1969.
De Monfort. Seven Gothic Dramas, 1789–1825. Ed. Jeffrey N. Cox. Athens: Ohio
UP, 1992. 231–314.
> A critical edition based on the 1798 first edition text. Also considers the texts
> of a manuscript from 1800 (Larpent Ms. 1287, see Primary/Manuscripts/
> Published, below) and Campbell's manuscript version (Huntington Ms.

32693, see Primary/Contemporary Miscellany, above). For the annotation of Cox's introduction to *De Monfort* and reviews of this book, see Secondary/ Critical, below.

The Family Legend. Female Playwrights of the Nineteenth Century. Ed. Adrienne Scullion. Everyman's Library. London: Dent; Rutland: Tuttle, 1996. 3–74.

Reprints the 1810 first edition.

PART I, SECTION B2 — PRIMARY WORKS/MODERN EDITIONS/NON-DRAMATIC WORKS

Individual volumes

The Family Legend *and* Metrical Legends of Exalted Characters. Ed. and introd. Donald H. Reiman. Romantic Context: Poetry. Significant Minor Poetry, 1789–1830. New York and London: Garland, 1976.

> Reprints the 1810 first edition of *The Family Legend* and an 1821 edition of *Metrical Legends*. For the annotation of the introduction, see Reiman, Secondary/Critical, below.

*Joanna Baillie: A Selection of Poems and Plays. Ed. Keith Hanley and Amanda Gilroy. Brookfield: Pickering and Chatto, 1997.

Joanna Baillie: Poems, 1790. Ed. and introd. Jonathan Wordsworth. Revolution and Romanticism, 1789–1834. Oxford and New York: Woodstock, 1994.

> Reprints *Poems: Wherein It Is Attempted . . .* , Baillie's first published work. For the annotation of the introduction, see Wordsworth, Secondary/Critical, below.

*——. *Poems.* Akros Pocket Classics Series 20. Edinburgh: Akros, 1995.

Selected poems and dramatic excerpts

Note: As above, I have listed the poems as they appear in each volume, including variations in titles and of spelling. I have substituted the first line of poems identified only as "Song."

Abrams, M. H. , ed. *The Norton Anthology of English Literature.* 6th ed. 2 vols. New York: Norton, 1993.

> Reprints "Up! quit thy bower" and "Woo'd and Married and A'."

Armstrong, Isobel, Joseph Bristow, with Cath Sharrock, ed. *Nineteenth-Century Women Poets: An Oxford Anthology.* Oxford: Clarendon, 1996. 50–73.

> Prints "A Winter's Day," "A Summer's Day," "To a Child," "London," "Lines to a Teapot," "Address to a Steamvessel," and "Volunteer's Song, Written in 1803."

*Ashfield, Andrew. *Romantic Women Poets, 1770–1838.* New York: Manchester UP, 1995.

> Prints "An Address to the Night: A Fearful Mind," "London," "Address to a Steamvessel," and excerpts from "A Winter Day," "A Summer Day," "Thunder," "Wind," and "The Traveller by Night in November."

Breen, Jennifer, ed. *Women Romantic Poets, 1785–1832: An Anthology.* Everyman's Library. London: Dent; Rutland: Tuttle, 1992. 43–71.

> Includes "A Winter's Day," "A Summer's Day," "A Reverie," "A Disappointment," "A Mother to Her Waking Infant," "A Child to His Sick Grandfather," "Hooly and Fairly," and "What voice is this, thou evening gale!"

Dixon, W. Macneille, ed. *The Edinburgh Book of Scottish Verse*. London: Meiklejohn and Holden, 1910. Granger Index Reprint Series. Freeport: Books for Libraries, 1971. 535–40.

> Contains "The Fisherman's Song," "The Outlaw's Song" from *Orra* ["The chough and crow to roost are gone"], "The Shepherd's Song," ["The gowan glitters on the sward"], and "Saw ye Johnnie Comin'."

Feldman, Paula R. ed. *British Women Poets of the Romantic Era: An Anthology*. Baltimore: Johns Hopkins UP, 1997.

> Prints "Wind," "Thunder," "The Kitten," "Up! Quit Thy Bower," "Woo'd and Married and A'," "Address to a Steam Vessel," "The Sun is Down," "Lines to a Teapot," and "The Maid of Llanwellyn."

Fullard, Joyce, ed. *British Women Poets 1660–1800: An Anthology*. Troy: Whitston, 1990. 56–7, 146–8, 228–9, 458–63.

> Presents "London," an excerpt from "Address to the Muses," and several songs: "Child, with many a childish wile," "Upon her saddle's quilted seat," "Wake awhile and pleasant be," "Come, form we round a cheerful ring," "O swiftly glides the bonny boat," and "High is the tower, and the watch-dogs bay."

Hale, Sarah Josepha. *Woman's Record; or Sketches of All Distinguished Women from the Creation to A.D. 1854, Arranged in Four Eras with Selections from Female Writers of Every Age*. 2nd ed. , rev. New York: Harper, 1855. Rpt. History of Women 1780. New Haven: Research, 1975. 574–7.

> Includes passages from the following: *De Monfort, Henriquez, Orra, Romiero*, "Lady Griseld Baillie," "Christopher Columbus," and "Address to Miss Agnes on Her Birthday."

Higonnet, Margaret Randolph, ed. *British Women Poets of the 19th Century*. New York: Meridian-Penguin, 1996. 143–67.

> Prints "A Winter's Day," "A Summer's Day," "A Reverie," "A Mother to Her Waking Infant," "Address to the Muses," "London," and "Verses Written in February 1827."

Johnson, Rossiter, ed. *Works from the British Poets, from Chaucer to Morris, with Biographical Sketches*. 3 vols. New York: Appleton, 1876. 2:16–34.

> Contains "To a Child," "Christopher Columbus," "Lady Griseld Baillie," and "Lord John of the East." Includes a portrait of Baillie as the frontispiece for volume two.

Jump, Harriet Devine, ed. *Women's Writing of the Romantic Period, 1789–1836: An Anthology*. Edinburgh: Edinburgh UP, 1997. 61–3.

> Prints two brief passages from the "Introductory Discourse."

Kerrigan, Catherine, ed. *An Anthology of Scottish Women Poets*. Edinburgh: Edinburgh UP, 1991. 172–76.

> Includes "Poverty Parts Good Company," "Tam O' the Lin," "Woo'd and Married and A'," and "The Shepherd's Song."

Lonsdale, Roger, ed. *Eighteenth Century Women Poets: An Oxford Anthology*. Oxford and New York: Oxford UP, 1989. 429–45.

Reprints "A Reverie," "A Mother to Her Waking Infant," "A Child to His Sick Grandfather," "The Horse and His Rider," and excerpts from "A Winter Day," "A Summer Day," "An Address to the Muses," and "Night Scenes of Other Times."

——. *The New Oxford Book of Eighteenth Century Verse*. Oxford and New York: Oxford UP, 1984. 770–75.

Includes "A Disappointment," "A Mother to Her Waking Infant," "A Child to His Sick Grandfather," and "The Horse and His Rider."

McCordick, David, ed. *Scottish Literature: An Anthology*. 3 vols. New York: Lang, 1996. 2:217–25.

Contains "Disappointment," "Woo'd and Married and A'," "Fy, Let Us A' to the Wedding," "It Fell on a Morning," "The gowan glitters on the sward," "Love's Wistful Tale," "Wake, Lady," and "The Black Cock."

McGann, Jerome J., ed. *The New Oxford Book of Romantic Period Verse*. Oxford and New York: Oxford UP, 1993. 592–8.

Prints "The Ghost of Fadon."

Miles, Alfred H., ed. *The Poets and Poetry of the Nineteenth Century*. 12 vols. London: Routledge, 1905–07. New York: AMS Press, 1967. 8:1–16.

Presents "The chough and crow to roost are gone" from *Orra*, "Saw Ye Johnny Comin'?," "The Maid of Llanwellyn," "Poverty Parts Gude Companie," "Fy, Let Us A' to the Wedding," "The gowan glitters on the sward," "It Was on a Morn," "Woo'd and Married and A'," and "Good Night, Good Night" from *The Phantom*.

Milford, H. S., ed. *The Oxford Book of English Verse of the Romantic Period, 1798–1837*. Oxford: Clarendon, 1935. 49–51.

A reprint of *The Oxford Book of Regency Verse*, below.

——. *The Oxford Book of Regency Verse, 1798–1837*. Oxford: Clarendon, 1928. 49–51.

Prints brief excerpts from *The Country Inn* and *Orra*.

Mitford, Mary Russell. *Recollections of a Literary Life; Or, Books, Places and People*. London: Bentley, 1851; New York: Harper, 1852. Rpt. Women of Letters. New York: AMS, 1975. 152–7.

Reprints "The Black Cock," "Woo'd and Married and A'," and "O welcome bat and owlet gray." For Mitford's critical evaluation, see Secondary/Critical, below.

Oliver, John W. and J. C. Smith, ed. *A Scots Anthology from the Thirteenth to the Twentieth Century*. Edinburgh and London: Oliver and Boyd, 1949. 359–60.

Prints "The Trysting Bush."

Patrick, David and J. Liddell Geddie, ed. *Chambers's Cyclopædia of English Literature*. New ed. 3 vols. London and Edinburgh: Chambers, 1927. 2:729–34.

Includes "The Shepherd's Song," selections from "The Kitten," "Address to Miss Agnes Baillie on Her Birthday," and scenes from *De Monfort, Orra*, and *Ethwald*.

Peacock, W., ed. *English Verse*. 5 vols. World's Classics. London: Oxford UP, 1930. 3:533–8.

Contains "The Fisherman's Song," "The Outlaw's Song" from *Orra* ["The chough and crow to roost are gone"], "The Shepherd's Song," ["The gowan glitters on the sward"], "Oh welcome, bat and owlet gray," and "Hay Making."

*Perkins, David, ed. *English Romantic Writers*. 2nd ed. New York: Harcourt, 1995.

Includes "A Reverie," "A Mother to Her Waking Infant," "Woo'd and Married and A'," "The Ghost of Fadon," "The Kitten," and passages from the "Introductory Discourse."

Petersohn, Frank. *Folksongs of Various Countries*. <http://ingeb.org/songs/maidofll.html>. 9 October 2002.

Prints "The Maid of Llanwellyn" with a link to a melody for the lyric.

Quiller-Couch, Arthur. *The Oxford Book of English Verse*. Oxford: Clarendon, 1901.

Includes "The Outlaw's Song" ["The chough and crow to roost are gone"].

Robertson, Fiona, ed. *Scott*. Vol. 3 of *Lives of the Great Romantics II: Keats, Coleridge, and Scott, By Their Contemporaries*. London: Pickering and Chatto, 1997. 20–22.

Reproduces "Lines on the Death of Sir Walter Scott."

Rogers, Charles. *The Scottish Minstrel: The Songs of Scotland Subsequent to Burns*. 2nd ed. Brooklyn: Swayne, 1870.

Contains "The Maid of Llanwellyn," "Good Night, Good Night," "Though richer swains thy love pursue," "Poverty Parts Gude Companie," "Fy, Let Us A' to the Wedding," "Hooly and Fairly," "The Weary Pund O' Tow," "The Wee Pickle Tow," "The gowan glitters on the sward," "Saw Ye Johnnie Comin," "It Fell on a Morning," and "Woo'd and Married and A'."

Stanford, Ann, ed. *The Women Poets in English: An Anthology*. New York: Hender and Hender-McGraw Hill, 1972. 101–02.

Prints "The Trysting Bush."

Tytler, Sarah and J. L. Watson. *The Songstresses of Scotland*. London: Strahan, 1871. 2:311–34.

Includes "Wi' Lang-Legg'd Tam," "The Merry Bachelor," "Woo'd and Married and A'," "It Fell on a Morn when We Were Thrang," "Fy, Let Us A' to the Wedding," "Hooly and Fairly," "The Weary Pund O' Tow," "Tam O' the Lin," "The Wee Pickle Tow," "The Lover's Watch," "Poverty Parts Good Company," and "Saw Ye Johnny Comin." For Tytler's and Watson's introduction to the poems, see Secondary/ Biography/Nineteenth, below.

Uphaus, Robert W. and Gretchen M. Foster, ed. *The "Other" Eighteenth Century: English Women of Letters, 1660–1800*. East Lansing: Colleagues, 1991. 343–58.

Prints excerpts from the "Introductory Discourse" from the 1799 second edition of *A Series of Plays*.

Ward, Thomas Humphry, ed. *The English Poets: Selections with Critical Introductions by Various Writers*. 5 vols. London: Macmillan, 1880. 4:221–6.

Prints "The Chough and Crow," "The Fisherman's Song," "They who may tell love's wistful tale," and "Woo'd and Married and A'." For the annotation of the "Critical Introduction," see Robinson, Secondary/Critical, below.

Wu, Duncan, ed. *Romantic Women Poets: An Anthology*. Oxford: Blackwell, 1997. 254–60.

    Prints "The gowan glitters on the sward," "What voice is this, thou evening gale," and "Tam o' the Lin."

——. *Romanticism: An Anthology*. 2nd ed. Oxford: Blackwell, 1998. 153–4.

    Prints a brief passage from the "Introductory Discourse."

PART I, SECTION B3 – PRIMARY WORKS/MODERN EDITIONS/LETTERS

Letters written by Baillie

Major collections

*Lambertson, Chester Lee, ed. "The Letters of Joanna Baillie (1801–1832)." Diss. Harvard University, 1956. *American Doctoral Dissertations* (1956).

Slagle, Judith Bailey. *The Collected Letters of Joanna Baillie.* 2 vols. Madison: Fairleigh Dickinson UP, 1999.

> Covers over 800 of Baillie's previously unpublished letters to various correspondents, including Mary Berry, Lady Byron, John Gibson Lockhart, Sir Walter Scott, George Thomson, and family members.

Published in collections or journals

Douglas, David, ed. *Familiar Letters of Sir Walter Scott.* 2 vols. Edinburgh: Douglas, 1894.

> Prints eight letters from Baillie to Scott; subjects include reactions to Scott's *House of Aspen, Rokeby,* and *The Bride of Lammermoor,* impressions upon meeting Maria Edgeworth, Abbotsford, the separation of Lord and Lady Byron, and Byron's *Giaour.* Also prints several letters from Scott to Baillie, see this section, below.

Lambertson, C[hester] L[ee], ed. "Speaking of Byron." *Malahat Review* 12 (1969): 18–42; 13 (1970): 24–46.

> Includes nine letters in volume twelve; subjects include Byron's *Corsair,* Byron's appreciation of *De Monfort* and his influence at Drury Lane, Scott's trip to France and subsequent poem on Waterloo, the Byrons' separation, and the future marriage of Baillie's niece. Presents seven letters in volume thirteen; subjects include Baillie's trip to Europe with her niece, the characters of Lord and Lady Byron, contemporary writers such as Byron and Edgeworth, publishing poetry, and Scott's reactions to and Baillie's revisions of "Christopher Columbus."

MacPherson, Gerardine. *Memoirs of the Life of Anna Jameson.* London: Longmans, 1878.

> Reprints three letters from Baillie to Jameson which include favorable comments on Jameson's "Winter Studies," expressions of sorrow concerning the death of Dr. Channing, and laments for the moral state of Scotland. For MacPherson's impressions of Baillie, see MacPherson, Secondary/Biography/ Nineteenth, below.

O'Reilly, W. H. , ed. "Unpublished Letters of Joanna Baillie to a Dumfriesshire Laird." *Dumfriesshire and Galloway Natural History and Antiquarian Society: Transactions and Journal of Proceedings* 18 (1934): 10–27.

Contains eleven letters (ranging from 1821 to 1827) from Baillie to General Alexander Dirom, a military leader, author, and friend. Subjects include mutual friends, invitations to visit, and literary matters such as: Baillie's thanks to Dirom for kind words about her *Metrical Legends* and *The Martyr*, her positive feedback on Dirom's own work, a discussion of Baillie's meetings with the publisher, Longman, on Dirom's behalf, a mention of Ahalya Baee as a "perfect female character," and a solicitation to Dirom for a poem to include in her 1823 *A Collection of Poems, Chiefly Manuscript*.

Partington, Wilfred, ed. *The Private Letter-Books of Sir Walter Scott: Selections from the Abbotsford Manuscripts, with a Letter to the Reader from Hugh Walpole*. London: Hodder and Stoughton; New York: Stokes, 1930.

Includes three letters by Baillie in which she discusses her niece's impending marriage, *Guy Mannering*, recent theatrical productions, and Scott's *Life of Napoleon*.

——. *Sir Walter's Post-Bag: More Stories and Sidelights from His Unpublished Letters*. London: Murray, 1932.

Presents extracts from several of Baillie's letters; subjects include William Wordsworth and Robert Southey, reactions to *The Knight of Snowdon*, London, her thoughts about producing an economical version of *The Family Legend*, the preservation of national forests, a French memorial to Voltaire, Lady and Lord Byron, Charles I, daily life, Scott's baronetcy, payment for poetry, and the journey from Abbotsford to London.

Sutton, Denys, ed. "Joanna Baillie and Sir George Beaumont, Bart." *Notes and Queries* 174 (1938): 146–8.

Includes three letters from Baillie to Sir George Beaumont in which Baillie solicits Beaumont's influence to help a Mr. Bell's election to the Royal Academy.

Letters written to Baillie

Colvin, Christina E. "Maria Edgeworth's Tours in Ireland, II. Killarney." *Studia Neophilologica* 43 (1971): 252–56.

Prints a letter from Edgeworth which details an 1825 journey she made with Sir Walter Scott, John Gibson Lockhart, Anne Scott, Captain Walter Scott, his wife, and Harriet Edgeworth. Details stops made in Killarney, Cork, Mallow, and Cashel. Calls Scott "the most agreeable companion possible."

Dibdin, James C. *The Annals of the Edinburgh Stage, with an Account of the Rise and Progress of Dramatic Writing in Scotland*. Edinburgh: Cameron, 1888.

Reproduces passages from two of Sir Walter Scott's letters concerning the production of *The Family Legend*.

Douglas, David, ed. *Familiar Letters of Sir Walter Scott*. 2 vols. Edinburgh: Douglas, 1894.

Presents several letters from Scott to Baillie; subjects include Scott's estimation of Francis Jeffrey, production of *The Family Legend*, dramatization of *The Lady of the Lake*, Abbotsford and renovations to it, Anna Barbauld,

Charles I, Baillie's change from "Miss" to "Mrs.," the Byrons and their separation, Byron's *Childe Harold's Pilgrimage*, Maria Edgeworth's *Harrington* and *Ormond*, the death of Scott's mother, and Scott's contribution to Baillie's *A Collection of Poems, Chiefly Manuscript*.

Lockhart, John Gibson. *The Life of Sir Walter Scott*. 10 vols. Edinburgh: Constable, 1903.

Presents several letters from Scott to Baillie; subjects include mutual literary friends, Scott's plans to visit Baillie in London, production of and reaction to *The Family Legend*, Scott's visit to Lady Rock and the surrounding Highland area, Scott's literary work, his critiques of *A Series of Plays* – especially volume three, Edinburgh and London society, Byron's *Childe Harold's Pilgrimage*, British royalty, and life at Abbotsford.

Plarr, Victor C. "Sir Walter Scott and Joanna Baillie." *Edinburgh Review* 216 (1912): 355–71; 217 (1913): 170–81.

Prints several letters from Sir Walter Scott to Joanna Baillie in volume 216; subjects include the Edinburgh production of *The Family Legend*, suggestions for minor revisions to the play, criticism of most of the actors, and details of the play's public reception. Prints seven letters in volume 217; details include Scott's illness, his appeal to Matthew Baillie for treatment, composition of the Waverly novels, and reactions to drafts of Baillie's *The Martyr* and her "witchcraft story" [*Witchcraft*].

PART I, SECTION C1 — PRIMARY
WORKS/MANUSCRIPTS/PUBLISHED WORKS

Note: In this section and the next, I have included listings only for complete plays or collections with more than one work. Individual poems or letters are not included. For more information on Baillie manuscripts, see David C. Sutton, ed. *Location Register of English Literary Manuscripts and Letters: Eighteenth and Nineteenth Centuries*. London: British Library, 1995.

The Beacon: A Serious Musical Drama in Two Acts. Ms. 1846. Henry E. Huntington Library, Larpent Collection of Plays. California, United States.
Constantine Paleologus. Ms. 1557. Henry E. Huntington Library, Larpent Collection of Plays. California, United States.
The Family Legend: A Tragedy. Ms. Press V, Shelf I. Abbotsford Library. Edinburgh, Scotland.
*[Miscellaneous Papers]. Henry W. and Albert A. Berg Collection of English and American Literature. New York Public Library. New York, United States.
  The catalog gives no manuscript numbers but states that the collection holds holograph revisions for *De Monfort*, manuscripts for "Fy, Let Us A' to the Wedding," "On the Death of a Very Dear Friend," and several letters.
Plays: [submitted to the Lord Chamberlain's Office]. Ms. Henry E. Huntington Library, Larpent Collection of Plays. California, United States.
  The *Location Register* states that the plays are dated from 1808 to 1815 but offers neither a manuscript number nor details on which plays.
Plays: [submitted to the Lord Chamberlain's Office]. Ms. 42934–42935. British Library. London, England.
  Again, no specific plays are listed, but as the *Index to Manuscripts in the British Library* gives the date as 1836, the plays are likely those of Baillie's *Dramas*, published that same year.
*[Poems]. Ms. Vol. 1. 44–48, 1. 75, and Vol. 2. 69. Royal College of Surgeons of England, Hunter-Baillie Collection. London, England.
  The *Location Register* states that these papers include "Lines to Agnes Baillie on Her Birthday," "To James Baillie, an Infant," "Sweet bird of promise, fresh and fair," and a fragment of *Ethwald*.

PART I, SECTION C2 – PRIMARY WORKS/MANUSCRIPTS/ UNPUBLISHED WORKS

*Memoirs Written to Please My Nephew William Baillie. Ms. 5613/68/1–6. Wellcome Institute for the History of Medicine. London, England.
*Prose Writings. Ms. Vol. 9. 10 and 9. 68–9. Royal College of Surgeons of England, Hunter-Baillie Collection. London, England.

The *Location Register* states these writings include "An Old Story," "The Lady and Her Two Maids," and "A Plan of a Comedy," among other items.

PART I, SECTION C3 – PRIMARY WORKS/ MANUSCRIPTS/LETTERS

Note: This section is meant to provide preliminary information on locations of Baillie's letters; it is not meant to be exhaustive. Rather, I intend only to give a sense of the volume of Baillie's correspondence as well as to point scholars to locations with significant amounts of Baillie materials. For more information regarding Baillie's letters, their locations, and manuscript numbers, see Judith Bailey Slagle, *The Collected Letters of Joanna Baillie*, listed in Primary/Modern/Letters, above. Thanks to Judith Slagle for sharing information from that work for this section of the bibliography.

Bodleian Library. Oxford University, England.
>   Contains letters written between 1814 and 1850, and includes Lady Byron, Mary Montgomery, and the Bishop of Salisbury as correspondents.

British Library. London, England.
>   Possesses nearly eighty letters (1804–1842) to George Thomson, for whom Baillie provided song lyrics.

Camden Local Studies and Archives Centre and Swiss Cottage Library. London, England.
>   Includes letters dating from 1813 to 1843, for which Margaret Holford Hodson and William Beattie appear as principal correspondents.

Edinburgh University Library. Edinburgh, Scotland.
>   Owns a dozen letters written to various correspondents, one of whom is Sir Walter Scott.

Houghton Library, Harvard University. Cambridge, Massachusetts, United States.
>   Contains nearly forty letters to Andrews Norton. Subjects include Baillie's opinions on American writers and American editions of her own plays.

Huntington Library. California, United States.
>   Includes fewer than two dozen letters to various recipients.

National Library of Scotland. Edinburgh, Scotland.
>   Possesses a large number of Baillie's letters, with over 150 to Sir Walter Scott alone; other correspondents include Anne Elliot, Anna Jameson, and John Gibson Lockhart.

Royal College of Surgeons. London, England.
>   Includes letters written between 1821 and 1851 with such correspondents as William Sotheby, Mary Berry, and family members.

University of Glasgow Library. Glasgow, Scotland.
>   Contains several letters to Lady Campbell, Baillie's cousin.

Wellcome Institute for the History of Medicine. London, England.
>   Possesses mainly letters to family and Mary Berry.

PART II, SECTION A1 – SECONDARY/BIOGRAPHY/
NINETEENTH CENTURY

Notes: There were no single volume biographies published during Baillie's life, and only one after her death. The following section lists biographical sketches of Baillie or brief descriptions of events in her life published when she was alive, just after her death, or by those who knew her during her life.

I have placed in this section – and the next – sources which are primarily factual. Many sources do, of course, provide some literary comment along with their depictions of Baillie's life. Those sources included in the following two sections, however, possess a stronger emphasis on Baillie's life rather than her work. Sources possessing a significant element of biography along with a stronger emphasis on critical comment are listed here and cross-referenced to Secondary/Critical, below.

Coleridge, Sara. *Memoir and Letters of Sara Coleridge*. Ed. Edith Coleridge. New York: Harper, 1874.
> Contains four letters written after 1830 which refer to Baillie. Describes Baillie's appearance and advanced age, and remarks that Baillie's 1836 *Dramas* are not as strong as the "Plays on the Passions." Expresses loss and grief following Baillie's death.

Cone, Helen Gray and Jeannette L. Gilder, ed. *Pen-Portraits of Literary Women*. 2 vols. Boston: Educational Publishing, 1900. 1:223–41.
> Reproduces descriptions of Baillie and appraisals of her work. Includes passages by Sarah Tytler and J. L. Watson, John Gibson Lockhart, Sara Coleridge, and Harriet Martineau.

"Death of Joanna Baillie." *Littell's Living Age* 29 (1851): 218.
> Provides an overview of Baillie's life and literary career and emphasizes the genius of *A Series of Plays* and their lack of theatrical success.

Edgeworth, Maria. *Letters from England, 1813–1844*. Ed. Christina Colvin. Oxford: Clarendon, 1971.
> Contains no letters to Baillie, but gives several of Edgeworth's letters in which Baillie appears. Subjects include: Edgeworth's visits with Baillie and her sister Agnes (several letters are written from their home), the sisters' hospitality, a trip with Baillie to see Anna Barbauld, a dinner party at which Baillie danced, the Baillie sisters' care for an ailing cat, the many visitors to the Baillies' home, and the sisters' consistent kindness. Calls Baillie "the most amiable literary woman I ever beheld."

Farrar, [Eliza]. *Recollections of Seventy Years*. Boston: Ticknor and Fields, 1866.
> Details a meeting with Baillie, and notes Baillie's grace, tact, and attention to guests. Recalls a story about Baillie and her sister attending the opera with Lord Byron.

Hutton, Laurence. *Literary Landmarks of London.* 4th ed. Boston: Ticknor, 1888.
Describes both homes in which Baillie lived while in London, including their
location and appearance. Also notes Baillie's burial place in Hampstead
Churchyard.

"Lord Jeffrey and Joanna Baillie." *International Monthly Magazine of Literature,
Art, and Science* 3 (1851): 312.
Gives a brief account of Baillie's friendship with Jeffrey, including her initial
refusal to be introduced to him and their friendship in later years.

MacPherson, Gerardine. *Memoirs of the Life of Anna Jameson.* London:
Longmans, 1878.
Recounts a childhood visit by the author (Jameson's niece) to see Baillie,
noting her kindness and simplicity. Reprints three letters from Baillie to
Jameson; for annotation, see Primary/Modern/Letters, above.

Martineau, Harriet. *Harriet Martineau's Autobiography.* 2 vols. 6th ed. Ed. Maria
Weston Chapman. Boston: Osgood, 1877.
Describes a brief meeting with Baillie, noting her patience and perseverance.

Robinson, Henry Crabbe. *Diary, Reminiscences, and Correspondence.* Ed.
Thomas Sadler. Boston: Houghton, 1876.
Brief references to Baillie note her kindness and intellect. Provides the story
relating Wordsworth's often quoted description of Baillie as the "model of an
English gentlewoman."

Sigourney, L. H. *Pleasant Memories of Pleasant Lands.* Boston: Munroe, 1842.
Tells of a visit to see Baillie whom the author found, at age 73, to be lively and
unfatigued by a walk in the cold.

Sprague, William B. *Visits to European Celebrities.* Boston: Gould and Lincoln,
1855.
Briefly describes the author's visit to Baillie when the latter was 72. Notes her
preference for the Scottish church over the English one and her devotion to
family. Concludes that Baillie is a "compound of intelligence, loveliness, and
venerable simplicity."

Tappan, Henry P. *Illustrious Personages of the Nineteenth Century.* New York:
Stringer and Townsend, 1853.
Provides a biographical chapter on Baillie with a focus on family members not
found in many other sources. Praises Baillie's moral example, Christian faith,
and her clear and forceful style. Also states that Baillie's plays are "better
suited to the sober perusal of the closet than the bustle and animation of the
theatre."

Ticknor, George. *Life, Letters, and Journals of George Ticknor.* 2 vols. Boston:
Osgood, 1876.
Narrates the author's 1835 introduction to Baillie, and describes her as living
"exactly as an English gentlewoman of her age and character should live."
Also briefly notes an 1838 meeting during which Baillie spoke kindly of Sir
Walter Scott and John Gibson Lockhart.

Tytler, Sarah and J. L. Watson. *The Songstresses of Scotland*. London: Strahan, 1871. 2:180–334.

  Provides a detailed biography of Baillie's life with special emphasis on Baillie's early life and her friendships with Sir Walter Scott and Mary Berry. Also reprints several of Baillie's poems; for list, see Primary/Modern/Non-dramatic/Selected, above.

**PART II, SECTION A2 – SECONDARY/BIOGRAPHY/
TWENTIETH CENTURY**

Note: In this section, I have included several, though by no means all, biographies of Sir Walter Scott. Although Baillie appears in many biographies of Scott, authors often only note in passing that she corresponded with Scott or that Scott helped stage *The Family Legend*. I have not listed those biographies of Scott which do not consider Baillie in detail.

Buchan, John. *Sir Walter Scott*. London, Toronto, and Melbourne: Cassell, 1932.
> Mentions Baillie as one of Sir Walter Scott's correspondents. Notes that Baillie once cared for Sophia Scott when her parents visited London.

Carhart, Margaret S. The Life and Works of Joanna Baillie. Yale Studies in English 64. New Haven: Yale UP, 1923.
> Offers the only full length biography of Baillie. Divides the book into six sections: "The Life of Joanna Baillie," "Literary Background," "Dramatic Theory," "Stage History," "Non-Dramatic Poetry," and "Joanna Baillie's Place in Literature." In "Life," emphasizes Baillie's literary milieux and her religion. In "Literary Background," traces both past and contemporary influences on Baillie's work, including contemporary history books, Greek drama, Robert Burns, and Shakespeare, while in "Dramatic Theory," heavily quotes and paraphrases Baillie's "Introductory Discourse." In "Stage History," details dates of performances, provides cast lists, surveys public reception, and notes revisions made during rehearsals for several of Baillie's plays. In "Non-Dramatic Poetry," offers a cursory look at main themes in Baillie's poetry. In the final chapter, concludes that Baillie "stands to-day as the greatest Scotch dramatist."

Carswell, Donald. *Sir Walter: A Four Part Study in Biography (Scott, Hogg, Lockhart, Joanna Baillie)*. London: Murray, 1930.
> Provides a chapter on Baillie's life. Emphasizes her family – especially her father and brother – and her early life. Details William Sotheby's introduction of Baillie to Sir Walter Scott and the subsequent friendship between the latter two. Also considers the literary stir caused by *A Series of Plays*, Scott's negative reaction to Baillie's *A View of the General Tenour . . .* , and Baillie's old age. Suggests that Baillie never achieved acclaim beyond the literati, and asserts that praise of her work resulted from Baillie's dramatic ideas, not her execution of them in her plays. Maintains that her plays, always thought to be unstageable, are, in the twentieth century, "not even readable."

Feldman, Paula R., ed. Introduction to "Joanna Baillie." *British Women Poets of the Romantic Era: An Anthology*. Baltimore: Johns Hopkins UP, 1997. 21–6.
> Provides an economical, inclusive, and sound biography of Baillie's life and publications. While discussing the publications of each of her volumes, consistently ties in contemporary reactions to Baillie's work to illustrate her popularity and high esteem.

Hill, Constance. *Maria Edgeworth and Her Circle in the Days of Buonaparte and Bourbon*. London and New York: Lane, 1910.

Discusses the friendship between Maria Edgeworth and Baillie, and prints Baillie's letter regarding her first impressions of Edgeworth. Tells of Edgeworth's 1818 extended visit with the Baillies, a public reading of one of Baillie's plays, and a dinner party at a Mr. and Mrs. Carr's. Also includes comments on Baillie by Sir Walter Scott, Lucy Aikin, and Anna Barbauld.

*Howells, Coral Ann. *Joanna Baillie and Her Circle, 1790–1850: An Introduction*. [London:] Camden Historical Society, 1973.

Howitt, William. *Homes and Haunts of the Most Eminent British Poets*. 2 vols. London: Bentley, 1847. Rpt. Belles Lettres in English. New York and London: Johnson, 1968.

Provides a vivid description of Baillie's birthplace, Bothwell, Scotland, noting its geography and culture. Briefly considers Baillie as a dramatic genius whose plays are "imagined to be more suitable for the closet than the stage."

Johnson, Edgar. *Sir Walter Scott: The Great Unknown*. 2 vols. New York: Macmillan, 1970.

Gives attention to the Edinburgh production of *The Family Legend* and the subsequent revival of *De Monfort*. Presents reactions from those who attended *The Family Legend*, including Scott, David Hume, and Robert Blair. Also notes briefly Baillie's unsuccessful appeals for Scott to intervene in the Byrons' separation. Discusses Scott's struggle to write a poem for Baillie's *A Collection of Poems, Chiefly Manuscript*.

Lockhart, John Gibson. *The Life of Sir Walter Scott*. 10 vols. Edinburgh: Constable, 1903.

Examines Baillie's friendship with Scott; details include their first meeting and Baillie's initial reaction to Scott, Baillie's visit to Abbotsford, *The Family Legend* and Scott's appraisals of it, and Scott's reactions to Baillie's other work, including *Orra* and her poetry.

MacCunn, Florence. *Sir Walter Scott's Friends*. London: Blackwood, 1909; New York: Lane, 1910.

Argues that Baillie was an original thinker whose sheltered life harmed the realism of her depictions of the passions. Details Baillie's family history and her literary friends. Gives special attention to Scott's friendship with Baillie, and argues that his praise of her is overgenerous.

McKerrow, Mary. "Joanna Baillie and Mary Brunton: Women of the Manse." *Living by the Pen: Early British Women Writers*. Ed. Dale Spender. Athene Series. New York: Teachers College, 1992. 160–74.

Offers a brief literary biography, and notes the publications of Baillie's works. Asserts that Baillie's greatest achievement was to write wide-ranging tragedies depicting the varieties of human passion while living "a relatively sheltered life." Discusses Baillie's anxiety regarding her participation in the male literary world.

Morre, Isabel, ed. *Talks in a Library with Laurence Hutton*. New York and London: Kinckerbocker-Putnam, 1911.

Recounts the brief story of Hutton's 1885 visit to Hampstead to find Baillie's house and grave. States that Hutton questioned two local inhabitants for information: one believed Baillie was still living, and the other had never heard of her.

Sutherland, John. *The Life of Sir Walter Scott: A Critical Biography*. Oxford and Cambridge (MA): Blackwell, 1995.

States that Scott attempted to promote Baillie "as Scotland's greatest living dramatist." Also describes Scott's efforts to produce *The Family Legend*, and notes his persuasion of Baillie to release production rights and his participation in rehearsals.

PART II, SECTION A3 – SECONDARY/BIOGRAPHY/ BIOGRAPHICAL DICTIONARIES

Note: In this section, I have limited listings to the most recent edition of a particular title. As such, although each edition of, for example, *The Oxford Illustrated Literary Guide to Great Britain and Ireland* includes Baillie, only the second is listed here.

Adams, W. Davenport. *Dictionary of English Literature, Being a Comprehensive Guide to English Authors and Their Works*. 2nd ed. London, Paris, and New York: Cassell, Petter, and Galpin, 1884. Rpt. Detroit: Gale, 1966. 50.

Allibone, S. Austin, ed. *A Critical Dictionary of English Literature, and British and American Authors, Living and Deceased, from the Earliest Accounts to the Middle Half of the Nineteenth Century*. 3 vols. Philadelphia: Childs, 1863. 1:100–01.

Baker, David Erskine, Isaac Reed, and Stephen Jones. *Biographica Dramatica; or A Companion to the Playhouse*. 3 vols. London: Longman, Hurst, Rees, Orme, and Brown, 1812. 1:15.

Barnhart, Clarence L. , ed. *The New Century Handbook of English Literature*. Rev. ed. New York: Appleton-Century-Crofts, 1967. 82.

Blain, Virginia, Patricia Clements, and Isobel Grundy, ed. *The Feminist Companion to Literature in English: Women Writers from the Middle Ages to the Present*. New Haven: Yale UP, 1990. 50–1.

Bold, Alan, ed. *Scotland: A Literary Guide*. London: Routledge, 1989. 45–6.

Browning, D. C. , comp. *Everyman's Dictionary of Literary Biography, English and American*. Rev. ed. Everyman's Reference Library. London: Dent; New York: Dutton, 1962. 30.

Buck, Claire, ed. *The Bloomsbury Guide to Women's Literature*. New York: Prentice Hall, 1992. 312.

Burroughs, Catherine. "Baillie, Joanna." *The Encyclopedia of Romanticism: Culture in Britain, 1780s–1830s*. Ed. Laura Dabundo. Garland Reference Library of the Social Sciences 1299. New York: Garland, 1992. 21–3.

Concise Dictionary of National Biography. London: Oxford UP, [1961]. 47.

de Ford, Miriam Allen. "Baillie, Joanna." *British Authors of the Nineteenth Century*. Ed. Stanley J. Kunitz. New York: Wilson, 1936. 28–30.

Door, Priscilla. "Joanna Baillie." *An Encyclopedia of British Women Writers*. Ed. Paul Schlueter and June Schlueter. New York and London: Garland, 1988. 15–16.

Drabble, Margaret, ed. *The Oxford Companion to English Literature*. Rev. ed. Oxford: Oxford UP, 1995. 60–1.

Drabble, Margaret and Jenny Stringer, ed. *The Concise Oxford Companion to English Literature*. Rev. ed. Oxford Paperback Reference. Oxford and New York: Oxford UP, 1996. 35.

Eagle, Dorothy, ed. *The Concise Oxford Dictionary of English Literature*. 2nd ed. Oxford: Clarendon, 1970. 33.

Eagle, Dorothy, and Hilary Carnell, comp. and ed. *The Oxford Literary Guide to the British Isles*. 2nd ed. Ed. Eagle and Meic Stephens. Oxford and New York: Oxford UP, 1992. 157–8.

Lindsay, Maurice. "Baillie, Joanna." *Reference Guide to English Literature.* 2nd ed. 3 vols. Ed. D. L. Kirkpatrick. St. James Reference Guides. Chicago and London: St James, 1991. 1:197–8.

Maison, Margaret. "Baillie, Joanna." *British Women Writers: A Critical Reference Guide.* Ed. Janet Todd. New York: Ungar-Continuum, 1989. 29–33.

Mann, David D., Susan Garland Mann, and Camille Garnier. *Women Playwrights in England, Ireland, and Scotland, 1660–1823.* Bloomington: Indiana UP, 1996. 45–7.

Morley, Frank. *Literary Britain: A Reader's Guide to Its Writers and Landmarks.* New York: Harper, 1980. 453–4.

Ousby, Ian, ed. *The Cambridge Guide to Literature in English.* Rev. ed. Cambridge: Cambridge UP, 1993. 52.

Ross, Marlon B. "Joanna Baillie." *British Romantic Poets, 1789–1832: First Series.* Ed. John R. Greenfield. Dictionary of Literary Biography 93. Detroit: Bruccoli Clark-Gale, 1990. 3–15.

Royle, Trevor. *Companion to Scottish Literature.* Detroit: Gale, 1983. 16. Rpt. of The Macmillan Companion to Scottish Literature. London: Macmillan, 1983.

——. *The Macmillan Companion to Scottish Literature.* London: Macmillan, 1983. 16.

——. *Mainstream Companion to Scottish Literature.* Edinburgh: Mainstream, 1993. 16.

Sampson, George. *The Concise Cambridge History of English Literature.* 3rd ed. Ed. R. C. Churchill. Cambridge: Cambridge UP, 1970. 497, 535.

Schnorrenberg, Barbara Brandon. "Joanna Baillie." *A Dictionary of British and American Writers, 1660–1800.* Ed. Janet Todd. London: Methuen, 1984. 35–6.

Shattock, Joanne, ed. *The Oxford Guide to British Women Writers.* Oxford: Oxford UP, 1993. 20–1.

Smith, George Bennet. "Baillie, Joanna." *The Dictionary of National Biography.* 24 vols. Ed. Leslie Stephen and Sidney Lee. Oxford: Oxford UP, 1917. 1:886–9.

Uglow, Jennifer S. , ed. *The Continuum Dictionary of Women's Biography.* New expanded ed. New York: Continuum, 1989. 42.

Watt, Homer A. and William W. Watt. *A Handbook of English Literature.* Everyday Handbook. New York: Barnes and Noble, 1959. 16. Rpt. of *A Dictionary of English Literature.* 1945.

Webster's New Biographical Dictionary. Springfield: Merriam-Webster, 1983. 67.

Wynne-Davies, Marion, ed. *Prentice Hall Guide to English Literature.* New York: Prentice Hall, 1990. 335.

PART II, SECTION B – SECONDARY WORKS/CRITICAL INTERPRETATIONS

Note: In this section, I have also listed reviews for books which contain at least a full chapter about Baillie but only reviews which specifically mention Baillie. For example, Ellen Donkin's *Getting into the Act* has several more reviews than those listed, but the reviews not listed do not consider Donkin's treatment of Baillie.

Anderson, Julie. "Spectacular Spectators: Regendering the Male Gaze in Delariviere Manley's 'The Royal Mischief' and Joanna Baillie's 'Orra." *Enculturation* 3.2 (2001). 20 May 2002. <http://www.uta.edu/huma/enculturation/3_2/anderson/index.html/>.
    Drawing from current film theory, argues that both Delariviere Manley's *The Royal Mischief* and Joanna Baillie's *Orra* present instances where the gazed upon, feminine self on stage reflects back to and engages viewers. States that at the end of *Orra*, the title character becomes both spectacle and spectator and, as such, challenges the masculine gaze of the audience.

"Autographs." *Mirror of Literature, Amusement, and Instruction* 13 (1831): 145–47.
    Reproduces Baillie's autograph along with those of other "Eminent Persons," including Felicia Hemans, Percy Bysshe Shelley, and William Wordsworth. Briefly suggests that Baillie's strong and firm handwriting "lacks the delicate feebleness of a lady's writing."

Badstuber, Alfred. *Joanna Baillie's Plays on the Passions*. Wiener Beiträge zur Englischen Philologie 34. Wien: Braumüller, 1911.
    Provides individual commentary on each of the "Plays on the Passions," with especial attention to *De Monfort* as "probably the best" of the thirteen. Includes brief introductory sections on Baillie's life and her dramatic theory, and concludes with a critical estimate of the place *A Series of Plays* occupies in English literature.

Bennett, Susan. "Genre Trouble: Joanna Baillie, Elizabeth Polack—Tragic Subjects, Melodramatic Subjects." *Women and Playwriting in Nineteenth-Century Britain*. Ed. Tracy C. Davis and Ellen Donkin. Cambridge: Cambridge UP, 1999. 215–32.
    Defines Helen as a representative woman trapped and objectified in the masculine world of *The Family Legend*. Examines how the multiple voices of *Witchcraft* embody and enact alternative models for women.

——. "Outing Joanna Baillie." *Women in British Romantic Theatre: Drama, Performance, and Society, 1790–1840*. Ed. Catherine Burroughs. Cambridge: Cambridge UP, 2000. 161–77.
    In a re-evaluation of Romantic closet dramas, proposes that Baillie's dramatic precepts place her at the forefront of nineteenth-century dramatic production theory. Puts forth *Constantine Paleologus* as a drama that effectively highlights Baillie's efforts to transform the closet drama into a theatrically viable genre by examining its interrogation of the boundaries between public and private spaces.

Boaden, James. *Memoirs of the Life of John Philip Kemble*. 2 vols. London: Longman, Rees, Orme, Brown, and Green, 1825. Rpt. New York and London: Blom, 1969.

    In a brief section, describes John Philip Kemble's desire to produce and act in De Monfort. Commends Kemble's acting, but criticizes the conflict between De Monfort and Rezenvelt as too slight for serious drama.

Bold, Valentina. "Beyond 'The Empire of the Gentle Heart': Scottish Women Poets of the Nineteenth Century." *A History of Scottish Women's Writing*. Ed. Douglas Gifford and Dorothy McMillan. Edinburgh: Edinburgh UP, 1997. 246-61.

    Briefly considers Baillie's poetry, and states that, although contemporaries overrated her poetry, they believed that Baillie produced a "moral influence" on literature.

Booth, Michael, ed. *Introduction. English Plays of the Nineteenth Century*. 5 vols. Oxford: Oxford UP, 1969. 1:1–28.

    Portrays Baillie as representative of Gothic melodrama. Asserts that Baillie's verse often deteriorates into "leisurely poetry for its own sake" and that *De Monfort* and *Henriquez* display the characteristic emotional excesses of Romantic theatre.

——— *Prefaces to English Nineteenth-Century Theatre*. Manchester: Manchester UP, 1980.

    Reprints the Introduction from *English Plays of the Nineteenth Century*, above.

Brewer, William D. "Joanna Baillie and Lord Byron." *Keats-Shelley Journal* 44 (1995): 165–81.

    Examines the biographical and literary connections between Baillie and Byron, and argues that their literary relationship explains Byron's "attitudes towards the roles of gender and power in female literary production." Explores Byron's admiration for and support of Baillie, and links this respect to Baillie's ability to create masculine protagonists such as Ethwald, Basil, and De Monfort. Suggests that through these characters, Baillie influences Byron's *Manfred* and *Marino Faliero*.

———. "The Prefaces of Joanna Baillie and William Wordsworth." *Friend: Comment on Romanticism*. 1.2–3 (1991–92): 34–47.

    Argues that although Baillie's "Introductory Discourse" shares similarities with William Wordsworth's "Preface" of 1800, Baillie avoids Wordsworth's "masculinist focus on the introspective process of an individual poet." Asserts that Baillie and Wordsworth advocate both the use of a simple style to depict common events and also the portrayal of the passions as motivation for human behavior. Shows that Baillie focuses on connecting with her audience while Wordsworth emphasizes the poet's independent and isolated mind. Drawing on the theories of Carol Gilligan and Nancy Chodorow, argues that this contrast derives from the gender difference between the two authors.

Burroughs, Catherine B. *Closet Stages: Joanna Baillie and the Theater Theory of British Romantic Women Writers*. Philadelphia: U of Pennsylvania Press, 1997.

    Explores early-nineteenth-century British women writers' representations of themselves, of other women, and their theories on the theatrical representation of women to show the influence contemporary gender expectations produced on dramatic practice. Uses Baillie as a representative female theatre theorist to demonstrate "the problems women theorists encounter when moving from 'the closet' to engage critics in public space." Emphasizes Baillie's dramatic and theoretical work as a means to examine her negotiation of self and gender representation in public and domestic spheres. States that Baillie's concern with depicting scenes from the closet connects with her desire to create intimate contact with the audience, her participation in and depiction of private theatricals, and her wish to alter theatre construction. Considers *De Monfort*, *Basil*, and *The Tryal* in detail.

Reviews:

Carlson, Julie. *Romantic Circles Reviews.* <http://www.rc.umd.edu/reviews/burroughs.html>

Crochunis, Thomas C. *Romanticism on the Net* 12 (December 1998). <http://users.ox.ac.uk/~scat0385/drama.html>

Dowd, Maureen A. *Theatre Journal* 50 (1998): 134–6.

——. "The English Romantic Closet: Women Theatre Artists, Joanna Baillie, and *Basil*." *Nineteenth-Century Contexts* 19 (1995): 125–49.

Argues that *Basil* explores a woman's participation in both "the informal stage of private life and the public arena of formal theatres." Drawing on the writings of Lord Byron and Mary Russell Mitford, shows that female playwrights and actors were caught between the societal conditioning for women to withdraw from attention and a personal desire to work under the public gaze in the theatre. Asserts that *Basil*'s Victoria attempts "to experiment with the performance of femininity" in private and public spaces and that Basil himself can neither negotiate nor differentiate the public and private arenas. Appears in a revised version as part of chapter four in *Closet Stages*.

——. "English Romantic Women Writers and Theatre Theory: Joanna Baillie's Prefaces to the *"Plays on the Passions."* *Re-visioning Romanticism: British Women Writers, 1776–1837*. Ed. Carol Shiner Wilson and Joel Haefner. Philadelphia: U of Pennsylvania Press, 1994. 274–96.

Asserts that Baillie's focus on "the potentiality of 'the closet'" anticipates modern feminist theatre. Following a survey of the theatre theories of Mary Wollstonecraft and Mary Russell Mitford, argues that Baillie attempts to create "a drama that actually dramatizes scenes from a character's closet," and hopes to foreground the domestic sphere and the feminine experience. Shows that Baillie's theatrical preferences, such as smaller stages, less over-emotive acting, and better lighting, share affinities with contemporary feminist and lesbian theatre, for these conditions help create a more personal and intimate environment. Further states that both Baillie and contemporary feminist and lesbian writers make women's lives the center of their dramas. Appears in a revised version as chapter three of *Closet Stages*.

——. "Joanna Baillie's Poetic Aesthetic: Passion and 'the Plain Order of Things'." *Approaches to Teaching British Women Poets of the Romantic Period*. Ed. Stephen C. Behrendt and Harriet Kramer Linkin. Approaches to Teaching World Literature. New York: MLA, 1997. 135–40.

Claims that like her dramas, Baillie's poems focus on the domestic closet as a mirror of societal conflicts. States that "Lines to a Teapot" concerns both the slave trade and the marriage market. Maintains that emphasizing the conflict inherent in domestic life, as Baillie does, helps students better understand the relationship between their educations and their lives.

——. "'Out of the Pale of Social Kindred Cast': Conflicted Performance Styles in Joanna Baillie's *De Monfort*." *Romantic Women Writers: Voices and Countervoices*. Ed. Paula R. Feldman and Theresa M. Kelley. Hanover: UP of New England, 1995. 223–35.

Argues that through the characters of Jane De Monfort and De Monfort, respectively, Baillie sets the Neoclassic acting style, here termed "statuesque stasis," against German Romanticism's "emotive" technique. Claims that De Monfort represents an anti-social force because he wishes to disrupt the interactions of polite society, which Baillie portrays most clearly through Jane De Monfort and Rezenvelt. States that Jane's and De Monfort's struggle to negotiate complex human relationships and gender roles mirrors Baillie's artistic efforts to create a drama of the private domestic realm also appropriate for the public stage. Appears in a revised version as part of chapter four in *Closet Stages*.

——. "'A Reasonable Woman's Desire': The Private Theatrical and Joanna Baillie's *The Tryal*." *Texas Studies in Literature and Language* 38 (1996): 265–84. (Reprinted in this volume.)

Places *The Tryal* in the context of privately produced plays, and states that such productions allowed women to participate in the theatre as directors and stage managers. Claims that Agnes, by directing the private play within *The Tryal*, attempts "to dramatize domestic space" as a way "to control the representation of women's social reality." Asserts that Withrington acts as a masculine model who views private theatricals as destabilizing the domestic feminine space. Appears in a revised version as chapter five of *Closet Stages*.

Cameron, Alasdair. "Scottish Drama in the Nineteenth Century." *The History of Scottish Literature*. Ed. Douglas Gifford. 4 vols. Aberdeen: Aberdeen UP, 1988. 3: 429–42.

Places Baillie among the foremost nineteenth-century Scottish dramatists, but argues that Baillie's plays suffer from an "awkward, overblown, and anglicized poetic style, which is rarely fitted to the subject." Criticizes Baillie's inconsistent use of Scots in *The Phantom*, but allows that in *Witchcraft* Baillie employs a more authentic and vibrant use of Scots.

Campbell, Thomas. *Life of Mrs. Siddons*. London: Wilson, 1839. Rpt. New York: Blom, 1972.

States that although *De Monfort* is pleasurable to read, the dramatic efforts of Sarah Siddons, John Philip Kemble, and Edmund Kean could not rescue the play from theatrical failure. Attributes Baillie's lack of success in production to her insufficient practical theatre experience. Briefly describes the sets of the original production, and notes the author's own positive reaction to Kean's 1821 revival.

Carlson, Julie A. "Remaking Love: Remorse in the Theatre of Baillie and Inchbald." *Women in British Romantic Theatre: Drama, Performance, and Society, 1790–1840*. Ed. Catherine Burroughs. Cambridge: Cambridge UP, 2000. 285–310.

Places Baillie and Elizabeth Inchbald in the tradition of the theatre of remorse, and argues that both challenge accepted, masculine views of

remorse in relation to the past and to revolutionary activity. Uses Henriquez
to illustrate that, in focusing on the effect of remorse, Baillie defines remorse
as masculine while showing that female beauty, maturity, and autonomy are
not mutually exclusive.

"Celebrated Female Writers, No. 1: Joanna Baillie." *Blackwood's Edinburgh
Magazine* 16 (1824): 162–78.

Responds to the *Edinburgh Review*'s negative review of the *Series of Plays*
(from 1803, for citation, see Primary/Contemporary/Multi-play, above).
Praises Baillie's genius as "inferior to no individual['s]" of the time, and
credits Baillie's "Introductory Discourse" with reforming and saving poetics
and drama from the "dull monotony" of contemporary conventions. Defends
Baillie's preference for character and mental action over plot as well as her
design to center a play around a single passion. Reprints extracts and/or
provides brief critical comments for *Count Basil*, *De Monfort*, *Ethwald*,
Rayner, *Orra*, *The Dream*, and *Constantine Paleologus*, calling the last
Baillie's "very finest" play.

Cox, Jeffrey N. "Baillie, Siddons, Larpent: Gender, Power, and Politics in the
Theatre of Romanticism." *Women in British Romantic Theatre: Drama,
Performance, and Society, 1790–1840*. Ed. Catherine Burroughs. Cambridge:
Cambridge UP, 2000. 23–47.

In an examination of the place of female writers in the literary and theatre
histories of Romanticism, locates Baillie at the center of literary, social, and
political circles. Demonstrates that while *The Family Legend* aimed to build
Scottish national pride, it also argued for a stronger alliance with England.

——. *In the Shadows of Romance: Romantic Tragic Drama in Germany, England,
and France*. Athens: Ohio UP, 1987.

In the fifth chapter, briefly considers *A Series of Plays* as the nineteenth
century's "most concerted attempt to ground tragedy in psychology." Argues
that because Baillie wishes to conserve the moral and didactic potential of
tragedy, she creates an unresolvable conflict between sympathizing with and
judgment of passionate characters. Considers *Orra* and *De Monfort*.

——, ed. Introduction. *Seven Gothic Dramas, 1789–1825*. Athens: Ohio UP, 1992.

Drawing on records of Sarah Siddons' portrayal of Jane De Monfort, argues
that Baillie critiques Gothic conventions and gender stereotypes. Asserts that
the tensions between Jane and the male characters of *De Monfort* frustrate
audience expectations for an emotive yet passive woman. Places Baillie
within the Gothic genre while showing how she works against the restrictive
roles for women within that genre.

Reviews:

Lindsay, David W. *Review of English Studies* ns 46 (1995): 281–2.

Patten, Janice E. *Theatre Journal* 45 (1993): 562–4.

Varma, Devendra. *Byron Journal* 21 (1993): 105–07.

Crochunis, Thomas C. "Authorial Performances in the Criticism and Theory of
Romantic Women Playwrights." *Women in British Romantic Theatre: Drama,
Performance, and Society, 1790–1840*. Ed. Catherine Burroughs. Cambridge:
Cambridge UP, 2000. 223–54.

Considers how Baillie and Elizabeth Inchbald performed as authors through
their print publications and dramatic productions, and examines how each
genre presented challenges in negotiating public and private identity. Uses

the "Introductory Discourse" to show that print publications allowed Baillie to create and control a context for her work that the theatre did not afford.

—— "The Function of the Dramatic Closet at the Present Time." *Romanticism On the Net* 12 (November 1998). [20 May 2002] <http://users.ox.ac.uk/~scat0385/bwpcro.html>

Examines different approaches to the term "closet drama," and uses Baillie as an example of an author whose plays are neither strictly closet dramas nor plays for the stage. Argues that Baillie and other women dramatists wrote "closet dramas" in order to reach a specific set of readers.

Curran, Stuart. "Romantic Poetry: The I Altered." *Romanticism and Feminism*. Ed. Anne K. Mellor. Bloomington: Indiana UP, 1988. 185–207.

Asserts that a masculine bias in Romantic studies has caused the marginalization of women writers such as Anna Barbauld and Charlotte Smith. Uses Baillie as a representative example of a highly published woman writer now largely forgotten by the academic community. Argues that of all texts, Baillie's *A Series of Plays* "exerted the most direct practical and theoretical force" on Romantic drama.

Davis, Tracy C. "The Sociable Playwright and Representative Citizen." *Romanticism On the Net* 12 (November 1998) [20 May 2002]. <http://users.ox.ac.uk/~scat0385/bwpcitizen.html>.

Argues that to reach a proper understanding of women's plays, they must be considered in the context of women's lives. Briefly considers Baillie as a playwright associated with domestic space but who aligned herself as such in order that she might more carefully control the appearance of her plays in public.

Donkin, Ellen. *Getting into the Act: Women Playwrights in London, 1776–1829*. London: Routledge, 1995.

In the final chapter, traces reasons for Baillie's literary rise and subsequent decline. Argues that Baillie's anonymous publication – which concealed her sex – played a large role in her initial popularity. Asserts that Richard Sheridan's reluctance to stage Baillie's plays, Baillie's consistent refusal to attend rehearsals, and male critics' bias against women playwrights all contributed to her fall from public favor.

Reviews:

Engle, Sherry D. *Theatre Journal* 48 (1996): 531–3.

Scullion, Adrienne. *Theatre Research International* 21 (1996): 264–5.

Donohue, Joseph W., Jr. *Dramatic Character in the English Romantic Age*. Princeton: Princeton UP, 1970.

In a chapter on "Romantic Heroism," portrays Baillie as a dramatic reformer who anticipates modern theatrical practice. Drawing on examples from *De Monfort*, argues that by presenting evil passion as an aspect of the soul rather than as a facet of fate, Baillie "effected . . . a transformation in the nature of dramatic character." Claims that Baillie's canonical exclusion results from a lack of audience acceptance of her radical innovations.

——. *Theatre in the Age of Kean*. Drama and Theatre Studies. Totowa: Rowman and Littlefield, 1975.

States that, along with Samuel Taylor Coleridge and William Wordsworth, Baillie holds the view that a connection exists between human nature and action. Claims that Baillie's dramaturgy, as expressed in the "Introductory

Discourse," remains "essentially untheatrical" as evidenced by the limited production of her plays. Asserts that *De Monfort* marks a moment of innovation for nineteenth-century Gothic drama because in the play Baillie takes special care to develop a complex psychology for the title character.

Druskowitz, Helen Von. *Drei englische Dichterinnen: Essays*. Berlin: Oppenheim, 1885.

Contains an essay on Baillie, in German.

Evans, Bertrand. *Gothic Drama from Walpole to Shelley*. University of California Publications 18. Berkeley: U of California Press, 1947.

In the eleventh chapter, calls for a revaluation of Baillie's plays. Argues that Baillie is quintessentially Gothic because she crowds most of her plays with dark and gloomy castle and convent settings, secret passageways, ruins, tolling bells, and remorseful and emotional protagonists. Asserts that in *Orra*, the title character's fear and eventual madness result from the combined effects of these Gothic elements.

Fawcett, Millicent Garrett. *Some Eminent Women of Our Times: Short Biographical Sketches*. London and New York: Macmillan, 1889.

Highlights Baillie's relationships with Sir Walter Scott and Sarah Siddons. States that Baillie's realistic women characters mark her style as feminine. Discusses *De Monfort* and its stage failure.

Fletcher, Richard M. *English Romantic Drama, 1795–1843*. New York: Exposition, 1966.

Portrays Baillie on the fringe of the Romantic drama, a scene dominated by William Wordsworth, Samuel Taylor Coleridge, and Lord Byron. States that like Coleridge and Wordsworth, Baillie hopes to create an artistic drama well-suited to the contemporary stage.

Frank, Parson. "Joanna Baillie." *Eclectic Magazine of Foreign Literature, Science, and Art* 23 (1851): 420–5.

Provides a general appreciation of Baillie's literary career, summarizing and providing brief laudatory comments on *De Monfort*, *Count Basil*, *Orra*, *The Family Legend*, and *Fugitive Verses*. Highlights Baillie's ability to create vivid characters, and notes the particular strength of De Monfort, Jane De Monfort, and Orra.

Franklin, Caroline. *Byron's Heroines*. Oxford: Clarendon, 1992.

In a short section of a chapter on "Heroic Heroines," traces Baillie's influence on Lord Byron's drama. States that Baillie and Lord Byron share ideas on feminine nurturing and that both emphasize sibling relationships. Considers *De Monfort* and *Constantine Paleologus*.

Friedman-Romell, Beth H. "Dueling Citizenships: Scottish Patriotism v. British Nationalism in Joanna Baillie's *The Family Legend*." *Nineteenth Century Theatre* 26 (1998): 26–49.

Examines the ways in which the Edinburgh production of *The Family Legend* paradoxically promoted Scottish national identity while also fostering identification with England and its culture. Explores the theatrical and political effects of the play through a consideration of its depictions of clothes, history, and gender. Concludes that Baillie constructed herself paradoxically, as both masculine and feminine as well as both Scottish and English.

——. "Staging the State: Joanna Baillie's 'Constantine Paleologus.'" *Women and Playwriting in Nineteenth-Century Britain*. Ed. Tracy C. Davis and Ellen Donkin. Cambridge: Cambridge UP, 1999. 151–73.

> Briefly summarizes productions and reviews of Constantine Paleologus at the Theatre Royal in Liverpool (1808), the Surrey Theatre in London (1817), the Theatre Royal in Edinburgh (1820), and the Theatre Royal in Dublin (1825), and then provides detailed analysis of the presentations of Valeria, Constantine, religion, and liberty in these stagings. Demonstrates that these productions replaced Baillie's interrogation of political, religious, and gender conventions with an "aggressively heterosexual, patriotic reading."

Gamer, Michael. "National Supernaturalism: Joanna Baillie, Germany, and the Gothic Drama." *Theatre Survey* 38.2 (1997): 49–88.

> Argues that Baillie attempts to combine spectacle and psychology, thus negotiating the boundary between public popularity and critical approval. Asserts that the creation of characters haunted by nothing "other than their own minds" allows Baillie to use Gothic tropes while directing audience attention away from spectacle and toward psychological perception of the supernatural. Further examines M. G. Lewis's *Castle Spectre* and August von Kotzebue's plays to demonstrate nineteenth-century critical bias against German conventions. Claims that in Ethwald, Baillie distances herself from such influences by "creating a series of dualisms . . . good versus evil, truth versus falsehood, Protestantism versus Catholicism, and Britain versus the Continent." Considers Ethwald, De Monfort, Rayner, and The Phantom in detail.

Gaull, Marilyn. *English Romanticism: The Human Context*. New York: Norton, 1988.

> In a brief passage, surveys Baillie's career. Also suggests that Baillie helped reform the theatre by directing it toward moral didacticism.

Genest, John, ed. *Some Account of the English Stage from the Restoration in 1660 to 1830*. 10 vols. Carrington: Bath, 1832. Rpt. Burt Franklin Research and Source Work Series 93. New York: Franklin, 1965.

> In volume seven, summarizes *De Monfort* and praises its "exquisitely beautiful language." In volume eight, provides plot summaries for the plays in each volume of *A Series of Plays* and those in *Miscellaneous Plays*. Praises Baillie's "masterly" characterizations, including Ethwald, Osterloo of *The Dream*, and Valdemar of *The Siege*. Criticizes Baillie's lack of practical knowledge of the stage, and repeatedly censures her "disgusting" tendency to allow characters to exit a scene only to enter the next without allowance for the passage of time.

Gilroy, Amanda. "From Here to Alterity: The Geography of Femininity in the Poetry of Joanna Baillie." *A History of Scottish Women's Writing*. Ed. Douglas Gifford and Dorothy McMillan. Edinburgh: Edinburgh UP, 1997. 143–57.

> Drawing on Frederick Rowton's 1848 anthology of women's poetry (see Primary/Contemporary/Works in Collections, above and this section, below) and on contemporary reviews of Baillie's work, examines "The Legend of Lady Griseld Baillie," "Sir Maurice: A Ballad," and Ahalya Baee to show how Baillie "negotiates the boundaries of space allotted to femininity." Considering the locations and events of each poem, asserts that "Lady Griseld" and "Sir Maurice" circumscribe the feminine within the domestic

sphere as well as under patriarchal power. Maintains that *Ahalya Baee* challenges the notion of separate gender spheres put forth by the earlier two poems.

Groves, David. "Beethoven and Scottish Poetry." *Bibliotheck* 15.2 (1988): 31–3.

Notes that Beethoven composed music for two of Baillie's lyrics for publication in George Thomson's *A Select Collection of Original Scotch Airs*.

Hamilton, Catherine J. *Women Writers: Their Works and Ways*. First Series. 1892. Essay Index Reprint Series. Freeport: Books for Libraries, 1971.

Offers a brief biographical essay with some critical evaluation. Claims Baillie's best attribute is her ability to depict the effects passions have on an individual's psyche. Discusses *De Monfort, Basil, Ethwald, Constantine Paleologus, Orra*, and *Henriquez*.

Hawkins, F. W. *The Life of Edmund Kean*. 2 vols. London: Tinsley, 1869. Rpt. New York: Blom, 1969.

Considers Kean's 1821 production of De Monfort and attributes its failure to the unsuitability of Baillie's plays for the stage. Notes Baillie's willingness to incorporate Kean's suggestions for revisions and her satisfaction with Kean's performance in the new version. Also highly praises Kean's interpretation of *De Monfort*.

Hazlitt, William. *Lectures on the English Poets*. London: Taylor and Hessey, 1818. Rpt. Lectures on the English Poets *and* The Spirit of the Age. Everyman's Library 459. London: Dent; New York: Dutton, 1910. 1–168.

Briefly criticizes Baillie's efforts to depict one passion per play as "heresies of dramatic art." Praises *De Monfort* for its "unity of interest," but heavily censures her comedies, especially *The Election*, for simplistic and heavy-handed moral didacticism.

Henderson, Andrea. "Passion and Fashion in Joanna Baillie's 'Introductory Discourse.'" *Publications of the Modern Language Association* 112 (1997): 198–213.

Argues that Baillie's emphasis on the passions arises from the "sympathy and sentimentality" of nineteenth-century business and consumer practices. Claims that Baillie's concern with physical appearance connects to a nineteenth-century focus on physiognomy. States that Baillie's artistic program "promotes a modern consumerist form of desire" which emphasizes both procurement and ownership of art objects.

Hoagwood, Terence Allan. "Elizabeth Inchbald, Joanna Baillie, and Revolutionary Representation in the 'Romantic' Period." *Rebellious Hearts: British Women Writers and the French Revolution*. Ed. Adriana Craciun and Kari E. Lokke. SUNY Series in Feminist Criticism and Theory. Albany: State U of New York Press, 2001. 293–316.

Uses Baillie's Constantine Paleologus as an example showing that the historical context surrounding the production of a work can influence that work's meaning outside of any authorial intent or emotional response by readers. Demonstrates, for example, that the play was changed each time it appeared on stage in an effort to sell more tickets to the production.

Inchbald, Elizabeth, ed. "Remarks [An Introduction to De Monfort]." *The British Theatre, or, A Collection of Plays*. Vol. 24. London: Longman, Hurst, Rees, and Orme, 1808. 3–6.

Asserts that *De Monfort* is a work of genius, but criticizes its lack of substantial reason for the title character's hatred for Rezenvelt. States that Baillie has created two excellent characters in Rezenvelt and Jane De Monfort.

Insch, A. G. "Joanna Baillie's *De Monfort* in Relation to Her Theory of Tragedy." *Durham University Journal* 23 (1961): 114–20.

Argues that Baillie's plays fail because the dramatist places depicting a passion and stating a moral message above developing character and plot. Maintains that this pattern results in a one-dimensional protagonist, De Monfort, while Rezenvelt appears more real because he need not be ruled by one passion alone. However, contends that *De Monfort* succeeds because Baillie invests the title character with pride as his tragic flaw.

Ireland, Joseph N. *Records of the New York Stage from 1750 to 1860.* 2 vols. New York: Morrell, 1866–7. Rpt. New York: Blom, 1966.

Includes cast lists for both the April 13, 1801, American premier of *De Monfort* and an 1809 revival.

"Joanna Baillie." *Bentley's Miscellany* 29 (1851): 453–7.

Provides an overview and general appreciation of Baillie's life and career. Lauds the "accuracy of her analysis of passion" and her ability to sustain a play based on a single emotion. Claims that Baillie's lack of theatrical success occurred because the plays were "not intended for the stage." Cites the flaws of Baillie's drama as her over-attention to detail and her use of Elizabethan language, but states that Baillie's genius rises above these imperfections.

Kucich, Greg. "Reviewing Women in British Romantic Theatre." *Women in British Romantic Theatre: Drama, Performance, and Society, 1790–1840.* Ed. Catherine Burroughs. Cambridge: Cambridge UP, 2000. 48–76.

Illustrates that the conflicted response to female dramatists in nineteenth-century periodicals reflects a larger social dispute over gender roles. Uses both positive and negative assessments of Baillie's work to show how Baillie represented both a promise of revival for Romantic-era drama as well as the threat to conventional gender stereotypes.

——. "Staging History: Teaching Romantic Intersections of Drama, History, and Gender." *Approaches to Teaching British Women Poets of the Romantic Period.* Ed. Stephen C. Behrendt and Harriet Kramer Linkin. Approaches to Teaching World Literature. New York: MLA, 1997. 88–96.

Shows how Baillie may be used in a course on Romanticism and gender. Places Baillie with other women writers – such as Maria Edgeworth, Catharine Macaulay, and Felicia Hemans – who attempt to create an "emotional interiority" distinct from masculine history. Shows that emotion can, for Baillie, manifest itself in communal expressions of feeling, as at the end of *De Monfort*.

Malina, Marilyn. "Scots Poetic Tradition: Wooing and Marriage in Poems by Ebenezer and Joanna B. Picken." *Selected Essays on Scottish Language and Literature: A Festschrift in Honor of Allan H. MacLaine.* Ed. Steven R. McKenna. Lewiston, NY: Mellen, 1992. 163–75.

States that Baillie's "Woo'd and Married and A'" influenced Joanna B. Picken's "An Auld Friend wi' a New Face." Argues that Picken more explicitly questions the institution of marriage than does Baillie.

286 Ken A. Bugajski

Mathur, Om Prakash. *The Closet Drama of the Romantic Revival*. Salzburg Studies
   in English Literature. Poetic Drama and Poetic Theory 35. Salzburg: Institut für
   Englische Sprache und Literatur, 1978.
   > In a brief section on Baillie, contends that Baillie's compartmentalization of
   > the passions, stereotypical plots, and weak characterizations result in
   > dramatic failure. Suggests that the *Miscellaneous Plays* are her most
   > successful works due to their variations in plot and character, and asserts
   > that Baillie's strongest attributes are her depictions of crowd scenes and her
   > poetic language. Considers *The Election, De Monfort, Basil, Rayner,
   > Constantine Paleologus*, and *The Family Legend*.

McCue, Kirsteen. "Women and Song, 1750–1850." *A History of Scottish Women's
   Writing*. Ed. Douglas Gifford and Dorothy McMillan. Edinburgh: Edinburgh UP,
   1997. 58–70.
   > Briefly considers Baillie as a Scottish songwriter, placing her among other
   > writers such as Anne Grant, Elizabeth Hamilton, and Jean Adam. Asserts that
   > songs allow socially refined women – like Baillie – "to grasp the physical
   > immediacy" of traditional ballads. States that Baillie's "Hooly and Fairly"
   > breaks with tradition by presenting a sarcastic and derisive view of marriage.

McMillan, Dorothy. "'Dr.' Baillie." *1798: The Year of the Lyrical Ballads*. Ed.
   Richard Cronin. London: Macmillan; New York: St. Martin's, 1998. 68–92.
   > Asserts that Baillie drew from examples of the career-oriented men in her
   > family, including her father and brothers, as examples in developing and
   > then following her own literary career. Views the *Series of Plays* as Baillie's
   > attempt to systematically investigate human emotion just as her brother,
   > Matthew Baillie, had scrutinized and categorized human anatomy.

Mellor, Anne K. "A Criticism of Their Own: Romantic Women Literary Critics."
   Questioning Romanticism. Ed. John Beer. Baltimore and London: Johns
   Hopkins UP, 1995. 29–48.
   > Asserts that Baillie, Anna Barbauld, Mary Wollstonecraft and other women
   > writers upheld coherent aesthetic theories opposed to those advanced by
   > their male contemporaries. Demonstrates that women espoused "the
   > workings of a rational mind," a fluid self immersed in a social context, and
   > reform through communal action. States that the *Series of Plays* show the
   > growth of feelings within a social context. This growth creates a connection
   > between characters and audience which culminates in the moral instruction
   > of the latter.

——. "Joanna Baillie and the Counter-Public Sphere." *Studies in Romanticism* 33
   (1994): 559–67.
   > Drawing on Jürgen Habermas's concept of the "public sphere" along with
   > Rita Felski's idea of the "counter-public sphere," maintains that Baillie uses
   > "the theatre to re-stage and revise the social construction of gender." Argues
   > that Baillie emphasizes the counter-public sphere, the "realm of feelings,
   > sympathy, and curiosity," and then shows how the central conflict in *Count
   > Basil* between honor and love is in fact "about the control of the public
   > sphere, a debate between two opposing methods of government." Further
   > argues that Baillie characterizes the "masculine public sphere" as dominated
   > by self-destructive egotism and pride while she offers the feminine counter-
   > public sphere as an alternative basis for action that is grounded in "rational
   > prudence" and "sympathetic understanding."

Meynell, Alice. *The Second Person Singular and Other Essays*. London: Milford, 1922. Essay Index Reprint Series. Freeport: Books for Libraries, 1968.

In a short essay on Baillie, states that her tragedies are well-constructed and provide a strong sense of closure. Contends that Baillie's comedies on the passions provide better dramatic entertainment and display Baillie's sharp wit, as in the "exceeding sweetness" of *The Tryal*'s heroines. Believes Baillie would have more readers if her comedies received more emphasis than her tragedies. Discusses *De Monfort* and *The Tryal*.

Millar, J. H. *A Literary History of Scotland*. New York: Scribners, 1903.

Praises Baillie's lyric power, and states that her best work is "The Chough and Crow" passage from *Orra*.

Mitford, Mary Russell. *Recollections of a Literary Life; Or, Books, Places, and People*. London: Bentley, 1851; New York: Harper, 1852. Rpt. Women of Letters. New York: AMS, 1975.

As did Wordsworth, praises Baillie as "the very pattern" of a distinguished woman and author. Lauds the strength of Baillie's plays, especially her female characters. Also admires Baillie's lyric abilities, and reprints several poems. For list, see Primary/Modern/Non-Drama/Selected, above.

Nicoll, Allardyce. *A History of Early Nineteenth-Century Drama, 1800–1850*. Cambridge: Cambridge UP, 1930.

In a chapter entitled "The Legitimate Drama," asserts that although Baillie's plays suffer from lapses in coherent plot construction and from too heavy a reliance on Elizabethan diction, her consistent development of one central emotion makes her plays "landmarks . . . in English theatre." Argues that Baillie's plays show potential because her dramatic technique improves with maturity, but states that Elizabethan influences continually hold back her art. Briefly considers *De Monfort*, *Ethwald* (part one), *Constantine Paleologus*, *The Family Legend*, *Orra*, and *The Dream*.

——. *A History of English Drama, 1660–1900*. 5 vols. Cambridge: Cambridge UP, 1955.

Reprints *A History of Early Nineteenth-Century Drama, 1800–1850* and *A History of Late Eighteenth-Century Drama, 1750–1800*, above and below, as volumes four and three, respectively.

——. *A History of Late Eighteenth-Century Drama, 1750–1800*. Cambridge: Cambridge UP, 1927.

Briefly considers the first volume of *A Series of Plays*, citing Baillie's focus on passion over character, her "tendency . . . towards the romantically abstract," and her false diction as flaws fatal to her plays.

*Nicoll, W. Robertson. *The Literary Associations of Hampstead*: Bolton House, Windmill Hill, and Metley Cottage. [London: Bookman], 1893.

Norton, M. "The Plays of Joanna Baillie." *Review of English Studies* os 23 (1947): 131–43.

Affirms that Baillie's most revolutionary technique is her consistent focus on only one humor per play. Believes that this innovation also becomes Baillie's greatest flaw because, "In seeking to reveal the passion, she loses sight of the man." States that the development of a single isolated emotion cannot sustain the interest of an audience full of many competing and conflicting emotions.

"Obituaries." *Harper's New Monthly Magazine* 2 (1851): 709.

> Commends Baillie's moral and simple life, and praises her literary works, comparing her stark emotional portrayals to Greek drama. Asserts that Baillie and William Wordsworth share responsibility for "the redemption of our poetry from that florid or insipid sentimentalism" of the early part of the century.

Page, Judith W. *Wordsworth and the Cultivation of Women.* Berkeley: U of California Press, 1994.

> In a chapter on Wordsworth's poetic vocation, briefly considers Baillie, and argues that although the "Introductory Discourse" influences Wordsworth's "Preface" of 1800, the two writers differ on their perceptions of their audiences. Suggests that Baillie hopes to teach her audience while Wordsworth attempts to earn the respect of his audience. Also contends that Baillie desires to create sympathy between the characters in her work and her audience while Wordsworth hopes to gain approval from critics.

Patten, Janice. "Joanna Baillie, A Series of Plays." *A Companion to Romanticism.* Ed. Duncan Wu. Oxford: Blackwell, 1998. 169–78.

> Gives a brief biography and family history, and asserts that in her plays Baillie suggests that "all cognition is based on passion," an idea itself based in the medicine familiar to Baillie's two uncles and brother. Details the psychological motivations in De Monfort and in the title character himself, and briefly considers the principal characters in *The Family Legend*, *Constantine Paleologus*, *Ethwald*, *The Martyr*, and *Orra*.

Pearson, Hesketh. *Sir Walter Scott: His Life and Personality.* New York: Harper, 1954. Rpt. London: Hamilton, 1987.

> Emphasizes Baillie's friendship with Sir Walter Scott. Challenges Scott's positive appraisal of Baillie's work, asserting that Scott's preference for blank verse drama and his admiration of Baillie's moral message led to his overestimation of her work. Also discusses Scott's efforts in the production of *The Family Legend*.

Purinton, Marjean D. "Revising Romanticism by Inscripting Women Playwrights." *Romanticism On the Net* 12 (November 1998). [20 May 2002] <http://users. ox.ac.uk/~scat0385/bwprevising.html>.

> Examines the ways in which consideration of women playwrights has changed perceptions of literary history, academic pursuits, teaching methods, the canon, and ideas about performance. Considers Baillie as a central figure in the re-evaluation, and further suggests staging her plays as a means to greater insight into Romantic drama.

——. *Romantic Ideology Unmasked: The Mentally Constructed Tyrannies in Dramas of William Wordsworth, Lord Byron, Percy Shelley, and Joanna Baillie.* Newark: U of Delaware Press, 1994.

> In the chapter on Baillie, demonstrates that she critiques gender "not as a biological function but as a cultural practice." Citing Mary Wollstonecraft, Maria Edgeworth, Mary Hays, Hannah More, and Clara Reeves, shows an oppressor/oppressed relationship between genders to be a widespread concern of nineteenth-century women. Argues that the concerns of these women writers "appear as latent content" in *De Monfort* and *Count Basil*. Interprets the two plays as works which depict men attempting to control women who are struggling to exert their independent will.

Reviews:

Schatz, Sueann. *Rocky Mountain Review* 49 (1995): 203–05.

Woodall, N. J. *Choice* 32 (1995): 937.

——. "Socialized and Medicalized Hysteria in Joanna Baillie's *Witchcraft*." *Prism(s)* 9 (2001): 139–56.

> Defines "techno-gothic drama" as that which uses theatrical techniques to investigate scientific concepts, and suggests that Baillie uses *Witchcraft* in such a manner as a means to challenge nineteenth-century medical theory on hysteria.

——. "Women's Sovereignty on Trial: Joanna Baillie's Comedy *The Tryal* as Metatheatrics." *Women in British Romantic Theatre: Drama, Performance, and Society, 1790–1840*. Ed. Catherine Burroughs. Cambridge: Cambridge UP, 2000. 132–57.

> Contends that the metadramatic elements of *The Tryal* expose the artificial nature of gender stereotypes and "enact revisionary treatments of female sovereignty in private and public spaces." Argues that *The Tryal* both challenges advice of eighteenth-century women's conduct books and instructs women in new modes of behavior.

Ranger, Paul. *"Terror and Pity reign in every Breast": Gothic Drama in the London Patent Theatres, 1750–1820*. London: Society for Theatre Research, 1991.

> Discusses William Capon's set design for the first production of *De Monfort*. Notes that Baillie's stage directions innovatively suggest hand held lanterns to help illuminate actors' faces more clearly. Surveys Edmund Kean's and John Philip Kemble's portrayals of *De Monfort*, and argues that Kean, though less dignified and technically adept than Kemble, brought more sustained energy to the role.

Reiman, Donald H. Introduction. The Family Legend *and* Metrical Legends of the Exalted Characters. By Joanna Baillie. Romantic Context: Poetry. Significant Minor Poetry, 1789–1830. New York and London: Garland, 1976. v–viii.

> Provides a brief description of Baillie's life, and surveys nineteenth-century reactions to her work. Claims that Baillie's blank verse is among the best of the Romantic period because it is "simple and natural, supple and original." Argues that like William Wordsworth, Baillie believes "ordinary life" possesses the potential for both "heroism and tragedy." Believes that Baillie may have achieved more if her later works had not been influenced by Sir Walter Scott's suggestions for subject matter.

——. Introduction. *Miscellaneous Plays*. By Joanna Baillie. Romantic Context: Poetry. Significant Minor Poetry, 1789–1830. New York and London: Garland, 1977. v–viii.

> Reprints the introduction from The Family Legend *and* Metrical Legends of the Exalted Characters, above.

——. Introduction. *A Series of Plays*. 3 vols. By Joanna Baillie. Romantic Context: Poetry. Significant Minor Poetry, 1789–1830. New York and London: Garland, 1977. i:v–viii.

> Reprints the introduction from The Family Legend *and* Metrical Legends of the Exalted Characters, above.

290 Ken A. Bugajski

Renwick, W. L. *English Literature: 1789–1815*. Oxford: Clarendon, 1963.

> Dismisses Baillie as one who lacks creativity and attempts to write beyond her ability. Provides the often quoted criticism that: "No real dramatist would deliberately sit down to write a whole series of *Plays on the Passions*."

Robertson, Fiona, ed. Introduction to Joanna Baillie's "Lines on the Death of Sir Walter Scott." *Scott*. Vol. 3 of *Lives of the Great Romantics II: Keats, Coleridge, and Scott, By Their Contemporaries*. London: Pickering and Chatto, 1997. 17–20.

> Describes the friendship between Scott and Baillie, and states that the two writers viewed each other as literary equals and did not, contrary to some current criticism, see their relationship as that of a master and apprentice. Argues that in "Lines on the Death of Sir Walter Scott," Baillie portrays her friend as the admirable and distinguished lord of Abbotsford while she simultaneously portrays him as a man who easily mixes with and offers friendship to all classes of people.

Robinson, A. Mary F. "Joanna Baillie." *The English Poets: Selections with Critical Introductions by Various Writers*. 5 vols. Ed. Thomas Humphry Ward. London: Macmillan, 1880. 4:221–2.

> Finds fault with Baillie's narrow dramatic didacticism, but praises her poetic simplicity and her Scottish ballads. For poems reprinted, see Primary/Modern/Non-Dramatic/Selected.

Ross, Marlon B. *The Contours of Masculine Desire: Romanticism and the Rise of Women's Poetry*. New York: Oxford UP, 1989.

> Depicts Baillie as a playwright caught in the middle of several conflicts. Argues that Baillie's dramatic theory exists between eighteenth-century sentimentality and rationality. Asserts that, like Wordsworth, Baillie attempts to integrate emotion and thought. Suggests that Baillie examines the masculine world of public affairs and its relationship to internal feelings. Concludes that Baillie believes that the lack of interaction between these two points of view threatens the stability of society.

Reviews:

Mellor, Anne K. *Studies in Romanticism* 31 (1992): 103–05.

Rowton, Frederic. *The Female Poets of Great Britain*. London: Longman, Brown, Green, and Longmans; Philadelphia: Carey and Hart, 1849. 287–306.

> Argues that Baillie is the foremost intellectual female poet of the age and that her writing possesses "vigour, clearness, and simplicity." Notes that Baillie precedes and heralds William Wordsworth, and asserts that she attempts to reform the theatre by leading it away from melodrama and towards poetry. For poems reprinted, see Primary/Contemporary/Works in Anthologies, above.

Rubik, Margarete. *Early Women Dramatists, 1550–1800*. English Dramatists. London: Macmillan; New York: St. Martin's, 1998.

> Asserts that in *De Monfort*, Baillie follows melodramatic conventions too closely, and thus the play remains unconvincing. States that, in contrast, *Count Basil*'s "sound characterization" contributes to a more effective drama. Also claims that although *The Tryal* lacks originality, it surpasses other contemporary comedies because of its humor and witty dialog.

Scullion, Adrienne. "Some Women of the Nineteenth-century Scottish Theatre: Joanna Baillie, Frances Wright, and Helen MacGregor." *A History of Scottish*

Women's Writing. Ed. Douglas Gifford and Dorothy McMillan. Edinburgh: Edinburgh UP, 1997. 158–78.

Defines Baillie's place in nineteenth-century Scottish theatre, and states that she helps initiate Scottish National Drama with *The Family Legend*. Claims that while Baillie manages *The Family Legend*'s stagecraft well, she produces a contrived plot and stereotypical characters. Briefly considers *Witchcraft* as complex and interesting drama. Also explores the gender dynamic in Baillie's work, placing her in alignment with Anne K. Mellor's idea of feminine Romanticism.

Simmons, James R., Jr. "'Small, Prim, and Quaker-like': Reinventing Joanna Baillie as Jane Eyre." *Brontë Society Transactions* 21. 4 (1994): 149–51.

Argues that Charlotte Brontë's descriptions of Jane Eyre's appearance influenced John Francis Waller's posthumous appreciation of Joanna Baillie (see Waller, this section, below).

Sotheby, William. *Tragedies*. London: Murray, 1814.

A short introductory letter dedicates this volume to Baillie.

Tobin, Terrence. *Plays by Scots, 1660–1800*. Iowa City: U of Iowa Press, 1974.

In a chapter on "Scots Abroad," asserts that Baillie's focus on a solitary emotion creates artificial and unsympathetic protagonists because she limits them to an *"idée fixe."* States that *De Monfort* most nearly fulfills Baillie's dramatic theory, but argues that the play fails because De Monfort never acts nobly, even though other characters describe him as such. Asserts that Jane De Monfort is the best conceived of Baillie's supporting characters because she is complex and virtuous but not without fault. Briefly considers *Basil* and *The Tryal*, criticizing them for their lack of complexity.

"The Tragedy Called *De Montford* [sic], and the Passion of Hatred, Illustrated by an Original Account." Signed "B." *Monthly Mirror* 9 (1800): 361–2.

Relates the story of an actual court case wherein a man confessed to murdering a former classmate due to a long-standing hatred of him. States that this case illustrates that *De Monfort*'s plot is neither too contrived nor too unbelievable, as some critics had charged. See also Wynn, this section, below.

Veitch, John. *The Feeling for Nature in Scottish Poetry*. 2 vols. Edinburgh and London: Blackwood, 1887.

Briefly notes Baillie's contributions to Scottish literature, stating that the "simplicity in theme, treatment, and language" of later nineteenth-century literature emerges due to Baillie's influence.

Waller, John Francis. "Leaves from the Portfolio of a Manager, No. IV: Joanna Baillie." *Dublin University Magazine* 37 (1851): 529–36.

Provides a first-person account of friendship with Baillie. Describes the playwright as "small, prim, and Quaker-like" (see Simmons, this section, above). Discusses the stage failure of both Kemble's and Kean's productions of *De Monfort*, attributing their failures to the play's strained emotions. Favorably considers the Edinburgh production of *The Family Legend*, and asserts the play possesses "action, vigor, and poetical dialogue" which make the play theatrically viable. Argues that *Constantine Paleologus* remains Baillie's most stageable play because of its story and vivid characterization. Reprinted in *Eclectic Magazine of Foreign Literature, Science, and Art* 23 (1851): 128–35.

Watkins, Daniel P. "Class, Gender, and Social Motion in Joanna Baillie's *De Monfort." Wordsworth Circle* 23.2 (1992): 109–17.

> Revises and expands "The Gait Disturb'd," below. Adds that in De Monfort, real and imagined knocking on doors represents the aristocracy's psychological anxiety about the rising middle class. Argues that the decadent party scenes function as the aristocracy's (futile) attempts to escape society's dissolving hierarchies.

——. "'The Gait Disturb'd of Wealthy, Honour'd Men': Joanna Baillie's De Monfort." *Nineteenth-Century Contexts* 15 (1991): 143–51.

> Argues that the class and gender conflicts of *De Monfort* highlight Baillie's political awareness. Claims that the personal conflict between De Monfort and Rezenvelt mirrors early nineteenth-century class conflicts. Concludes that De Monfort's psychological instability reflects the "rapidly-increasing social change" of the nineteenth century.

——. *A Materialist Critique of English Romantic Drama.* Gainesville: UP of Florida, 1993.

> In the chapter on Baillie (which further refines the previous two essays), argues for Baillie's primary importance because she dramatizes the "social and historical pressures" of her era. Drawing on Marxist theory, states that the main conflict in *De Monfort* is one of class, exemplified through the aristocratic De Monfort and his bourgeois rival, Rezenvelt. Also asserts that the second important struggle for power occurs between genders, with women subject to men regardless of class. Concludes that De Monfort is the embodiment of the aristocracy, caught between a deteriorating class structure and the collapse of distinct gender roles.

Reviews:

> Cox, Jeffrey N. *Criticism* 36 (1994): 464–7.
> Crochunis, Thomas C. *Nineteenth Century Theatre* 24 (1996): 42–55.
> Jewett, William. *Studies in Romanticism* 34 (1995): 309–15.
> Moody, Jane. *Review of English Studies* ns 47 (1996): 600–01.
> Purinton, Marjean D. *Southern Humanities Review* 30 (1996): 290–93.

Whyte, Walter. "Joanna Baillie (1762–1851)." *The Poets and Poetry of the Nineteenth Century.* 12 vols. Ed. Alfred H. Miles. London: Routledge, 1905. New York: AMS, 1967. 8: 1–16.

> Introductory note provides biographical information, and argues that although Scott overrates Baillie's plays, they possess the merits of creativity, dignified verse, and graceful heroines. Asserts that Baillie will be remembered primarily for her lyrics and songs. Reprints nine poems; for list, see Miles, Primary/Modern/Non-Drama/Selected, above.

*Wordsworth, Jonathan, ed. *Ancestral Voices: Fifty Books from the Romantic Period. Revolution and Romanticism, 1789–1834.* Oxford: Woodstock, 1991.

> Reprints and revises the introduction to Joanna Baillie: *A Series of Plays,* below.

——. Introduction. Joanna Baillie: *Poems. Revolution and Romanticism, 1789–1834.* Oxford and New York: Woodstock, 1994. n. pag.

> Argues that, like the dramas which were to follow, Baillie's poems attempt to depict one prevailing passion or mood. Places Baillie within the Scottish poetic tradition. Notes her influence on William Wordsworth, and claims that Baillie anticipated – if not invented – the lyrical ballad form.

———. "Joanna Baillie: *Poems*, 1790." *The Bright Work Grows: Women Writers of the Romantic Age. Revolution and Romanticism, 1789–1834.* Poole and Washington D.C.: Woodstock, 1997. 58–66.

Reprint of the above introduction with revisions. Offers specific comparisons between Baillie's and William Wordsworth's verse.

———. Introduction. Joanna Baillie: *A Series of Plays.* Oxford and New York: Woodstock, 1990. n. pag.

Considers the success of *A Series of Plays*, and links Baillie's "Introductory Discourse" and *De Monfort* to William Wordsworth's "Preface" and early poetry. Briefly considers *Count Basil, The Tryal,* and *De Monfort,* asserting that the last best fulfills Baillie's theatre theory.

Worth, Christopher. "'A Very Nice Theatre at Edinr.': Sir Walter Scott and Control of the Theatre Royal." *Theatre Research International* 17 (1992): 86–95.

Examines the historical significance of Scotland's Theatre Royal in relation to Sir Walter Scott's efforts to create a national identity for Scotland. Discusses *The Family Legend* as an important early production in the theatre.

Wynn, Frances Williams. *Diaries of a Lady of Quality, from 1797 to 1844.* 2nd ed. Ed. A. Hayward. London: Longman, Green, Longman, Roberts, and Green, 1864.

Relates the story of long-lasting hatred and murder given in "The Tragedy Called *De Montford* [sic]," *Monthly Mirror* 9 (1800): 361–2, this section, above. Also provides editorial notes defending the authenticity of the story. A review of this book, *Edinburgh Review* 119 (1864): 305–39, also reprints the story.

Yudin, Mary F. "Joanna Baillie's Introductory Discourse as a Precursor to Wordsworth's Preface to *Lyrical Ballads*." *Compar(a)ison* 1 (1994): 101–11.

Argues that Baillie's "Introductory Discourse" and William Wordsworth's "Preface" are linked by a focus on both "middle and lower class subjects" and "quotidian events." Notes that both authors concern themselves with the depiction and description of authentic emotions. Argues that the "Introductory Discourse" raised public expectations which Baillie's subsequent plays failed to reach, thus contributing to her fall from popularity and eventual exclusion from the canon.

Zall, Paul M. "The Cool World of Samuel Taylor Coleridge: The Question of Joanna Baillie." *Wordsworth Circle* 13 (1982): 17–20.

Provides a brief biography of Baillie. Asserts that her plays are ridiculous, though *De Monfort* is "less ludicrous than most." Discusses the staging and revising of *De Monfort*, especially noting the revisions made by John Philip Kemble and Sarah Siddons. Argues that Baillie's plays failed because she knew little of contemporary theatre practice.

Ziegenrucker, Emil. *Joanna Baillie's "Plays on the Passions".* Hamburg-Barmbeck: Starck, 1909.

Provides a descriptive and critical study of Baillie's drama. Devotes a chapter to the works from *A Series of Plays*, as well as *Romiero, The Alienated Manor,* and *Henriquez*. Provides bibliographical and biographical essays together with a discussion of Baillie's views of comedy, tragedy, and dramaturgy.

PART II, SECTION C – SECONDARY WORKS/DISSERTATIONS

Note: Not all dissertations were available through inter-library loan. In cases where an abstract exists for a dissertation I could not obtain, I have written an annotation based on the abstract. These sources are marked with a †.

†Berliner, Donna Gaye. "The Female Romantic Imagination." Diss. U of Texas at Dallas, 1994. *DAI* 55 (1995): 368.
   Considers Baillie, Felicia Hemans, and Letitia Landon as self-supporting women. Examines nineteenth-century opinions of Baillie's work, and asserts that Baillie's overt sentimentality challenges standard readings of the Romantic period.

*Carhart, Margaret Sprague. "The Life and Work of Joanna Baillie." Diss. Yale University, 1921. *ADD* L1923.
   For an annotation of the book based on this dissertation, see Carhart, Secondary/Biography/Twentieth, above.

†Colombo, Claire Miller. "'You all may boast the censor's art': Censorship and Authority in Romantic Drama." Diss. U of Texas at Austin, 1997. *DAI* 59 (1998): 180.
   In an examination of the ways in which early nineteenth-century playwrights sought to increase their own authority, examines Baillie's "Introductory Discourse," suggesting that because it remained outside of a censor's scope, this preface allowed Baillie to construct her own context for reading and understanding her work.

†Dowd, Maureen Anne. "'The monster melo-drame': Spectacle, Sensationalism, and the Cultural Performances of Joanna Baillie, Lady Morgan, and M. E. Braddon." Diss. Loyola U of Chicago, 1999. *DAI* 60 (1999): 1571.
   Considers "issues of gender, genre, class, and nationalism" in relation to Baillie's melodramatic works. Includes a chapter on *Rayner*, suggesting that through it Baillie uses German melodramatic techniques in order to provide a model of British patriotism to a middle-class audience.

†Dwyer, Karen. "Joanna Baillie Plays the Passions: Literature, Science and Medicine." Diss. U of Notre Dame, 2000. *DAI* 61 (2000): 618.
   Places Baillie and her *Series of Plays* at the center of a convergence of nineteenth-century literary, scientific, and medical thought. After a brief biography of Baillie, examines her participation in psychological, medical, and moral debates, and concludes with a detailed look at *Orra*.

†Friedman-Romell, Beth H. "Producing the Nation: Nationalism and Gender in the Theatre of Hannah Cowley, Elizabeth Inchbald, and Joanna Baillie." Diss. Northwestern U, 1999. *DAI* 60 (2000): 4251.
   Investigates how plays and productions by Hannah Cowley, Elizabeth Inchbald, and Joanna Baillie helped construct and reinforce ideas of British Nationalism. Argues that an understanding of Baillie must take into account printed text, production strategies, and public reception.

Gamer, Michael Crews. "Popular Stigmas and Appropriate Authors: High Romanticism's Hidden Gothic." Diss. U of Michigan, 1993. *DAI* 54 (1994): 2588.
   In a chapter on Baillie, argues that Baillie utilizes Gothic conventions while distancing herself from their lack of sophistication. States that Baillie "markets herself as a socially benign and culturally legitimate alternative" to

the excess of Gothic theatre. Asserts that Baillie avoids "supernatural spectacles" in an effort to reform drama. Also suggests that Baillie attempts to continue Shakespearean styles in a new context and explores Baillie's influence on Samuel Taylor Coleridge's revisions to *Remorse*. Considers *Basil, De Monfort, Ethwald, Orra,* and *The Phantom.*

Judson, Barbara Louise. "Passion and the Public Sphere: A Study of the Political Significance of Female Sexuality in British Romanticism." Diss. U of Virginia, 1995. *DAI* 57 (1996): 233.

Asserts that Baillie attempts to "rehabilitate" femininity by removing "women's autonomous sexuality" from public life as well as by emphasizing the "sanctity of maternity" in private life. States that *De Monfort* promulgates "Tory evangelical ideology" by espousing the virtue of reason and "passionlessness." Claims, however, that even as Baillie marks Jane De Monfort as chaste and forbidden, masculine desire for her simultaneously increases.

†Kutrieh, Marcia Geib. "Popular British Romantic Poets." Diss. Bowling Green State U, 1974. *DAI* 34 (1974): 2229a.

Considers Baillie among 17 other British women poets, and provides a biographical sketch of her. Defines Baillie as an important author because of her large reading public.

Lamb, Virginia Blackwell. "Joanna Baillie's *Plays on the Passions* Viewed in Relation to Her Dramatic Theories." Diss. Kent State U, 1973. *DAI* 34 (1974): 406a.

Contends that Baillie's effectiveness as a writer of moral tragedies emerges from her ability to depict ordinary people under extraordinary levels of passion. States that Baillie rejects satirical, sentimental, and circumstantial comedies because these do not provide moral edification. Shows that Baillie developed "characteristic comedy" to instruct readers and to develop sympathetic curiosity in them, just as in tragedy. Places Baillie's dramatic theory in context with other writers such as Samuel Taylor Coleridge and William Hazlitt. Considers *Basil, The Beacon, De Monfort, The Dream, Ethwald, Henriquez, Orra,* and *Romiero.*

*Lambertson, Chester Lee. "The Letters of Joanna Baillie, (1801–1832)." Diss. Harvard U, 1956. *ADD* (1956): X1956.

†Mears, Richard McMath. "Serious Verse Drama in England: 1812–1850." Diss. U of North Carolina-Chapel Hill, 1953. *DA* (1954).

In a short section on Baillie, examines *Orra* in relation to her dramatic theories. States that *Orra* suffers because other passions – such as pride – play important roles in the play. Also believes that the presence of a Gothic villain frustrates the entirely internal development of fear. Claims that Baillie's plays anticipate later drama in several ways, including her portrayals of "Byronic" heroes. Asserts that Baillie's movement from "Gothic drama to religious drama to prose tragedy" parallels larger dramatic trends in the early nineteenth century.

Noble, Aloma. "Joanna Baillie as Dramatic Artist." Diss. U of Iowa, 1983. *DAI* 44 (1984): 1974.

Provides a survey of Baillie's life, the theatrical conventions of the Romantic age, and Baillie's dramatic theory, and concludes that Baillie's greatest strength lies in her characterization. Argues that *De Monfort* illustrates "the nature of humanity" and the "Biblical principle" of the struggle against powers of evil. Contends that by focusing on the human mind in *De Monfort*, Baillie creates a tragedy without political, class, or economic concerns. Asserts that Baillie's comedy *The Tryal* anticipates the realism of twentieth-century comedy.

Patten, Janice Elma. "Dark Imagination: Poetic Painting in Romantic Drama." Diss. U of California, Santa Cruz, 1992. *DAI* 53 (1992): 3225.

> In a chapter on Baillie, argues that Baillie's concept of dramaturgy rests on a foundation of character as it is perceived in nineteenth-century medicine and psychology. States that Baillie's plays manifest internal realities and conflicts. Asserts that Baillie explores the "perceptions of the mind" as related to actual "emotional experience." Considers *Constantine Paleologus*, *De Monfort*, and *The Family Legend*.

†Pipkin, John George. "'The Line Invisible': Intertextuality and the Men and Women Poets of British Romanticism (Charlotte Smith, Joanna Baillie, Mary Tighe, William Wordsworth, Samuel Taylor Coleridge, John Keats)." Diss. Rice U, 1997. *DAI* 58 (1997): 887.

> Examines the interconnections between the "Introductory Discourse" and Wordsworth's "Preface," arguing that Baillie's "aesthetic theory . . . anticipates Wordsworth's valorization of powerful emotions, natural language, and rustic themes." Asserts that Baillie's notion of sympathetic curiosity contributed to Wordsworth's desire to write the "Preface."

Purinton, Marjean Delene. "Ideology Unmasked and Fictions Revealed: The Mentally Constructed Tyrannies of English Romantic Drama." Diss. Texas A&M U, 1991. *DAI* 53 (1992): 162.

> For an annotation of the book based on this dissertation, see Purinton, Secondary/Critical, above.

†Sim, S. "'Memory's Wizard Pencil': The Perpetuation of an Ethos in Early Nineteenth-Century Representation of Renaissance Drama." Diss. U of Stirling, 1991. Index to Theses Accepted for Higher Degrees by the Universities of Great Britain and Ireland (and the Council for National Academic Awards) 42 (1993): 42–5208.

> Explores connections between *A Series of Plays* and Renaissance drama, and asserts that Baillie attempts to "reconstitute and sanitize issues and themes" of the earlier period. Argues, however, that Baillie's literary allusions undermine her moral aims.

Yudin, Mary F. "Women Dramatists of the Nineteenth Century and the Domestic Drama: Joanna Baillie, Charlotte Birch-Pfeiffer, and Gertrudis Gomez de Avellaneda." Diss. Pennsylvania State U, 1995. *DAI* 57 (1996): 164.

> Claims that Baillie reshapes nineteenth-century theatre by attempting "to unite the lyricism of the past with the morality of the present." Asserts that *The Beacon* subverts melodramatic convention by redefining the heroine and by creating a sympathetic villain. States that, contrary to her other plays, *Constantine Paleologus* represents men as reasonable and women as sentimental. Shows that *Orra* explores the horror of the supernatural and that it locates terror within the domestic sphere. Also asserts that *Orra*'s madness allows her to subvert masculine power structures.

Works cited

Addelson, K. P. (1993) "Knower/Doers and Their Moral Problems," in L. Alcoff and E. Potter (eds) *Feminist Epistemologies*, New York: Routledge, 265–94.

Aikin, L. (1864) *Memoirs, Miscellanies and Letters*, P. H. Le Breton (ed.), London: Longman, Green, Longman, Roberts & Green.

Aikin, L. (1996) *Epistles on Women, Exemplifying Their Character and Condition in Various Ages and Nations*, in A. K. Mellor and R. E. Matlak (eds) *British Literature: 1780–1830*, New York: Harcourt.

Allaback, S. and Medlicott, A., Jr. (1978) *A Guide to the Microfilm Edition of the European Journals of George and Anna Ticknor in the Library of Dartmouth College*, Hanover, New Hampshire: Dartmouth College Library.

Altick, R. D. (1978) *The Shows of London*, Cambridge: Belknap Press of Harvard University Press.

Anderson, B. (1991) *Imagined Communities: Reflections on the Origin and Spread of Nationalism*, 2nd ed., London: Verso.

Anderson, M. G. (2002) *Female Playwrights and Eighteenth-century Comedy: Negotiating Marriage on the London Stage*, New York: Palgrave.

Anderson, W. E. K. (ed.) (1972) *The Journal of Sir Walter Scott*, Oxford: Clarendon.

Aristotle (1984) *Poetics*, trans. I. Bywater, in *The Complete Works of Aristotle*, J. Barnes (ed.), vol. 2, Princeton: Princeton University Press.

Arnold, T. (1782–86; 2nd ed. 1806) *Observations on the Nature, Kinds, Causes, and Prevention of Insanity*, 2 vols, Leicester: Robinson and Caddell; London: Richard Phillips.

Arnold, T. (1809) *On the Management of the Insane*, London.

Artaud, A. (1958) *The Theatre and its Double*, trans. M. C. Richards, New York: Grove Press.

Aspinall, A. (1938) *The Letters of George IV, 1812–1830*, 4 vols, Cambridge: Cambridge University Press.

Athenaeum (Jan. 1836): 4–5.

Auerbach, N. (1990) *Private Theatricals: The Lives of the Victorians*, Cambridge, MA: Harvard University Press.

Austen, J. (1966) *Mansfield Park*, Tony Tanner (ed.), London: Penguin.

Austen, J. (1985) *Northanger Abbey*, London: Penguin.

Backscheider, P. R. (1993) *Spectacular Politics: Theatrical Power and Mass Culture in Early Modern England*, Baltimore: Johns Hopkins University Press.

Baillie, J. (1798) *A Series of Plays*, London: T. Cadell, Jun. & W. Davies.

Baillie, J. (1836) "On the Character of Romiero," *Fraser's Magazine* (December): 748–9.

Baillie, J. (1840) *Fugitive Verses*, London: Moxon.

Baillie, J. (1851) *The Dramatic and Poetical Works of Joanna Baillie: Complete in One Volume*, London: Longman, Brown, Green, and Longmans.

Baillie, J. (1853) *The Dramatic and Poetical Works of Joanna Baillie*, 2nd ed., London: Longman, Brown, Green, and Longmans.

Baillie, J. (1976) *Joanna Baillie: The Dramatic and Poetical Works*, Hildesheim: Georg Olms Verlag.

Baillie, J. (1990) *A Series of Plays 1798*, facsimile reprint, Oxford and New York: Woodstock Books.

Baillie, J. (1997) *A Selection of Plays and Poems*, A. Gilroy and K. Hanley (eds), London and Brookfield, VT: Pickering & Chatto.

Baillie, J. (2001) *Plays on the Passions*, P. Duthie (ed.), Peterborough, Ontario: Broadview.

Baillie, Lady G. (1911) *Household Book, 1692–1733*, R. Scott-Moncrieff (ed.), Edinburgh: Scottish History Society Publications.

Baillie, M. (1793) *Morbid Anatomy of some of the most important parts of the human body*, London: J. Johnson and G. Nicol.

Baillie, M. (1797) *Morbid Anatomy of some of the most important parts of the human body* [2nd ed. corrected and considerably enlarged], London: J. Johnson and G. Nicol.

Baillie, M. (1798) *An appendix to the first edition of the Morbid Anatomy of some of the most important parts of the human body*, London: J. Johnson and G. Nicol.

Baillie, M. (1799–1802) *A series of engravings, accompanied with explanations, which are intended to illustrate the morbid anatomy of some of the most important parts of the human body: divided into ten fasculi*, London: printed by W. Bulmer for J. Johnson and G. and W. Nicol.

Baillie, M. (1825a) *Lectures and Observations on Medicine*, London: Richard Taylor.

Baillie, M. (1825b) *The Works of Matthew Baillie, M.D. to which is prefixed an Account of his Life, collected from authentic sources*, 2 vols, James Wardrop (ed.), London: Longman, Hurst, Orme, Brown, and Green.

Baillie, M. (1896) "An Autobiography, entitled 'A Short Memoir of my Life, with a view of furnishing authentic materials'," James Blake Bailey (ed.), *The Practitioner* (July): 51–65.

Bann, S. (1995) *Romanticism and the Rise of History*, New York: Twayne.

Barker-Benfield, G. J. (1992) *The Culture of Sensibility: Sex and Society in Eighteenth-Century Britain*, Chicago: University of Chicago Press.

Baron-Wilson, Mrs. C. (1839) *Memoirs of Harriot, Duchess of St. Albans*, 2 vols, London: Henry Colburn.

Battie, W. (1758) *A Treatise on Madness*, London: J. Whiston.

Belenky, M. F., Clinchy, B. M., Goldberger, N. R., and Tarule, J. M. (1986) *Women's Ways of Knowing: The Development of Self, Voice and Mind*, New York: Basic Books.

Bell, C. (1806) *Essays on the Anatomy of Expression in Painting*, London: Longman, Hurst, Rees, and Orme.

Benjamin, W. (1968) "Theses on the Philosophy of History," in H. Arendt (ed.) *Illuminations*, New York: Schocken Books.

Bennett, S. (2000) "Outing Joanna Baillie," in C. Burroughs (ed.) *Women in British Romantic Theatre: Drama, Performance, and Society 1790–1840*, Cambridge: Cambridge University Press: 161–77.

Beresford, J. (1825) *The Miseries of Human Life; or The Groans of Timothy Testy and Samuel Sensitive*, 10th ed., vol. 1, London: P. Wright and Son.

Berrios, G. and Porter, R. (eds) (1995) *A History of Clinical Psychology: The Origin and History of Psychiatric Disorders*, London: Athlone.

Blackwood's Edinburgh Magazine 5 (1819) (Sept.): 686–8.

Blair, H. (1783; facsimile reprint 1965) *Lectures on Rhetoric and Belles Lettres*, H. F. Harding (ed.), vol. 1, Carbondale and Edwardsville: Southern Illinois University Press.

Boaden, J. (1827) *Memoirs of Mrs. Siddons*, 2 vols, London: Henry Colburn.

Booth, M. R., Southern, R., Marker, F., Marker, L.-L., Davies, R. (1975) *The Revels History of Drama in English. Volume VI. 1750–1850*, London: Methuen.

Boswell, J. (1950) *Boswell's London Journal 1762–1763*, F. A. Pottle (ed.), New York: McGraw-Hill.

Brewer, W. D. (1991) "The Prefaces of Joanna Baillie and William Wordsworth," *The Friend: Comments on Romanticism* 1: 34–47.

Brewer, W. D. (1995) "Joanna Baillie and Lord Byron," *Keats-Shelley Journal* 44: 165–81.

Brissenden, R. F. (1974) *Virtue in Distress: Studies in the Novel of Sentiment from Richardson to Sade*, New York: Harper and Row.

British Women Playwrights around 1800 (2003), M. Eberle-Sinatra and T. C. Crochunis (eds), <http://garamond.stanford.edu/mirrors/romnet/wp1800/>. Online, 30 April 2003.

Brooks, P. (1976) *The Melodramatic Imagination: Balzac, Henry James, Melodrama and the Mode of Excess*, New Haven: Yale University Press.

Brown, C. C. (1985) *John Milton's Aristocratic Entertainments*, Cambridge: Cambridge University Press.

Brunton, M. (1992) *Emmeline with Some Other Pieces*, C. Franklin (ed.), London: Routledge/Thoemmes Press.

Burney, F. [Madame d'Arblay] (1957) *Edwy and Elgiva*, M. J. Benkovitz (ed.), Hamden: Shoe String Press.

Burroughs, C. B. (1994) "English Romantic Women Writers and Theatre Theory: Joanna Baillie's Prefaces to the Plays on the Passions," in C. S. Wilson and J. Haefner (eds), *Re-Visioning Romanticism: British Women Writers, 1776–1837*, Philadelphia: University of Pennsylvania Press: 274–96.

Burroughs, C. B. (1996) "Review: Marjean D. Purinton, *Romantic Ideology Unmasked: The Mentally Constructed Tyrannies in the Dramas of William Wordsworth, Lord Byron, Percy Shelley and Joanna Baillie*," *Keats-Shelley Journal* 45: 206–8.

Burroughs, C. B. (1997) *Closet Stages: Joanna Baillie and the Theater Theory of British Romantic Women Writers*, Philadelphia: University of Pennsylvania Press.

Burroughs, C. B. (1998) "Teaching the Theory and Practice of Women's Dramaturgy," *Romanticism on the Net* 12. Online. <http://www-sul.stanford.edu/mirrors/romnet/articles.html#12>.

Burton, A. (1995) "'Invention Is What Delights Me': Jane Austen's Remaking of English History," in D. Looser (ed.) *Jane Austen and Discourses of Feminism*, New York: St. Martin's Press.

Burwick, F. (1996) *Madness and the Romantic Imagination*, University Park: Pennsylvania State University Press.

Bushe, C. K. (1825) *The Private Theatre of Kilkenny, with Introductory Observations on Other Private Theatres in Ireland, before it was opened*, n. loc.: n. pub.

Butler, J. (1990) *Gender Trouble: Feminism and the Subversion of Identity*, New York: Routledge.

Bynum, W. (1981) "Rationales for Therapy in British Psychiatry, 1780–1835," in A. Scull (ed.) *Madhouses, Mad-Doctors, and Madmen: The Social History of Psychiatry in the Victorian Era*, Philadelphia: University of Pennsylvania Press: 35–57.

Cabanis, P.-J.-G. (1981) *On the Relations Between the Physical and Moral Aspects of Man*, trans. Margaret Duggan Saidi, George Mora (ed.), 2 vols, Baltimore: Johns Hopkins University Press.

Campbell, T. (1834) *Life of Mrs. Siddons*, 2 vols, London: Effingham Wilson, Royal Exchange.

Carhart, M. S. (1923, rpt. 1970) *The Life and Work of Joanna Baillie. Yale Studies in English*, Vol. 64, New Haven: Yale University Press.

Carlson, J. A. (1988) "A New Stage for Romantic Drama," *Studies in Romanticism* 27: 419–27.

Carlson, J. A. (1994) *In the Theatre of Romanticism: Coleridge, Nationalism, Women*, Cambridge: Cambridge University Press.

Carlson, J. A. (1999) "Like Me: An Invitation to Domestic/Tragedy", *South Atlantic Quarterly* 98. 3: 331–53.

Carlson, J. A. (2002) "Hazlitt and the Sociability of Theatre," in G. Russell and C. Tuite (eds), *Romantic Sociability: Social Networks and Literary Culture in Britain 1710–1840*, Cambridge: Cambridge University Press, 145–65.

Carlson, M. (1989) *Places of Performance: The Semiotics of Theatre Architecture*, Ithaca, NY, and London: Cornell University Press.

Carr, I. (1992) "'Not on the outward appearance . . . but on the heart' Matthew Baillie and Cardiology," *Canadian Journal of Cardiology* 8.1: 78–82.

Carter, M. (1987) *Specter or Delusion?: The Supernatural in Gothic Fiction*, Ann Arbor, London: UMI Research Press.

Carver, A. (1966) *The Story of Duntisbourne Abbots*, Gloucester: Albert E. Smith.

Case, S.-E. (1988) *Feminism and Theatre*, New York: Methuen.

Castle, T. (1993) *The Apparitional Lesbian: Female Homosexuality and Modern Culture*, New York: Columbia University Press.

Channing, W. H. (1848) *Memoir of William Ellery Channing with Extracts from his Correspondence and Manuscripts*, 3 vols, London: J. Chapman.

Cheeke, S. (1998) "Shelley's *The Cenci*: Economies of a Familiar Language," *Keats-Shelley Journal* 47: 142–60.

Clayden, P. W. (1887) *The Early Life of Samuel Rogers*, London: Smith, Elder & Company.

Coburn, K., Christenson, M. and Harding, A. J. (eds) (1957–<c2002) *The Notebooks of Samuel Taylor Coleridge*, 5 vols, New York, Princeton, NJ, and London: Bollingen Series, Princeton University Press.

Code, L. (1993) "Taking Subjectivity into Account," in L. Alcoff and E. Porter (eds), *Feminist Epistemologies*, New York: Routledge.

Coleridge, S. T. (1983) *Biographia Literaria*, J. Engell and W. J. Bate (eds), 2 vols, Princeton: Princeton University Press.

Colley, L. (1992) *Britons: Forging the Nation, 1707–1837*, New York: Yale University Press; London: Pimlico.

Collins, P. H. (1990) *Black Feminist Thought: Knowledge, Consciousness and the Politics of Empowerment*, Boston: Unwin Hyman.

Conolly, L. W. (1976) *The Censorship of English Drama 1737–1824*, San Marino, CA: The Huntington Library.

Conway, S. (ed.) (1994) *The Correspondence of Jeremy Bentham*, Oxford: Clarendon.

Corum, R. (1998) *Understanding Hamlet*, Westport, CT: Greenwood Publishing.

Cox, J. M. (1804) *Practical Observations on Insanity: In Which Some Suggestions Are Offered Towards an Improved Mode of Treating Diseases of the Mind [...] to Which Are Subjoined, Remarks on Medical Jurisprudence as Connected with Diseased Intellect*, London: Baldwin and Murray.

Cox, J. N. (ed. and intro.) (1992) *Seven Gothic Dramas, 1789–1825*, Athens, OH: Ohio University Press.

Cox, J. N. (2000) "Baillie, Siddons, Larpent: Gender, Power, and Politics in the Theatre of Romanticism," in C. Burroughs (ed.) *Women in British Romantic Theatre: Drama, Performance, and Society, 1790–1840*, Cambridge: Cambridge University Press: 23–47.

Cox, J. N. and Gamer, M. (eds) (2003) *The Broadview Anthology of Romantic Drama*, Peterborough, ON: Broadview.

Crainz, F. (1995) *The Life and Works of Matthew Baillie, MD, FRS L&E, FRCP, etc. (1761–1823)*, Santa Palomba: Peliti Associati.

Craven, E. B. (1914; orig. 1826) *The Beautiful Lady Craven: The Original Memoirs of Elizabeth Baronness Craven afterwards Margravine of Anspach and Bayreuth and Princess Berkeley of the Holy Roman Empire (1750–1828)*, 2 vols, London: John Lane The Bodley Head.

Craven, E. B. (1991) *Mémoires*, Édition Presentée et Annotée par Jean-Pierre Guicciardi, Paris: Mercure de France.

Crochunis, T. C. (1998) "The Function of the Dramatic Closet at the Present Time," *Romanticism on the Net* 12, special issue on "British Women Playwrights around 1800"<http://www-sul.stanford.edu/mirrors/romnet/articles.html#12> .

Crochunis, T. C. (2000) "Authorial Performances in the Criticism and Theory of Romantic Women Playwrights," in C. Burroughs (ed.) *Women in British Romantic Theatre: Drama, Performance, and Society, 1790–1840*, Cambridge: Cambridge University Press: 223–54.

Crompton, L. (1985) *Byron and Greek Love: Homophobia in 19th-Century England*, Berkeley: University of California Press.

Cumberland, R. (1788) "Remarks upon the Present Taste for Acting Private Plays," in *The European Magazine, and London Review*, 14.

Cumberland, R. (1807) *Memoirs of Richard Cumberland. Written by Himself*, 2 vols, London: Lackington, Allen & Company.

Curran, S. (1970) *Shelley's Cenci: Scorpions Ringed with Fire*, Princeton, NJ: Princeton University Press.

Curran, S. (1993) "Women Readers, Women Writers," in S. Curran (ed.) *The Cambridge Companion to British Romanticism*, Cambridge: Cambridge University Press.

Darwin, E. (1794–96) *Zoonomia: or, The Laws of Organic Life*, 2 vols, London: J. Johnson.

Darwin, E. (1806) *The Poetical Works of Erasmus Darwin, M.D., F.R.S.*, 3 vols, London: J. Johnson.

Davis, T. C. (1999) "The Sociable Playwright and Representative Citizen," in T. C. Davis and E. Donkin (eds) *Women and Playwriting in Nineteenth-Century Britain*, Cambridge: Cambridge University Press: 15–33.

Davis, T. C. and Donkin, E. (eds) (1999) *Women and Playwriting in Nineteenth-Century Britain*, Cambridge: Cambridge University Press.

Day, W. P. (1985) *In the Circles of Fear and Desire: A Study of Gothic Fantasy*, Chicago: University of Chicago Press.

Derrida, J. (1994) *Specters of Marx*, trans. P. Kamuf, New York and London: Routledge.

Devrell, M. (1792) *Mary, Queen of Scots: An Historical Tragedy, or, Dramatic Poem*, London: Stockdale.

Dibdin, J. C. (1888) *The Annals of the Edinburgh Stage*, Edinburgh: Richard Cameron.

Dictionary of American Biography (1929), A. Johnson (ed.), 20 vols, New York: Charles Scribner's Sons.

Dictionary of National Biography (1938–), L. Stephen and S. Lee (eds), 22 vols, London: Oxford University Press.

Dobson, J. (1969) *John Hunter*, Edinburgh: Livingstone.

Dolan, J. (2001) *Geographies of Learning: Theory and Practice, Activism and Performance*, Middletown, CT: Wesleyan University Press.

Donkin, E. (1995) *Getting into the Act: Women Playwrights in London, 1776–1829*, New York: Routledge.

Donohue, J., Jr. (1970) *Dramatic Character in the English Romantic Age*, Princeton, NJ: Princeton University Press.

Dowd, M. (1998) "'By the Delicate Hand of a Female': Melodramatic Mania and Joanna Baillie's Spectacular Tragedies," *European Romantic Review* 9: 469–500.

Dowd, M. A. (1998) "Review: Catherine Burroughs, *Closet Stages: Joanna Baillie and the Theater Theory of British Romantic Women Writers*," *Theatre Journal* 50.1: 134–6.

Downer, A. S. (1943) "Nature to Advantage Dressed: Eighteenth-Century Acting," *Publications of the Modern Language Association* 58: 1002–37.

Downer, A. S. (1946) "Players and Painted Stages: Nineteenth-Century Acting," *Publications of the Modern Language Association* 61: 522–76.

Dublin University Magazine (1851) 37 (April): 529–36.

Duran, J. (1991) *Toward a Feminist Epistemology*, Savage, MD: Rowman and Littlefield.

Duthie, P. (2001) "Introduction," in J. Baillie, *Plays on the Passions*, P. Duthie (ed.), Peterborough, ON: Broadview Press.

Dutton, T. (1801) "Review of *De Monfort*," *Dramatic Censor* 2: 112–18, 127–33.

Duyckinck, E. and Duyckinck, G. (1856) *Cyclopædia of American Literature*, 2 vols, New York: C. Scribner.

Edgeworth, M. (1971) *Letters from England, 1813–1844*, C. Colvin (ed.), Oxford: Clarendon Press.

Edgeworth, M. (1980) *Castle Rackrent*, Oxford: Oxford University Press.

Edinburgh Monthly Review (1819) 2 (Nov.): 574–81.

Edinburgh (Scots) Magazine (1821) 8 (Jan.–June): 260–5.

Ehrenreich, B. and English, D. (1973) *Witches, Midwives, and Nurses: A History of Women Healers*, New York: Feminist Press.

Erdman, D. V. (1939) "Byron's Stage Fright: The History of His Ambition and Fear of Writing for the Stage," *English Literary History* 6 (1939): 219–43; reprinted in R. Gleckner and B. Beatty (eds) (1997) *The Plays of Lord Byron: Critical Essays*, Liverpool: Liverpool University Press. 5–31.

Evenden, M. (1993) "Inter-mediate Stages: Reconsidering the Body in 'Closet Drama'," in C. B. Burroughs and J. D. Ehrenreich (eds) *Reading the Social Body*, Iowa City: University of Iowa Press: 244–69.

Ezell, M. J. M. (1993) *Writing Women's Literary History*, Baltimore: The Johns Hopkins University Press.

Ferrier, J. (1795) *Medical Histories and Reflections*, 2 vols, London: Cadell and Davies.

Ferrier, J. (1803) "Review: Joanna Baillie, *A Series of Plays: in which it is attempted to delineate the stronger Passions of the Mind*, Vol. 2," *Monthly Review* 43: 31–9.

Ferris, L. (1989) *Acting Women: Images of Women in Theatre*, New York: New York University Press.

Fitzgerald, P. (1871) *Lives of the Kembles*, 2 vols, London: Tinsley Brothers.

Flaherty, G. (1990) "Empathy and Distance: Romantic Theories of Acting Reconsidered," *Theatre Research International*, 15.2: 125–41.

Forbes, D. (1985) *Hume's Philosophical Politics*, Cambridge: Cambridge University Press.

Fradenburg, L. (1992) *Marriage, City, Tournament: Arts of Rule in Medieval Scotland*, Madison: University of Wisconsin Press.

Francis, B. (1950) *Fanny Kelly of Drury Lane*, London: Rockliff Publishing.

Fraser, F. (1986) *Emma, Lady Hamilton*, New York: Random House.

Fraser's Magazine (1836) "Review: Joanna Baillie, *Dramas*, 3 vols," (February): 236–49.

Friedman-Romell, B. H. (1998) "Dueling Citizenships: Scottish Patriotism v. British Nationalism in Joanna Baillie's *The Family Legend*," *Nineteenth Century Theatre* 26: 25–49.

Friedman-Romell, B. H. (1999) "Staging the State: Joanna Baillie's *Constantine Paleologus*," in T. C. Davis and E. Donkin (eds) *Women and Playwriting in Nineteenth-Century Britain*, Cambridge: Cambridge University Press: 151–73.

Gamer, M. (1997) "National Supernaturalism: Joanna Baillie, Germany, and the Gothic Drama," *Theatre Survey* 38.2: 49–88.

Gamer, M. (2000) *Romanticism and the Gothic: Genre, Reception, and Canon Formation*, Cambridge: Cambridge University Press.

Garber, M. (1995) *Vice Versa: Bisexuality and the Eroticism of Everyday Life*, New York: Simon and Schuster.

Gaull, M. (1988) *English Romanticism: The Human Context*, New York: Norton.

Genest, J. (1832) *Some Account of the English Stage from the Restoration in 1660 to 1830*, 10 vols, Bath: Carrington.

Gilbert, S. M. and Gubar, S. (1979) *The Madwoman in the Attic: the Woman Writer and the Nineteenth Century Literary Imagination*, New Haven and London: Yale University Press.

Gilroy, A. (1997) "From Here to Alterity: The Geography of Femininity in the Poetry of Joanna Baillie," in D. Gifford and D. McMillan (eds) *A History of Scottish Women's Writing*, Edinburgh: Edinburgh UP.

Gleckner, R. and Beatty, B. (eds) (1997) *The Plays of Lord Byron: Critical Essays*, Liverpool: Liverpool University Press.

Goodman, K. R. (1992) "The Sign Speaks: Charlotte von Stein's Matinees," in K. R. Goodman and E. Waldstein (eds) *In the Shadows of Olympus: German Women Writers Around 1800*, Albany, NY: State University of New York Press: 71–93.

Gordon, A. (1997) *Ghostly Matters: Haunting and the Sociological Imagination*, Minneapolis and London: University of Minnesota Press.

Goshen, C. E. (1967) *Documentary History of Psychiatry: A Source Book on Historical Principles*, New York: Philosophical Library.

Grant, A. (1803) *Poems on Various Subjects*, Edinburgh and London: Longman and Company.

Grant, A. (1806) *Letters from the Mountains; being the Correspondence with her Intimate Friends between the Years 1773 and 1803*, 3 vols, London: Longman and Company.

Grant, A. (1808) *Memoirs of an American Lady with Sketches of Manners and Scenery in America as They Existed Previous to the Revolution*, 2 vols, London: Longman and Company.

Grant, A. (1811) *Essays on the Superstitions of the Highlanders of Scotland, with Translations from the Gaelic*, 2 vols, London: Longman and Company.

Greig, J. A. (1948) *Francis Jeffrey of The Edinburgh Review*, Edinburgh: Oliver and Boyd.

Griffinhoof, A. (pseud.) (1830) *Memoirs of the Life of Madame Vestris*, privately printed.

Guildhall Library Pamphlet FO 3155 (n.d.) London: Guildhall Library.

Haakonssen, K. (1989) *The Science of a Legislator: The Natural Jurisprudence of David Hume and Adam Smith*, Cambridge: Cambridge University Press.

Hardwicke, Countess of (1831) *The Court of Oberon, or The Three Wishes*, London: n. pub.

Haslam, J. (1809) *Observations on Madness and Melancholy, including practical Remarks on these Diseases, together with Cases; and an Account of the morbid Appearances on Dissection*, 2nd ed., London: Callow.

Hays, M. (1803) *Female Biography; or Memoirs of Illustrious and Celebrated Women, of All Ages and Countries*, vol. 1, London: Richard Phillips.

Hazlitt, W. (1930–34) *The Complete Works of William Hazlitt*, P. P. Howe (ed.), vol. 18, London: J. M. Dent and Sons, Ltd.

Heller, J. R. (1990) *Coleridge, Lamb, Hazlitt, and the Reader of Drama*, Columbia, MO: University of Missouri Press.

Henderson, A. (1997) "Passion and Fashion in Joanna Baillie's 'Introductory Discourse'," *Publications of the Modern Language Association* 112: 198–213.

Herder, J. G. von (1800) *Outlines of the Philosophy of the History of Man*, trans. T. Churchill, London: J. Johnson.

Hillhouse, J. A. (1839) *Dramas, Discourses, and Other Pieces*, 2 vols, Boston: C.C. Little and J. Brown.

Hilliard, R. F. (1990) "*Clarissa* and Ritual Cannibalism," *Publications of the Modern Language Association* 105: 1083–97.

Historical and Genealogical Account of the Clan Maclean, from its first settlement at Castle Duart, in the Isle of Mull to the present period (1838), by a Seneachie, London: Smith, Elder & Company; Edinburgh: Laing and Forbes.

Hoagwood, T. A. (1997) "Elizabeth Inchbald, Joanna Baillie, and Revolutionary Representation in the 'Romantic' Period," unpublished paper presented at MLA, Washington, DC.

Hoagwood, T. A. (2001) "Elizabeth Inchbald, Joanna Baillie, and Revolutionary Representation in the 'Romantic' Period," in A. Craciun and K. Lokke (eds), *Rebellious Hearts: British Women Writers and the French Revolution*, Albany, NY: State University of New York Press.

Holman, L. E. (1935) *Lamb's 'Barbara S–': The Life of Frances Maria Kelly, Actress*, London: Methuen.

Holmström, K. G. (1967) *Monodrama, Attitudes, Tableaux Vivants: Studies on Some Trends of Theatrical Fashion 1770–1815*, Uppsala, Stockholm: Almqvist & Wiksell.

Hume, D. (1978) *A Treatise of Human Nature*, 2nd rev. ed., L. A. Selby-Bigge (ed.), P. H. Nidditch (rev. ed.), Oxford: Clarendon Press.

Hume, D. (1987) "Of Tragedy," *Essays Moral, Political, and Literary*, 2nd rev. ed., E. F. Miller (ed.), Indianapolis: Liberty Fund.

Hunter-Baillie papers (Royal College of Surgeons, London).

Hutcheson, F. (1726; facsimile reprint 1990) *An Inquiry into the Original of our Ideas of Beauty and Virtue*, 2nd ed., in *Collected Works of Francis Hutcheson*, vol. 1, Hildesheim: Georg Olms.

Inchbald, E. (1806–9) "Prefaces" to *The British Theatre*, 25 vols, London: Hurst, Robinson.

Jaggar, A. M. (1989) "Love and Knowledge: Emotion in Feminist Epistemology," in A. M. Jaggar and S. R. Bordo (eds), *Feminist Reconstructions of Being and Knowing*, New Brunswick, NJ: Rutgers University Press.

Jameson, A. (1832) *Characteristics of Women: Moral, Political, and Historical*, vol. 1, London: Saunders and Otley.

Jameson, F. (1995) "Marx's Purloined Letter," *New Left Review* 209: 75–109.

Jane Austen Songs (1989) Patricia Wright, soprano, and Jon Gillaspie, forte, Sussex: Pavilion. CD Recording.

Jeffrey, F. (1805) "Miss Baillie's Miscellaneous Plays," *The Edinburgh Review*, 5: 405–21.

Jeffrey, F. (1812) *Edinburgh Review*, February: 265–6.

Jenkins, I. and Sloan, K. (eds) (1996) *Vases and Volcanoes: Sir William Hamilton and His Collection*, London: British Museum Press.

Jermyn, L. (1825) "A Memoir of Mrs. Elizabeth Cobbold," in *Poems by Mrs. Elizabeth Cobbold. With a Memoir of the Author*, Ipswich: J. Row.

Jewett, W. (1997) *Fatal Autonomy: Romantic Drama and the Rhetoric of Agency*, Ithaca, NY: Cornell University Press.

Jipson, J. and Munro, P. (1999) "Deconstructing Feminist Pedagogy: Seeing That Which Is Ordinarily Obscured by the Familiar," in L. K. Christian-Smith and K. S. Kellor (eds) *Everyday Knowledge and Uncommon Truths: Women of the Academy*, Boulder, CO: Westview Press.

"Joanna Baillie's *Metrical Legends*" (1821) *Monthly Review* 96: 72–81.

Johnson, E. (1970) *Sir Walter Scott: The Great Unknown*, 2 vols, New York: Macmillan.

Johnson, R. B. (1926) "Introduction," in R. B. Johnson (ed.) *Bluestocking Letters*, London, John Lane The Bodley Head.

Keenan, T. (1997) *Fables of Responsibility: Aberrations and Predicaments in Ethics and Politics*, Stanford, CA: Stanford University Press.

Kelly, G. (1990) "Revolutionary and Romantic Feminism: Women, Writing and Cultural Revolution," in K. Hanley and R. Selden (eds) *Revolution and English Romanticism: Politics and Rhetoric*, New York: St. Martin's Press.

Kelly, G. (1993) *Women, Writing and Revolution 1790–1827*, Oxford: Clarendon.

Klancher, J. P. (1987) *The Making of English Reading Audiences, 1790–1832*, Madison, WI: University of Wisconsin Press.

Klein, L. (1995) "Gender and the Public/Private Distinction in the Eighteenth Century: Some Questions about Evidence and Analytic Procedure," *Eighteenth-Century Studies* 2.1: 97–109.

Kobler, J. (1960) *The Reluctant Surgeon: A Biography of John Hunter*, New York: Doubleday.

Lamb, C. (1903–05) "On the Tragedies of Shakspeare, Considered with Reference to their Fitness for Stage Representation," in E. V. Lucas (ed.) *The Works of Charles and Mary Lamb*, 7 vols, London: Methuen.

Lansdown, R. (1992) *Byron's Historical Dramas*, Oxford: Oxford University Press.

Leacroft, R. (1988) *The Development of the English Playhouse*, Ithaca: Cornell University Press.

Le Breton, P. H. (ed.) (1864) *Memoirs, Miscellanies and Letters of the Late Lucy Aikin*, London: Longman, Green, Longman, Roberts, and Green.

Lessing, G. E. (1962; orig. publ. 1769) *Hamburg Dramaturgy*, trans. V. Lange, New York: Dover Publications.

"Life of Joanna Baillie." (1853) *The Dramatic and Poetical Works of Joanna Baillie, in One Complete Volume*, 2nd ed., London: Longman.

Liu, A. (1989) *Wordsworth: A Sense of History*, Stanford, CA: Stanford University Press.

Lockhart, J. G. (1837–38) *Memoirs of the Life of Sir Walter Scott, Bart*, 7 vols, Edinburgh: Cadell.

Lockhart, J. G. (1842) *Memoirs of the Life of Sir Walter Scott*, new ed., Edinburgh: Cadell.

London Review (1788) "To the Editor of the *European Magazine*. Plan for a Fashionable Rosciad; and some account of Mr. Fector's Private Theatre at Dover," 14.

Longman's Dictionary of Geography (1966) D. Stamp (ed.), London: Longmans, Green, and Company.

Looser, D. (2000) *British Women Writers and the Writing of History, 1670–1820*, Baltimore: Johns Hopkins University Press.

Lynch, M. (1991) *Scotland: A New History*, London: Century.

Macalpine, I. and Hunter, R. (1969) *George III and the Mad-Business*, London: Allen Lane; New York: Pantheon.

Macaulay, C. (1763–83) *The History of England, from the Accession of James I to that of the Brunswick Line*, 8 vols, London: J. Nourse.

Macaulay, C. (1790) *Letters on Education: With Observations on Religion and Metaphysical Subjects*, London: C. Dilly.

Maclaren, A. (1809) *The Private Theatre: or, the Highland Funeral*, London: A. Macpherson.

McMillan, D. (1998) " 'Dr' Baillie," in R. Cronin (ed.) *1798: The Year of the Lyrical Ballads*, Houndmills: Macmillan.

Macpherson, J. (1996) *The Poems of Ossian and Related Works*, H. Gaskill (ed.), with an introduction by F. Stafford, Edinburgh: Edinburgh University Press.

Mandeville, B. (1970) *The Fable of the Bees*, P. Harth (ed.), London: Penguin.

Marchand, L. (ed.) (1975–82) *Byron's Letters and Journals*, 12 vols, Cambridge, MA: Belknap Press, Harvard University Press.

Marshall, D. (1986) *The Figure of Theater: Shaftesbury, Defoe, Adam Smith, and George Eliot*, New York: Columbia University Press.

Mather, G. R. (1894) *Two Great Scotsmen: The Brothers William and John Hunter*, Glasgow: James Maclehose and Sons.

Meisel, M. (1983) *Realizations: Narrative, Pictorial, and Theatrical Arts in Nineteenth-Century England*, Princeton: Princeton University Press.

Mellor, A. K. (1994) "Joanna Baillie and the Counter-Public Sphere," *Studies in Romanticism* 33: 559–67.

Mellor, A. K. (2000) *Mothers of the Nation: Women's Political Writing in England, 1780–1830*, Bloomington: Indiana University Press.

Mellor, A. K. and Matlak, R. E. (eds) (1996) "Count Basil" (1798 edn), *British Literature, 1780–1830*, Fort Worth: Harcourt Brace: 458–94.

Meynell, A. C. (1968; orig. 1922) *The Second Person Singular*, Freeport, NY: Books for Libraries Press.

Micale, M. K. (1995) *Approaching Hysteria: Disease and Its Interpretations*, Princeton: Princeton University Press.

Minnich, E. K. (1990) *Transforming Knowledge*, Philadelphia: Temple University Press.

"Miss Baillie's Plays" (1805) *The Literary Journal, or Universal Review of Literature Domestic and Foreign* 5: 49–64.

"Miss Baillie's Plays" (1813) *The Eclectic Review* 10: 21–32, 167–86.

"Miss J. Baillie's Series of Plays. Vol. II" (1802) *The British Critic* 20: 284–90.

Monthly Magazine (1800) "Review of *De Monfort*," 9: 487.

Moody, J. (1999) "Illusions of authorship," in T. C. Davis and E. Donkin (eds) *Women and Playwriting in Nineteenth-Century Britain*, Cambridge: Cambridge University Press. 99–124.

Moore, T. (1827) "Review of C. K. Bushe's *The Private Theatre of Kilkenny . . .* ," *Edinburgh Review* 46: 368–90.

Morley, E. J. (ed.) (1938) *Henry Crabb Robinson on Books and their Writers*, 3 vols, London: J. M. Dent and Sons.

Morning Post (1800) "Review of *De Monfort*," 30 April.

Moylan, P. A. (1999) "Sophia and Sophistry: Gender and Western Civilization," in M. Mayberry and E. C. Rose (eds) *Meeting the Challenge: Innovative Feminist Pedagogies in Action*, New York: Routledge.

Mullan, J. (1990) *Sentiment and Sociability: The Language of Feeling in the Eighteenth Century*, corrected paperback ed., Oxford: Clarendon Press.

Murray, Lady (of Stanhope) (1824) *Memoirs of the Lives and Characters of the Right Honourable George Baillie of Jerviswood and of Lady Grisell Baillie*, printed at Edinburgh.

Namaste, K. (1996) "From Performativity to Interpretation: Toward a Social Semiotic Account of Bisexuality," in D. E. Hall and M. Pramaggiore (eds) *RePresenting Bisexualities: Subjects and Cultures of Fluid Desires*, New York: New York University Press: 70–95.

Newey, K. (2000) "Women and history on the Romantic stage: More, Yearsley, Burney, and Mitford," in C. Burroughs (ed.) *Women in British Romantic Theatre: Drama, Performance, and Society, 1790–1840*, Cambridge: Cambridge University Press.

Nicoll, A. (1927) *A History of Late Eighteenth-Century Drama, 1750–1800*, Cambridge: Cambridge University Press.

Nicoll, A. (1930) *A History of Nineteenth-Century Drama, 1800–1850*, 2 vols, Cambridge: Cambridge University Press.

Nicoll, A. (1955) *A History of Early English Drama 1660–1900*, vol. 4, Cambridge: Cambridge University Press.

O'Brien, K. (1997) *Narratives of Enlightenment: Cosmopolitan History from Voltaire to Gibbon*, Cambridge: Cambridge University Press.

Osborne, R. (ed.) (1982) *The Borderers* by William Wordsworth, Ithaca, NY: Cornell University Press.

Otten, T. (1972) *The Deserted Stage: The Search for Dramatic Form in Nineteenth-Century England*, Athens, OH: Ohio University Press.

Park, L. J. (1838) *Joanna of Naples*, Boston: Hilliard, Gray.

Park, L. J. (1838) *Miriam: A Dramatic Poem*, 2nd ed. Boston: H. P. Nichols.

Park, R. (ed.) (1980) *Lamb as Critic*, London: Routledge and Kegan Paul.

Pascoe, J. (1997) *Romantic Theatricality: Gender, Poetry, and Spectatorship*, Ithaca: Cornell University Press.

Patten, J. E. (1992) "Dark Imagination: Poetic Painting in Romantic Drama," unpublished diss., University of California, Santa Cruz.

Peachey, G. C. (1924) *A Memoir of William and John Hunter*, Plymouth: William Brendon and Son.

Peake, R. B. (1827; orig. 1818) *Amateurs and Actors: A Musical Farce in Two Acts*, London: John Cumberland.

Phillips, M. S. (2000) *Society and Sentiment: Genres of Historical Writing in Britain, 1740–1820*, Princeton: Princeton University Press.

Philp, M. (ed.) (1993) *Political and Philosophical Writings of William Godwin*, 7 vols, London: William Pickering.

Pinel, P. (1806) *A Treatise on Insanity*, trans. Dr. D. Davis, Sheffield: Cadell and Davies.

Playhouse Aires: Eighteenth-Century English Theatre Music (1996) The London Oboe Band, directed by Paul Goodwin, France: Harmonia Mundi. CD Recording.

Pocock, J. G. A. (1985) *Virtue, Commerce, and History: Essays on Political Thought and History, Chiefly in the Eighteenth Century*, Cambridge: Cambridge University Press.

Porter, J. (1810) *The Scottish Chiefs*, London: Longman & Co.

Porter, R. (1987) *Mind-Forg'd Manacles: A History of Madness in England from the Restoration to the Regency*, London: Athlone Press.

Powell, J. (1787) *Private Theatricals: A Farce. In Two Acts*, n. loc.: n. pub.

Praz, M. (1951) *The Romantic Agony*, trans. Angus Davidson, 2nd ed., London: Oxford University Press.

Purinton, M. D. (1994) *Romantic Ideology Unmasked: The Mentally Constructed Tyrannies in Dramas of William Wordsworth, Lord Byron, Percy Shelley, and Joanna Baillie*, Newark: University of Delaware Press.

Purinton, M. D. (1998) "The Sexual Politics of *The Election*: French Feminism and the Scottish Playwright Joanna Baillie," *Intertexts* 2.2: 119–30.

Purinton, M. D. (2000) "Women's Sovereignty on Trial: Joanna Baillie's Comedy *The Tryal* as Metatheatrics," in C. B. Burroughs (ed.) *Women in British Romantic Theatre: Drama, Performance, and Society, 1790–1840*, Cambridge: Cambridge University Press.

Purinton, M. D. (2001) "Socialized and Medicalized Hysteria in Joanna Baillie's *Witchcraft*," *Prism(s): Essays in Romanticism* 9: 139–56.

Quarterly Review (1836) "Review: Joanna Baillie, *Dramas*, 3 vols," (January): 83–108.

Reiman, D. (1977) "Introduction," Joanna Baillie, *A Series of Plays*, vol. 1. New York: Garland: v–viii.

"Remarks on the Plays on the Passions by Joanna Baillie" (1818) *Edinburgh Magazine and Literary Miscellany (Scots Magazine)*, new series 2: 517–20.

"Review of *The Family Legend* (1810) *Scots Magazine and Edinburgh Literary Miscellany*, 72: 103–7.

"Review of a Series of Plays, Vol. I" (1799) *British Critic and Quarterly Theological Review* 8: 284–90.

Richards, S. (1993) *The Rise of the English Actress*, New York: St. Martin's Press.

Richardson, A. (1988) *A Mental Theater: Poetic Drama and Consciousness in the Romantic Age*, University Park: Pennsylvania State University Press.

Richardson, A. (2001) *British Romanticism and the Science of the Mind*, Cambridge: Cambridge University Press.

Richardson, S. (1985) *Clarissa, or the History of a Young Lady*, A. Ross (ed.), Hammondsworth: Penguin Books.

Robinson, H. C. (1869) *Diaries, Reminiscences, and Correspondence of Henry Crabb Robinson, Barrister-At-Law, F.S.A*, 3 vols, Dr. T. Sadler (ed.), London: Macmillan.

Rosenfeld, S. (1978) *Temples of Thespis: Some Private Theatres and Theatricals in England and Wales, 1700–1820*, London: Society for Theatre Research.

Ross, M. B. (1989) *The Contours of Masculine Desire: Romanticism and the Rise of Women's Poetry*, Oxford: Oxford University Press.

Russell, G. (1995) *The Theatres of War: Performance, Politics, and Society, 1793–1815*, Oxford: Clarendon Press.

Schama, S. (1995) *Landscape and Memory*, London: Harper Collins.

Schmitt, J.-C. (1998) *Ghosts in the Middle Ages: The Living and the Dead in Medieval Society*, trans. T. L. Fagan, Chicago and London: University of Chicago Press.

Schneider, L. (1987) *Paradox and Society: The Work of Bernard Mandeville*, New Brunswick and Oxford: Transaction Books.

Scott, J. (1988) *Gender and the Politics of History*, New York: Columbia University Press.

Scott, J. (ed.) (1996) *Feminism and History*, Oxford: Oxford University Press.

Scott, W. (1831) *Letters on Demonology and Witchcraft, Addressed to J. G. Lockhart, Esq.*, 2nd ed., London.

Scott, W. (1894) *Familiar Letters*, 2 vols, Edinburgh: David Douglas.

Scott, W. (1932–37) *The Letters of Sir Walter Scott*, H. J. C. Grierson and others (eds), 12 vols, London: Constable.

Scott, W. (1950) *The Journal of Sir Walter Scott*, Edinburgh: Oliver & Boyd.

Scott, W. (1981) *Letters of Malachi Malagrowther*, preface and essay by P. H. Scott, Edinburgh: Blackwood.

Scott, W. (1984, rpt) *Familiar Letters of Sir Walter Scott*, vol. 1, New York: Houghton Mifflin.

Scull, A. (1993) *The Most Solitary of Afflictions. Madness and Society in Britain 1700–1900*, New Haven: Yale University Press.

Scullion, A. (ed.) (1996) *"The Family Legend"* (1810 ed.), *Female Playwrights of the Nineteenth Century*, London: J. M. Dent: 3–74.

Scullion, A. (1997) "Some Women of the Nineteenth-century Scottish Theatre: Joanna Baillie, Frances Wright, and Helen MacGregor," in D. Gifford and D. McMillan (eds) *A History of Scottish Women's Writing*, Edinburgh: Edinburgh University Press: 161–5

Shapiro, A.-L. (ed.) (1994) *Feminists Revision History*, New Brunswick: Rutgers University Press.

Shaver, C. and Shaver, A. (1979) *Wordsworth's Library: A Catalogue*, New York: Garland.

Shelley, P. B. (1977) *Shelley's Selected Poetry and Prose*, D. Reiman and S. B. Powers (eds), New York: Norton.

Siddons, H. (1968) *Practical Illustrations of Rhetorical Gesture and Action; Adapted to the English Drama: From a Work on the Subject by M. Engel*, 2nd ed., New York: Benjamin Blom.

Simpson, M. (1998) *Closet Performances: Political Exhibition and Prohibition in the Dramas of Byron and Shelley*, Stanford, CA: Stanford University Press.

Siskin, C. (1988) *The Historicity of Romantic Discourse*, Oxford: Oxford University Press.

Skultans, V. (1975) *Madness and Morals: Ideas on Insanity in the Nineteenth Century*, London: Routledge & Kegan Paul.

Slagle, J. B. (ed.) (1999) *The Collected Letters of Joanna Baillie*, 2 vols, Madison, NJ: Fairleigh Dickinson University Press; London: Associated University Presses.

Slagle, J. B. (2002) *Joanna Baillie: A Literary Life*, Madison and Teaneck, NJ: Fairleigh Dickinson University Press.

Smith, A. (1984) *The Theory of Moral Sentiments*, D. D. Raphael and A. L. Macfie (eds), Indianapolis: Liberty Fund.

Smith, B. G. (1998) *The Gender of History: Men, Women, and Historical Practice*, Cambridge, Massachusetts: Harvard University Press.

Snodgrass, C. (1999) "Narrating Nations, Negotiating Borders: The Scottish Romantic Novel in Blackwood's Circle," unpublished diss., Texas A&M University.

Somerville, M. (2001) *Queen of Science: The Personal Recollections from Early Life to Old Age of Mary Somerville with Selections from her Correspondence, by her Daughter, Martha Somerville* (orig. publ. London: John Murray, 1873), D. McMillan (ed.), Edinburgh: Canongate.

Stafford, F. (1988) *The Sublime Savage: A Study of James Macpherson and the Poems of Ossian*, Edinburgh: Edinburgh University Press.

Steiner, G. (1961) *The Death of Tragedy*, New York: Knopf.

Stephens, J. R. (1992) *The Profession of the Playwright: British Theatre 1800–1900*, Cambridge: Cambridge University Press.

Straznicky, M. (1998) "Recent Studies in Closet Drama," *English Literary Renaissance* 28: 142–60.

Stuart, Lady L. (1985) *Memoire of Frances, Lady Douglas*, J. Rubenstein (ed.), Edinburgh: Scottish Academic Press.

Sturgess, K. (1987) *Jacobean Private Theatre*, London and New York: Routledge.

Sweet, N. (1994) "History, Imperialism, and the Aesthetics of the Beautiful: Hemans and the Post-Napoleonic Moment," in Favret , M. A. and Watson, N. J. (eds) *At the Limits of Romanticism: Essays in Cultural and Materialist Criticism*, Bloomington: Indiana University Press.

Ticknor, A. and Hillard, G. S. (1876) *Life, Letters, and Journals of George Ticknor*, 2 vols, Boston: J. R. Osgood.

Times (1800) "Review of *De Monfort*," 30 April: n. pg.

Tobin, T. (1974) *Plays by Scots, 1660–1800*, Iowa City, IA: University of Iowa Press.

Toepfer, K. (1991) *Theatre, Aristrocracy, Pornocracy: The Orgy Calculus*, New York: Performing Arts Journal.

Transactions of the Wordsworth Society (1966), London: W. Dawson.

Trilling, L. (1950) "Freud and Literature," *The Liberal Imagination: Essays on Literature and Society*, New York: Viking.

Turner, V. (1982) *Ritual to Theatre: The Human Seriousness of Play*, New York: Performing Arts Journal Publications.

Tytler, S. and Watson, J. L. (1871) *The Songstresses of Scotland*, 2 vols, London: Strahan and Co.

Van Sant, A. J. (1993) *Eighteenth-Century Sensibility and the Novel: The Senses in Social Context*, Cambridge: Cambridge University Press.

Veith, I. (1993) *Hysteria: The History of a Disease*, Chicago: University of Chicago Press.

Wang, S. (1990) *The Theatre of the Mind: A Study of Unacted Drama in Nineteenth-Century England*, New York: St. Martin's Press.

Wardrop, J. (1825) "The Life of Dr. Baillie," in vol. 1 of M. Baillie, *The Works of Matthew Baillie, M.D.*, London: Longman, Hurst, Orme, Brown, and Green.

Wasserman, E. (1947) "The Sympathetic Imagination in Eighteenth-Century Theories of Acting," *Journal of English and German Philology*, 46: 264–72.

Watkins, D. P. (1993) *A Materialist Critique of English Romantic Drama*, Gainesville: University Press of Florida.

Westfall, S. R. (1990) *Patrons and Performance: Early Tudor Household Revels*, Oxford: Clarendon Press.

White, H. (1973) *Metahistory: The Historical Imagination in Nineteenth-Century Europe*, Baltimore: Johns Hopkins University Press.

Whitney, L. (1973) *Primitivism and the Idea of Progress in English Popular Literature of the Eighteenth Century*, New York: Octagon.

Williams, P. (1991) *Alchemy of Race and Rights*, Cambridge, MA: Harvard University Press.

Wilshire, B. (1982) *Role Playing and Identity: The Limits of Theatre as Metaphor*, Bloomington, IN: Indiana University Press.

Wilson, M. S. (1987) "*Ut Pictura Tragoedia*: An Extrinsic Approach to British NeoClassic and Romantic Theatre," *Theatre Research International* 12: 201–20.

Wollstonecraft, M. (1792) *A Vindication of the Rights of Woman*; reprinted (1997) in D. L. Mcdonald and K. Scherf (eds), *The Vindications: The Rights of Men, the Rights of Woman*, Peterborough, ON: Broadview Press.

Wollstonecraft, M. (1795) *A Historical and Moral View of the French Revolution*, London: J. Johnson.

Women Writers: Their Works and Ways (1892–93), 2 vols, London and New York: Ward, Lock, Bowden, and Company.

Wordsworth, J. (1990) "Introduction," *Joanna Baillie: A Series of Plays* (1798), Oxford: Woodstock Books.

Wordsworth, J. (ed.) (1994) *Poems, 1790*, New York: Woodstock.

Wordsworth, W. (1967) *The Letters of William and Dorothy Wordsworth*, E. de Selincourt, rev. C. L. Shaver (eds), vol. 1, 2nd ed., Oxford: Clarendon Press.

Yearsley, A. (1791) *Earl Goodwin, an Historical Play*, London: G. G. J. Robinson.

Young, A. (1995) *The Example of France: A Warning to Britain*, in G. Claeys (ed.), *Political Writings of the 1790s*, vol. 4, London: William Pickering.

Yudin, M. F. (1994) "Joanna Baillie's Introductory Discourse as a Precursor to Wordsworth's Preface to *Lyrical Ballads*," *Compar(a)ison* 1: 101–11.

Zall, P. M. (1982) "The Cool World of Samuel Taylor Coleridge: The Question of Joanna Baillie," *The Wordsworth Circle* 13.1: 17–20.

Žižek, S. (1996) "'There Is No Sexual Relationship,'" in R. Saleci and S. Žižek (eds) *Gaze and Voice as Love Objects*, Durham, NC: Duke University Press: 208–49.

Index

eBooks – at www.eBookstore.tandf.co.uk

A library at your fingertips!

eBooks are electronic versions of printed books. You can store them on your PC/laptop or browse them online.

They have advantages for anyone needing rapid access to a wide variety of published, copyright information.

eBooks can help your research by enabling you to bookmark chapters, annotate text and use instant searches to find specific words or phrases. Several eBook files would fit on even a small laptop or PDA.

NEW: Save money by eSubscribing: cheap, online access to any eBook for as long as you need it.

Annual subscription packages

We now offer special low-cost bulk subscriptions to packages of eBooks in certain subject areas. These are available to libraries or to individuals.

For more information please contact webmaster.ebooks@tandf.co.uk

We're continually developing the eBook concept, so keep up to date by visiting the website.

www.eBookstore.tandf.co.uk

Printed in Great Britain
by Amazon

44306232R00192